www.wadsworth.com

www.wadsworth.com is the World Wide Web site for Thomson
Wadsworth and is your direct source to dozens of online resources.

At *www.wadsworth.com* you can find out about supplements,
demonstration software, and student resources. You can also send
email to many of our authors and preview new publications and
exciting new technologies.

www.wadsworth.com
Changing the way the world learns®

Writer's Resources

Sentence Skills with Readings

Writer's Resources

Sentence Skills with Readings

Julie Robitaille
Sante Fe Community College

Robert Connelly
Santa Fe Community College

THOMSON

WADSWORTH

Australia • Brazil • Canada • Mexico • Singapore • Spain • United Kingdom • United States

Writer's Resources: Sentence Skills with Readings
Julie Robitaille, Robert Connelly

Publisher: *Michael Rosenberg*
Acquisitions Editor: *Stephen Dalphin*
Development Editor: *Laurie Runion*
Editorial Assistant: *Cheryl Forman*
Technology Project Manager: *Joe Gallagher*
Senior Marketing Manager: *Mary Jo Southern*
Marketing Assistant: *Dawn Giovanniello*
Advertising Project Manager: *Patrick Rooney*
Senior Project Manager, Editorial Production: *Lianne Ames*
Senior Print Buyer: *Mary Beth Hennebury*
Permissions Editor: *Bob Kauser*
Production Service: *Lachina Publishing Services*

Text Designer: *Diane Beasley*
Photo Manager: *Sheri Blaney*
Photo Researcher: *Cheri Throop*
Cover Designer: *Andrew Ogus*
Cover Printer: *Transcontinental*
Compositor: *Lachina Publishing Services*
Printer: *Transcontinental*
Cover Art: *Constellation,* 1943 by Alexander Calder, © 2005 Estate of Alexander Calder/Artists Rights Society (ARS), New York
Photo Credit: CNAC/MNAM/Dist. Réunion des Musées Nationaux/Art Resource, NY

Printed in Canada
1 2 3 4 5 6 7 09 08 07 06 05

Library of Congress Control Number: 2005926688

Student Edition with Readings: ISBN 1-4130-1003-2

Credits appear on page I-9, which constitutes a continuation of the copyright page.

Thomson Higher Education
25 Thomson Place
Boston, MA 02210-1202
USA

For more information about our products, contact us at:
Thomson Learning Academic Resource Center
1-800-423-0563
For permission to use material from this text or product, submit a request online at http://www.thomsonrights.com
Any additional questions about permissions can be submitted by e-mail to
thomsonrights@thomson.com

Contents

Introduction: Aiming for Success   1

Part I   Introduction to College Writing   11

Part II Grammar, Mechanics, and Punctuation   75

Chapter 3   Capitalization   77

Chapter 4   Problem Words   91

Chapter 5   Word Use and Choice   113

Chapter 6   Identifying Subjects and Verbs   131

Chapter 7   Subject–Verb Agreement   149

Chapter 8   Verb Tenses   171

Chapter 9　Adjectives and Adverbs　193

Chapter 10　Sentence Parts and Types　205

Chapter 11　Sentence Fragments　213

Chapter 12   Run-on Sentences   233

Chapter 13   Sentence Combining   255

Chapter 14   Pronoun Agreement   273

Appendix 1   Spelling and Dictionary Skills   A-1

Appendix 2   Parts of Speech   A-9

Appendix 3   ESL Skills   A-23

Writer's Resources

Sentence Skills with Readings

Preface

It is our pleasure to present *Writer's Resources: Sentence Skills with Readings.* This textbook, our third in the *Writer's Resources* series, will introduce your students to the power of language and help them develop their own writing power.

We have found that one of the heaviest burdens of teaching and learning in an entry-level writing course is the sheer amount of grammar, punctuation, and rhetorical rules that must be taught and learned. Trying to make these rules interesting and engaging is challenging. Beginning writing classes can often feel more like torture than learning. In *Writer's Resources: Sentence Skills with Readings,* we have tried to address this silent killer of student and teacher enthusiasm in a number of ways.

First, we begin with the firm belief that writing matters. We learn what we think, express what we know, and explore ideas through writing. In every chapter in Parts 1 and 2, we spotlight writers who have made a difference with their writing. The **Spotlight on Writers** feature includes well-known writers and celebrities and ordinary young people who have made a difference through their writing. This feature serves as a reminder that writing matters, and it keeps students focused on the most important reason they are learning the basic skills.

We also use the substantial skill practice, exercises, and test material to impart interesting information taken from newspapers and magazines. Since so much class time is spent on skill and drill material, we want to expose students to college-level ideas while they practice. We use continuous discourse in most of the practices, review exercises, editing tests, and skill tests.

Most importantly, at the end of every skill chapter in Part 2, we provide writing topics drawn from the subject matter developed in the review exercises. Connecting students' reading in the exercises with their writing will help prepare them for later college assignments. Each **Practicing Your Writing Power** feature gives students an opportunity to explore topics of interest, such as friends, travel, and school experiences, as well as topical subjects such as bullying in schools.

It is our sincere hope that you will find *Writer's Resources: Sentence Skills with Readings* an ally in developing your students' writing.

Power of Language Features

- **Spotlight on Writers**—unique to the market—draws attention to individuals, famous and ordinary, who have used writing to change the world. These human-interest stories will engage students and help them connect writing skills with a sense of power. These examples will motivate and inspire students as they develop the sentence skills necessary to write clearly and correctly. Featured writers include hip-hop artist Chuck D, talk show host Oprah Winfrey, civil rights leader Martin Luther King, Jr., horror writer Stephen King, singer/songwriter Bob Dylan, environmental writer Rachel Carson, along with four writers who contribute essays in the readings section, Sandra Cisneros, Malcolm X, Marian Wright Edelman, and William Zinsser.

- **Practicing Your Writing Power**—another feature unique to this market—ties the writing topics to topics developed in the review exercises in order to stimulate students' thinking. This feature, found at the end of each chapter, provides writing topics that prompt students to use their writing skills to discover more clearly what they think and feel about issues in their own lives. Writing about ourselves is a powerful way to generate enthusiasm for writing. These writing prompts will be easy to respond to after students have completed chapter Review Exercises that provide timely information about the topics.

- **Model paragraphs and essays** written by students show what college writing looks like. Often students learn best by example, and these eight sample paragraphs and two essays—the topics of which are typical of entry-level assignments—demonstrate the writing concepts they are learning. Exercises follow each model to help students explore the writing concepts they are learning to use in their writing.

- **Skill Previews** at the beginning of every chapter introduce students to the topic of the chapter and allow them to assess how much they know about that topic.

- **Practice and Review Exercises** give students valuable practice using the skills they are learning. Some of the exercises are **Working Together Exercises** that encourage students to work alongside classmates. Because such practice can seem boring and removed from meaningful writing, we have worked hard to make the content of the practices interesting. We mostly use continuous discourse on topics drawn from the newspaper and magazines. Information on topics ranging from health to history and popular culture will stimulate student thinking, increase their awareness of contemporary issues, and demonstrate how college-level ideas are expressed in writing.

- **Combined Editing Tests** combine all the skills students are learning into editing tests that will help them improve their ability to edit their own writing. These editing exercises start with the basic skills and progress to advanced tests that include all the skills. Using these editing tests, students will improve their editing process gradually through the term. Like the other exercises in the book, we have chosen topics of interest to students such as computer viruses and public speaking.

- **CD Connection** points to more in-depth instruction and practice on the *Writer's Resources* CD-ROM, the popular interactive multi-media presentation of all the topics covered in the text. The depth of the CD expands the textbook significantly by providing hundreds of additional pages of instruction, examples, exercises, and additional concepts such as rhetorical patterns. Students will enjoy the audio explanations, animated examples, and extensive practice that will help them improve their writing skill and boost their power.

How the Textbook Is Organized

Introduction: Aiming for Success

This short section introduces students to the power of language and helps them develop the habits that will make them successful college students such as keeping a journal, developing a positive attitude, taking notes, setting a schedule, and using their resources.

Part I   Introduction to College Writing

Chapter 1 provides in-depth coverage of the paragraph, which is the building block of college essays. Students will follow the writing process of a student, Tony, as he develops a paragraph. They will use the same writing process to create a well-developed paragraph using strong sentence structure.

Chapter 2 presents an overview of the essay. Students will make the connection between the paragraph and the essay when Tony shows them how he expanded his paragraph from Chapter 1 into a college essay.

Part II   Grammar, Mechanics, and Punctuation

This section includes nineteen chapters of grammar, mechanics, and punctuation that provide the most important rules and concepts students need to write effective sentences. All rules are numbered for easy reference, and practice using each rule is provided after each rule. Unlike other textbooks for this course, *Writer's Resources* prepares students for later writing courses by defining and using the grammatical vocabulary that they will use throughout college.

Each chapter in Part II includes

- **Skill Preview** that introduces chapter topics.
- **Spotlight on Writers** that will help students connect writing skills with a sense of power.

- **Practice Exercises** that allow students to use concepts and to check their answers in the back of the text.
- **Working Together Exercises** that encourage students to work collaboratively.
- **Review Exercises** that combine all the rules for each skill.
- **Editing Exercises** that give students practice finding target errors in a passage.
- **Skill Tests** that allow students to check their comprehension of the concepts taught in each chapter.
- **Practicing Your Writing Power** prompts that encourage students to think and write critically about topics of interest.
- **CD Connection** that points to more in-depth instruction and practice on the *Writer's Resources* CD-ROM.
- **Student Answer Key** (at back of book) that allows students to check their understanding of concepts.

Part III   Review Tests

Combined Editing Tests and **Mastery Tests** give students practice applying (in both editing and multiple choice formats) all the skills acquired in Part II.

Part IV   Readings

Part IV of the text includes **ten professional readings.** These articles will inspire students as they begin their college careers. The professional readings are followed by vocabulary exercises, comprehension questions, discussion questions, and writing topics. Many of the readings spotlight the power of language theme of the text with authors such as Malcolm X, Sandra Cisneros, William Zinsser, and Marian Wright Edelman.

Appendices

Appendix 1, **Spelling and Dictionary Skills,** gives students a tutorial on improving their spelling and on using the dictionary to avoid errors in their writing. Appendix 2, **Parts of Speech,** provides background information on grammatical concepts and terminology used in writing classes. Appendix 3, **ESL Skills,** addresses particular language issues that many writers, both international and American, have in learning to use Standard English. Appendix 4, **Paragraph Writing Checklists,** provide materials that will help students write paragraphs.

Supplements

Writer's Resources Instructor's Manual

The instructor's manual and test bank that accompanies *Writer's Resources* includes the following: discussion of how to use the book; discussion of teaching the paragraph and essay; teaching suggestions; sample schedule; group activities; portfolio suggestions; handouts for the beginning of the term, and assorted handouts for paragraph and essay writing; **additional tests (three for each skill); and additional Diagnostic and Mastery Tests.**

Writer's Resources CD-ROM

This CD provides multimedia lessons on all the topics covered in the textbook. Students can use the CD to review concepts covered in class, to get additional practice on skills (with instant feedback), and to explore concepts in greater depth. In addition, it presents expanded lessons on the writing process, the paragraph, the essay, rhetorical patterns and grammatical skills.

Writer's ResourcesNow™

This web-based study system combines the multimedia resources of the *Writer's Resources* 2.0 CD-ROM with the course management capabilities of Thomson's iLrn system. Each chapter of the textbook is accompanied by a Pre-test, personalized Study Plan, and Post-test within *Writer's ResourcesNow*. After completing a chapter in the textbook, students may take an online Pre-test to assess their proficiency in the skills covered in the chapter. The student then receives a personalized Study Plan that is based on the results of the Pre-test and contains links to appropriate multimedia tutorials and interactive practice exercises drawn from the *Writer's Resources* 2.0 CD-ROM. After working through their Study Plans, students complete a follow-up Post-test to assess their mastery of the material. The scores of the Pre-test and Post-test are tracked in an instructor gradebook, so that instructors may monitor their students' progress through the course.

Acknowledgments

We benefited from the insightful reviews of the text. We are indebted to our reviewers who were kind enough to take the time and give attention to our project. Many thanks to the following reviewers who offered constructive suggestions and helped make decisions about the structure and content of the text:

E. Ferol Benavides, *Anne Arundel Community College*

Dorothea Burkhart, *Davidson County Community College*

Judy Covington, *Trident Technical College*

Sarah Garman, *Miami-Dade College*

Victoria Gay, *Columbia State Community College*

Catherine Gorvine, *Delgado Community College*

Sandra Griffin, *Western New Mexico University*

Judy Haberman, *Phoenix College*

Heather Jeddy, *Northern Virginia Community College*

Sarah Lahm, *Normandale Community College*

M. Diane Langston, *Floyd College*

Christine Mitchell, *Delgado Community College*

Jamie Moore, *Scottsdale Community College*

Stephanie Powers, *Florida Community College at Jacksonville*

Jessica Rabin, *Anne Arundel Community College*

Jinhao Wang, *South Texas Community College*

Wendy Jo Ward, *Miami-Dade College*

Thurmond Whatley, *Aiken Technical College*

We also wish to thank the people who have contributed to the making of *Writer's Resources: Sentence Skills with Readings*. First, our long-time editor at Wadsworth, Steve Dalphin, conceived this textbook and gave us valuable insight into the needs of the market, and Laurie Runion, who is our Development Editor, guided us through the review and editing process and encouraged us to do our best work. Other folks at Wadsworth who helped birth this book include Lianne Ames, Production Project Manager, Mary Jo Southern, Marketing Manager, Michele Tomiak, copyeditor, Diane Beasley, designer, Joe Gallagher, Technology Product Manager, and Sheila McGill, Project Manager at Lachina Publishing Services.

Finally, in our personal lives, Julie wishes to thank her husband, Steve, and her two boys, Jean Paul and Jordan, for their support. Bob thanks his partner, Claudia Munnis, for her support and understanding throughout.

About the Authors

Julie Robitaille received a B.A. in English from Emory University, an M.A. in English literature from the University of North Carolina at Chapel Hill, and an M.A. in creative writing from the University of Florida. For twenty years, she directed the

Writing Lab at Santa Fe Community College in Gainesville, Florida. In addition to teaching, she enjoys writing a variety of fiction and non-fiction and renovating old houses.

Bob Connelly received a B.A. from the University of Florida and an M.A. in English literature from the University of Chicago. He has been teaching writing for over twenty-five years at Santa Fe Community College. Bob also writes fiction, runs and swims, and practices meditation.

A Note to Students

It is our pleasure to present *Writer's Resources: Sentence Skills with Readings.* This textbook will introduce you to the power of language and help you develop your own writing power. Because the sentence is the basic unit of all writing, developing college writing skills begins with learning to write clear and correct sentences. By using this book, you will review and strengthen your punctuation and grammar skills, and learn to put sentences together into well-developed paragraphs and essays. However, this textbook will do more than teach you the basic mechanics of college writing.

What you will learn this term is that writing is one of the most powerful forces in the world. Language has the power to change the world, and writing has always been a vehicle for discovering what we think and for communicating important ideas. You will experience both aspects of the power of language as you build your writing skills.

Power of Language Features

- **Spotlight on Writers** boxes tell about writers, famous and ordinary, who have changed the world through their writing. Their examples will motivate and inspire you as you develop the sentence skills necessary to write clearly and correctly. Featured writers include hip-hop artist Chuck D, talk show host Oprah Winfrey, civil rights leader Martin Luther King, Jr., horror writer Stephen King, singer/songwriter Bob Dylan, environmental writer Rachel Carson, Children's Defense Fund founder Marian Wright Edelman, and writing coach William Zinsser.
- **Practicing Your Writing Power** at the end of each chapter provides writing topics that prompt you to use your writing skills to discover more clearly what

you think and feel about issues in your own life. Writing about yourself is a powerful way to generate enthusiasm for writing. These writing prompts will be easy to respond to after you complete chapter Review Exercises that provide timely information about the topics.

- **Model paragraphs and essays** written by students like you show you what college writing looks like. Often we learn best by example, and these eight sample paragraphs and two essays demonstrate the writing concepts you are learning. Exercises follow each model to help you explore the writing concepts you are learning to use in your writing.

- **Skill Previews** at the beginning of every chapter introduce you to the topic of the chapter and help you figure out how much you know about that topic.

- **Practice and Review Exercises** give you valuable practice using the skills you are learning. Some of the exercises are **Working Together Exercises** that encourage you to work alongside classmates. Because such practice can seem boring and removed from meaningful writing, we have worked hard to make the content of the practices interesting. Information on topics ranging from health to history and popular culture will stimulate your thinking, increase your awareness of contemporary issues, and demonstrate how college-level ideas are expressed in writing.

- **Combined Editing Tests** combine all the skills you are learning into editing tests that will help you improve your ability to edit your own writing. These editing exercises start with the basic skills and progress to advanced tests that include all the skills. Using these editing tests, you will improve your editing process gradually through the term.

- **CD Connection** points to more in-depth instruction and practice on the *Writer's Resources* CD-ROM, the popular interactive multi-media presentation of all the topics covered in the text. You will enjoy the audio explanations, animated examples, and extensive practice that will help you improve your writing skill and boost your power.

How the Textbook Is Organized

Introduction: Aiming for Success

This short section introduces you to the power of language and helps you develop the habits that will make you a successful college student such as keeping a journal, developing a positive attitude, taking notes, setting a schedule, and using your resources.

Part I   Introduction to College Writing

Chapter 1 provides in-depth coverage of the paragraph, which is the building block of college essays. You will follow the writing process of a student like you, Tony, as he develops a paragraph. You will use the same writing process to create a well-developed paragraph using strong sentence structure.

Chapter 2 presents an overview of the essay. You will make the connection between the paragraph and the essay when Tony shows you how he expanded his paragraph from Chapter 1 into a college essay.

Part II   Grammar, Mechanics, and Punctuation

This section includes nineteen chapters of grammar, mechanics, and punctuation that provide the most important rules and concepts you need to write effective sentences. All rules are numbered for easy reference, and practice using each rule is provided after each rule. Unlike other textbooks for this course, *Writer's Resources with Readings* prepares you for later writing courses by defining and using the grammatical vocabulary that you will use throughout college.

Each chapter in Part II includes

- **Skill Preview** that introduces chapter topics.
- **Spotlight on Writers** that will help you connect writing skills with a sense of power.
- **Practice Exercises** that allow you to use concepts and to check your answers in the back of the text.
- **Working Together Exercises** that encourage you to work collaboratively.
- **Review Exercises** that combine all the rules for each skill.
- **Editing Exercises** that give you practice finding target errors in a passage.
- **Skill Tests** that allow you to check your comprehension of the concepts taught in each chapter.
- **Practicing Your Writing Power** prompts that encourage you to think and write critically about topics of interest.
- **CD Connection** that points to more in-depth instruction and practice on the *Writer's Resources* CD-ROM.
- **Student Answer Key** (at back of book) that allows you to check your understanding of concepts.

Part III   Review Tests

Combined Editing Tests and **Mastery Tests** give you practice applying (in both editing and multiple choice formats) all the skills acquired in Part II.

Part IV   Readings

Part IV of the text includes **ten professional readings.** These articles will inspire you as you begin your college career. The professional readings are followed by vocabulary exercises, comprehension questions, discussion questions, and writing topics.

Appendices

Appendix 1, **Spelling and Dictionary Skills,** gives you a tutorial on improving your spelling and on using the dictionary to avoid errors in your writing. Appendix 2, **Parts of Speech,** provides background information on grammatical concepts and terminology used in writing classes. Appendix 3, **ESL Skills,** addresses particular language issues that many writers, both international and American, have in learning to use Standard English. Appendix 4, **Paragraph Writing Checklists,** provide materials that will help you write paragraphs.

About the Authors

Julie Robitaille received a B.A. in English from Emory University, an M.A. in English literature from the University of North Carolina at Chapel Hill, and an M.A. in creative writing from the University of Florida. For twenty years, she directed the Writing Lab at Santa Fe Community College in Gainesville, Florida. In addition to teaching, she enjoys writing a variety of fiction and non-fiction and renovating old houses.

Bob Connelly received a B.A. from the University of Florida and an M.A. in English literature from the University of Chicago. He has been teaching writing for over twenty-five years at Santa Fe Community College. Bob also writes fiction, runs and swims, and practices meditation.

Introduction Aiming for Success

This introduction will help you

- ☞ Introduce yourself to your classmates and instructor
- ☞ Understand the power of language
- ☞ Keep a journal: practice your writing power
- ☞ Develop the right attitude
- ☞ Get organized
  - Use a notebook
  - Take notes
  - Schedule study time
- ☞ Use your resources
  - Instructor, classmates, labs, textbook, *Writer's Resources* CD-ROM
  - Online practice

Most students come to college because they want a better life. Each of us has dreams and goals about the way we would like our lives to be. As you begin college, you are starting one of the greatest journeys of your lives. You are leaving behind one life and starting a new life that will require new skills, attitudes, and behaviors. Our dreams and goals help define us and motivate us. Sharing those goals is one of the best ways to get to know one another.

Succeeding in this class is the first step toward achieving your goals. This class is important both because it will help you establish the habits that will make you a successful college student and because it will give you the language skills needed to succeed in college and in life.

WRITING ASSIGNMENT 1

In three to four paragraphs, introduce yourself to your instructor and your class-mates by describing your career and personal goals. What dreams and goals have brought you to college? How do you hope your life will be different in five years?

Example of Writing Assignment 1

Tony Anderson, who shares his writing process in Chapter 2, "The Paragraph," intro-duces himself.

My career goal is to become a counselor so that I can help kids like me figure out what they want in life and get started on the right track. I'd like to help kids make the right decisions instead of wasting their time in high school the way I did. If I had tried harder in high school, I would have learned much more than I did. Unfortunately, I didn't have any ambition then, and all I cared about was hanging out with my friends. I will be successful if I can reach kids who are stalled the way I was. I want to help them by encouraging them to believe in themselves, set goals, and reach for their dreams. I hope not just to be successful, but also to be a decent person, one that gives back to his community. A second, personal goal is to meet the woman of my dreams and raise a happy, healthy family.

The Power of Language

Language is one of the most important tools you will ever learn to use. Language is what makes us uniquely human, what sets us apart from animals, what enables us to think, and what enabled civilization to develop.

Have you ever heard the saying "The pen is mightier than the sword"? It means that language and our ability to express our ideas in writing are far more powerful and persuasive than physical force. Language can win people's hearts and minds, something that guns and violence can never do.

Language is one of the most powerful tools any individual has at his or her dis-posal. Language can and has been used to

- Persuade a nation to go to war
- Overthrow a political system without going to war
- End segregation
- Change laws
- Win love
- Get good grades
- Get a job
- Get a promotion or raise

Spotlight on Writers

Power of Language

Harriet Beecher Stowe

"If it were your Harry, mother, or your Willie, that were going to be torn from you by a brutal trader, tomorrow morning,—if you had seen the man, and heard that the papers were signed and delivered, and you had only from twelve o'clock till morning to make good your escape,—how fast could you walk? How many miles could you make in those few brief hours, with the darling at your bosom,—the little sleepy head on your shoulder,—the small, soft arms trustingly holding on to your neck?"

Harriet Beecher Stowe (1811–1896) is best-known for her antislavery novel *Uncle Tom's Cabin.* The novel was an immediate best-seller, and Stowe toured the United States and Europe, speaking out against the evils of slavery. The novel is credited with stirring wide popular support for the abolition of slavery and for the Civil War. Abraham Lincoln is reported to have called her "the little lady who made this big war."

In this excerpt from Chapter 7 of *Uncle Tom's Cabin,* Stowe dramatizes the injustice and tragedy of slavery when the slave Eliza flees after hearing that her child will be taken away from her and sold.

- Create a record of your life
- Figure out what you feel and think

Throughout the text, we feature individuals who have used the power of language through their writing, speeches, or songs to accomplish a goal. Some of these individuals are famous writers, singers, and celebrities, and some are everyday citizens, but each illustrates how writing can open doors and move mountains.

Gaining control of language will make you a far more powerful individual. Learning how to express your ideas and feelings in writing will give you the power to figure out what you think and believe, to express your thoughts and feelings, and to persuade others to understand and share those ideas and feelings.

As any college graduate will tell you, gaining control of language is the key to being successful in school. Learning the course material is only half the battle because instructors give grades based on a student's ability to communicate his or her understanding of course material in writing. Most classes require essay exams, reports, and papers, and many of these writing assignments must be completed in class. Learning to write clearly will make succeeding in school much easier.

Writing also plays an important role in getting and keeping a good job. Employers consistently say that they are looking for employees who can communicate clearly. They are unlikely to hire an applicant who does not demonstrate strong writing skills. Once hired, employees need to be able to write clearly in order to communicate with clients, co-workers, and supervisors. Common on-the-job writing tasks include writing directions, reports, letters, explanations, and memos. Being able to write well can mean the difference between promotion and nonpromotion. Clear writing can often determine more than promotion, however. For example, the clarity of law enforcement officers' reports can make or break a case, and the accuracy of records kept by medical personnel can mean the difference between life and death. The ability to communicate clearly in writing is essential to success in the workplace.

Improving your language skills will take time and effort, but most of all, it will take developing the right attitude and developing the habits that will help you be successful.

Keep a Journal: Practicing Your Writing Power

Nothing improves your writing like doing it regularly. The best way to get better at writing is to write every day or at least several times a week. The more you write, the more you will see how useful writing can be, how it can help you think, how it can help you develop and clarify your ideas. At the end of each chapter, you will find an assignment called Practicing Your Writing Power that will help you use writing to develop and express your ideas. One of the magical things about writing is that the more you write, the better you will get at it.

Develop the Right Attitude

"If you think you can or if you think you can't, you are right." Will Rogers

Will Rogers reminds us that attitude is the single biggest determiner of success. People who believe they can succeed do succeed. People who don't believe in themselves don't succeed.

First, you need to believe in yourself enough to try. Next, you shouldn't be discouraged by the obstacles you encounter. Everyone encounters obstacles, large and small. The difference between those who succeed and those who fail is that those who succeed keep trying despite the obstacle.

Get Organized

Even if you have the right attitude, you will need to translate your attitude into action.

Successful people develop habits that will help them succeed. The habits listed below will help you succeed in this and any class.

Use a Notebook

Buy a loose-leaf notebook and dividers for this class. Set up dividers for handouts, class notes, writing assignments, and any other divisions your instructor suggests. Every time your instructor gives you a handout, date it, hole punch it, and put it in your notebook. Most important assignments, dates, and concepts are covered on handouts, and the best way to be sure you don't lose any important information is to keep all handouts in your notebook.

Take Notes

Taking notes in class will help in two ways: it will make sure that you don't miss important information, and it will help you stay focused during class.

For every class you attend, date a piece of notebook paper, and write down the following:

- Anything your instructor writes on the board. If it's important enough for your instructor to write on the board, it's important enough to be in your notes.
- Any information your instructor covers in class, including directions for assignments, definitions, procedures, and so on. If your instructor covers it, he or she expects you to know the information, and you may have no other way to get the information if you don't write it down in class.

Schedule Study Time

Most first-time college students aren't used to having to do significant amounts of schoolwork outside of class, and few students have the luxury of going home to uninterrupted study time. In fact, most students must balance the demands of school, work, family, and social life. It takes real effort to schedule study time and then to follow that schedule, but it is absolutely essential to your success in college.

You should plan to study from thirty minutes to an hour outside of class for every hour you spend in class. Scheduling regular study time will mean making sacrifices. You may need to cut down on the number of hours you work or the number of hours you watch TV or the number of hours you spend with friends and family, but in the end, the trade-off will be worth it.

When will you schedule study time for this class?

_____

What problems do you foresee studying thirty to sixty minutes outside of class for every hour of class?

_____
_____
_____
_____

Monitor Your Progress

To succeed, you must keep track of how well you are doing and make changes if you are not succeeding. Get in the habit of checking in with yourself on a weekly basis about your progress in this (or any) class.

Evaluate Your Weekly Progress by Examining the Following Areas:

Attendance: How many days did you miss class this week?

_____

What could you do in the future to avoid the problem that caused you to miss class?

_____

Homework: How many assignments were you unable to complete before the class in which they were due? What could you do not to miss assignments in the future?

_____

Attitude: Rate your attitude for the week. (1 = lowest, 5 = highest)

1 2 3 4 5

What can you do to help keep your attitude positive and focused?

_____

Grades: Record any and all grades you received on tests or assignments. What could you do in the future to maintain or improve your grades?

_____

Use Your Resources

Successful students are active students. They use the resources that are available to help them succeed. Following are the most important resources for your success.

Instructor

Your instructor is your single best resource for success. Be sure you know your instructor's name, office hours, office phone, and e-mail address.

Instructor's name: _____

Office location: _____

Office hours: _____

Phone: _____

E-mail address: _____

If you have questions about the course or about your progress, don't hesitate to ask your instructor. If you are not available during your instructor's office hours, talk with him or her before or after class or e-mail him or her with questions. Instructors want to answer student questions, but they won't be able to help if you don't ask for help.

It's always a good idea to notify your instructor in advance if you will miss class, and you should always inform an instructor when you will miss an exam. Many instructors will not allow students to make up missed work or exams unless the instructor has been notified in advance.

List three ways your instructor might be able to help you this semester.

_____

_____

_____

Classmates

Your classmates will also be a valuable resource in helping you succeed in this course. First, your peers can be valuable tutors and study partners. Many students set up out-of-class study groups to learn material and review for tests. Getting to know your classmates' names is the first step in forming a bond with your peers. Make an effort to learn your classmates' names by taking notes as they introduce themselves or are introduced by others. Write down their names, and jot down anything that will help you remember them (hair color, distinguishing features, etc.).

Your classmates can also be a resource if you miss class. Get the phone number and/or e-mail address of several students in your class who are willing to be a resource for you (and vice versa) if any of you should miss class. If you must miss class, be sure you call or e-mail a classmate or your instructor to get the assignments, and be sure you complete the assignments before you return to class. Once you return, ask to see a classmate's notes and the answers to any exercises that were reviewed in class.

Classmate Contacts

Name _____   Name_____

Phone_____   Phone _____

E-mail_____   E-Mail _____

Working with Classmates

Learning to work effectively with others is important both in school and in the workplace. Employers consistently rate the ability to get along with others as one of the most valued characteristics in an employee. This semester you will have the opportunity to work with your classmates in groups and in pairs.

Here are some guidelines for effective cooperation.

1. Treat your classmates as you would like to be treated, with respect. Listen when they speak, and don't interrupt. Try to appreciate their viewpoints or experiences, even if different from your own.

2. If you are working in a group, divide the tasks equally among group members. Each group member will be expected to contribute his or her fair share of the final project.

List three ways that your classmates might be able to help you this semester.

_____

_____

_____

Labs

Many schools have resource centers or labs where students can get individual help or tutoring if they are having trouble in a class. Find out the location and hours of the writing center or lab on your campus, and visit the lab to find out what services it offers students.

Writing center location: _____

Writing center hours: _____

Your Textbook

Writer's Resources: Sentence Skills can help you succeed in your English class, especially if you use it effectively. The key is to use your book. To absorb the knowledge in a book, you need to be active. Write in your book: highlight, underline, and write notes and questions in the margins, but most important, be sure you complete your assignments before you go to class. This textbook is intended to be written in, and you should plan on answering all the practices and exercises in the book. After each skill rule, you will find a short practice that enables you to see whether you understand the rule and can apply it. The answers to these practices are located in the back of the book (pp. A-53–A-93). Doing the practices after each skill and checking your answers will help you gauge whether or not you are "getting it," absorbing the skills you are trying to learn.

Instructors can't cover every rule in the same detail that your textbook will, so you can't expect to learn the rules simply by attending class. If you have completed the practices in the book, you will know which rules are most difficult for you, and you can ask your instructor for additional help or explanation of those rules, or you can visit your campus writing center or use _Writer's Resources_ CD-ROM for additional help and practice with the skill. Many instructors cover the answers to reviews and tests in class (answers not in the back of the book), so if you miss class, you should check with a classmate to find the right answers for review exercises and tests.

Before a test, use the review exercises and tests in your textbook to brush up on the rules and to see which rules gave you the most difficulty.

Writer's Resources CD-ROM

The CD-ROM that accompanies your textbook provides additional instruction, with audio and visual reinforcement, and provides many additional practice exercises with feedback after each item. The CD-ROM is a great way to get additional help and practice. Using the CD-ROM is like having a writing center available in the convenience of your own home.

USING THE CD-ROM

We suggest that you store the CD-ROM in a hard case to avoid cracking the disc. To use the CD-ROM, insert it in the CD-ROM drive, and select the My Computer icon on the desktop. Next, select the Writer's Resources icon. At the opening screen, you may select to take a tour of the program, a two-minute explanation of the contents and functionality of the CD-ROM, or you may go directly to the menu by selecting the large blue arrow labeled "Continue to Contents." The Contents menu screen enables you to choose the area of the program you wish to enter. The grammar, punctuation, and mechanics lesson, in the green bar at the bottom of the screen, contains interactive lessons on twenty-one skill areas. Select an area by clicking on its name. The menu for each skill lists the topics and practices covered in the lesson, and you can select any topic or practice by clicking on it.

Each lesson contains numerous three- to five-item practices, which can be repeated, a Review Resources screen with links to review the entire lesson, and ten-item Exercises sets that review the concepts for the entire lesson. Exercises sets can be repeated with new items each time. Many lessons contain Writing Practices that allow you to compose your own sentences. You may print your scores for a session by selecting the Report tab at the top of the screen. If you would like to print your scores, type your name, and select Print. If your instructor wants you to report your scores online (only exercise sets are reported), select the Save Online tab, and enter your predetermined login ID and password. Note: To save scores online, you must first establish a login ID and password through iLrn®, Blackboard®, or WebCT™.

Remember: Your scores will not be saved on the CD-ROM, so you must either print scores or save them online before you exit the CD-ROM after each session.

Online Practice

Additional practice tests are available online through iLrn, Blackboard, or WebCT. Your instructor will tell you if he or she requires or recommends that you access online practice tests and how to do so.

Part I Introduction to College Writing

You will use your writing skills in most courses you take in college. In fact, your ability to express yourself effectively in writing will determine your grades in many courses. Most of your writing will be in the form of paragraphs and essays. You will be required to write paragraph responses on exams, and most college papers will be in the form of essays. In all your assignments, your professors will expect you to use the writing process to brainstorm ideas to write about, formulate a main idea for your paragraphs and essays, generate support for your main idea, and construct a conclusion.

In this part of the textbook, you will learn to write a paragraph in Chapter 1 and an essay in Chapter 2. The paragraph and essay are closely related because the basic format for both is the same. Indeed, the paragraph format you learn to use in Chapter 1 is the same format that you will use in the body paragraphs in your essays. In Chapter 2, you will learn to construct an essay from paragraphs like the ones you learned in Chapter 1; in addition, you will learn to write introductory paragraphs and concluding paragraphs to introduce and conclude your essay.

It is our hope that by the end of this course you will be able to write well-developed paragraphs and that you will understand the format of the essay.

Chapter 1 The Paragraph

In this chapter you will

- Learn about the paragraph format
- Practice using the parts of the paragraph
- Use the writing process to write paragraphs

Skill Preview

The paragraph is the building block of all college writing. Many college assignments, including short-answer exams, call for paragraph-length responses. Essays, the most common college writing assignment, are built one paragraph at a time. The best way to prepare to succeed with college writing assignments is to master the paragraph.

In this chapter, you will learn to use the writing process to write paragraphs that have the three marks of good writing: **development, unity,** and **coherence.** Development means developing the paragraph with enough strong, supporting sentences to convince the reader of the paragraph's main idea. Unity means that all the sentences in the paragraph support the main idea. Coherence means that the relationships between the supporting sentences are clear.

To help you get the hang of paragraph writing, Tony Anderson, a student like you, shares one paragraph he wrote and shows you the steps he followed to develop his paragraph. You will follow the same steps in the writing process as you begin writing your own paragraphs.

A Student's Best Friend

    Computers offer students many advantages. First, most col-
lege instructors expect students to turn in typed papers, and
word processing programs allow students to compose, save, and
revise their writing easily, and students can eliminate
errors by using the spell check and grammar check functions.
Next, because Internet search engines such as Google and
Yahoo put the resources of the World Wide Web at a student's
fingertips, researching information for assignments no longer
involves late nights at the library. Computers can also aid
students with their homework by giving them access to CD-ROM
tutorials and online testing sites such as iLrn, WebCT, and

Blackboard. Moreover, the computer can save students time and money while keeping them in touch with instructors, class-mates, and family through e-mail, instant messaging, and online discussion boards. Additionally, students can use their computers to take advantage of the convenience and cost savings of shopping over the Web for everything from CDs and textbooks to plane tickets. Last but not least, students can relax after a long day by listening to their favorite music, playing games, or watching a DVD on their computer. Computers do indeed provide students with many benefits.

Tony's paragraph shows many of the characteristics of college-level writing. His **development** of the main idea includes enough details, facts, and examples to convince the reader of the computer's advantages. For example, he mentions a specific search engine, *Google,* and the names of online testing sites such as *WebCT.* Also, the paragraph achieves a **unity** of purpose because all the sentences support the main idea. Finally, the paragraph creates **coherence** by using transitions such as *additionally, also,* and *last but not least* to make clear the relationship between supporting sentences.

PREVIEW ACTIVITY   To become familiar with the paragraph format, underline the first sentence of Tony's paragraph and label it *topic sentence.* Then, underline the last sentence and label it *conclusion.* Finally, draw a bracket from the second line of the paragraph to the line before the conclusion and label all the sentences between the topic sentence and conclusion *supporting sentences.*

Spotlight on Writers

Power of Language

Marjorie Stoneman Douglas

"There are no other Everglades in the world. They are, they have always been, one of the unique regions of the earth; remote, never wholly known. Nothing anywhere else is like them. . . ."

Marjorie Stoneman Douglas (1890–1998) is best-known for her book *Everglades: River of Grass,* which drew attention to the Everglades as a unique national treasure. Throughout her life she fought for the preservation of the Everglades and the fragile ecosystem on which their existence depends. Her persuasive use of language influenced environmentalists and politicians to help protect the Everglades. A former governor of Florida called her "the poet, the sledge-hammer advocate, the constant conscience of the Everglades for half a century."

Paragraph Form

A paragraph is a series of sentences that develops a main idea. While paragraphs can be any length, most college paragraphs are between five and ten sentences. When the paragraph stands alone as a piece of writing, it may need a **title.** The main idea of the paragraph is usually stated in the **topic sentence.** The body of the paragraph provides **supporting sentences** that explain or prove the main idea. The **conclusion** is the last sentence of the paragraph, and it summarizes the paragraph or adds a final supporting sentence.

The Parts of the Paragraph

Title

✓ Presents a unique name for the paragraph

✓ Is usually a fragment written a line or two above the topic sentence in the middle of the page

✓ Has the first, last, and all important words capitalized

Topic Sentence

✓ States the main idea of the paragraph

✓ Expresses an opinion, feeling, attitude, or point of view

✓ Often is the first sentence of the paragraph

Supporting Sentences

✓ Develop the main idea

✓ Prove, explain, or illustrate the main idea in the topic sentence

✓ Include three to five (or more) supporting sentences

✓ Use specific details, including facts, examples, and descriptive language

Conclusion

✓ Restates the main idea in different words or

✓ States the significance of the support or

✓ Presents a final support

CD Connection

Power of Language

On *Writer's Resources* CD-ROM, see *The Paragraph* in Writing Elements for more information on the parts of the paragraph: topic sentence, support, and conclusion.

The Writing Process

Paragraphs like Tony's are developed one step at a time using the writing process. You will follow the same steps in the writing process to write your own paragraph.

Steps in the Writing Process

Step 1: Narrowing the topic to a tentative main idea

Step 2: Generating ideas

Step 3: Developing and organizing ideas

Step 4: Drafting

Step 5: Revising

Step 6: Editing

Using the writing process will help you develop your ideas, organize them, and present them clearly because you will focus on one issue at a time during each step in the process. Many students try to write papers in one draft, but such papers don't usually turn out well because the students don't give themselves time to develop their ideas fully, and they don't revise their writing or edit it to eliminate errors.

In the early stages of the writing process, you will focus on making sure your ideas are well **developed.** Next, you will check to make sure all your ideas are **unified** in supporting your main idea. Then, you will focus on making your paragraph **coherent** so that the reader understands how the sentences relate to one another.

Step 1: Narrowing the Topic to a Tentative Topic Sentence

Many topics you will be given in college will be broad subjects that you must narrow down in order to develop effectively. If you are given a broad topic, your first step must be to narrow the topic to a topic sentence. You may revise your tentative topic sentence later, after you have generated supporting ideas.

THE PARAGRAPH TOPIC

Either your instructor or you will choose a topic to develop in a paragraph. The topic is the general subject of your paragraph. The topic may be a few words or a writing prompt of a few sentences. Following are a number of typical writing topics.

Paragraph Topics

Advantages or disadvantages of computers or cell phones

Advantages or disadvantages of living in your hometown

A movie you would or would not recommend

A good or bad teacher

The benefits or drawbacks of owning a pet

A good or bad roommate

A job that you enjoyed or didn't enjoy

A place of business you would or would not recommend

Instructor's choices:

_____

_____

_____

THE TOPIC SENTENCE

The topic sentence states the **main idea** of the paragraph. Because the body of the paragraph will develop the main idea, the topic sentence is generally **not a factual statement but a statement of opinion** that calls for development or explanation. The topic sentence usually expresses the writer's **feeling, attitude, or point of view about the writing topic.**

Practice 1   Label each sentence as fact or opinion. Put a check mark next to the sentence that would make the best topic sentence. Then, underline the opinion words in the best topic sentence.

1. _____   A. My pet is a golden retriever.

    _____   B. My golden retriever, Sandy, is a wonderful pet.

2. _____   A. Algebra was my favorite class last year.

    _____   B. I took algebra last year.

3. _____   A. Mr. Beckman was my boss at Quick Pick.

    _____   B. Mr. Beckman was a great boss.

4. _____   A. Josh was a terrible roommate.

    _____   B. Josh was my roommate last semester.

5. _____   A. I lived in Pinewood Apartments for two years.

    _____   B. Pinewood Apartments are great for students.

Practice 2   Choose the best topic sentence for each topic. Remember that the topic sentence must be a complete sentence as well as an opinion.

1. Topic: teachers

   A. A wonderful teacher

   B. Mr. Crabbe is a great history teacher.

   C. Mr. Crabbe was my eighth grade teacher.

2. Topic: cell phone

   A. There are many advantages to owning a cell phone for teenagers.

   B. Advantages of owning a cell phone for teenagers.

   C. Many teenagers own cell phones.

3. Topic: roommates

   A. My roommate is Deidre Jenkins.

   B. Deidre Jenkins is an awesome roommate.

   C. The best roommate I could ever have.

4. Topic: role models

   A. My father is an outstanding role model for me.

   B. An outstanding role model in my life.

   C. Thomas Pinkerton is my father.

5. Topic: pets

   A. One of the best dogs for a family.

   B. I own a golden retriever.

   C. My golden retriever is a great family dog.

GENERATING A TOPIC SENTENCE FROM THE TOPIC

One strategy to narrow a general topic to an opinion that you can develop in a paragraph is to consider the **audience** (the group of people you are addressing) and your **purpose** (why you are addressing them).

Tony was given the topic of *the advantages or disadvantages of computers*, and he narrowed the topic by considering how computers can help students.

Topic: Advantages or disadvantages of computers
Audience: Students
Tentative topic sentence: Computers offer students many advantages.

Practice 3   Narrow the topic by considering different audiences or groups of people you might address, and write a main idea that states that the topic is an advantage or disadvantage for that group of people. Choose from the following audiences for each item: students, families, children, businesspeople, and the elderly.

Example:
Topic: Advantages or disadvantages of computers
Audience: Children
Tentative topic sentence: Computers offer children many advantages.

1. Topic: Advantages or disadvantages of cell phones
   Audience: _____
   Tentative topic sentence: _____

2. Topic: Advantages or disadvantages of living in your hometown
   Audience: _____
   Tentative topic sentence: _____
   _____

3. Topic: Benefits or drawbacks of owning a pet
   Audience: _____
   Tentative topic sentence: _____

4. Topic: A place of business you would or would not recommend
   Audience: _____
   Tentative topic sentence: _____

5. Topic: A good or bad movie
   Audience: _____
   Tentative topic sentence: _____

Another way to narrow a general topic is to think of a **specific example of the topic.** If you are given a general topic such as *movies,* a good way to narrow the topic may be to think of a specific example that you are familiar with. Once you've come up with an example, you can make a statement that expresses an opinion about your narrowed topic.

Practice 4   Choose a specific example of each general topic, and decide whether it is a positive or negative example of the general topic.

Example:
Topic: A good or bad movie
Example: *The Return of the King*
Topic sentence: *The Return of the King* is a great movie.

1. Topic: A good or bad teacher
   Example: _____
   Topic sentence: _____

2. Topic: Benefits or drawbacks of owning a pet
   Example: _____
   Topic sentence: _____

3. Topic: A good or bad roommate
   Example: _____
   Topic sentence: _____

4. Topic: A good or bad job that you have held
   Example: _____
   Topic sentence: _____

5. Topic: A place of business you would recommend
   Example: _____
   Topic sentence: _____

WRITING PRACTICE 1

Determine your topic and tentative topic sentence.
Topic: _____
Tentative topic sentence: _____
_____

Step 2: Generating Ideas

Once you have narrowed the topic to a tentative topic sentence, you are ready to generate ideas to support your topic sentence. Supporting ideas are specific facts, ideas, or examples that prove or illustrate the main idea stated in your topic sentence.

Tips on Generating Ideas

Visualize or imagine a picture of the topic you are writing about. Imagine what the person, place, or thing looks like.

See the topic in your mind's eye and be aware of all the senses—sight, hearing, taste, smell, and touch.

Don't worry about writing correctly. Don't even try to write in complete sentences, and don't worry about grammar, spelling, or punctuation. Simply get your ideas down on paper.

Writers use brainstorming strategies such as **brainstorming/listing, free writing, dividing,** and **clustering** to come up with ideas to support their main idea. These techniques are effective because they can help you discover what you think, how you feel, and what you have to say about a topic.

BRAINSTORMING OR LISTING

Alone or in a group, focus on the topic, and come up with as many ideas as possible to support your topic sentence.

Tony started brainstorming by seeing how many ideas he could come up with on the advantages of using computers.

> Advantages of computers for students:
>   play games
>   buy stuff
>   record music
>   play music
>   do schoolwork
>   instant message
>   pay bills
>   visit web sites for my favorite teams

FREEWRITING

Focus on your topic sentence and write everything that comes to mind, no matter how important or unimportant, about why you feel the way you do about the topic. Write as much and as fast as you can for five minutes.

> I don't think that I could live without my computer. In fact, I wish I had a new one. I want to get a bigger monitor, but I guess I can live with the one I have. I'm using it right now to write my paper, and I do a lot of schoolwork with it. I don't think I could get by in school if I didn't have it. Maybe I should write about how the computer helps me get my work done. I could even include how I e-mail and listen to music while doing homework. There's a lot of stuff students like me use it for.

CLUSTERING

Start by writing your topic sentence in the middle of the page. Then write down words or images you associate with your main idea in the topic sentence. These words may be parts of your topic. Next, cluster or group related ideas together by drawing lines around them and drawing lines between them.

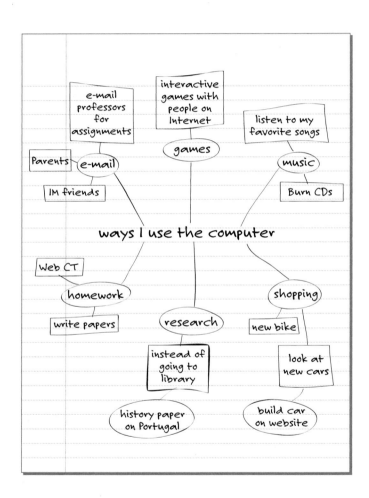

DIVIDING

Divide your topic into its component parts (the parts of a movie, of a job, of a class). Perhaps you can divide your topic chronologically according to what happens first, second, and third. Thinking of the parts of your topic can help you think of supports for your main idea.

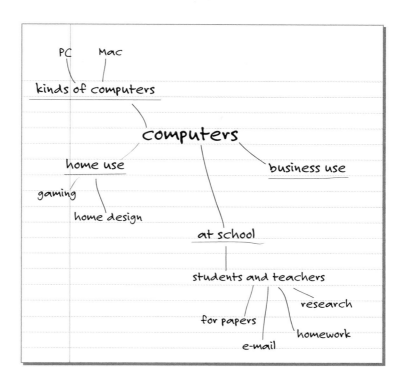

Practice 5 *Working Together*

1. In groups of three to five students, generate ideas for how computers might be an advantage or disadvantage for *one* of the following groups of people: shoppers, businesspeople, schoolchildren, families, retirees, or gamers. After generating ideas, each group should share the ideas generated with the rest of the class.

2. In groups of three to five students, generate ideas for how living in your hometown might be an advantage or disadvantage for *one* of the following groups: students, families, businesses, children, athletes, singles, or retirees. After generating ideas, each group should share the ideas generated with the rest of the class.

WRITING PRACTICE 2

On your own paper, write your tentative topic sentence, and then use one or more of the brainstorming strategies to generate ideas to support your tentative topic sentence.

CD Connection

Power of Language

On *Writer's Resources* CD-ROM, see "Writing Process: First Steps" for more information on narrowing a topic, formulating a topic sentence, and generating ideas.

Step 3: Developing and Organizing Ideas

Before you write supporting sentences for your topic sentence, you must develop the supporting ideas and organize them. You will flesh out your supporting ideas with specific facts or examples, and you may want to explain how the ideas relate to the topic sentence. In this stage of the writing process, you are concentrating on getting your ideas down on paper in preparation for writing supporting sentences.

CREATING A PARAGRAPH MAP OR OUTLINE

Many students prefer to start the process of organizing their ideas as they are developing their ideas. You can list the ideas you have generated, or you can create a map or outline of your ideas. As you develop your supporting ideas, you will add additional information to your map or outline. By mapping your ideas on paper, you can avoid getting writer's block and not knowing what to write. Also, a map or outline helps you keep on track once you start writing your rough draft. Developing and organizing your ideas will save you time and frustration when you start writing sentences because you will have all your ideas and words on paper in front of you.

Paragraph Map

Topic sentence:_____

_____

Area of Support	Specific Details	Relation to Opinion
1. _____	_____	_____
2. _____	_____	_____
3. _____	_____	_____
4. _____	_____	_____
5. _____	_____	_____
6. _____	_____	_____

Paragraph Outline

Topic sentence:_____

_____

I. Supporting idea 1 _____
    A. Specific detail or example _____
    B. Explain how idea supports topic sentence_____

II. Supporting idea 2_____
    A. Specific detail or example _____
    B. Explain how idea supports topic sentence_____

III. Supporting idea 3 _____
    A. Specific detail or example _____
    B. Explain how idea supports topic sentence_____

IV. Supporting idea 4 _____
    A. Specific detail or example _____
    B. Explain how idea supports topic sentence_____

V. Supporting idea 5_____
    A. Specific detail or example _____
    B. Explain how idea supports topic sentence_____

To create strong support for your topic sentence, you should use a step-by-step process. Using a map or outline, you will

1. List the **general ideas** you generate to support your main idea.
2. Add **specific details and examples** for each general idea.
3. Make sure **the supporting ideas clearly support** the topic sentence**.**

ADD SPECIFIC DETAILS AND EXAMPLES

Once you have generated ideas to support your tentative topic sentence, you are ready to build your support by adding specific details and examples to your map or outline. Specific details are words, facts, statistics, details, or examples that will make the supporting ideas more concrete and understandable to the audience. Readers want detailed information, not generalities. For example, if you are stating that your hometown is great for college students, readers won't be satisfied reading that your hometown offers lots of recreation—they want specific examples of the recreation. To be well developed, your writing must have enough specific details to convince the reader of your main idea.

Model

Tony added specific details to the list of ideas he had generated. He thought of specific ways the computer helps him with papers, research, classwork, communication, and shopping.

```
Papers
How does the computer help?-->word
processor with spell-check and grammar-
check
Anything else the computer does with
paper?-->save docs and revise easily

Research
How does computer help with research?
-->Internet search engines-->Google

Homework
What homework is done with the
computer?-->CD-ROM for writing, WebCT, iLrn
testing
```

Practice 6   Match specific details to the corresponding area of support.

I. Topic: Your hometown
    Topic sentence: Reedsville is a fantastic town for athletes.

Area of Support	Specific Details
1. great weather	_____ A. Intramural sports, city leagues
2. numerous facilities	_____ B. Indoor and outdoor pools, tracks, recreation parks and fields
3. other athletes	_____ C. Lots of dedicated athletes and trainers
4. organized group sports	_____ D. Ability to train outdoors year-round
5. great sports medicine facilities	_____ E. Sports massage, physical therapy, trained doctors

II. Topic: Good or bad role model
    Topic sentence: Halle Berry is a great role model.

Area of Support	Specific Details
1. Kind and generous to fans	_____ A. Never misses work, never is late to set or uncooperative

2. Likes to help others

_____ B. Always signs autographs and answers fan mail

3. Behaves well in public

_____ C. Polite and considerate of others

4. Respects others

_____ D. Works for charities and encourages girls to stay in school

5. Works hard

_____ E. Never drunk in public, never behaves inappropriately

III. Topic: Good or bad neighbors
    Topic sentence: The Shaneys were terrible neighbors.

Areas of Support	**Specific Details**
1. Loud	_____ A. Pile trash in corner of yard, never mow or weed yard, junk cars on blocks
2. Messy yard	_____ B. Play loud music late at night
3. Borrow things without asking	_____ C. Yard tools and chairs disappear and reappear in their yard
4. Bad people as guests	_____ D. Hoodlums and drug dealers hanging around
5. Animals	_____ E. Their dogs attacked our cat

WRITING PRACTICE 3

In a group or alone, generate specific details for each area of support you generated for your main idea, and add them to your map or outline.

MAKE SURE THE SUPPORTING IDEAS CLEARLY SUPPORT THE TOPIC SENTENCE

The next step in building a strong paragraph is to examine your topic sentence and your supporting ideas to make sure they match. At this stage in the writing process, you are working to make sure that your paragraph is **unified,** that everything in it supports your topic sentence.

1. You must examine your topic sentence to make sure it covers all the supporting ideas you have generated. Your topic sentence should be an umbrella statement that covers everything you develop in your paragraph. In other words, it should be general enough to cover all of your supporting sentences.
2. You must examine the supporting ideas you have generated to make sure that they clearly support your topic sentence.

Evaluating Your Topic Sentence

Make sure the topic sentence expresses an opinion, not a fact, about the topic.

Make sure the topic sentence is broad enough to cover everything developed in the paragraph.

Make sure the topic sentence is a complete sentence.

Practice 7   Select the topic sentence that best expresses the main idea of *all* the details generated in the brainstorming list.

1. Narrowed topic: Disadvantages of owning a dog

Brainstorming list:

- Dog hair everywhere and accidents on rug
- Time consuming to walk and play with
- Expensive—vet bills, food
- Loud barking keeps you and neighbors awake at night
- Nasty disposition, growl or bite people

Topic sentences:

    A. A dog can be messy and time consuming.

    B. Dogs can be noisy.

    C. Dogs require lots of time and are expensive.

    D. Owning a dog can have many disadvantages.

2. Narrowed topic: advantages of roommates

Brainstorming list:

- Reliable in paying rent
- Help with chores around house
- Share bills
- Someone to go out with at night
- Help with homework
- Take turns cooking

Topic sentences:

    A. I shared an apartment with Aaron for a year.

    B. Aaron was a great roommate.

    C. I could rely on Aaron to pay his bills on time.

    D. Aaron was lots of fun because we could go out together.

3. Narrowed topic: Disadvantages of cell phones

Brainstorming list:

- Bad reception or no signal
- Battery always going dead
- High monthly charges
- Easy to forget to turn it off in class or movie
- No uninterrupted study time—friends can always bother you

Topic sentences:

A. Cell phones can be expensive and a nuisance.

B. There are many disadvantages to cell phones.

C. There are many disadvantages to cell phones for students.

D. Cell phones give students little privacy.

Developing Unified Supporting Sentences

Compare each supporting sentence to your topic sentence.

Ask yourself how the information you have generated explains or proves the main idea in the topic sentence. If your supporting sentence doesn't clearly support your topic sentence, either add information to make it support your topic sentence, or delete it.

Express the relationship of the supporting ideas to the topic sentence in a word or phrase.

Once you have examined and revised your topic sentence, you are ready to examine your supporting ideas to make sure that they develop the main idea in your topic sentence. Your goal should be to make sure every sentence in your paragraph clearly supports your topic sentence.

Don't assume that the reader will automatically understand how your supporting sentences prove your topic sentence. Many supporting ideas can be either positive or negative, depending on how they are presented. For example, if your main idea is that your hometown is great for college students, and one of your supports is that lots of other students are in town, you should not assume that the reader will automatically see how having lots of students in town is an advantage. Your reader might conclude that having lots of other students in town is a disadvantage because of the trouble in finding a parking place or getting into restaurants or movies. You may need to explain how or why the details you've included support your topic sentence.

To make sure that your supporting sentences clearly support your topic sentence, include enough information to **make clear the relationship between**

the supporting idea and the main idea. You may need to show how the information and details you give prove the opinion stated in the topic sentence.

Tony examined each of his support sentences and challenged himself to explain how the details he included proved that computers are an advantage for students.

Papers
How are spell-check, grammar-check, and the save and revise functions a benefit when writing a paper?--?avoid errors

Research
What is the advantage of doing research on the computer?-->no more late nights at the library

Homework
What is the advantage of doing homework like the CD-ROM and WebCT on the computer? -->work at home on tests

Communication
Why do students like using e-mail and instant messaging?--?save time and money

Shopping
What's the advantage of shopping online? -->save money

Entertainment
What benefits do students get from music, games, and movies on the computer?--?relax

Practice 8   The following support ideas were generated to support the topic *The disadvantages of being the oldest child*. Decide how each idea could be negative. Next, write a new sentence that makes the relationship between the supporting detail and the topic sentence clear.

Topic sentence: I experienced many disadvantages as the oldest child in my family.

1. I was spoiled by my parents and grandparents.
   How could being spoiled be negative?

   _____

Write a revised support sentence that clearly explains the disadvantage.

_____

_____

2. My parents were strict with me.
   How could having to live with strict rules be negative?

   _____

   Write a revised support sentence that clearly explains the disadvantage.

   _____

   _____

3. My parents had high expectations of me.
   How could your parents' expectations be negative?

   _____

   Write a revised support sentence that clearly explains the disadvantage.

   _____

   _____

4. I was expected to babysit my younger brother and sister.
   How could having to babysit be negative?

   _____

   Write a revised support sentence that clearly explains the disadvantage.

   _____

   _____

5. I was the first child in my family to do things like drive and go out on dates.
   How could being the first to do things be negative?

   _____

   Write a revised support sentence that clearly explains the disadvantage.

   _____

   _____

Practice 9   Add an explanation of how the details support the topic sentence for each support area in the following outlines. The first item has been completed as an example.

1. Topic sentence: Reedsville offers athletes many advantages.
   I. Area: great weather
      A. Details: sunny most of the year and temperatures between 40 and 90 degrees
      B. Explain how details support topic sentence: ability to train outdoors year-round
   II. Area: numerous facilities
      A. Details: indoor and outdoor pools, tracks, recreation parks and fields

      B. Explain how details support topic sentence (How are facilities an advantage to athletes?):

   _____

  III. Area: contact with other athletes
      A. Details: lots of other dedicated athletes and trainers
      B. Explain how details support topic sentence (Why are contacts with athletes and trainers an advantage?):

   _____

  IV. Area: organized group sports
      A. Details: intramural sports, city leagues
      B. Explain how details support topic sentence (How do intramurals and leagues help athletes?):

   _____

  V. Area: great sports medicine facilities
      A. Details: sports massage, physical therapy, trained doctors
      B. Explain how details support topic sentence (How are great sports medical facilities an advantage for athletes?):

   _____

2. Topic sentence: There are many disadvantages to riding a bicycle to school.
   I. Area: weather
      A. Details: over 80 degrees in summer and below freezing in winter
      B. Explain how details support topic sentence: arrive at school sweaty or numb
   II. Area: fatigue
      A. Details: use too much energy
      B. Explain how details support topic sentence (How would arriving at school tired be a disadvantage?):

   _____

  III. Area: no space to carry anything
      A. Details: art portfolios or laptops
      B. Explain how details support topic sentence (How is lack of carrying space a disadvantage for students?):

   _____

  IV. Area: time consuming
      A. Details: takes thirty minutes to an hour to reach school
      B. Explain how details support topic sentence (Why is lost time a disadvantage?):

   _____

  V. Area: accidents
      A. Details: cars don't see bicyclists
      B. Explain how details support topic sentence (How would getting into an accident be harmful?):

   _____

3. Topic sentence: The Shaneys are terrible neighbors.
   - I. Area: loud
     - A. Details: play loud music late at night and dogs bark all night long
     - B. Explain how details support topic sentence: we had trouble getting any sleep
   - II. Area: messy yard
     - A. Details: pile trash in corner of yard, never mow or weed yard, junk cars on blocks
     - B. Explain how details support topic sentence:

     _____

   - III. Area: borrow things without asking
     - A. Details: yard tools and chairs disappear and reappear in their yard
     - B. Explain how details support topic sentence:

     _____

   - IV. Area: bad people as guests
     - A. Details: hoodlums and drug dealers hanging around
     - B. Explain how details support topic sentence:

     _____

Practice 10 Underline the topic sentence, and identify the sentences in the paragraph that do not support the topic sentence. Next, decide what information you could add to make the nonsupports into supports.

Woman's Best Friend

My golden retriever, Sandy, is a fantastic dog.[1] She loves to entertain me by doing tricks like retrieving sticks or balls, rolling over, and shaking hands.[2] I bought her from a friend who breeds and shows golden retrievers.[3] My friend Janet has won several Best of Show prizes with her dogs.[4] Sandy keeps me company by following me around the house and lying down at my feet, and with her in the house, I never feel alone.[5] If someone comes near the house, she warns me by barking, and I feel safe with her standing guard.[6] Because I've owned her since she was a puppy, Sandy loves me.[7] She senses when I'm upset or angry and tries to comfort me by laying her soft muzzle on my lap, and I sometimes think she is my best and truest friend.[8]

1. Nonsupport #1 is sentence number ____.
   What information could you add to make it support the topic sentence?

   _____

   Rewrite the sentence to make it support the opinion expressed in the topic sentence.

   _____

   _____

2. Nonsupport #2 is sentence number _____.
   What information could you add to make it support the topic sentence?

   _____

   Rewrite the sentence to make it support the opinion expressed in the topic
   sentence.

   _____

   _____

WRITING PRACTICE 4

Examine all the supporting sentences in your paragraph map to make sure that
they develop the main idea in the topic sentence. If any supporting sentences don't
clearly support your main idea, either revise your main idea, add information to
make the ideas support the main idea, or delete the supporting idea. Try to make
the relationship clear with a word or phrase that explains how each support relates
to your main idea in the topic sentence.

ORDERING SUPPORTING SENTENCES

Once you are sure that the ideas you have generated support your main idea, you
are ready to determine the order of your supporting ideas. Making sure that your
supporting ideas are clearly organized will make your paragraph **coherent** to the
reader. As you write your paragraph, you will help make the relationship between
and within your ideas clear to the reader by using **transitions,** which are words
and phrases that show the relationship between ideas.

First, you have to decide the order in which you want to present your supporting ideas. The three most common and useful ways to order your supporting
sentences are **chronological order, listing,** and **order of importance.**

Chronological Order

Chronological order means that you present your supporting ideas in order of the
time at which they happen. Chronological order is often used in telling or narrat-
ing a story.

Example of Chronological Order

The writer tells the story of discovering her gift. She starts in seventh grade and
proceeds through time to graduation.

My Gift

I *first* discovered I had a talent for singing when I was in
the *seventh grade.* My choir teacher picked me out the first

day of practice and said I sounded like a young Aretha
Franklin. She offered to give me voice lessons after church
in exchange for my help mowing and raking her yard. *Throughout high school,* I performed solos in church every Sunday.
One of the proudest moments of my life was when I sang *Graduation* as my classmates marched in for our *graduation* ceremony. The sound of their applause filling my ears is something I will never forget. It will continue to inspire me to
develop and use the gift I have been given.

Listing

If you don't feel the order of your supports is particularly important, you can simply list them. The transitions that you would use at the beginning of some of the
supports would explain that the supports are organized in a list.

Transitions That Show Time Order or List Order	
First	Next
Second	Also
Third	Moreover
Finally	In addition
Last	In conclusion

Example of Listing

The writer lists three benefits of riding a bicycle to school. The benefits have no
particular order, so the writer uses transitions simply to note the first, second, and
final support.

The Advantages of Riding a Bike to School

Riding a bicycle to school gives students many important
benefits. *First,* parking is easy with a bike because cyclists
don't have to hunt for a parking space blocks from their
classroom but instead can usually lock up their bike in a
stand next to their building. *Also,* bike riders get great
exercise for their legs, and the aerobic workout strengthens
their heart and lungs. *Finally,* riding a bicycle to school
can save students twenty to fifty dollars per week on the

```
average cost of driving their car. Students will find that
there are many advantages to riding a bike to school.
```

Order of Importance

Writers often organize their supporting ideas in order of importance. You can organize your ideas from least important to most important or from most important to least important.

Another variation is to open and close with strong supports to get the reader's attention and to end on a strong note. You can use many of the same transitions as you would if you were listing. However, you would also signal to the reader the order of importance with transitions that communicate the relative importance of the supports.

Transitions That Show Order of Importance

Most importantly
Least importantly
Significantly
Best of all

Example of Order of Importance

```
           The Benefits of Pedaling to School
    Riding a bicycle to school gives students many important
benefits. Significantly, riding a bicycle to school can save
students 20 to 50 dollars per week on the average cost of
driving their car. Also, parking is easy with a bike because
cyclists don't have to hunt for a space in a parking lot
several blocks from their classroom but instead can usually
lock up their bike in a stand next to their building. Most
importantly, bike riders get great exercise for their legs,
and the aerobic workout strengthens their heart and lungs.
Pedaling to school has many advantages.
```

Note: A comma follows transitions at the beginning of sentences. (See Chapter 18, page 331 for information about using commas with transitions.) Also, it is not necessary to introduce every support with a transition. Often writers use a transition in the first, middle, and last supports.

RHETORICAL PATTERNS—OTHER WAYS TO ORGANIZE SUPPORTS

Writers often choose prescribed patterns to develop their paragraphs. Three common patterns are **narrative** for telling a story, **description** for describing people and things using the five senses, and **example or illustration** for giving examples. At the end of this chapter are sample student models of these rhetorical patterns as well as student paragraphs that use chronological order, listing, and order of importance to organize support. In addition, the *Writer's Resources* CD-ROM discusses all eleven rhetorical patterns in the "Rhetorical Pattern" section.

Practice 11   Underline the transitions and identify the organizational patterns of the following paragraphs.

1.   Value Drugs on 13th Street is my favorite drugstore. First, the pharmacy is always well staffed with two or three trained pharmacists, and it is open late in the evening, on weekends, and during holidays, making it convenient for me if anyone in my family gets sick unexpectedly. Second, this well-stocked pharmacy offers both generic and name brand medicines, so I end up saving five to ten dollars per prescription by choosing a generic brand. Because the service is fast, I generally don't have to wait, but if I do, I can choose to relax in one of the comfortable chairs the store provides, browse the large selection of magazines and paperback books, try on sunglasses, or pick out bargains in the seasonally discounted merchandise. If my two-year-old son is with me, no one seems to mind if we spend time playing with the endless array of toys in the toy aisle. Best of all, the pharmacists know us, so I don't always have to carry my insurance card with me when I pick up prescriptions, and people who wait on me are always friendly and smiling. Value Drugs is the drugstore I recommend.

A. Chronological
B. Listing
C. Order of importance

2.   Miami, Florida, is a great place for runners. Weather is always a key factor for the avid runner, and the climate here is perfect for running year-round. Also, there are miles of running trails and sidewalks scattered all over Miami, so runners can run safely and enjoy beautiful scenery. In the rare case of bad weather, there are many indoor training facilities, and they include a vast selection of state-of-the-art equipment to fit anyone's needs. If an injury should occur, top medical facilities are minutes away with an experienced medical staff on site. Moreover, there are many associations of runners who run together; therefore, there are plenty of people who enjoy running here in Miami, so if running alone is an issue, there is no need to worry about personal safety. If running is a main hobby for someone, Miami, Florida, is the place to be.

A. Chronological
B. Listing
C. Order of importance

3.   Rosa Parks is called the mother of the civil rights movement because of her role in the Montgomery Bus Boycott. In December 1955, Rosa Parks refused to give up her seat to a white man on a crowded evening bus in Montgomery, Alabama. Her protest led to her arrest and subsequently ignited a yearlong boycott of the city bus system. The protest was led by Dr. Martin Luther King and was so effective that it crippled the bus system, drew international attention to segregation in Montgomery, and one year later, led to a United States Supreme Court ruling that segregation on the Montgomery buses was unconstitutional. Rosa Parks and her husband both lost their jobs as a result of their roles in the protest, and they had to move to Detroit to escape harassment. She has no doubts, however, that her actions were worth the cost. For forty years, she has remained active in the civil rights movement and spoken to groups across the country. She also founded the Rosa and Raymond Parks Institute for Self-Development in Detroit to help motivate young people. She remains determined to make conditions better for all young people.

A. Chronological
B. Listing
C. Order of importance

USING TRANSITIONS

The organization of your supports will vary from paragraph to paragraph, and you can choose to organize a given paragraph in a number of ways. What matters most is that you clearly communicate your method of organization to the reader. Transitions help readers follow your ideas and understand the paragraph's organization.

Practice 12   1. **Fill in the blanks in the following paragraph with one of the transitions provided to show that the events are arranged in chronological order. Use each transition only once.**

Eventually, First, Then, Next

Choosing an apartment is a time-consuming process. _____, it is wise to determine how much money will be available each month for rent and utilities, and apartment hunters should not forget the initial costs of moving in such as deposits for security, usually equal to one month's rent, and for electric and cable hook-ups if renters choose to have them. _____, tenants can then begin looking through the local newspapers to find apartments that fit into their budget. _____, they will need to call and speak to the managers of the apartments in their price range. _____, renters will need to visit each one to check out the neighborhood, the availability of laundry facilities, and the condition of the apartment. After tenants have decided on the apartment that best suits them, they will need to sit down with the manager and have her explain the lease. They should make sure that they understand just what types of damage they will be liable for and how long the lease will be in effect. It takes a lot of time and effort to find a new apartment, but the hard work pays off when apartment hunters find the right place to live.

2. Fill in the blanks in the following paragraph with one of the transitions provided to show that the events are arranged in order of importance.

Most importantly, First, Second

My decision to return to school has had a big impact on my life. _____, because of the added expense of books and tuition, I have even less spending money than I did before I came back to school. This has meant that I have had to postpone making big purchases such as replacing the dishwasher when it broke, and I have had to cut back on small expenses such as going out to eat and going to the movies. _____, not only do I have less money than I did, but I also have less time. Rather than watching TV after dinner, I now study. Gone are the days when I could spend hours hanging out with my friends. These days most of my free time is spent studying and completing reading and writing assignments for my classes. _____, going back to school has changed the way I see myself. Through my experiences in school, I have gained a new respect for myself. I have learned I can set my mind to something and do it, and this new confidence in myself far outweighs the temporary inconveniences of not having as much time or money as I once did.

3. Fill in the blanks in the following paragraph with one of the transitions provided to show that the events are arranged in a list. Use each transition only once.

Moreover, Finally, Also, Another

Cars are now equipped with technological advances that make them more responsive to the driver and the road. _____, with compact disc players and telephones in many cars, the driving environment is more like a living room than an automobile. Many newer cars even have heaters in the seats and rearview mirrors. The steering column and seat positions are controlled by a computer that can remember a person's favorite settings and return to them with the push of a button. _____, computers control every engine function through sensors strategically placed, and some high-tech cars even use computers to help the suspension components react to road conditions as they are encountered. _____ new technological advancement allows for the continued running of an engine with no water in the cooling system. _____, even tires are manufactured for specific tasks like hot weather or snow and mud conditions which makes the entire car, from the ground up, a very high-tech engineering feat.

Model

Tony decided to list his supports, and he penciled in transitions that will show that he is listing supports.

Topic sentence: Computers benefit students.

Area of Support	Specific Details	Relation to Opinion
1. First, Papers	spell-check, grammar-check, save and revise	avoid errors
2. Next, Research	search engines (Google, Yahoo)	no more late nights in library
3. Also, homework	CD-ROM, Web-CT, BCA testing	work at home on tests
4. Moreover, Communication	e-mail, messaging, discussion boards	save time/money
5. Additionally, Shopping	buy CDs, textbooks, plane tickets	save money
6. Last but not least, Entertainment	listen to music, games, watch movies	relax

WRITING PRACTICE 5

Complete a map or outline for your paragraph by deciding the order of your supports. Signal the organization of your supports by using transitions.

Step 4: Drafting

Once you have generated the ideas for your paragraph, you are ready to write a draft of the paragraph. The main task at this point is to write sentences using the ideas in your map or outline.

Tips on Drafting

✓ Use most of the ideas on the map.

✓ Express the ideas for each support in one or two sentences.

✓ Use transitions to help you include information.

✓ Create sentence variety by using different sentence patterns.

✓ Don't worry about neatness or English errors until you complete a draft.

As Tony wrote the first draft of his paragraph, he tried to use all the ideas on his map. He didn't worry about making English errors while writing this first draft because he would correct them later during the revision process.

Computers: A Student's Best Friend

Computers offer students many advantages. *First,* there are papers to type. Spell-check, grammar-check, and save and revise come with the computer. These programs help writers avoid errors. *Next,* research uses the Internet. Search engines such as Google and Yahoo are for students to use to research information for assignments. Which means no more late nights in the library. *Also,* computers can be used to do homework like CD-ROM, Web-CT, BCA testing, so students can work at home on tests. *Moreover,* communicating through e-mail, instant messaging, and discussion boards can save students time and money. *Additionally,* students can buy CDs, textbooks, and plane tickets and save money. *Last but not least,* another use for computers is entertainment, students can listen to music, games, and watch movies in order to relax.

Practice 13   Put a check mark next to the sentence that best expresses the ideas on the map.

Topic sentence: Mr. Greeley is a good neighbor.

I. Friendly
   A. Waves at me when we pass each other before or after work
   B. Makes me feel welcome in neighborhood
      ___ 1. Mr. Greeley is very happy when he waves to me.
      ___ 2. I feel welcome in my neighborhood because Mr. Greeley waves to me when we pass each other before or after work.

II. Beautiful yard
    A. Mows yard every week and never leaves trash out
    B. Inspires me to keep up my yard
        ____ 1. When I see Mr. Greeley picking up trash every day and mowing his grass every Saturday, I am inspired to keep up my yard.
        ____ 2. I love Mr. Greeley's beautiful yard, and he never leaves trash out in his yard.

III. Lets me borrow stuff
    A. Tools and food
    B. Always feel like I have what I need
        ____ 1. He lets me borrow tools and food.
        ____ 2. Mr. Greeley always lets me borrow anything I need like tools to finish a chore or an ingredient to make a favorite recipe.

IV. Watches my place
    A. Lets me know if someone comes to visit
    B. Would call police or fire department if anything went wrong
        ____ 1. My wonderful neighbor will let me know if someone visits me while I am away, and I feel safe knowing that he would call the police or the fire department if anything went wrong at my house.
        ____ 2. Mr. Greeley notices if someone comes to visit.

V. Covers for me in an emergency
    A. Takes me to get my car from garage and watches kids if I am late
    B. Like a parent or partner to me
        ____ 1. Mr. Greeley has been like a parent or partner to me because in an emergency he will take me to get my car from the garage and watch my kids when I am late.
        ____ 2. I appreciate the way Mr. Greeley helps me with my car and my kids when I need him.

Practice 14   Use the following map to write sentences of support. Try to use all the ideas in the map.

Topic sentence: There are many disadvantages to riding a bicycle to school.

I. Weather
    A. Over 80 degrees in summer and below freezing in winter
    B. Arrive at school sweaty or numb

Support sentence:

_____

_____

II. Fatigue
    A. Use too much energy
    B. Fall asleep during class

Support sentence:

_____

_____

III. No space to carry anything
  A. Art portfolios or laptops
  B. Come to class unprepared

  Support sentence:

  _____

  _____

IV. Time consuming
  A. Takes thirty minutes to an hour to reach school
  B. Late for class unless students leave early

  Support sentence:

  _____

  _____

V. Accidents
  A. Cars don't see bicyclists
  B. Danger of serious accidents with cars

  Support sentence:

  _____

Practice 15   **Put a check mark next to the supporting detail with the best specific details to support the topic sentence.**

1. Topic sentence: Greenville is a wonderful place to retire.

   A. There are lots of options for health care in Greenville.

   B. The health care facilities for seniors include three major hospitals, hundreds of doctors and other health care professionals, and a dozen living facilities just for seniors.

2. Topic sentence: Greenville is a fantastic place to attend college.

   A. Students will have little trouble finding part-time jobs in the many restaurants and stores, and managers are willing to work around students' schedules.

   B. Because businesses thrive in Greenville, students can easily find a part-time job.

3. Topic sentence: Greenville is a great town for sports fans.

   A. There are many sports bars where sports fans can watch games.

   B. Sports fans have six sports bars to choose from where they can watch games on big screen TVs while enjoying their favorite food and beverage.

4. Topic sentence: Greenville is a great town for kids.

   A. Kids can play soccer.

   B. Kids can choose to participate in many organized sports such as soccer, JV football, or little league baseball.

5. Topic sentence: Greenville is a great town for businesses.

    A. Business owners can purchase land to build or expand a business in Greenville for half of what they would have to pay in a larger city.

    B. The cost of land in Greenville is low compared to other parts of the country.

THE CONCLUSION

The conclusion of the paragraph is the last sentence in the paragraph. It usually reminds the reader of the main idea in the topic sentence. Writers may also use the conclusion to state the significance of the information presented in the supports or to present a final support sentence.

The Conclusion

Is the last sentence of the paragraph (usually only one sentence in length)

Reminds reader of the main idea

May explain the significance of the supports

May be a final supporting sentence

Does not usually list all the supporting ideas

Does not start a new argument

THE TITLE

The title of a paragraph gives the piece of writing a name. The title should be different from the writing topic, and it is usually a sentence fragment. The first and last words and all important words in the title should be capitalized. Because the title is the first thing a reader sees, writers try to make it catchy or interesting. A good title will give the reader an idea of the writing's topic and main idea. Often the important words in the topic sentence make a good title.

Topic sentence: A computer can be a student's best friend in college.
Title: A Student's Best Friend in College

WRITING PRACTICE 6

Write a draft of your paragraph by creating a sentence or sentences for each area of supports on your map or outline. Incorporate your specific details and, where appropriate, the relationship to the opinion expressed in the topic sentence.

Step 5: Revising

Revising means re-examining your writing to see how it could be improved. At this stage in the writing process, you are working on improving the coherence of your writing to make your ideas as easy as possible for the reader to follow. You do not need to worry about correcting grammar and punctuation errors at this stage in the writing process because you will tackle those issues after you have finished revising your writing.

You may wish to ask your instructor or a classmate to read your paper and give you feedback on the strong and weak points. If it is not possible to get feedback on your paper, use the Paragraph Revision Checklist on page A-48 to help you re-examine your paper.

When revising their work, writers **use transitions within and between sentences** to make the relationship among their ideas clear. Good writers also **vary the sentence structure** to keep their writing interesting for the reader. See Chapter 13: "Sentence Combining," page 255, for practice with these skills.

In revising his paragraph, Tony tried to combine short sentences, and he tried to vary the types of sentences he used.

Support Sentence 2:

Next, research uses the Internet. Search engines such as Google and Yahoo are for students to use to research information for assignments. There are are no more late nights in the library.

Next, Internet search engines such as Google and Yahoo put WWW within reach, and researching information is easy with no late nights at the library.

Next, because Internet search engines such as Google and Yahoo put the resources of the World Wide Web at a student's disposal, researching information for assignments no longer involves late nights at the library.

Don't forget—use complex sentence!

Tony followed the suggestions of his instructor and classmates in revising his paragraph. The italicized phrases show his changes.

Computers: A Student's Best Friend

Computers offer students many advantages. First, *most college instructors expect students to turn in typed papers, and word processing programs allow students to compose,* save, and revise their writing easily as well as spell-check and grammar-check their work to *eliminate* errors. Next, *because* Internet search engines such as Google and Yahoo *put the resources of the World Wide Web at a student's disposal, researching information for assignments no longer involves* late nights at the library. Computers can *also aid students* in their homework *by giving them access to CD-ROM tutorials and online testing sites such as* WebCT, BCA, or Blackboard. Moreover, *the computer can save students time and money while keeping them in touch with instructors, classmates, and family through* e-mail, instant messaging, and online discussion boards. Additionally, students can *take advantage of the convenience and cost savings of shopping for everything from* CD's and textbooks to plane tickets. Last but not least, *students can relax after a long day by listening to their favorite music, playing games, or watching a DVD on their computer.*

WRITING PRACTICE 7

If possible, get feedback on your paragraph from peers or your instructor. If not, analyze the strengths and weaknesses of your paragraph using the Paragraph Revision Checklist on p. A-48, and revise your draft using transitions where appropriate and the sentence variety guidelines.

Step 6: Editing

Once you are satisfied with the content and organization of your writing, you are ready to correct grammar, spelling, and punctuation errors. Using an editing checklist such as the one on the next page can help you catch and correct errors in your English. When you edit, you should read your paragraph five or six times, focusing on one type of error each time—fragments, verb errors, comma errors, spelling errors, and so on—paying particular attention to errors you have had trouble with in the past.

EDITING CHECKLIST

As you learn about the following skills, add them to your checklist.

1. Check for run-ons and fragments. Is one complete sentence—and no more than one complete sentence—between every two periods? (Identify the subject and the verb, and make sure the word group makes sense.)

2. Check every verb. Do subjects and verbs agree? Is proper verb tense used? Be sure to check the problem phrases such as *there is/there are* and pay attention to singular subjects such as *everyone*.

3. Use the dictionary or computer spell check to catch capitalization errors and misspellings. Remember, however, that the spell check will not catch errors with problem words such as *there/their.*

4. Remember your personal list of errors. Check your writing for any of these errors.

5. Check for apostrophes in contractions and possessives.

6. Check commas.

7. Check pronouns. Do they agree with their antecedents? Is the reference clear?

8. Look for any missing words or letters by reading the writing slowly from the last sentence to the first.

WRITING PRACTICE 8

Edit your paragraph using the Editing Checklist above.

CD Connection

Power of Language

On *Writer's Resources* CD-ROM, see "Writing Process: Writing a Paragraph" for more information on organizing, drafting, revising, and editing a paragraph.

REVIEW EXERCISE 1

Fill in the blank with the letter of the best choice to complete the sentence.

1. Most college paragraphs are at least _____ sentences long.
   A. 7
   B. 5
   C. 3
   D. 4

2. The main idea of the paragraph is called the _____.
   A. topic
   B. thesis
   C. topic sentence
   D. title

3. The topic sentence expresses _____.
   A. a personal feeling
   B. an opinion
   C. the writer's point of view
   D. all of the above

4. The topic sentence is very often _____.
   A. the last sentence of the paragraph
   B. the second sentence of the paragraph
   C. the first sentence of the paragraph
   D. the third sentence of the paragraph

5. Most successful writers _____.
   A. write only one draft of their paragraph
   B. brainstorm and map their paragraph on paper before beginning to write
   C. compose their paragraph in their heads before writing
   D. think of a title first

6. Effective supporting sentences _____.
   A. include specific details
   B. relate to the topic sentence
   C. develop the main idea
   D. all of the above

7. Writers plan their paragraph using _____.
   A. a map or outline
   B. a tape recorder
   C. the textbook
   D. a friend's help

8. Transitions are used to _____.
   A. relate ideas within a paragraph
   B. relate ideas between sentences
   C. create a visual picture
   D. all of the above

9. Supporting sentences in the paragraph can be organized _____.
   A. chronologically

   B. in a list

   C. by order of importance

   D. all of the above

10. The conclusion to the paragraph _____.
    A. starts a new argument

    B. comes in the middle of the paragraph

    C. comes at the end of the paragraph

    D. is a sentence fragment

Sample Student Paragraphs

Power of
Language

Paragraph 1

Natalie Knight

Bad Break-up

Divorce can be harmful to children.[1] When many parents divorce, some tend to remarry; therefore, the children have to adjust to a new stepmother or stepfather.[2] For example, new parents may have different rules than the children's real parents, and children can become confused or even angry at the new parents.[3] After many divorces, children must move with one of their parents to a new town or even out-of-state.[4] Moving can be a problem because kids will have to leave old friends and make new ones, and children may really miss the other parent and feel lonesome and sad.[5] Some children even feel that they are to blame for their parents' divorce, and the guilt can cause them to be depressed and vulnerable.[6] Most children hate for their parents to get divorced.[7]

Discussion:
Most paragraphs present three to five separate supporting details. Writers may choose to use only one sentence to express a supporting detail, or they may use more than one sentence. In the previous paragraph, Natalie provides three separate supports for her topic sentence. She expresses some of her supporting details in one sentence and some in two sentences.

Activity:
Identify the sentence numbers that express each supporting idea. Some supporting details may use more than one sentence.

Supporting detail #1 about new step-parents: _____

Supporting detail #2 about moving: _____

Supporting detail #3 about guilt: _____

Paragraph 2

Evan Locker

Laptops: Portable Gifts

Laptops are great for students.[1] Laptops offer students a computer that students can take with them to class, so students can take notes in class and print out their notes when they get home.[2] Laptops are one-fifth the size of a normal computer, and the small size makes it easy for students to carry their laptops around in their backpacks.[3] Furthermore, new laptop hard drives come with fifty mega-bites more than an old desktop machine; therefore, students can save more papers, surf the web, and research papers more easily than at home on a desktop computer.[4] Also, laptops come with a wireless web, so students can be anywhere and access the Internet or instant message friends between classes.[5] Laptops are ideal for students.[6]

Discussion:
Evan keeps the topic sentence (1) simple, yet it clearly responds to the topic. It promises to explain to the reader why laptops are great. His conclusion restates the topic sentence in different words. Most importantly, each support discusses one benefit of the laptop, such as portability, size, memory, and wireless connectivity. Evan gives concrete information about laptops and then in the same sentence explains how each benefit is "great" for students.

Activity:
Underline the specific information in each supporting detail about the laptop, and double underline the words that explain how the specific information proves that *laptops are great for students.*

Example:
Laptops offer students <u>a computer that students can take with them to class</u>, so <u>students can take notes in class and print out their notes when they get home</u>.

Paragraph 3

Nicole Budget

Healthy Choice

Subway Station, a super sub shop on University Avenue, is a great food place.[1] Subway Station offers a variety of delicious sandwiches, garden fresh salads, and healthy vegetable wraps, so customers never get bored with the huge menu selection.[2] In addition, Subway Station's low-fat food is loaded with plenty of energy-boosting ingredients to keep hearts pumping and weight off.[3] Subway Station is one of the cheapest fast-food restaurants around; for example, a customer can get a large sub, chips, and an ice-cold drink for under five dollars.[4] Regular customers get a generous meal deal card that they can redeem for free food after they purchase ten meals.[5] Subway Station is truly a fantastic business that offers the best food.[6]

Discussion:

One of the most effective ways that writers sway the reader is by using descriptive words, mainly adjectives and adverbs. In this paragraph, Nicole must prove that Subway Station is "a great food place." In each supporting detail, she uses vivid adjectives and adverbs such as "delicious" and "garden fresh" to help make her point.

Activity:

Write the descriptive words in each supporting detail that help Nicole make her point. The first words in number 1 and number 2 have been provided.

1 super,_____

2 delicious, garden fresh,_____

3 _____

4 _____

5 _____

6 _____

Paragraph 4

Sparky Vilsaint

Cheating Doesn't Help

Academic dishonesty is harmful to a student's academic performance.[1] First of all, a student is not learning by copying off someone else's paper, and he or she won't understand the concepts needed to go to the next level of study.[2] Even though a student may get away with cheating once, the next time may not be as easy as the last; for example, classmates may hide their answers on the next test.[3] If a student is caught cheating on a test, the penalties can be failure on the test or in the course, and academic dishonesty may be noted on a student's record and follow him or her through school.[4] Most importantly, cheating in schools starts a dangerous habit that can lead to other cheating such as in marriage or business.[5] Cheating is not a good idea.[6]

Discussion:
Sparky's paragraph presents a strong argument against academic dishonesty because he provides very specific drawbacks to cheating and then explains how each drawback is harmful to students.

Activity:
Underline the specific information in each supporting detail about cheating, and double underline the words that explain how the specific information proves that *academic dishonesty is detrimental to a student's academic performance.*

Example:
First of all, a student is <u>not learning by copying off someone else's paper</u>, and he or she <u>won't understand the concepts needed to go to the next level of study.</u>

Paragraph 5

Phil Trautwein

Dis-Owning a Dog

There are many disadvantages to owning a dog.[1] First, a lot of dogs shed their hair all year long, and the hair gets all over the rug and furniture, so the house always looks dirty.[2] Also, puppies and young dogs will chew on table and chair legs, urinate on rugs and beds, and jump up on visitors to the house.[3] Because a dog takes a lot of time to feed, walk, play with, and clean, dog owners are always late for appointments.[4] Moreover, when a dog gets sick, the vet bills can be outrageous, and even when a dog is healthy, its food can cost as much as it would to feed another member of the family.[5] Finally, having a dog makes it difficult to go away for a night or weekend because a dog is not always welcome at hotels or friends' houses.[6] People should think about the drawbacks before getting a dog.[7]

Discussion:

Phil uses transitions at the beginning of most of the supporting details to alert the reader to a new support for his topic sentence. A transition is usually one to three words followed by a comma. Many transitions, such as *first, also,* and *last,* tell the reader the order of the supporting details, and others signal the importance of the support, such as *most importantly.*

Activity:

Write the transition that begins most of the supporting details. (One supporting detail does not start with a transition word, so don't write anything on that line.)

Sentence 2: _____

Sentence 3: _____

Sentence 4: _____

Sentence 5: _____

Sentence 6: _____

Example Paragraph 6

Cornelius Ingram

The Oldest Child

I hate being the oldest child in my family and having to take care of my younger brother and sister.[1] Since I am the oldest child out of three and still live at home, I am asked to baby-sit my younger brother and sister two or three nights each week when my parents go out.[2] After dinner every night, I am expected to clean up after them; for example, I must wipe off the table, wash the dishes, and sweep the floor before I go up to do my homework.[3] It is not easy being the only child who drives because my brother and sister want me to take them everywhere they want to go such as friends' houses or school games and dances.[4] In fact, my girlfriend broke up with me after I stood her up for an important date when I was stuck at the middle school waiting for my brother's school bus to return from a field trip.[5] Being the oldest is no fun.[6]

Discussion:

An example paragraph uses examples or illustration to develop or support the topic sentence. Cornelius provides examples of how he must take care of his brother and sister to explain why he hates being the oldest. His supporting details are very strong because they are so specific and concrete. For additional samples of example paragraphs and a discussion of example as a rhetorical mode, see *Writer's Resources* CD-ROM, "Rhetorical Patterns, Illustration or Example."

Activity:

Make a list in your own words of the examples Cornelius gives of different ways he has to take care of his brother and sister.

Example #1: _____

Example #2: _____

Example #3: _____

Narrative Paragraph 7

Tony Anderson

A Hard Lesson

I learned a valuable lesson about work habits in my first term in college.[1] In high school, I didn't have to work very hard to pass my classes, so I never developed good study habits.[2] When I started college, I was thrilled to be on my own, and I had trouble saying no when my friends asked me to go out and party.[3] Because I stayed out late, I missed quite a few of my early classes during the first few weeks of my first term.[4] As a result, I fell behind in my assignments. When I missed an exam at midterm, I realized I had better start making it to class.[5] Unfortunately, by that point in the semester, I was so far behind that I didn't think I could catch up.[6] Later that term, I had to drop my classes, which meant I wasted several hundred dollars in tuition and a semester's worth of time.[7] I'm determined not to let that happen again, and this semester I'm saying no to parties and yes to my schoolwork.

Discussion:
Tony's paragraph is a narrative. It tells the story of his experience during his first semester in college. Narrative writing is organized chronologically, in the order in which the events took place. Writers use time markers such as *later* to alert the reader that the supporting details are organized in time. Notice that Tony organizes his sentences from the beginning to the end of the term. For additional examples of narrative paragraphs and essays and a discussion of narration as a rhetorical mode, see *Writer's Resources* CD-ROM, "Rhetorical Patterns, Narration."

Activity:
Underline the time markers and transitions that Tony uses to lead the reader through his narrative. *Hint: Transitions and time markers may come anywhere in the sentence.*

Example: <u>Unfortunately</u>, <u>by that point in the semester</u>, I was so far behind that I didn't think I could catch up.

Descriptive Paragraph 8

Beth Kamisky

A Walk on the Beach

My favorite time to be at the beach is early in the morning in summer.[1] I try to get to the beach before the sun comes up so that I can see the first rays of light staining the horizon gold and orange.[2] Sometimes the sun comes up like a giant orange ball, and sometimes it is hidden behind clouds, outlining them in gold and sending shafts of golden light spilling over the water.[3] A cool breeze ruffles my hair as I walk down the beach and my toes sink into the cool, wet sand.[4] As I walk, I can hear the steady roll of waves breaking on the beach and the screech of sea gulls overhead.[5] The salty smell of the ocean and seaweed clears my mind, and I feel my worries and troubles melt away.[6] Nothing relaxes me like an early morning walk on the beach.[7]

Discussion:

Notice that Beth's description of her walk on the beach focuses on one place, one season, and one time of day. Descriptions paint a word picture of a place, a person, or an object, and they rely heavily on an appeal to the five senses of sight, hearing, touch, smell, and taste. Notice how Beth appeals to the sense of sight in sentences 2 and 3, the sense of touch in sentence 4, the sense of hearing in sentence 5, and the sense of smell in sentence 6. Descriptions also rely on concrete, specific language and strong verbs (see Chapter 5, "Word Choice," for more information on word choice). A description should also be unified in evoking a single mood or emotion. Beth's description shows us how walking on the beach relaxes her. For additional examples of descriptive paragraphs and a discussion of description as a rhetorical mode, see *Writer's Resources* CD-ROM, "Rhetorical Patterns, Description."

Activity:

1. Underline the appeal to the senses in Beth's paragraph. What details help us see, feel, hear, touch, and smell the scene she is describing?
   Example: I try to get to the beach before the sun comes up so that I can <u>see the first rays of light staining the horizon gold and orange.</u>
2. Circle the specific nouns, strong verbs, and colorful adjectives and adverbs that Beth uses to describe her walk on the beach.

   Example: A cool breeze ruffles my hair as I walk down the beach and my toes sink into the cool, wet sand.

Chapter 2 The Essay

In this chapter you will

- Learn about the differences between the paragraph and the essay
- Study the process of writing the essay
- Learn the parts of the essay

Skill Preview

The essay is the most common form of college writing. Like the paragraph, the essay presents a main idea and develops it. The essay's main idea is called a thesis or thesis statement. It is presented in an introductory paragraph. This first paragraph of the essay begins with background information about the topic and ends with the thesis statement. The support for the thesis statement is presented in a number of paragraphs that follow the introduction. Each support paragraph develops one major support for the thesis. These body paragraphs contain a topic sentence and supporting sentences that develop the topic sentence. The essay ends with a conclusion, usually of one paragraph. The conclusion restates the thesis and reminds the reader of the main points.

In Chapter 1 you learned how to write a paragraph. The format you learned corresponds to the format of the body or support paragraphs in the essay. Therefore, you are already familiar with how to write most of the paragraphs in the essay. The two parts of the essay that you must learn how to write are the introduction and conclusion.

In this chapter, as in the previous chapter, you will examine some writing by Tony Anderson. You will look at an essay Tony wrote that is based on the ideas he developed in the paragraph you read in Chapter 1. You will follow the steps of the writing process to write an essay of your own.

```
             Computers, a Student's Best Friend

    In the past twenty-five years, computers have revolution-
ized society. It's hard to imagine how our society would
function without computers, and it's particularly difficult to
imagine how students could function without computers. It's
hard to believe that before computers, students had to do
their research by looking all over campus for articles and
```

books. They also had to type their papers, and if they made an error, they had to retype the paper. They didn't have access to tutorial and testing programs that could help them learn coursework outside of class. If they wanted to contact instructors, they had to try to catch them in their office, and staying in touch with friends and family meant writing letters or paying for long distance phone calls. Thank goodness, all of that has changed. Computers help students research and write papers, complete schoolwork, and communicate with their professors, classmates, and family.

First, computers are useful in researching and writing papers and reports. Search engines such as Yahoo and Google make researching any topic easy. All students have to do is type in the topic they are interested in, and they can find hundreds of sources, often from the convenience of their home. Once they have located information for a report, the word processor allows them to write and revise their papers without having to start over every time they make a change. They can also save the paper to a disk so that nothing is lost. Perhaps most important, the software will check for spelling and grammar errors so that the paper will be clean and error free. Formatting is simple, and the paper or report always looks professional. Students can save time and improve their chances of getting a good grade by using computers to do their research and word-processing.

Not only do computers help with papers, but they can also help students master course work. Many college textbooks now come with CD-ROMs that offer extra practice and illustrated lessons. For example, *Writer's Resources* has an interactive CD-ROM that provides out-of-class opportunities for students to learn and practice their writing skills. Many courses also use Internet programs such as Web CT and Blackboard to post information and test students. Instead of having to go to the library to locate information for research essays, students can use search engines such as Google and Yahoo to find hundreds of articles on their topic, and all from the convenience of their own home. In addition, by using the Internet, students can access the school library to order or reserve books. It is almost impossible to imagine completing the course work for many college courses without using the computer.

Finally, computers make communication with instructors, classmates, friends, and family cheap and easy. If students miss class or have a question for an instructor, they can e-mail their instructor to explain their absence, get missed assignments, ask questions, or make an appointment for an office visit. Of course, students also use e-mail and instant messaging to connect with one another about school and to communicate with friends and family. Using e-mail can keep students connected to distant friends and family while saving hundreds of dollars on long distance phone bills. Moreover, students can stay in touch with their peers by posting questions on online message boards or by becoming involved in online discussion groups. The computer allows students to stay connected to the important people in their lives.

Technology has helped reshape our society in the last twenty-five years, and today, computers are indispensable to college students. Computers have revolutionized the way college students do business, and they have made our jobs as students a lot easier by helping us produce professional papers, access coursework outside of class, and stay in touch easily and inexpensively.

Spotlight on Writers

Power of
Language

Langston Hughes

"We younger Negro artists now intend to express our individual dark skinned selves without fear or shame."

"No great poet has ever been afraid of being himself."

Langston Hughes (1902–1967) began writing poetry in the eighth grade and became part of the Harlem Renaissance in the 1920s, writing poetry as he listened to jazz and blues in the clubs of Harlem. In his sixteen books of poetry, two novels, twenty plays, and numerous short stories and essays, he shared the African American experience with readers throughout the world. In an early essay, he argued for Black identity and pride, and he encouraged young writers to claim their identity.

Tony's essay exhibits many of the characteristics of college-level essays. His introduction begins with background information that introduces the topic of *computers and students.* He ends his introduction with the thesis that his essay will develop, which is that *computers help students,* and he lists the ways he will develop his thesis by mentioning the main ideas of his support paragraphs. In each support paragraph, Tony begins with a topic sentence that announces the main idea of the paragraph, and then he develops the main idea with a number of supports. Throughout the essay, Tony uses transitions to help the reader understand the relationship among ideas. Finally, Tony's last paragraph concludes the essay by reminding the reader of his thesis and the main points he made to support the thesis.

PREVIEW ACTIVITY In the margin, label the first paragraph *Introduction.* Then, label the second paragraph *Support Paragraph 1,* label the third paragraph *Support Paragraph 2,* and label the fourth paragraph *Support Paragraph 3.* Finally, label the final paragraph *Conclusion.*

The Differences Between the Paragraph and the Essay

The Paragraph	*The Essay*
✓ Main idea in topic sentence	✓ Main idea (called the thesis statement) in the introductory paragraph
✓ Three to five supporting sentences	✓ Three or more paragraphs of support (These paragraphs follow the paragraph format you learned in Chapter 1)
✓ One sentence of conclusion	✓ One concluding paragraph that restates the thesis and reminds the reader of major points

The Process of Writing an Essay

The process of writing an essay is similar to the process of writing a paragraph. Most writers generate ideas for their essays using the techniques described in Chapter 1 on pages 20–23, and they outline their essays before they begin writing. Also, many writers wait to write the introductory paragraph until after they have written the supporting paragraphs. Writers can then determine the most effective way to begin the essay with background information.

Tony's Outline

I. Introduction
   A. Background information
      1. computers revolutionized society, especially for students
      2. how life was hard for students before computers
   B. Thesis: Computers help students research and write papers, complete school-work, and communicate with their professors and classmates.

II. Major Support 1: Papers and Reports
   A. Write and revise without starting over
   B. Save paper on disk so nothing lost
   C. Simple formatting
   D. Spell check and grammar check

III. Major Support 2: Coursework
   A. Textbooks with CDs
   B. Internet programs like WebCT and Blackboard
   C. Completing research using Internet
      1. Google.com
      2. Yahoo.com
   D. Access school library to order books

IV. Major Support 3: Communication
   A. E-mail professors
      1. get assignments
      2. make appointments
   B. Participate in online discussion boards
   C. E-mail other students and friends and family

V. Conclusion (You don't need to outline the conclusion.)

CD Connection

Power of Language

WP 3.1-39: *Writing an Essay* in Writing Process provides a discussion of the writing process for essays, shows many examples of student essays, and gives lots of practice in using the writing process.

Practice 1   Working alone or with a partner, use Tony's outline to label the parts of Tony's essay. Underline Tony's thesis in the first paragraph of his essay, and label it *thesis statement*. Next, look in the second paragraph for the key words in the outline next to Roman numeral II, *papers and reports.* These words appear in the topic sentence of the second paragraph. Underline the sentence where these two key words appear together in the second paragraph, and label it *topic sentence.* Then go to the third and fourth paragraphs and underline the topic sentence for each paragraph. The topic sentence of each support paragraph will contain the key words next to the Roman numerals in the outline: *coursework* and *communication.*

The Parts of the Essay

Parts of the Essay

Title
- ✓ Unique name for the essay
- ✓ Usually a fragment centered a line or two above the first line
- ✓ The first, last, and all important words capitalized

Introduction
- ✓ Background information
- ✓ Thesis sentence (the main idea of the essay)

Body Paragraphs
- ✓ Two to five paragraphs (or more) that develop the thesis
- ✓ Each paragraph develops one major support that is stated in the topic sentence
- ✓ Each paragraph develops the major support point with specific or concrete details, including facts, statistics, and descriptive language

Conclusion
- ✓ Restates the main idea in different words and reminds the reader of the main supports

CD Connection

Power of
Language

WE 6.1-40: *The Essay* in Writing Elements provides a discussion of the essay parts and characteristics along with lots of examples of student essays and practice using the essay parts.

The Introduction

The purpose of the introduction is to get the reader interested in the topic of the essay and to prepare the reader to understand the main idea of the essay. The first part of the introductory paragraph introduces the topic and presents background information to help the reader understand the main idea, or thesis, of the essay. The second part of the introductory paragraph is the thesis, which is presented at the end of the introductory paragraph. After the thesis statement or included in the thesis statement, you may also list the major supporting points that you will cover in the essay.

BACKGROUND INFORMATION

There are many ways to get the reader interested in your topic and present background information to help your reader understand your main idea. Two of the most common techniques are to present a **story or anecdote** or to present **important facts** about your topic.

Example of Story or Anecdote for Background Information

background information anecdote

For some people, the senior prom is the culmination of four years of high school and is more important and certainly more memorable than graduation. They proudly display their prom pictures on their mantels, and they remember prom night as one of the best in their lives. It didn't quite work that way for me. I changed schools my senior year because my parents moved from one area of Atlanta to another. As a result, my date for the prom was a girl I had met in my English class but who I barely knew. I still have the picture of the two of us that night, but I don't have the heart to display it because even though I look good in my tux and she looks beautiful in her blue satin dress and orchid corsage, I can't look at the picture without remembering that just after the flash went off, she turned away in anger. Unfortunately, my

Thesis   senior prom was a disaster.

Example of Important Facts for Background Information

background information anecdote

My dad didn't have a college degree, but he was an intelligent man. He could fix most things, from cars to toasters to radios, and he had a knack for nurturing growing things such as crops and animals and children. My father was well liked and well respected in our community, and nobody deserved his reputation more than he did. Most of the things I learned of value in my childhood came from watching my father and learning from him. By setting a good example for me, my father

Thesis   showed me the meaning of honesty, hard work, and generosity.

CD Connection

Power of Language

WE 6.6-15: *The Essay* in Writing Elements provides numerous student and professional examples of these and many more introductory techniques.

THE THESIS

The thesis should state the main idea that the essay will develop. The thesis should be an umbrella statement that covers everything that will be developed in the essay, in the same way as a topic sentence is an umbrella statement that covers everything that will be developed in a paragraph. The thesis may also name the primary supports that you will use to develop the thesis. If you include the main support points in your thesis, be sure to express the supports in parallel structure. (See Chapter 17, page 315.)

Practice 2   Circle the letter of the thesis that best expresses the support ideas.

1. Topic: Disadvantages of smoking

   Support ideas:

   People don't want to be around smokers.

   No one wants to kiss a smoker.

   Most people and businesses won't allow smokers to smoke inside.

   Smokers get sick more often.

   Smokers feel terrible about themselves.

   Possible thesis statements:

   A. Smoking can damage your health.

   B. Smoking harms a smoker's physical, mental, and social life.

   C. Smoking is bad for you.

2. Topic: Alcoholism

   Support ideas:

   Alcoholics miss or are late for work.

   They have trouble getting work done.

   Alcoholics tend to be abusive of family members.

   Many alcoholics get divorced.

   No one wants to go out with an alcoholic.

   Alcoholics lose their driver's license.

   Possible thesis statements:

   A. Alcoholics create lots of problems for themselves.

   B. Alcoholics are unhappy people.

   C. Alcoholism can affect a drinker's work, family, and social life.

3. Topic: Choosing a college

Support ideas:

See a counselor during the junior year of high school.

Visit a number of colleges during the summer between junior and senior year.

Talk to parents about financial matters before deciding which school to attend.

Apply to at least three to five schools.

Discuss options with parents.

Start making applications during the first months of senior year.

Possible thesis statements:

A. Choosing a college involves making choices about where to live.

B. The process of choosing a college should begin in the junior year of high
    school and continue through senior year.

C. Choosing a college is interesting.

The Body Paragraphs

The body paragraphs support the essay's main idea or thesis. Each body paragraph develops one main point, stated in a topic sentence, and the topic sentence should be developed with specific supporting sentences. If your thesis statement names the main points your essay will develop, your body paragraphs should develop those points in the order in which they are listed in the thesis. You should also use transitions with your topic sentences to signal the order and relationship among the main points your essay will develop.

Thesis: Smoking harms a smoker's physical, mental, and social life.

Topic sentence #1: First, smoking can damage a smoker's health.
Topic sentence #2: Not only can smoking affect a smoker's physical health, but it can
                   also harm a smoker's mental health.
Topic sentence #3: Finally, smoking can damage a smoker's social life.

Practice 3   Determine the order of thesis and topic sentences in the following outlines.

1. A. First, a leash law would help ensure the safety of animals.
   B. Perhaps most important, a leash law would help protect innocent people.
   C. Not only would a leash law protect animals, but property as well.
   D. Chapel Hill should pass a leash law in order to protect animals, property, and
      people.

    I. Thesis = _____
    II. Topic sentence #1 = _____
    III. Topic sentence #2 = _____
    IV. Topic sentence #3 = _____

2. A. Students would feel safer in the parking areas if the lots were better lighted.
   B. Also, lighting would make the campus more attractive at night.
   C. Not only would students feel safer if parking areas were better lit, but theft and vandalism would be reduced as well.
   D. Winnipeg Community College should improve lighting throughout the campus in order to improve safety, discourage vandalism, and make the campus more attractive.

    I. Thesis = _____
    II. Topic sentence #1 = _____
    III. Topic sentence #2 = _____
    IV. Topic sentence #3 = _____

3. A. First, applicants should wear clothing that is appropriate for the job they are seeking.
   B. Next, applicants should make certain that their appearance is neat and clean.
   C. Job applicants should present themselves well in an interview.
   D. Lastly, job candidates should project a positive attitude in their interview.

    I. Thesis = _____
    II. Topic sentence #1 = _____
    III. Topic sentence #2 = _____
    IV. Topic sentence #3 = _____

The Conclusion

The conclusion of an essay summarizes the essay or draws the essay to a close. The conclusion is generally not as long as the introduction. Two to three sentences are generally acceptable in a short essay of four to six paragraphs. The two most common techniques used in conclusions are to **refer to the story or information in the introduction** and to **emphasize the important points** made in the essay.

Disaster Prom

    By the time I dropped my date off after the prom, she was so furious that she refused to say goodnight let alone kiss me goodnight. Needless to say, she never went out with me again. I spent two hot summer months mowing my brother's lawn to pay for borrowing his car, and when my prom picture arrived in the mail, I put it in a drawer without looking at it. All in all, my senior prom was an experience I would just as soon forget.

This conclusion refers to the story that began the introduction.

An Admirable Man

There aren't many men like my dad, and the older I get, the more I come to appreciate and admire him. The old saying "Actions speak louder than words" is certainly true of my father. He didn't preach about how to be a good person, but he was one. I learned to value honesty, hard work, and generosity from watching him and from the example he set. I only hope I can set as good an example for my children.

This conclusion emphasizes the important points of the essay.

REVIEW EXERCISE 1

Fill in the blank with the letter of the best choice to complete the sentence.

1. The introductory paragraph usually starts with the _____.
   A. thesis statement
   B. background information
   C. list of supports

2. Techniques for writing background information include _____.
   A. tell an anecdote
   B. give facts about the topic
   C. both of the above

3. The thesis statement states _____.
   A. the subject of the essay
   B. the opinion of the essay
   C. the support of the essay
   D. the conclusion of the essay

4. The thesis statement _____.
   A. should be a fact
   B. may include a list of the major supports

C. must be the first sentence of the essay

D. can never be the last sentence of the introductory paragraph

5. Paragraphs in the body of the essay usually start with _____.

A. a topic sentence

B. a thesis statement

C. an anecdote

6. The topic sentences of the body paragraphs must _____.

A. support the thesis statement

B. state an important fact about the topic

C. both of the above

7. In the body of the essay, _____.

A. there should be only one paragraph

B. there may be three or more paragraphs

C. there must be five paragraphs

D. there must be seven paragraphs

8. The body paragraphs contain _____.

A. a topic sentence

B. supporting details

C. a conclusion

D. all of the above

9. The conclusion paragraph usually _____.

A. refers to the background information

B. emphasizes the main points of the essay

C. either of the above

10. An outline to the essay _____.

A. should be written before the essay is written

B. should be written after the essay is written

C. must be written in complete sentences

D. none of the above

Sample Student Essays

Power of
Language

Essay 1

Tony Anderson

Modern Nuisance

Almost everyone seems to have a cell phone these days. It is hard to be in any public place without the irritation of hearing a cell phone ring or hearing someone talking loudly into a cell phone. Glance around in traffic and three out of four drivers will be talking on a cell phone. Cell phones are so widespread that middle and high schools have had to ban them on campus because of the disruption they cause. Certainly, cell phones have added convenience to our lives, but at what price? Cell phones may be popular, but they come with hidden drawbacks. Cell phones are more expensive, unreliable, and unsafe than most people realize.

First, cell phones are far more expensive than most people realize. A basic cell phone policy starts at thirty dollars per month, and some policies cost as much as one-hundred dollars a month. Most policies don't include text messaging or Internet access, and these add-ons can add twenty dollars to the monthly bill. Although some policies offer free long distance within a home district, if cell phone users call from outside their district, they are hit with roaming charges and sky-high charges for each minute of use. In addition to the policy, consumers must purchase their own phone, which can cost from twenty-five dollars to several hundred dollars, and if owners lose or damage their cell phone, they have to pay to replace it. Next, cell phone paraphernalia such as car chargers, earphone jacks, and fancy faceplates can easily cost an additional fifty dollars. In addition to all these costs, most consumers don't realize that taxes will add another thirty percent to their bill, so a seventy-dollar policy will cost them one hundred dollars per month. Overall, a cell phone can cost well over a thousand dollars per year.

Despite all that customers pay for cell phone service, that service is often unreliable. Many cell phones don't have coverage in rural areas, and even in cities, cell phone users may hit dead spots, may pick up static, or may not pick up a signal inside buildings. The advertisement that features a man asking, "Can you hear me now?" is no joke for most cell phone users because for far too many of them, the answer is No. In addition to poor coverage, cell phones only hold a charge for a couple of hours, so they often go dead when the user least expects it. If a battery isn't properly calibrated or is old, it won't hold a charge at all, making the cell phone useless. In reality, cell phones aren't as convenient as many people claim.

The biggest problem with cell phones, however, is the danger they pose to their users and others. Drivers who place or answer calls while driving endanger themselves and other drivers. When drivers fumble for a phone, dial a phone, or write down a number, they take their eyes off the road, which can all too easily cause an accident. Insurance and cell phone companies warn consumers not to use cell phones while driving, but these warnings have little effect on drivers. Even walking with an ear bud in and talking on the phone can lead to accidents with other pedestrians, cyclists, or cars. In addition, heavy cell phone users are at greater risk of developing brain cancer than others. Although most cell phone users don't realize it, talking on their phone could be endangering their own lives and the lives of others.

More people should stop and think twice before they commit to a cell phone policy. Consumers often end up spending more than they think, getting poorer service than they expect, and endangering their safety and well being by getting hooked on cell phones. Thinking twice could save consumers money, hassles, and health problems.

Discussion:
Tony's essay follows the classic structure of a five-paragraph essay. The first paragraph is an introduction. It begins with background information to get the reader's attention. The first paragraph ends with the thesis statement that Tony will develop in the body of the essay. The last sentence of the introduction lists the ideas Tony will cover in each of the body paragraphs.

The body of the essay also is clearly structured. The topic sentence of each body paragraph begins each body paragraph, and the sentences in each body paragraph support the topic sentence that begins the paragraph.

Activity:
In the first paragraph, underline the thesis statement, and circle the three major details to be covered in the body of the essay. Then, underline the topic sentences in each body paragraph. Label the last paragraph *Conclusion*.

Essay 2

Chris Vaughn

My Journey

My journey is to work toward getting a masters degree in business. I have been working since I was fourteen and have been the supervisor or manager at every job I have had. I am also good at listening to people and helping them with their problems, so I would like to find a way that I could incorporate business and psychology into my work. My ultimate goal is to be able to make more money than I have been able to in the past in order to take care of my family better and not have to worry about how I am going to pay the bills from one day to the next. I also want to finish college as no one else in my family ever did.

I'm leaving all the people in my life behind me who have always been so negative toward my goals and desires. I promised myself years ago when I first left school that I would go back to finish school, but something has always gotten in the way. After being the manager of a video store for three years and not being able to advance any further because of my lack of education, I realize it was time for me to go back to school.

I face a number of obstacles on my journey. It would be helpful if my children were more cooperative when it comes to my studying. They do try sometimes, but other times they are just preoccupied with being boys. It would also be helpful if I didn't have to worry so much about the bills getting paid all the time. Alas, those obstacles are part of being me.

Over the years, I have gotten very bitter. I worked hard in all my jobs. I even set records for sales and loss prevention and received awards in most of my jobs. Yet, I still haven't been able to move up any further than manager, and I have never been able to get paid what I am truly worth. Overall, I want to leave the bitterness behind me since I am on my journey to a better life and a better me.

When I start feeling like everything is closing in, I stop and think about my kids. I think about how I want their lives to be and how I want them to see their mother. I want them to be proud of me in everything I do, and I hope that part of me rubs off on them and that they always do their best, don't quit, and don't let anyone tell they that they can't achieve what they want.

Discussion:
Although Chris's essay is not a traditional academic essay with a stated thesis and stated topic sentences, the essay does develop a central idea, as does each support paragraph. Overtly stated thesis and topic sentences are necessary for clarity in most academic writing, but many of the essays you read in magazines will use implied (not directly stated) main ideas.

Activity:
Read the essay on page 73 and answer the following questions.

1. What is the central idea of the introductory paragraph?

_____

2. What is the central idea of paragraph 2?

_____

3. What is the central idea of paragraph 3?

_____

4. What is the central idea of paragraph 4?

_____

5. What is the central idea of paragraph 5?

_____

Part II Grammar, Mechanics, and Punctuation

Good writing begins with strong sentences that use a variety of sentence patterns to express ideas clearly and correctly. This part of the textbook will help you to develop sound sentence structure and to avoid English errors.

College writers are expected to use a variety of sentence structures and to present lots of information in their sentences. To gain these skills, you will learn to identify the subject and verb of the sentence in order to make sure you are writing complete sentences and not sentence fragments or run-on sentences. Then you will learn to combine ideas into strong sentences using different sentence patterns. In addition, you will learn to recognize and avoid common English errors. Reducing errors in your writing is important because errors distract the reader and may even keep the reader from understanding your ideas.

The chapters in this part offer lots of practice using the concepts and skills being taught. The learning activities include

- ☞ Short practice sets following most explanations of concepts (with answers at the back of the text)
- ☞ CD Connection that directs you to more information and practice on the *Writer's Resources* CD-ROM
- ☞ Review exercises covering all the concepts covered in the chapter
- ☞ Editing tests using the concepts in passages
- ☞ Tests for your instructor to assign
- ☞ Journal topics that give you actual writing practice.

Chapter 3   Capitalization

In this chapter, you will learn the rules for capitalizing the

- First word of sentences and quoted sentences
- Proper names of people
- Proper names of places
- Proper names of things

Skill Preview

To avoid errors with capitalization, writers should use a capital letter for the first word of sentences and the proper names of people, places, and things. Although that may sound simple, there are many rules to review in order to avoid confusion about what should and should not be capitalized.

Read the passage below and capitalize the letters that should be capitalized.

last friday night, cheryl jones and i went on a date to the lakeview mall. first, we had dinner at rigatelli's italian restaurant. i ordered veal parmesan, and cheryl ordered chicken florentine. after dinner we decided to go see the latest air bud movie because cheryl and i both love golden retrievers. afterwards, we decided to get ice cream at ben and jerry's. she ordered a chocolate sundae, and i ordered a cherry garcia cone.

Compare your corrections with the corrected capitals in the following passage.

Last Friday night, Cheryl Jones and I went on a date to the Lakeview Mall. First, we had dinner at Rigatelli's Italian Restaurant. I ordered veal Parmesan, and Cheryl ordered chicken Florentine. After dinner we decided to go see the latest Air Bud movie because Cheryl and I both love golden retrievers. Afterwards, we decided to get ice cream at Ben and Jerry's. She ordered a chocolate sundae, and I ordered a Cherry Garcia cone.

If you correctly identified many of the letters that should be capitalized in the paragraph (there are twenty-six), you probably already know many of the rules for capitalization. This lesson will acquaint you with all the rules and give you practice perfecting your knowledge.

Spotlight on Writers

Power of Language

Thomas Paine

"These are the times that try men's souls. The summer soldier and the sunshine patriot will, in this crisis, shrink from the service of their country. But he that stands it now deserves the love and thanks of man and woman."

"The harder the conflict, the more glorious the triumph."

In 1776, Thomas Paine (1739–1809) wrote *Common Sense,* which justified the separation of the American colonies from England. His writing is credited with strengthening public support for the Revolutionary War. When the American army was losing the war, George Washington had another of Paine's essays, *The Crisis,* read aloud to his troops on the banks of the Delaware River. Paine's words so inspired the troops that they crossed the Delaware, defeated the British troops, and turned the tide in the Revolutionary War.

Sentence Beginnings

1.1 Capitalize the **first word of sentences.**

The track meet is tomorrow.

1.2 The first word of a **quoted sentence** should be capitalized.

When I ran into Hank, he asked, "How is your dad?"

Practice 1   Capitalize the letters that should be capitalized. Write the correct answer in the space provided.

1. joaqin asked me if I had seen the latest movie. _____

2. rooney asked me out on a date. _____

3. when I returned to class, Mr. Peabody asked, "where were you yesterday?" _____

4. jean paul offended me when he asked, "what happened to your hair?" _____

5. my mother looked at me and asked, "where have you been? _____

Proper Nouns

Names of specific people, places, and things are considered proper nouns, and all proper nouns should be capitalized.

Proper Names of People

2.1 **Proper names** of people should be capitalized.

Sandra asked **Mr. Morton** if there would be questions about **Napoleon** on the test.

2.2 **Proper titles** are capitalized if they are used to replace someone's name or are part of a proper name.

Capitalize	**Do Not Capitalize**
How are you feeling today, **Dad**?	**My dad** is my best friend
When is your appointment with **Doctor Ashley**?	You need to see a **doctor**.
I asked **Uncle Joe** to fix my leaky faucet.	**My uncle** is a plumber

(If a word such as *my* or *the* comes before the title, the title is not replacing a proper name.)

2.3 The pronoun *I* is considered a proper name and should be capitalized.

My uncle and **I** plan to hike the Appalachian Trail when **I** return from school.

Practice 2 Capitalize the letters that should be capitalized. Write the correct answer in the space provided

ron weasley _____ doctor _____

my favorite uncle _____ my father _____

sandy perkins _____ mrs. Sandros _____

aunt sarah _____ professor snape _____

prince william _____

Proper Names of Places

3.1 Proper names of **specific geographic features** and **proper place names** should be capitalized.

Directions: In the space to the right of each category, write an example of your own that would be capitalized.

Capitalize	**Do Not Capitalize**	**Your Example**
Indian Ocean	the ocean	_____
Rocky Mountains	the mountains	_____
Lake Alice	a deep lake	_____
Amazon River	a long river	_____

3.2 Names of **cities, counties, states, regions, countries, continents,** and **planets** should be capitalized.

Prepositions are not capitalized in proper names unless they are the first or last word of the name.

Directions: In the space to the right of each category, write an example of your own that would be capitalized.

Capitalize	Do Not Capitalize	Your Example
Rome	a big city	_____
Dekalb County	five counties	_____
Michigan	a large state	_____
the West	west Texas	_____
England	a large country	_____
Europe	both continents	_____
Mars	two planets	_____

3.3 Directional words ending in -*ern* (western, northern, southern, eastern) are not capitalized. The words *north, south, east, west* are **not** capitalized if they refer to a direction, but **regions of the country are capitalized** when they name the geographical region.

Capitalize: Many retirees spend the winter in the **South.**
Do not capitalize: Many retirees head **south** in the winter.

Practice 3   Capitalize the letters that should be capitalized. Write the correct answer in the space provided.

altuna river _____   the polluted river _____

southern canada _____   the sangre de cristo _____
                                         mountains
grand canyon _____

time square _____   california _____

france _____   berlin _____

Proper Names of Things

4.1 Proper names of **institutions, businesses, federal agencies** (as well as their abbreviations), **buildings,** and **historical monuments** should be capitalized.

Capitalize	Do Not Capitalize	Your Example
Dekalb High School	my high school	_____
Rigatoni's Restaurant	an expensive restaurant	_____
University of Florida	a university	_____
Burger King	a fast food restaurant	_____
Internal Revenue Service (IRS)	a government agency	_____
the New York Yankees	a baseball team	_____
the Eiffel Tower	a skyscraper	_____
the Lincoln Memorial	a famous monument	_____

4.2 Capitalize **brand or trade names of products.**

Capitalize	Do Not Capitalize	Your Example
Campbell's Chicken Soup	chicken soup	_____
Excedrin	aspirin	_____
Tylenol	acetaminophen	_____

Practice 4   Capitalize the letters that should be capitalized. Write the correct answer in the space provided.

montgomery middle school _____

federal bureau of investigation (fbi) _____

my favorite barbecue restaurant _____

buckingham palace _____

the toronto blue jays _____

tide detergent _____

university of california _____

community college _____

the jefferson memorial _____

the mall _____

4.3 **Days, months,** and **holidays** are capitalized. Seasons are **not** capitalized.

Capitalize	Do Not Capitalize	Your Example
Wednesday	today	_____
Sunday	many days	_____
February	next month	_____
Christmas	spring	_____
Mother's Day	summer	_____
Labor Day	fall	_____
Martin Luther King Day	winter	_____

Practice 5   Capitalize the letters that should be capitalized. Write the correct answer in the space provided.

November _____   saturday _____

Sunday _____   fourth of july _____

winter snowstorm _____   thanksgiving _____

june _____   holiday _____

fall _____   spring _____

4.4 Names of **languages, nationalities,** and **specific school courses** should be capitalized.

Capitalize	Do Not Capitalize	Your Example
French	a foreign language	_____
History 101	history	_____
Introduction to Computing	a computer class	_____

4.5 Specific **historical events** and any **eras or periods in history** should be capitalized.

Capitalize	Do Not Capitalize	Your Example
the Civil War	the last world war	_____
the French Revolution	the twentieth century	_____
the Renaissance	the seventeenth century	_____

4.6 The first word, last word, and all important words in the **titles of books, poems, articles, essays, newspapers, magazines, movies, television shows, songs, and musical groups** should be capitalized. Prepositions are not capitalized unless they are the first or last word of the title.

Capitalize	Do Not Capitalize	Your Example
War and Peace	my favorite book	_____
The Days of Our Lives	a soap opera	_____
The New York Times	a leading newspaper	_____
Boot-Scoot Boogie	a country and western song	_____
The Beatles	a rock and roll band	_____

Practice 6 Capitalize the letters that should be capitalized. Write the correct answer in the space provided.

portuguese _____   the vietnam war _____
the spanish civil war _____   history _____
my favorite situation comedy _____   a punk rock group _____
the washington post _____   the supremes _____
jazz _____   drawing 101 _____

4.7 Capitalize only the words of animal and plant names that refer to a specific place, person, or language.

Capitalize	Do Not Capitalize	Your Example
African elephant	elephant	_____
Bengal tiger	tiger	_____
German shepherd	shepherd	_____
Scottish terrier	terrier	_____
Chihuahua	bulldog	_____
American bald eagle	eagle	_____
Dutch elm	elm	_____

Practice 7 Capitalize the letters that should be capitalized. Write the correct answer in the space provided.

bottlenose dolphin _____   shrimp cocktail _____
florida panther _____   daffodils _____
hammerhead shark _____   chestnut trees _____
pansies _____   english bull dog _____
sugar snap peas _____   black bear _____

CD Connection

On *Writer's Resources* CD-ROM, see *Capitalization* in Grammar/Punctuation/
Mechanics 3.1–3.28 for more information and practice with capitalization.

REVIEW EXERCISE 1

Identify the capitalization in the following sentences as correct (C) or incorrect (I),
and correct capitalization errors in the space provided.

_____ 1. My history and french teachers are leading a student trip to Europe this
summer. _____

_____ 2. Students will study history, art, architecture, and languages. _____

_____ 3. Some parents like my mom and my dad will accompany our group and
have the opportunity to study the cultures, foods, and peoples of the
countries on our tour. _____

_____ 4. The group will spend one week each in london and rome. _____

_____ 5. The group will visit two western European countries: England and Italy.
_____

_____ 6. Some of the favorite destinations in London are the tower of London,
Buckingham palace, and Trafalgar square. _____

_____ 7. The Thames River flows through London, and students will have the
opportunity to take a barge ride through the city and surrounding
counties. _____

_____ 8. While in England, students will stay at bed and breakfast inns and eat
British food like kidney pie. _____

_____ 9. In Rome, no one will want to miss the coliseum. _____

_____ 10. Students will also have a chance to sample Italian foods like risotto
and gnocchi. _____

REVIEW EXERCISE 2

Identify the capitalization in the following sentences as correct (C) or incorrect (I),
and correct any capitalization errors in the space provided.

_____ 1. Every year Foothills High School holds a fall carnival to raise money for
the school. _____

_____ 2. The carnival is held around the time of Halloween on the last Friday
afternoon in october. _____

_____ 3. The parent-teacher association (pta) organizes the booths,
vendors, and activities. _____

_____   4. Kids love to dress up in costumes, and they especially like to try to dunk Mr. Hill, our Principal, at the dunking booth. _____

_____   5. Last year, some parents asked Mom to organize the bake sale. _____

_____   6. She raised twenty dollars by raffling off a three-layer german chocolate cake. _____

_____   7. Companies like ibm often donate money to sponsor booths. _____

_____   8. My english teacher volunteered to have an arm wresting contest with the coach. _____

_____   9. Our home economics teacher raffles off bouquets of roses, and our spanish teacher raffles off posters. _____

_____   10. This year the carnival raised over a thousand dollars for the Foothills Blue Devils. _____

CAPITALIZATION EDITING TEST 1

Working alone or in groups of two or three, correct the twenty capitalization errors in the passage.

Jackson Hole

My vacation to Jackson hole, Wyoming, was fantastic. After settling into our Hotel, we explored the many Downtown Shops. The next day we took a raft trip down the snake river and saw beaver, canada geese, trumpeter swans, osprey, and a bald eagle. Just outside of town is grand teton national park with hundreds of miles of hiking trails, lakes, and mountains to be explored. We took a ferryboat across Jenny lake. The next day we drove to Yellowstone national park and had a chance to see the most famous geyser in the world, old faithful, shoot a plume of water a hundred and fifty feet in the air. As we drove south out of yellowstone, we saw herds of Bison grazing in the plains. I felt as if I were in the movie *The Man Who dances with wolves.*

CAPITALIZATION EDITING TEST 2

Correct the twenty capitalization errors in the passage.

```
                          Ethnic Foods


    These days americans can choose from a variety of Restau-

rants featuring food from all over the world. Chain restau-

rants such as taco bell and olive garden have made ethnic

food as easy to enjoy as traditional fast food items such as

Hamburgers and fries. Today even many small towns have

chinese, mexican, and Italian restaurants. Whereas twenty

years ago, Hometown restaurants didn't serve anything more

exotic than Spaghetti, today these restaurants often feature

dishes such as sweet and sour pork and shrimp fried rice.

Diners no longer have to travel to big cities such as new

york or san francisco to find restaurants that specialize in

indian, vietnamese, or ethiopian food. Today, ethnic food is

as common as Apple Pie.
```

Practicing Your Writing Power

Power of Language

What type of ethnic food do you like? Write about the types of restaurants you like to go to and the dishes you most enjoy. When you finish writing, go back and edit your writing for capitalization.

© Thomson Corporation/Heinle Image Resource Bank

Name _____
Section _____ Score _____

CAPITALIZATION TEST 1

Identify the capitalization in the following sentences as correct (C) or incorrect (I), and correct any capitalization errors in the space provided.

_____ 1. My Mother is taking her sister Elaine to France in August. _____

_____ 2. They are both taking a french class in order to learn the language.

_____

_____ 3. They have already purchased their tickets on American airlines.

_____

_____ 4. Their flight takes off from Hattsfield International Airport in Atlanta and lands at Charles DeGaulle Airport in Paris.

_____ 5. They will take a boat tour on the Seine, the River that runs through Paris.

_____

_____ 6. My father hopes she won't spend too much money in the stores on the Champs Elysees.

_____ 7. Dad hopes Mother spends more time in the museums than in the department stores.

_____ 8. She has always wanted to dine at a famous three-star restaurant named Causson.

_____ 9. She particularly wants to see the most famous painting in the world, the mona lisa by Michelangelo. _____

_____ 10. They plan to visit the Eiffel Tower and other famous landmarks.

Name _____

Section _____ Score _____

CAPITALIZATION TEST 2

Identify the capitalization in the following sentences as correct (C) or incorrect (I), and correct any capitalization errors in the space provided.

_____ 1. My family recently moved from Illinois to Georgia.

_____ 2. Because my daughter is in High School, it was particularly hard for her to leave her friends. _____

_____ 3. Her new school, Decatur senior high, is huge compared to her old school. _____

_____ 4. The Principal, Ms. Charbonet, welcomed my daughter personally to school and gave her a tour of the buildings. _____

_____ 5. Her new school offers subjects such as astronomy, spanish, and interior design. _____

_____ 6. The gymnasium holds over four hundred students, and the basketball team, the Hornets, is unbeaten.

_____ 7. Even though everyone has been nice, she still misses her best friend, Charlene, and her coach, Mrs. Benson.

_____ 8. Our Beagle, Patches, has had just as much trouble adjusting as my daughter has. _____

_____ 9. I told her that if she gets involved in activities such as band and chorus, she will feel better.

_____ 10. No matter what I say, she is counting the days until we go back to Illinois on vacation this Summer. _____

Name _____
Section _____ Score _____

CAPITALIZATION TEST 3

Identify the capitalization in the following sentences as correct (C) or incorrect (I), and correct any capitalization errors in the space provided.

_____ 1. Maine has sixty-four working lighthouses, more than any other State in the country. _____

_____ 2. Lighthouses are no longer necessary for shipping safety because boats now use global positioning system (gps) for navigation.

_____

_____ 3. However, the lighthouses are a symbol of the state's History. _____

_____ 4. In June 1998, Senator Olympia Snowe turned over ownership of twenty-eight lighthouses to various state agencies, towns, and nonprofit organizations.

_____ 5. The program, called the Maine Lights Program, has saved many Lighthouses. _____

_____ 6. The program came about after a fire damaged the lighthouse on the Southern tip of Green Island. _____

_____ 7. When the coast guard planned to tear down the damaged lighthouse, citizens decided to save their light. _____

_____ 8. It took three years and an act of Congress to save the lighthouse.

_____ 9. The Maine Lights Program is supervised by the Maine historic preservation commission. _____

_____ 10. Now many other states are looking into creating similar programs under the supervision of the national park service. _____

Name _____

Section _____ Score _____

CAPITALIZATION TEST 4

Identify the capitalization in the following sentences as correct (C) or incorrect (I), and correct any capitalization errors in the space provided.

_____ 1. The Everglades, located in the Southern part of Florida, is home to many interesting plants and animals. _____

_____ 2. Marjorie Stoneman Douglas wrote a book about the Everglades called *River of Grass.*

_____ 3. Water moves from north to south across its partially submerged grasses.

_____ 4. Perhaps the most famous and feared creature in the Everglades is the Alligator, but Florida panther, black bear, and white-tail deer are also inhabitants of this watery world. _____

_____ 5. Common birds include the bald eagle, osprey, hawk, and numerous wading birds such as blue heron, spoonbill and ibis.

_____ 6. The everglades is also home to rare and beautiful plants. _____

_____ 7. The big cypress swamp state preserve is the only place in the continental United States that the rare ghost orchid grows.

_____

_____ 8. The movie *Adaptation* focuses on the search for this rare and hard-to-find orchid.

_____ 9. The movie is loosely based on the book *the orchid thief* by Susan Orleans.

_____

_____ 10. This magnificent and vital natural wonder should be restored and preserved.

Chapter 4 Problem Words

In this chapter, you will learn about the most commonly confused words through

- Definitions
- Memory hooks
- Examples

Below we have included two lists of the most commonly confused words. The words are divided into two lists so that you can focus on about twenty word pairs at a time.

LIST 1		LIST 2	
Accept/Except	Their/There/They're	Advice/Advise	Choose/Chose
An/And	Thorough/Through	Affect/Effect	Complement/
Its/It's	Throw/Threw		Compliment
Know/No	Though/Thought	All ready/Already	Fair/Fare
Passed/Past	To/Too/Two	All together/	Hear/Here
Peace/Piece	Use to/Used to	Altogether	
Principal/Principle	Weather/Whether	Bare/Bear	Hole/Whole
Right/Write	Woman/Women	Blew/Blue	Lay/Lie
Steal/Steel	Would (could, should,	Brake/Break	Loose/Lose
	must) Have/Would	By/Buy	Stationary/
	(could, should,		Stationery
	must) Of	Capital/Capitol	Weak/Week
Suppose/	Your/You're		
Supposed to			
Than/Then			

Skill Preview

Words that sound alike but have different spellings and meanings present problems for writers because such words are easily confused. It takes special attention to spot errors with these problem words in our own and others' writing.

Working alone or in a group, circle the thirteen problem word errors in the passage below.

The whether up North has been colder then usual this passed weak. All you here about on the news is how their have been snowstorms and ice storms threwout New England. Experts advice that if the whether doesn't brake, there could be serious affects. More people are in danger of loosing there lives in the all ready hard-hit northern states.

Compare the problem words you found to the corrections in the passage below. Go back and highlight any problem words you missed.

The weather up North has been colder than usual this past week. All you hear about on the news is how there have been snowstorms and ice storms throughout New England. Experts advise that if the weather doesn't break, there could be serious effects. More people are in danger of losing their lives in the already hard-hit northern states.

Words that **sound alike but have different spellings and different meanings** can cause spelling errors for writers and can cause misunderstanding for readers. Spell check programs won't catch errors with these commonly confused words because each word exists in the spell checker's dictionary, and spell check programs can identify only misspelled words, not misused words. The only way to catch errors with these problem words is to learn the meaning of each word and to proofread your writing carefully for misuses of these words.

The problem words have been divided into two lists so that they will be easier to learn. We suggest that you complete the exercise pairs after each word set and

Spotlight on Writers

Power of Language

Martin Luther King, Jr.

"I have a dream that my four little children will one day live in a nation where they will not be judged by the color of their skin but by the content of their character."

Martin Luther King, Jr., (1929–1968) wrote hundreds of speeches, sermons, and essays condemning segregation and calling on all Americans to live up to the assertion in the Declaration of Independence that "all men are created equal." His persuasive use of language stirred leaders and the American public to condemn the injustice of segregation and eventually led to the passage of the Civil Rights Act of 1964, which outlaws discrimination on the basis of race, color, religion, or national origin.

check your answers in the back of the book. Write the words that you miss on a review sheet. This will help you determine which words will be most difficult for you to master.

Ways to Remember the Difference Between Problem Words

1. Use a **memory hook:** Associate an image or sound with each word as a way to hook your memory into remembering the word's meaning.
2. Remember an **example** for each word that illustrates the difference between it and the words with which it is confused.

LIST 1

Directions: Study the problem words below, and then fill in the blanks in the practice sentences and check your answers on pages A-57–A-58.

Accept means to take or receive what is offered.

accept = acceptance

I will *accept* the award tonight.

Except means what is left out or excluded.

X in except = not

I like most vegetables *except* lima beans.

1. I _____ most offers _____ those that come with strings attached.

2. Yasmin can't _____ the fact that she passed all her courses _____ math.

An is an article meaning one or any and is used before words that begin with a vowel (a, e, i, o, u) or silent h sound.

An apple a day keeps the doctor away.

An American eagle landed in a tree near our house.

And means plus.

And = +

Ham *and* eggs are a traditional American breakfast.

3. ___ hour ago Jack gave me ___ old book ____ several letters.

4. ___ owl flew over ___ old house ____ landed on a branch.

Its is the singular possessive pronoun meaning belonging to it.

Its (no apostrophe) = his, her, their

The monkey scratched *its* neck.

It's is the contraction of it is or it has.

💡   It's = it is or it has

It's raining.

It's been raining all day.

5. _____ been a long time since I met a parrot that knew _____ name.

6. _____ time to find the book that has lost _____ cover.

Know means to have knowledge of.

💡   Know = knowledge

I am confident I *know* the answer.

No means zero.

💡   No = 0

There are *no* more apples on the shelf.

7. Jerry doesn't _____ how to take ____ for an answer.

8. There is ____ reason not to _____ the multiplication tables.

Passed is the past tense of the verb *pass*.

💡   Passed = -ed verb ending

Jimmy *passed* the football to Devin.

Past means time that has already gone by or is the adverb meaning *by* or *beyond*.

💡   Past = time or position

Rosario walked *past* the movie theater every day this *past* week.

9. In the _____ I have had good grades because I have _____ my exams.

10. This _____ month, Joaquin _____ his driving test.

Peace means tranquility.

💡   "Peace on Earth!"

I need some *peace* and quiet.

Piece means a part of something.

💡   "piece of pie"

I received a good *piece* of news yesterday.

11. The _____ agreement was written on a _____ of paper.

12. It is _____ful on this _____ of property.

Principal means main or most important.

(💡)   **principal = main**

The *principal* reason that Jasmine is healthy is because she exercises regularly.

Principle means a rule or law.

(💡)   **principle = rule**

Enrique lives by his *principles*.

13. The instructor explained the _____ reasons for testing the _____ of physics.

14. The _____ rule involved is the _____ of fair play.

Right can mean correct, the opposite of left, or something that is due to a person by law.

(💡)   **right = correct or "might does not make right."**

I want to get the *right* answer.

Write means to put words on paper.

(💡)   **"write looks like scribble."**

I like to *write* in my journal every morning.

15. The teacher asked that we _____ the _____ answers on a sheet of paper.

16. _____ down the name and phone number of the person to your _____.

Steal means to rob.

(💡)   **steal = illegal**

The suspect was caught *stealing* the money.

Steel means a hard metal.

(💡)   **The ee in steel is doubled to make it strong like the metal.**

My sister has nerves of *steel*.

17. I promise not to _____ any _____ tools.

18. The _____ beams will not be easy to _____.

Suppose means assume.

💡 No **d** means *suppose* is a **verb** in present tense.

I *suppose* you are right.

Supposed to means ought to or should.

💡 *Supposed to* is always preceded by a form of *to be* and followed by *to* plus a verb infinitive: is supposed to go.

I am *supposed to* be home by eleven.

19. I _____ I am _____ to go to every practice.

20. I don't _____ you know what time we are _____ to be there, do you?

Than is used to make comparisons.

💡 than = comparison

Lynn likes ice cream better *than* she likes cake.

Then means for a moment in time.

💡 Then = time

I want to think about it, and *then* I'll decide.

21. We can decide _____ if driving would be faster _____ walking.

22. I like orange juice more _____ apple juice.

Their is a possessive pronoun meaning belonging to them.

💡 their = heir

Their car is parked on the grass.

There can mean a place, or can begin a sentence: There is/There are.

💡 there = not here

We won't stop until we get *there*.

They're is the contraction of "they are."

💡 they're = they are

They're coming over at eight.

23. _____ going to visit Bob and Melissa in _____ new home.

24. The twins left _____ books over _____.

Thorough means complete or entire.

💡 *Thorough* has an **o** for complete.

Jermaine did a *thorough* job preparing for the test.

Through means finished, or in one side and out the other, or in the midst of something.

Be careful when you go *through* a swinging door.

25. Have you gone _____ your textbook and taken _____ notes?

26. I will have to work _____ the evening in order to do a _____ job.

Throw means to launch an object.

When will you *throw* out the trash?

Threw is the past tense of the verb *throw.*

Emmanuel *threw* a touchdown pass.

27. After he _____ five good passes, I knew he could _____ the ball.

28. When I asked him to _____, he _____ a curve ball.

Though is the short form of *although* or a part of *even though.*

Though I'd like to go, I need to study.

Thought is the past tense of the verb *think.*

Elena *thought* she could make a difference by volunteering.

29. I hadn't _____ to answer his call _____ I should have realized it was important.

30. Even _____ Shane answered quickly, I knew he hadn't _____ carefully.

To is a preposition that indicates direction or a part of the infinitive verb form (to be, to go, to do).

Tasha is going *to* the theater *to* see a play.

Too means excessively, extremely, or also.

    too = too many o's or also.

If it's not *too* late, I'd like to go, *too.*

Two is the number.

The game lasted for over *two* hours.

31. We plan _____ see _____ movies on Saturday.

32. It's _____ late _____ go _____ a show.

Use to means to utilize and is present tense.

The Sponge I *use to* clean the sink is missing.

Used to means having the habit and is past tense.

💡   **It always includes to + verb (used to eat).**

Sandra *used to* be my friend.

33. My mother _____ cook with lots of butter.

34. I know how to _____ a rake, but I'm not _____ working this hard.

Weather means outdoor air conditions.

Cold *weather* has caused power outages in some states.

Whether indicates alternatives.

Carmen cannot make up her mind *whether* or not to take the class.

35. We will play _____ or not the _____ is good.

36. The _____ may determine _____ or not we win.

Woman is the opposite of *man* in the singular form.

I know a *woman* who won the lottery.

Women is the plural form of *woman*.

💡   **women and men**

Many more *women* have entered the workforce.

37. One _____ I know joined a _____ rights group.

38. The youngest _____ in my _____ club was elected president.

Would have, could have, should have, and **must have** are verb phrases.

I *should have* written a thank-you note.

Would of, could of, should of, and **must of:** The *of* that follows the verbs begins a prepositional phrase.

💡   *Of* **will be separated from the verb with a comma.** *Of* **is almost never used after these verbs. (***Have* **is almost always used after these verbs.)**

Sandra must, of course, be late.

39. My teacher would, ___ everyone in the school, be the one to say I could _____ passed.

40. I should _____ known that you would, ___ all people, be late.

Your is the possessive pronoun meaning belonging to you.

Have you completed *your* assignment?

You're is the contraction of you are.

You're (you are) lucky to be here.

41. _____ the luckiest of all _____ friends.

42. _____ going to be late if you don't finish _____ homework.

WRITING PRACTICE

On your own sheet of paper, write a sentence with each problem word.

Working Together

In small groups or with the entire class, read the sentences you have written for problem words. Ask other students to decide the correct spelling of the word used in the sentence.

Name _____

Section _____   Score _____

LIST 1, TEST 1

Identify the sentences as correct (C) or incorrect (I), and then correct all problem word errors.

_____   1. Every morning, I walk through a playground on the way to school.

_____   2. The other day, I saw two boys throw a peace of paper on the ground.

_____   3. It looked like blue stationery, but before I could get to it, it blew away in the wind.

_____   4. If your not used to seeing people litter, it's a shock.

_____   5. I was madder then I thought I would have been to see them littering.

_____   6. I wanted to give them back there trash and tell them not to litter again.

_____   7. I wanted them to except responsibility for their actions.

_____   8. However, I didn't know whether they dropped it on purpose or not.

_____   9. A elderly woman who was walking her dog must have seen them litter, too.

_____   10. She explained the principle of accepting responsibility for your actions.

Name _____

Section _____   Score _____

LIST 1, TEST 2

Identify the sentences as correct (C) or incorrect (I), and then correct all problem word errors.

_____   1. Its sometimes difficult for my son to accept, but I want him to live by certain principles.

_____   2. The principal rule is that he should finish his work and then go out.

_____   3. There are many reasons he should of gotten his work done sooner.

_____   4. I will accept no more than two excuses a day.

_____   5. He's not suppose to go out until he is through with his homework.

_____   6. Though he accepts the principle of the idea, he says it will be harder then I think to buy movie tickets at the last minute.

_____   7. He won't be through with his homework until ten, and by then it will be too late.

_____   8. He and his friends are supposed to go a movie downtown.

_____   9. Their coming by to pick him up at half-past seven.

_____   10. I still haven't decided whether I will let him go.

LIST 2

Directions: Study the problem words, complete the exercises for each set of words, and check your answers on page A-58.

Advice is a noun that means a recommendation.

I asked my counselor for *advice* on the right courses to take for my major.

Advise is a verb that means to counsel.

The counselor *advised* me to take three English courses.

1. My friend _____d me to take easy classes, but I didn't think it was good _____.

2. My _____ to you is not to listen to what anyone _____ you to do.

Affect is a verb that means to influence or bring about a change.

💡 affect = action

I was *affected* by Martin Luther King, Jr.'s speeches.

Effect is a noun that means a result.

💡 effect = result

There were serious *effects* from the storm.

3. The _____ of Hurricane Andrew _____ the town for years.

4. I was _____ by the speaker's warnings about the _____ of global warming.

All ready means that everyone or everything is prepared.

💡 *all ready* can be read as "ready."

We will leave when we are *all ready.*

Already means before, or previously, or by this time.

💡 *already* cannot be read as "ready."

I have *already* completed my reading assignment.

5. Having _____ sold twenty boxes of cookies, the Girls Scouts were _____ to leave.

6. I have _____ completed my homework, so I am _____ to go to the movie.

All together means everything or everyone together.

💡 all together can be read as "together."

We will meet *all together* in the mall at eight o'clock.

Altogether means completely or entirely.

💡 altogether cannot be read as "together"

Jordan is not *altogether* sure where he put his books.

7. If you keep your papers _____, you will be _____ certain where to find them.

8. I am _____ certain of my answer because we studied _____ last night.

Bare means uncovered or just enough.

I can *barely* understand the directions.

Bear means the wild animal or to carry, to hold up, or to endure.

Black *bears* can *bear* long winters because they hibernate.

9. I can't _____ to study anymore because I _____ly got any sleep last night.

10. After a long winter, there is _____ly enough food for a wild _____ to eat.

Blew is the past tense of *blow*.

The wind *blew* the leaves off the tree.

Blue is the color.

💡 blue = color or hue

The sky is clear *blue*.

11. The wind _____ the clouds out of the _____ sky.

12. My friend _____ it when he told his date he didn't care for her _____ dress.

Brake means a device to stop movement.

💡 a brake on a car

When the *brakes* failed, I hit a tree.

Break means an interruption.

Most students look forward to spring *break*.

13. I'm trying to _____ the bad habit of resting my foot on the _____ as I drive.

14. Let's take a coffee _____ while the mechanic fixes the _____.

By is a preposition.

I drove *by* the store.

Buy means to purchase.

I like to *buy* groceries that are on sale.

15. If we stop _____ the theater before we go to dinner, we can _____ our tickets in advance.

16. You can sit _____ me if you _____ raffle tickets.

Capital means the main or most important.

Capital punishment is controversial.

Capitol means the government building.

💡   capit**ol** = d**o**me

The dome on the *capitol* is covered in gold.

17. We drove to our nation's _____ and stood in line to see the _____ rotunda.

18. I don't mind spending some of my _____ to visit the legislators' offices in the _____ building.

Choose means to pick out.

💡   *Choose* has two o's to choose from.

How do you *choose* the right shoes?

Chose is the past tense of *choose* and is pronounced with a long *o*.

I *chose* not to have dessert after dinner last night.

19. If I want to, I can _____ to go to the same movie I _____ to go to last night.

20. Yesterday I _____ one color, but today I _____ another.

Complement means to make complete or something that completes or makes perfect.

💡   complement = make complete

Complementary colors go well together.

Compliment means praise.

💡   compliment = praise

Thank you for your kind *compliment*.

21. My bedspread _____ the blue rug.

22. I'd like to _____ you on the hat that _____ your shoes.

Fair means just, good, blond, pale, or carnival. (*Fair* is used for all meanings except money.)

Discrimination is *unfair.*

Fare means the ticket price.

The plane *fare* to Seattle had increased.

23. It's _____ to charge one _____ on the weekend and another during the week.

24. The _____ to ride on the tilt-a-whirl at the _____ is one dollar.

Hear means to perceive by ear.

💡 **hear = ear**

Did you *hear* my directions?

Here means location.

💡 **here = not there**

I have lived *here* for five years.

25. Did you _____ how long they will be staying _____?

26. I won't be _____ after ten.

Hole means an opening.

Be careful of the *hole* in the sidewalk.

Whole means entire or complete.

My kids ate a *whole* loaf of bread.

27. There was a _____ in the bag, and now my _____ report is missing.

28. The cost of the _____ trip to Europe left a _____ in my budget.

Lay means to place or put. In present tense, if you can substitute *place* or *put* for *lay,* then *lay* is correct.

💡 **lay = place or put**

I always *lay* my keys on the table.

Lie means to recline.

💡 **lie = recline**

I'd like to *lie* down in a hammock and take a nap.

29. Students are asked to _____ their books on the floor during an exam.

30. People who _____ out in the sun too long will get sunburned.

Loose can mean free.

My son's front tooth is *loose* and is about to fall out.

Lose can mean unable to keep.

💡 **lose = lost**

I don't want to *lose* sight of my goals.

31. You may _____ a dog that runs around _____.

32. My ring is _____, and I don't want to _____ it.

Stationary means not moving.

The boy stood as *stationary* as a statue.

Stationery means writing paper.

💡 **stationery = paper**

Wedding invitations are usually printed on white *stationery.*

33. The report about the _____ weather front was printed on white _____.

34. Don't try to write on _____ unless your car is _____.

Weak means the opposite of strong.

If I don't exercise, I feel *weak.*

Week means seven days.

Everyone likes short *weeks* and long *weekends.*

35. Because I was feeling _____ after surgery, my doctor recommended I take a _____ off work.

36. After a _____ of hiking in the mountains, I discovered that my knees were _____.

CD Connection

Power of
Language

On *Writer's Resources* CD-ROM, see *Problem Words* in Grammar/Punctuation/ Mechanics for more information and practice with problem words.

WRITING PRACTICE

On your own sheet of paper, write a sentence with each problem word.

 Working Together

In small groups or with the entire class, read the sentences you have written for problem words. Ask other students to decide the correct spelling of the word used in the sentence.

Practicing Your Writing Power

Power of Language

© Thomson Corporation/Heinle Image Resource Bank

Choose one of the following topics:

1. Write about your chosen major. Do you know what is required and what courses you will have to take? Have you visited a guidance counselor to plan your courses? When you have finished writing, go back and edit your writing for problem word errors.
2. Write about how the weather affects your mood. When you have finished writing, go back and edit your writing for problem word errors.

Name _____

Section _____   Score _____

LIST 2, TEST 1

Identify the problem words in the following sentences as correct (C) or incorrect (I), and then correct the errors.

_____   1. A winter storm blew into New England last week.

_____   2. People have been adviced to stay indoors until there is a break in the

storm.

_____   3. Homes and businesses are in danger of loosing power.

_____   4. Millions of people have been affected by the storm.

_____   5. The hole northeast has already suffered the worst weather in a decade.

_____   6. By the end of the week, more then fifty people were hospitalized.

_____   7. Residents have had to bare a whole week of freezing temperatures.

_____   8. Unless temperatures rise, more people are in danger of losing their lives.

_____   9. Here in the capital, many residents are choosing to stay indoors.

_____   10. Everyone is hoping for fare weather and blue skies.

Name _____

Section _____   Score _____

LIST 2, TEST 2

Identify the problem words in the following sentences as correct (C) or incorrect (I), and then correct the errors.

_____   1. My son's safety patrol will visit Washington, D.C., our capitol, this spring.

_____   2. The trip will last one hole week.

_____   3. The bus fare for the trip is over one hundred dollars.

_____   4. School officials are hoping that twenty parents will chose to make the trip as chaperones.

_____   5. Some parents feel it is all together too much responsibility.

_____   6. Others do not think it is fare to ask chaperones to pay their own way.

_____   7. Crowds are expected around the capitol because Congress is in session.

_____   8. The students have been advised to wear matching shirts so that we will not loose anyone in the crowds.

_____   9. Most kids see the trip as a welcome break from school.

_____   10. The effect of a whole week in our capital should be educational.

Name _____

Section _____   Score _____

PROBLEM WORDS LISTS 1 AND 2, TEST 1

Identify the problem words in the following sentences as correct (C) or incorrect (I), and then correct the errors.

_____ 1. Even though the spring term has barely started, I am all ready looking forward to spring break.

_____ 2. The weather in St. Paul is cold and snowy, and the weather can effect your mood.

_____ 3. It makes me feel blue an throws me into a depression that makes me question why I'm in school.

_____ 4. Like most students, right now I'm trying not to lose my mind, and I'm counting the weeks until the break.

_____ 5. I know I'm not supposed to be affected by the weather.

_____ 6. It doesn't seem fare that we have to live through a winter that is so much more difficult than it is in other places.

_____ 7. It's difficult to except that it is sunny there and snowy here.

_____ 8. I have taken the advise of my friends and made plans to go somewhere sunny for spring break.

_____ 9. If the plane fare isn't more than two hundred dollars, I will buy a plane ticket to Key West, Florida.

_____ 10. I hope the weather will not be altogether to hot in Florida so that I can lie out in the sun for the whole week.

Name _____

Section _____   Score _____

PROBLEM WORDS LISTS 1 AND 2, TEST 2

Identify the problem words in the following sentences as correct (C) or incorrect (I), and then correct the errors.

_____ 1. Last weak, I went to see a counselor for advise on chosing my courses.

_____ 2. She asked whether I had all ready decided on a major.

_____ 3. I told her I was not altogether certain, but I thought I was interested in medicine.

_____ 4. She complemented me on my choice.

_____ 5. Then she advised me that I would have to take many math and science classes by the time I graduate.

_____ 6. Unfortunately, I bearly passed algebra, and I don't believe I can bear to take chemistry.

_____ 7. It doesn't seem fair that I should have to take such hard courses whether I like them or not.

_____ 8. I know I should except the fact that it's not going to be a piece of cake getting a degree that will lead to a job that pays a fair salary.

_____ 9. I hope that I don't loose sight of my goals.

_____ 10. However, I don't want to spend my hole life in school.

Chapter 5 Word Use and Choice

In this chapter, you will

- ☛ Learn to use specific rather than general words
- ☛ Learn to choose words with the right denotation or meaning
- ☛ Learn to avoid the pitfalls of
  - Nonstandard language
  - Double negatives
  - Slang
  - Wordiness
  - Omitted letters and words

Skill Preview

Writers should be aware of their choices of words. Language that might be appropriate between friends would be inappropriate with a supervisor, and much of the language that we use in speech isn't appropriate in academic writing.

Directions: Working alone or in groups of two or three, circle the words and phrases in the passage below that seem inappropriate for academic writing.

Our vacation at the beach wasn't no good on account of we had bad experiences. First off, being that the weather was crummy, we couldn't go nowhere. Then the beach was crowd with a lot of people, meaning that we couldn't barely find no place to put are blanket. When we went out to eat, the prices were totally off the wall and the food was gross. The whole experience was a bummer. Will never go back to that beach no more.

Next, read the corrected passage below and circle any inappropriate words that you did not catch in the first passage when you read it.

Our vacation at the beach wasn't any fun because we had bad experiences. First, because the weather was rainy, we couldn't go anywhere. Then the beach was crowded with a lot of people, so we couldn't find any place to put our blanket. When we went out to eat, the prices were expensive and the food was terrible. The whole experience was a disappointment. Will never go back to that beach again.

Effective Word Choice

College writers try to use language that is clear, correct, and precise. To communicate effectively, writers should avoid using nonstandard (incorrect) words and phrases, double negatives, slang, and profanity. In college, writers must also edit their writing carefully to avoid wordiness and to catch any omitted letters or words.

Specific and General Words

Specific language communicates more clearly than general language. General words, such as *things, stuff,* or *people,* won't help the reader see a picture of what you have in mind. After all, there are all kinds of things, stuff, and people. Use specific words to create images for the reader.

1.1 Use **specific nouns** where appropriate.

General	Specific
things	CDs
stuff	books and papers
people	John and Alicia
animal	humpback whale
river	Columbia River
car	Mustang convertible

Spotlight on Writers

Power of
Language

Rachel Carson

"The beauty of the living world I was trying to save has always been uppermost in my mind—that, and anger at the senseless, brutish things that were being done. I have felt bound by a solemn obligation to do what I could—if I didn't at least try I could never be happy again in nature. But now I can believe that I have at least helped a little. It would be unrealistic to believe one book could bring a complete change."

Rachel Carson (1907–1964) was a scientist who was best-known for her best-selling book *Silent Spring* (1962), in which she warned that the overuse of pesticides was destroying bird life and upsetting the balance of nature. *Silent Spring* is credited with changing the way we view our relationship with the natural world, and the uproar created by Carson's book helped push through environmental legislation to curb the widespread use of pesticides such as DDT.

1.2 Use **active verbs** where appropriate.

Whenever possible, replace general verbs such as is/are, was/were, has/have, does/do with specific verbs that fit the scene you are describing.

General	Specific
She *put* flowers in a vase.	Maria *arranged* irises in a long-stemmed, crystal vase.
An animal *was* in the water.	A bottlenose dolphin *rode* our wake.
The river *was* long.	The Columbia River *snaked* for miles to the horizon.

Notice how both the nouns and verbs in the sentences on the right are specific.

Practice 1 For each pair of words, circle the words that are more specific.

1. building/courthouse

2. crow/bird

3. has/owns

4. Rocky Mountains/mountains

5. does/studies

6. dog/Irish setter

7. politician/person

8. goldfish/animal

9. school/Wyles Elementary

10. ladybug/insect

Practice 2 Rewrite the following sentences, making them more concrete and specific.

Example:
Topic: Some things on TV are bad for people.
More specific: The sugarcoated cereals advertised during cartoons encourage kids to develop unhealthful eating habits.

1. The things they show on TV are bad.
   (What things are bad? In what way are they bad?)

   _____

2. The animal came close to the child.
   (What animal? How close to the child was it? What did the animal and child look like?)

   _____

3. The room was beautiful.
   (What room? Describe the room's beauty so that the reader can see it in the mind's eye.)

   _____

4. When I saw the man, I had a good feeling.
   (What man and what was the good feeling?)

_____

5. A person walked into the room and put something on the desk.
   (What person? Describe the way he or she walked or use another more descriptive word for walk. What thing did he or she put on the desk? Describe the desk.)

_____

Denotation

2.1 Choose words that have the right **denotation,** or literal meaning.

If you're not absolutely sure the word you have in mind is the right one, look it up in the dictionary. You are better off choosing a word you are familiar with rather than one you think sounds sophisticated.

Commonly Confused Words

Be aware of the difference in meaning between these commonly confused words:

idea/ideal

Ideal = perfect   Example: This is the *ideal* place to live.
Idea = thought   Example: I had a good *idea.*

are/our

Are = present plural of verb "to be"   Example: We *are* friends.
Our = personal pronoun meaning   Example: Those are *our* cards.
belonging to us

want/won't

Want = to desire   Example: Do you *want* dessert?
Won't = will not   Example: Chandra *won't* answer the phone.

were/where

Were = past tense of was   Example: We *were* late for the party.
Where = question word for location   Example: *Where* are you from?

will/we'll

Will = future of the verb "to be"   Example: Sandra *will* go at ten.
We'll = we will   Example: *We'll* go to the grocery store.

Practice 3 Circle the correct word in parentheses in each sentence. Use a dictionary if you need to.

1. They (were/where) leaving school when they (were/where) in an accident.

2. (Will/We'll) return from the store by five o'clock.

3. I (want/won't) a chocolate ice cream cone.

4. All (are/our) notes (were/where) lost in the fire.

5. (Were/Where) did you buy those shoes?

6. I don't (mine/mind) cleaning the house.

7. I want to work for a (respective/respectable) business.

8. My parents (encouraged/incouraged) me to work hard.

9. I (want/won't) to be successful.

10. I made a (regretful/regrettable) decision to drop out of school.

Ineffective Word Choice

Take care to avoid pitfalls such as nonstandard words and phrases, double negatives, slang, wordiness, and omitted letters and words in your writing.

Nonstandard Usage

3.1 Avoid **nonstandard usage** (incorrect words and phrases that may be commonly used).

Some words are used incorrectly by lots of people, but the words are still incorrect. The dictionary will have these words labeled as nonstandard or incorrect.

✗ Nonstandard/Incorrect	✓ Standard/Correct
ain't	am not
gonna	going to
wanna	want to
would of/could of/should of	would have/could have/should have
drive thru	drive through
alright	all right
being that	because
on account of	because
so ____(tired, full, etc.) until	so ____ that
theirselves	themselves

✗ Nonstandard/Incorrect	✓ Standard/Correct
hisself	himself
neck in neck	neck and neck
one in the same	one and the same
stock and trade	stock in trade
tongue and cheek	tongue in cheek
irregardless	regardless
could care less	couldn't care less
misunderestimated	underestimated
hone in on	home in on

Practice 4   Rewrite the following sentences by eliminating nonstandard usage.

Example:

✗ Steve ran so fast until he exhaust hisself. (nonstandard)

✓ Steve ran so fast that he exhausted himself. (standard)

1. I'm gonna go irregardless of what my parents say.

   _____

2. Jerome don't wanna go to school on account of he don't feel good.

   _____

3. Being that we won the game, were gonna go to the drive thru an buy shakes.

   _____

4. On account of I didn't have no ideal how long the project was gonna take, I misunderestimated how much time I would need.

   _____

   _____

5. I could care less if they ain't gonna pay for theirselves.

   _____

Double Negatives

4.1 Avoid the use of two negatives in a sentence.

Nonstandard	Standard
✗ Kim is not no star player.	✓ Kim is not a star player.
✗ I don't like no cats.	✓ I don't like cats.
✗ Suli is not doing no more homework.	✓ Suli is not doing any more homework.

Practice 5   Cross out the double negatives from the following sentences, and then write in the correct word to replace it.

1. Jerome doesn't have no _____ time to waste.

2. Sandy won't go to no _____ office party.

3. I'm not interested in no _____ date.

4. The teacher won't give us no _____ extra credit.

5. Don't bring no _____ problems around here.

Slang

5.1 Avoid **slang** (informal words that have a specific meaning to a group of people) and **profanity** (language that is disrespectful or vulgar).

Slang may be colorful, but it is generally considered inappropriate for most writing. One of the problems with slang is that the writer runs the risk of the audience not understanding the intended meaning.

✗ Slang	
anyways	crib
awesome	ride
bad	dis (disrespect)
dude	far out
bro (brother)	gross
bummed	gnarly
chill	hood (neighborhood)
cool	rad (radical)

Practice 6   Rewrite the following sentences to eliminate slang.

1. Pedro wanted to chill in his crib.

   _____

2. I want to cruise in a totally awesome ride.

   _____

3. The prof introduced us to a totally rad idea.

   _____

4. I'm bummed over my low grade.

   _____

5. The dude claimed he was king of the hood

Wordiness

6.1 Avoid **wordiness,** the use of words that do not contribute to meaning.

Often writers end up using more words than they need. In writing, it's best to be concise, which means using the fewest words necessary to communicate clearly.

Wordy: ✗ As far as I am concerned, due to the fact that students are adults, they should be able to make their own decisions and do what they want with their time, so class attendance should be optional.

Concise: ✓ Because students are adults, class attendance should be optional.

6.2 Avoid **unnecessary phrases.**

Unnecessary phrases do not add to the meaning of a sentence.

✗ Unnecessary Phrases	
In my opinion	Due to the fact
I think	Because of the fact that
As far as I'm concerned	Like for instance
Obviously	First off
It goes without saying	Each and every
At this point in time	

6.3 Avoid **intensifiers.**

Intensifiers are also considered wordy. For example, what is the difference between writing that you are angry or *really* angry? The intensifier does not add meaning for the reader.

Wordy: ✗ I'm so happy because when I saw Max downtown he was really friendly.

Concise: ✓ I'm happy because when I saw Max downtown he was friendly.

✗ Intensifiers	
So (as in so nice)	Really
Extremely	Quite
Very	

Practice 7   Rewrite the following sentences to eliminate wordiness.

1. Like for instance, when I study past history, the thing that interests me is learning and reading about the places where events and things happened and took place.

   _____

2. Each and every time I make future plans, some unexpected surprise comes along that changes everything I have planned and what I'm doing.

   _____

3. I would like to work for maybe two or three years or thereabouts in my chosen field of business.

   _____

4. In actual fact, it will take me well over more than two years to complete my degree due to the fact that I will need to take several college prep classes on account of my high school background was not too good.

   _____

   _____

5. My advisor recommended to me that I should not take more than three classes each and every term due to the fact out of necessity and to pay my bills I have to be working at the same time I am attending school.

   _____

   _____

Missing Letters and Words

7.1 Avoid missing letters and words.

You must read over your writing carefully to make sure that you have not left out letters and/or words you intended to include. Sometimes important words such as the subject or the verb are left out of a sentence. More often, endings are left off of nouns and verbs, and small words such as articles and prepositions are left out of the sentence. One way to avoid leaving out words and letters is to focus on each word as you read.

Practice 8

Insert the missing words and letters above the sentences using a ^ to mark the spot you are inserting the words or letters.

1. Many of my friend work at the same time they go school.

2. When have to work late during the week, I'm sleepy in class next day.

3. Since no on supporting me, I have to work to pay my bills.

4. I work twenty hour during week and eight hours on Saturday.

5. It is hard to complete all homework when I have work so many hour.

CD Connection

Power of Language

On *Writer's Resources* CD-ROM, see *Word Choice* in Writing Elements/Words for more information and practice with word choice.

Practice 9 *Working Together*

Working alone or in groups of two or three, write four sentences that contain language that might be appropriate between friends but that would not be appropriate in academic writing. Make sure you do not write anything that might be considered offensive to other group members.

Practice 10   Trade the sentences you wrote in Practice 9 with another group, and rewrite each other's sentences using the principles of word choice learned in this chapter. Share your sentence revisions with the other group or with the class.

REVIEW EXERCISE 1

Working alone or in groups of two or three, cross out the italicized words or phrases and replace them with more effective words.

1. My *roomy flipped out* when he saw the *total zero's I'd scored on my grades.*

_____

2. He doesn't *get it* that *at this point in time* I *ain't got no particular* interest in school.

_____

3. *In actual fact,* he has these *totally rad* ideas about how I should be *cruising.*

_____

4. I wanted to say, "*Bummer,* I *like* wasn't paying *no* attention to school."

_____

5. Instead, for *about the first time in like my entire lifetime,* I kept my *trap* shut.

_____

6. He *like did the preacher number about no more partying* until my grades improved.

_____

7. He *laid a downer on me* when he said I couldn't use his car *no more.*

_____

8. *It goes without saying* that the *unbelievable total* unfairness *of it all bummed me out* for days.

_____

9. *Due to the fact that* I couldn't *party with the bros,* I *actually cracked* my books for the first time *in forever.*

_____

10. After *a relatively short period of* only a few weeks *more or less,* my grades *did a wheelie and shot for the moon.*

_____

REVIEW EXERCISE 2

Cross out the italicized words or phrases and replace them with more effective words.

1. *In this day and time, so very* many students find adjusting to life *away from their family in college* difficult *to adjust to.*

_____

2. *Due to the fact that* they don't have *no* experience living on their own *without family or roommates,* they have *so much* trouble adjusting to life on their own.

_____

3. Some *newbies* feel *like* they have *to do a song and dance* to impress other *dudes.*

_____

4. They think it's *way cool* to *chug an over the top number of beers* and get *wasted.*

_____

5. *Most of the time* they end up *cutting the fool* and *tossing their cookies.*

_____

6. *On account of* they *don't know no* better, they try to drive home and could end up in a *horror* show by getting in an accident.

_____

_____

7. In class the next day, they are *zoned out* and *clueless.*

_____

8. *Needless to say,* at the end of the term, they have *bombed* their classes.

_____

9. They find themselves *bounced back to the minors* and *flipping burgers* in their home *joint.*

_____

_____

10. *Irregardless of what their friends say, student* need to behave *responsible in order that* they can stay in school.

_____

EDITING FOR WORD CHOICE 1

Working alone or in groups, circle the most appropriate choice within the parentheses. When you see [delete], it means that the best choice is simply to cut the italicized word or phrase.

School Daze

In my opinion ([delete]/I think), high school was an

extremely ([delete]/really) difficult *and really trying*

([delete]/very trying) time in my life. My parents always (incouraged/encouraged) me to work hard in school, but I was more (interesting/interested) in sports and dating (than/then) in schoolwork. (Like for instance/For instance), when I was (a/an) sophomore, I (decided/decide it) to try out for the track team. I made a (promise/promist) to myself to be the (fast/fastest) runner in the school. (Regrettable/Regrettably), I (neglected/negligent) to do my homework (an/and) my grades dropped. *In actual fact* ([delete]/In reality), I hope I (learn/learned) (an/a) lesson from my experiences. Now, *at this point in time* ([delete]/today), I am a better student because *of the fact that* ([delete]/on account of) I learned my lesson the hard way. *Due to the fact that I had this experience,* ([delete]/I believe) I have grown up, and now I am ready to be a serious student.

EDITING FOR WORD CHOICE 2

Circle the most appropriate choice within the parentheses.

To Whom It May Concern:

I would like to (acquire/inquire) about the job opening (advertise/advertised) in yesterday's paper. (You/Your) advertisement (mentioned/mention) the need to dress (appropriate/appropriately) for the job of restaurant host. (Does/Dose) the position (intail/entail) dressing (formerly/formally)? Would (their/there) be special clothes or (a/an) uniform I would need to (where/wear)? If so, who would be (responsible/responsibly) for the purchase and cleaning of the uniform? I am very much (interest/interested) in the position and would like more information if (possible/passable). I have three years of (experience/experienced) working in the restaurant business as a busboy and waiter. (Beside/Besides) that experience, I am (real/really) good with people (on account of the fact that/because) I am a friendly and (likable/likely) person.

(Respectably/Respectfully) yours,

Practicing Your Writing Power

Power of Language

© Thomson Corporation/Heinle Image Resource Bank

1. How might learning to use specific, correct language improve your chances of success in school and in the work world? What kinds of errors have you become more aware of and learned to avoid by completing this chapter?
2. Write a letter to a friend about what college is like. Then write the same ideas to parents and choose different language. Be aware of how your choice of words differs between the two letters you write.

WORD CHOICE TEST 1

Circle the most appropriate word in parentheses.

1. Sunny is a (sharp/sharply) (dress/dressed) man.

2. Students (aint/aren't) in the habit of doing (no/any) studying

    before an exam.

3. Mike (misunderestimated/underestimated) how much (money/dough)

    he needed.

4. Paul, run (quick/quickly) (an/and) get me my hat.

5. Saturday was a (gloriest/glorious) day for a picnic, and the students enjoyed (their-

    selves/themselves).

6. When I get my degree, my life will change (tremendous/tremendously), and I will

    be (in the clover/wealthy).

7. I (should of/should have) finished my work before I (went out/partied down).

8. There was an (extreme/extremely) loud explosion that (totally blew my mind/fright-

    ened me).

9. Eleanor (dissed/talked back to) her boss and was (canned/fired).

10. The boy was (respectable/respectful) of his teachers until he (wigged out/lost his

    temper).

WORD CHOICE TEST 2

Circle the most appropriate word in parentheses.

1. (We'll/Will) finish all (are/our) work before we go out.

2. Nick was (bummed/disappointed) that he didn't (ace/get an A on) his

   math test.

3. (Being that/Because) we are friends, we like to (do things/chill)

   together.

4. Margo and Josie (won't/want) know (were/where) to meet us.

5. Ms. Ketchum (ain't/isn't) (gonna/going to) give us a make-up test.

6. (On account of/Because of) her injury, Melissa doesn't (won't/want)

   to play.

7. The players don't want to do (nothing/anything) that will make the coach (lose

   it/get mad).

8. My brothers embarrassed (theirselves/themselves) by (playing the

   fool/misbehaving).

9. The (food/grub) at the cafeteria is (gross/disgusting).

10. (Will/We'll) see you at ten on the corner (were/where)

    we agreed to meet.

Name_____
Section _____ Score _____

WORD CHOICE TEST 3

Insert the two missing words and/or letters in each of the following sentences. Use a ^ to show where the missing words and/or letters should be placed.

1. I started school when was five year old.

2. My kindergarten teacher was kind an sweet woman.

3. After that, my teacher didn't seem interested in their student.

4. They too many student to keep up with.

5. Some of the teacher look exhausted.

6. Then I move to small town.

7. In my new school, the class were smaller and the teacher happier.

8. I made lots of friends and played football most my junior an senior year.

9. Then on day, I was on the way to school, and I got into auto accident.

10. I was injured an couldn't play football the rest of year.

Name_____

Section _____ Score _____

WORD CHOICE TEST 4

Eliminate unnecessary words and phrases from the following sentences. Rewrite your sentence on the lines below.

1. In my opinion, students of all sorts should do their best to get involved and become active in school politics and activities such as clubs on campus.

   _____

2. It goes without saying that students who are involved in campus activities experience more success in their classes and are more successful in school than students who do not choose to get involved in what is happening on campus.

   _____

   _____

3. First off, studies show that for the most part and generally, students who get involved in campus activities are not as likely to leave school or drop out of school as students who do not get involved.

   _____

   _____

4. At this point in time it seems apparent that it is very extremely important for students who want to succeed to set aside some time each and every day to participate and get involved in campus activities.

   _____

5. As far as I'm concerned, in order to increase his or her chances of becoming successful, each and every student should strive his or her best to get involved.

   _____

Chapter 6 Identifying Subjects and Verbs

In this chapter, you will learn how to identify

☞ The subject of the sentence

☞ The complete verb

☞ Problem subjects and verbs

Skill Preview

Subjects and verbs are the most important parts of sentences. You use them every time you communicate a complete thought.

Fill in the blank with a subject for the sentence.

The _____ in my house is broken.
Most _____ like to dance.
_____ is my friend.

Fill in the blank with a verb for the sentence.

The bus _____ at Main Street every half hour.
Most students _____ on the weekends.
Miranda _____ after class.

We use subjects and verbs naturally in our communication. Learning to identify the subjects and verbs in sentences will help you avoid the major sentence structure errors of run-ons and fragments (Chapters 11 and 12) and avoid verb errors (Chapter 7). In addition, being aware of the subject and verb of the sentence will help you use varied sentence patterns that depend on the placement of the subject and the verb.

Spotlight on Writers

Power of
Language

Mattie Stepanek

"I want people to know my life philosophy, to remember to play after every storm."

Mattie Stepanek (1991–2004) died of a rare form of muscular dystrophy; he was only 13 years old. Mattie had three wishes: to have his poems published, to meet his hero Jimmy Carter, and to share his message of peace on *The Oprah Winfrey Show*. All three wishes were granted before he died. When Oprah asked Mattie why these three experiences were so important to him, he explained that talking about his ideas and publishing his feelings in his books would make them last forever. His three books of poetry, *Heartsongs, Journey through Heartsongs,* and *Hope through Heartsongs,* are all best-sellers.

The Most Important Parts of a Sentence

The subject and complete verb express the main idea of the sentence. The **subject** of the sentence tells who or what the sentence is about. The **verb** expresses the action or the state of being of the subject.

     S   V
The carpenter <u>measures</u> the cabinets before installing them.
    S   V
The flag <u>was fluttering</u> in the wind.
  S   V
She <u>has seemed</u> excited all week.

- Notice that the subjects in these sentences come before the verb and are nouns (carpenter, flag) or pronouns (she).
- The action verb (was fluttering) and the state of being verb (has seemed) include more than one word in these examples. (See "Parts of Speech," page A-9 for more information about nouns and verbs).

Finding the Subject and the Verb

1.1 To find the subject of the sentence, ask who or what the sentence is about.

1.2 To find the verb of the sentence, ask what the subject is doing or what word expresses the state of being of the subject.

        S   V
On weekends, the store <u>opens</u> at eight.

Who or what is the sentence about? _____

What is the store doing, or what word expresses its state of being? _____

S   V
Some children from our neighborhood <u>remain</u> in the backyard.

Who or what is the sentence about? _____

What are the children doing, or what word expresses their state or being?

_____

More about Subjects

2.1 The **simple subject** of the sentence is the noun (person, place, thing, or idea) the sentence is about without any modifiers or descriptive words.

S   V
A large gray car <u>is turning</u> around at the corner.

S   V
Some experienced teachers <u>will not accept</u> late assignments.

- The simple subject is always a person or thing. The word for the subject answers *who* or *what* the sentence is about.
- The words that describe the person or thing are not part of the simple subject. The common descriptive words in these examples are a *large gray* and *some experienced.*

Common Descriptive Words That Modify the Subject	
The	Few
A	His
An	Her
Many	Their
Some	Our

2.2 Pronouns can be the subject of the sentence.

S   V
He and Nora <u>have gone</u> to dinner.

S   V
Everyone <u>wants</u> to own a cell phone.

Common Subject Pronouns	
He	We
She	Everyone
It	Someone
They	Anyone

No one	Everybody
Everything	Somebody
Something	Anybody
Anything	Nobody
Nothing	

More about Verbs

3.1 The **complete verb** of the sentence includes all the forms of the verb, including helping or auxiliary verbs.

For example, there are many possible forms of a common verb such as *turn*.

Forms of the Verb *Turn*	
Turns	Has turned
Turn	Has been turned
Can turn	Is turned
Would turn	Won't turn
Should turn	Will turn
May turn	Will have turned
Is turning	Would have turned
Was turning	Could have turned
Turned	

3.2 States-of-being verbs do not express an action of the subject. The most common states-of-being verbs are *is, are, was, were, am, be, been, feel, look, appear, smell, seem, remain, sound,* and *become.*

　　　　　S　　V
The class <u>is</u> in the library.
　　　　　　S　　　　V
The teacher <u>looks</u> tired.
S　V
I <u>feel</u> good today.

The subjects of these sentences are not completing an action. Instead, the verbs express the state of being of the subjects.

3.3 Present participles and past participles always need a helping verb in order to be complete.

　　　　　　S　　　　　　　V
The mailman <u>is delivering</u> the mail right now.
　S　　　V
He <u>has taken</u> the test.

3.4 Infinitives begin with *to* and are never the verb of the sentence.

S V
I <u>have</u> to cook dinner tonight.

     S   V
The cake <u>has begun</u> to bake in the oven.

 S   V
I also <u>have agreed</u> to wash the dishes.

3.5 Modifiers and words that describe the verb (adverbs) are not part of the verb.

   S   V
James quickly <u>answered</u> the question.

Common Descriptive Words That Modify the Verb

Almost	Sometimes	Usually
Very	Often	Rarely
Really	Never	Actually
Always	Ever	Clearly
Also	Mostly	Still

Practice 1   Circle the simple subject and underline the complete verb of each sentence.

1. Telephone service is becoming less expensive for the consumer.

2. Many phone companies have lowered their rates recently.

3. Some communities are paying less now for local service than they were five years ago.

4. Competition has helped to lower the rates.

5. Also, wireless phone companies have reduced their long distance rates.

6. Many consumers pay nothing for long distance phone calls on nights and weekends.

7. Everyone may give up land phones altogether.

8. Group plans make wireless service really inexpensive for families.

9. Consumers have many options when choosing phone service.

10. Telephone service is cheaper than ever for Americans.

Practice 2   Circle the simple subject and underline the complete verb of each sentence.

1. Many American homeowners have found an easy way to get extra cash.

2. They are getting money from their homes.

3. Local banks have been lending homeowners money on the equity in their homes.

4. This is called home refinancing.

5. Wise homeowners will watch for low interest rates.

6. Then, they may call a number of banks to find the lowest loan rate.

7. Financial experts recommend getting three or more loan quotes.

8. Some consumers have saved a lot of money by getting lower interest rates on their home loans.

9. You should consult your bank for details about your loan.

10. Almost anyone can benefit from lower interest rates.

Problem Subjects and Verbs

GERUNDS AND INFINITIVES

4.1 Gerunds (the –*ing* form of the verb) and **infinitives** (the base form of the verb beginning with *to*) are called verbals because they act as nouns and can be the subject of the sentence.

S   V
Walking <u>provides</u> good exercise.

S   V
To eat a balanced meal every day <u>is</u> a challenge for Americans with busy lives.

IMPLIED SUBJECTS

5.1 The subject *you* is implied, meaning understood, but not stated in **command sentences.**

(**You**) <u>Stop</u> teasing the cat!

(**You**) <u>Turn</u> left at the corner.

Practice 3   Circle the subject and underline the complete verb in the following sentences. If the subject **you** is implied, write in *you* before the verb.

1. Taking tests <u>can be</u> stressful.

2. Remembering a few tips <u>can help</u> students with tests.

3. *You* Don't <u>wait</u> until the last minute to study.

4. *You* <u>Try</u> to get a good night's sleep the night before.

5. *You* Finally, <u>take</u> your time on tests.

PREPOSITIONAL PHRASES

6.1 Prepositional phrases often come between a subject and verb. The **subject** of the sentence is **never found in a prepositional phrase.** For more about prepositional phrases, see "Parts of Speech," page A-9.

The (children) ~~in my family~~ <u>are</u> all tall and thin.

(One) ~~of the students~~ <u>comes</u> to class early every day.

Common Prepositions			
About	Behind	In	Outside of
Above	Below	In addition to	Over
According to	Beneath	Inside	Since
Across	Beside	In spite of	Through
After	Besides	Instead of	Throughout
Against	Between	Into	To
Along	Beyond	Like	Toward
Along with	By	Near	Under
Among	Despite	Of	Until
Around	Down	Off	Up
As	During	On	Upon
As far as	Except	On account of	With
At	For	On top of	Within
Before	From	Out	Without

Practice 4   Cross out the prepositional phrases in the following sentences, circle the subject, and underline the complete verb.

1.   A number of stores in town have begun to stay open all night long.

2.   Along with a grocery store and a drug store, a department store in the shopping mall offers late night hours to customers.

3. People in my family enjoy shopping late at night instead of watching television.

4. Shoppers in the deserted aisles can appear mysterious.

5. In addition to people who work late, students from the local college shop during the wee hours of the morning.

6. At one store in the mall, employees play progressive music after 10 P.M.

7. By the end of the night, customers can be seen dancing in the aisles.

8. On Halloween, trick-or-treaters from every neighborhood come to the mall for a party after closing time.

9. From midnight until two in the morning, older kids in costume are allowed to skateboard along the walkways of the mall.

10. For many people, shopping at all-night stores can be amusing.

Practice 5   **Cross out the prepositional phrases in the following sentences, circle the simple subject, and underline the complete verb.**

1. As early as May, fans from around the country look forward to the college football season.

2. Throughout the summer, followers of the different teams get ready for the first game.

3. Articles about the top teams appear in newspapers and magazines.

4. National polls of sportswriters rank the top teams in each conference.

5. Along with guessing the top teams, everyone with an interest in football tries to guess who will be the best players in the country.

6. Throughout the season, games between the best teams will be broadcast on television.

7. The most loyal fans will travel with their team to games all over the nation.

8. Between August and December, college teams will play over five thousand football games.

9. Near the end of the season, teams with the best records will be invited to bowl games.

10. After the season, the best players of the year are chosen for special recognition.

COMPOUND SUBJECTS AND VERBS

7.1 A sentence may contain more than one subject and verb.

> S   S   V   V
> Tico and Carlotta take a trip each year and travel to a foreign country.

7.2 Compound sentences have two sets of subjects and verbs.

> S   V   S   V
> The meeting ended early, so we went to lunch.

Practice 6   Circle the subjects and underline the complete verbs in the following sentences. There may be more than one subject and/or verb in each sentence.

1. Many people love to travel to foreign countries, but they should remember to take their passports.

2. Also, some countries require shots for diseases and recommend certain medications to bring along on the trip.

3. Magda and Johan are visiting from Holland and are touring America for three months.

4. They take their passports everywhere and also carry their international driver's licenses.

5. Tourists everywhere must carry picture identification, and everyone also should carry an international credit card for emergencies.

REVERSE-ORDER SUBJECTS AND VERBS

8.1 When sentences begin with *There* or *Here,* the verb comes before the subject. *There* and *Here* are *not* the subject of the sentence.

> V   S
> There are many nice houses on our street.
> V   S
> Here comes my brother.
> V   S
> There is some snow on the ground today.

8.2 In questions, the verb, or part of the complete verb, comes before the subject.

> V   S   V
> Will you take me to the store?
> V   S   V
> When does the movie start?
> V   S
> Are you our new boss?

Practice 7   Circle the subjects and underline the complete verbs in the following sentences.

    1.   Have you ever traveled to a foreign country?

    2.   Here are a few reasons to visit a foreign country.

    3.   There is a different culture to study.

    4.   There will be new foods and customs to explore.

    5.   Where can we find American food?

DEPENDENT CLAUSES

9.1 The main subject and verb of the sentence are not found in a dependent clause. However, a dependent clause does contain a subject and a verb.

You will recognize a dependent clause by the subordinating conjunction or relative pronoun that begins a dependent clause.

Subordinating Conjunctions	
Because	Unless
Since	When
Although	While
Even though	After
If	Before

Relative Pronouns	
That	Whichever
Which	Whoever
Who	Whomever
Whom	Whose

Dependent Clause
Because I am the oldest child, my parents <u>expect</u> me to set a good example.

Dependent Clause   *Dependent Clause*
When class is over, students <u>talk</u> with the professor if they have questions.

                  Dependent Clause
The team that wins the most games <u>will receive</u> a trophy.

Practice 8   Cross out the prepositional phrases and dependent clauses in the following sentences, circle the simple subjects, and underline the complete verbs.

1. There is a digital revolution in America's schoolrooms.

2. Wireless phones and handheld digital assistants are now seen as essential back-to-school supplies for students across America.

3. Most students now carry cell phones, so schools are beginning to change their policies about phones in the classroom.

4. Students who own cell phones and personal digital assistants (PDAs) are bringing them to class and are using them during class.

5. Because cell phones can be disruptive, many teachers have prohibited them in class.

6. However, PDAs and laptop computers can be useful to students who want to take notes or complete research assignments.

7. Here are some of the best ways for students to use their electronic devices.

8. Cell phones can be used to record assignments, and laptops can be used to take notes or compose papers in class.

9. Also, because many cell phones connect to the Internet, they can be used to research information.

10. Probably within five years, there will be teachers who require students to bring cell phones and laptops to class, and electronic devices will be as common in the classroom as paper and pencil.

Practice 9   *Working Together*

Write one sentence for each topic below, using your own paper. Then, switch papers with a partner and circle the subject and underline the complete verb in each other's sentences. Check your answers together.

1. a recent movie you have seen
2. a class you have this term
3. taking tests
4. your car
5. your job

CD Connection

Power of Language

On *Writer's Resources* CD-ROM, see *Subject-Verb Identification* in Grammar/ Punctuation/Mechanics for more information and practice with subjects and verbs.

REVIEW EXERCISE 1

Circle the simple subject and underline the complete verb of each sentence. Cross out prepositional phrases and dependent clauses.

1. Getting exercise is so important to our health.

2. Everyone can't find an hour a day to exercise.

3. Now, some fitness experts recommend as little as thirty minutes a day of moderate exercise.

4. There are many ways to exercise effectively in just half an hour.

5. Jogging has been a very popular form of exercise.

6. During lunch breaks at work or school, you can go outside and walk briskly.

7. Health clubs offer thirty-minute workouts on exercise machines.

8. Physical fitness trainers suggest a cardiovascular workout three times per week, and they also suggest strength training twice per week.

9. Of course, a proper diet can help everyone to stay in shape.

10. Eat lots of vegetables and drink plenty of water all day long.

11. It is important to find an exercise and diet program that works for you.

REVIEW EXERCISE 2

Circle the simple subject and underline the complete verb of each sentence. Cross out prepositional phrases and dependent clauses.

1. Most teachers don't allow cell phones in the classroom.

2. For one thing, most teachers and students are annoyed at the interruption of a ringing cell phone.

3. The loud ring of a phone can be distracting to other students.

4. Everyone in the class will look at the student with the ringing phone.

5. Also, there is a risk of students getting answers on tests.

6. Students sometimes will find ways to type instant messages quietly under their desks.

7. However, most teachers do understand the value of carrying a phone, so schools have been wrestling with how to control the use of phones at school.

8. Many schools across the country have banned cell phones in class and have limited their use on campus to the halls and cafeteria.

9. On the other hand, innovative schools across the country are encouraging students to use PDAs, or handheld computers, to take notes.

10. Schools must determine fair rules for using phones and PDAs.

SUBJECT-VERB IDENTIFICATION EDITING TEST

Alone or working with a partner, circle the subject of the sentence and underline the complete verb.

Good Buys

In October 1999, *Forbes Magazine* published a list of "100 Things Worth Every Penny." Objects include a good pillow and comfortable running shoes, but other objects are more unusual, such as a custom-made tuxedo. Surprisingly, a good pedicure made the list. The writers of the article have included a good waiter or waitress on the list. There are more surprising people on the list, such as a private tour guide and a computer guru, but a good divorce lawyer is the most surprising addition to the list. The magazine also recommends heated car seats and warm towels. The writers have added to the list a yellow Labrador retriever and a portrait of our children. Porsche, Levi's, and Krispy Kreme are some of the name brands that make the list. The most unusual entry happens to be a hot-air balloon flight over the Serengeti Plain in Africa. Read *Forbes Magazine* for the entire list of good buys.

Practicing Your Writing Power

Power of Language

© Thomson Corporation/Heinle Image Resource Bank

What things do you own that you think are worth every penny of their cost? Choose two things you own that you believe are important to your happiness and explain why. You may wish to include some service that you purchase, such as grooming for hair or nails, membership to a health club, or a cell phone service.

Name _____

Section _____ Score _____

SUBJECT-VERB IDENTIFICATION TEST 1

Circle the simple subject and underline the complete verb of each sentence.

1. Americans of all ages are overweight.

2. According to a recent study, the majority of adults in this country need to

   lose weight.

3. The problem has gotten so bad that doctors are prescribing exercise during yearly

   checkups.

4. The primary care physician or a nurse should measure every patient's body mass

   and waist.

5. After looking at the measurements, the health-care professional will discuss the

   patient's activity level and will make recommendations.

6. Don't worry if you are told to exercise regularly.

7. The dangers of excess weight include heart disease and diabetes.

8. There are many ways to take off unwanted pounds.

9. Try walking more instead of always using the car.

10. Anyone can lose pounds.

Name _____

Section _____ Score _____

SUBJECT-VERB IDENTIFICATION TEST 2

Circle the simple subject and underline the complete verb of each sentence.

1. Unfortunately, a high school diploma doesn't always prepare students for college or the work world.

2. A group of distinguished educators and civic leaders has studied the problem and made some recommendations.

3. These experts believe that students need to take better writing and math courses in high school.

4. High-school exit requirements should be strengthened to include skills demanded in college and the workplace.

5. In many states, there are exit exams to test students' skills.

6. However, schools should not rely solely on exams to assess student progress.

7. Taking harder courses in high school could help most students to succeed in college.

8. Enroll in college preparatory classes if you want to strengthen your skills.

9. Core courses and electives help students to prepare for college and work.

10. By changing the educational system, we can ensure success for all students.

Name _____

Section _____ Score _____

SUBJECT-VERB IDENTIFICATION TEST 3

Circle the simple subject and underline the complete verb of each sentence.

1. Cranes belong to a family of large birds with long legs and necks.

2. These graceful birds live in marshy areas in many parts of the world.

3. There are a few different species of cranes in the United States and Canada.

4. One of the most common cranes in America is the sandhill crane.

5. These beautiful birds can reach heights of 5 feet and can have wingspans of

   7 feet.

6. Minnesota, Michigan, and Wisconsin provide the summer home for these birds.

7. During the winter, males and females fly south to Tennessee, Georgia, and Florida.

8. When watching for cranes, get up early to see them feed in ponds and

   wetlands.

9. Unfortunately, some species of cranes have become rare because of the loss of

   marshes and wetlands.

10. In fact, destruction of their breeding grounds presents the greatest threat to

    cranes' survival.

SUBJECT-VERB IDENTIFICATION TEST 4

Circle the simple subject and underline the complete verb of each sentence.

1. Treating back pain costs Americans more than 25 billion dollars each year.

2. This enormous amount of money represents more than two percent of our nation's total health-care bill.

3. The costs of treating back pain promise to continue increasing as patients try costly new therapies.

4. Problems with the back are one of the ten most common reasons for visits to the doctor.

5. Incredibly, 70 percent of adults have had back pain at some point in their lives.

6. There are all sorts of therapies that claim to reduce back pain.

7. Traditional medicine offers braces and surgery.

8. Massage and acupuncture are less traditional alternatives and are very popular.

9. Everyone with back pain must decide on a course of treatment.

10. Do your own research before deciding on how to treat back pain.

Chapter 7   Subject–Verb Agreement

In this chapter, you will

- ☛ Learn the rules of subject-verb agreement
- ☛ Learn to avoid errors with problem subjects and problem verbs

Skill Preview

The subject–verb agreement rules described in this chapter apply only to present tense. Much of the writing you will do in college will use other tenses, such as the past tense. The rules for using other tenses correctly are described in Chapter 8, "Verb Tenses."

To succeed in college, students must use Standard English subject–verb agreement. Although many people do not use standard subject–verb agreement in their speech, verb errors are considered serious errors in writing. Learning the rules for subject–verb agreement can be difficult, especially if you grew up around adults who did not use standard subject–verb agreement in their speech. The first step in learning to use Standard English subject–verb agreement is to identify the types of verb agreement errors that will be difficult for you to spot.

Read the passage below and circle subject–verb agreement errors.

Reading books are a wonderful hobby. Even though it be
difficult to find the time to read, reading books are the
best way to spend free time because books helps improve your
vocabulary and your knowledge about the world. They is also
fun to read. My favorite kind of book are adventure stories.
When I read spy stories, I learn about history, politics, and
geography. Best of all, spy stories is the most exciting kind
of story to read.

Compare your circles with the corrected verbs in the following passage.

Reading books is a wonderful hobby. Even though it is
difficult to find the time to read, reading books is the

best way to spend free time because books help improve your
vocabulary and your knowledge about the world. They are also
fun to read. My favorite kind of book is adventure stories.
When I read spy stories, I learn about history, politics, and
geography. Best of all, spy stories are the most exciting
kind of story to read.

Which verb errors did you miss?

Spotlight on Writers

Power of
Language

Marian Wright Edelman

"If you don't like the way the world is, you change it. You have an obligation to
change it. You just do it one step at a time."

Marian Wright Edelman (1939–) grew up in the segregated South and
attended college in Atlanta, Georgia, where she took part in civil rights protests
alongside Martin Luther King, Jr. She later graduated from Yale Law School and
became the first black woman admitted to the bar in Mississippi. She was so
outraged by the poverty she encountered in Mississippi that she helped organize the Poor People's March on Washington, D.C., and she later became the
founder and president of the Children's Defense Fund, a world-renowned advo-
cacy group for young people.

If subject–verb agreement is difficult for you, you will want to follow a three-
step process to avoid verb errors in your writing.

Three Steps to Avoiding Verb Errors

1. Identify the subject and the verb (discussed in Chapter 6).
2. Determine whether the subject is singular (one person or thing) or plural
   (more than one).
3. Apply the present tense subject–verb agreement formula for third person:

Singular subject	>	*-s* on verb	**One dog barks.**
Plural subject	>	no *-s* on verb	**Two dogs bark.**

Singular and Plural Subjects

1.1 A **singular** subject refers to **one** person or thing.

an excellent class	she
a wild animal	the movie
a good book	a motorcycle

Notice that the articles *a* and *an* are used with singular subjects.

1.2 A **plural** subject refers to **more than one** person or thing. Most plural subjects end in an **-s**.

excellent classes	they
wild animals	the movies
good books	motorcycles

1.3 Some plural subjects do not end in an **-s**. They are **irregular plurals** because they do not follow the rule that plural subjects end in an **-s**.

men	people
women	police
children	

Practice 1   Identify the following words as either singular (S) or plural (P).

1._____ cats   2._____ bike

3._____ woman   4._____ police

5._____ children   6._____ tree

7._____ men   8._____ noise

9._____ eyes   10._____ mice

Subject–Verb Agreement Rules

2.1 **Subjects** and **verbs** must **agree** in number.

In the present tense, the verb has no ending unless the subject is third-person singular. If the subject is third-person singular, the verb takes an -s or -es ending.

	Singular	Plural
1st person	I run	We run
2nd person	You run	You run
3rd person	**He/She/It** run**s**	They run
	A student run**s**	Students run

Notice that the singular subjects **I** and **you** take no ending on the verb.

> 💡 This memory hook may help you remember the correct endings for third-person verbs.
> Remember that **I** and **You** are not third person and take no ending on the verb.
>
> **A singular subject** (the word *singular* begins with s) takes a verb with an **-s ending**.
>
> | Singular subject | -s on verb |
> |---|---|
> | He/She/It/The student | walk**s.** |
>
> **A plural subject** (the word *plural* doesn't begin with s) takes a verb with **no -s.**
>
> | Plural subject | no -s on verb |
> |---|---|
> | They/The students | walk. |

Practice 2   In the following passage, circle the subjects and identify whether they are singular or plural by writing an **S** or a **P** over them. Next, underline the verbs and circle the S endings on third-person singular verbs.

The modern American supermarket has become a one-stop shopping center for the entire family. While the neighborhood supermarket still sells the usual groceries, it also now offers a variety of choices from around the world such as Italian olive oils and pastas, Asian noodles, and South American plantains. The store bakery bakes everything from breads to donuts and birthday cakes, and because we can fill prescriptions while we shop, supermarkets have become our primary drug stores. Videos, flowers, and even perfumes are a few of the expanded lines of merchandise that grocery stores stock. Also, most stores provide stamps, check cashing, and photo processing, and they house a deli that makes sandwiches and salads for busy workers on the go. Shopping is becoming a pleasure at supermarkets these days.

Problem Subjects

PREPOSITIONAL PHRASES

3.1 The subject is never found in a prepositional phrase.

Because prepositional phrases may come between the subject and the verb, they may distract students from the subject and cause errors with subject–verb agreement.

For a list of common prepositions and a definition and examples of prepositional phrases, see page 137.

S   V
The flowers ~~in the basket~~ <u>are</u> white.

Even though *basket* appears immediately before the verb *are,* the flowers are what is white, not the basket.

S   V
The papers ~~on the table~~ <u>have</u> to be signed by the boss.

Even though *table* appears immediately before the verb *have,* the papers have to be signed, not the table.

Practice 3   Cross out the prepositional phrases in the following sentences. Circle the subject, label it as singular (S) or plural (P), and underline the correct verb.

1. The <u>leaves</u> on the tree (is/<u>are</u>) turning brown.

2. The <u>cars</u> on the freeway (creates/<u>create</u>) pollution.

3. <u>One</u> of my classes (<u>is</u>/are) difficult.

4. The <u>clouds</u> in the sky (moves/<u>move</u>) quickly.

5. The <u>student</u> in the front of the room (<u>belongs</u>/belong) to my drama club.

6. The <u>teachers</u> at my school (is/<u>are</u>) strict.

7. The <u>dents</u> on my car (looks/<u>look</u>) terrible.

8. The <u>papers</u> in my notebook (is/<u>are</u>) well organized.

9. <u>Each</u> of the boys (plays/<u>play</u>) soccer.

10. <u>Some</u> of my answers (is/<u>are</u>) correct.

INDEFINITE PRONOUNS

Some indefinite pronouns are singular, some are plural, and some can be either singular or plural, depending on the meaning of the sentence.

4.1 Most indefinite pronouns are singular and take a verb with an -s ending.

S   V
Everything <u>runs</u> smoothly.

S   V
Everybody <u>is</u> late.

Singular Indefinite Pronouns			
"-one"	**"-body"**	**"-thing"**	**Others**
any**one**	any**body**	any**thing**	each
everyone	everybody	everything	either
no one	nobody	nothing	neither
one	somebody	something	someone

Practice 4　Underline the correct verb in the following sentences.

1. Everything (go/goes) wrong in the morning.

2. Someone (is/are) reading out loud.

3. Nothing (pleases/please) my mother.

4. Each of my friends (belongs/belong) to a health club.

5. Everyone I know (is/are) coming to the party.

4.2 Some indefinite pronouns are **always plural.**

　S　　　　　V
Both of us <u>have</u> to leave.

　S　　　　　　　V
Several of my books <u>are</u> valuable.

Plural Indefinite Pronouns
both
few
many
several

Practice 5　Underline the correct verb in the following sentences.

1. Many of my instructors (assigns/assign) homework.

2. Both of my dogs (is/are) tame.

3. Several of my best friends (works/work) on the weekend.

4. (Few) of my study habits (is/are) effective.

5. Many Americans (wants/want) to lose weight.

4.3 Some subjects can be **either singular or plural,** depending on the meaning of the sentence.

The meaning generally comes in the prepositional phrase that follows these subjects.

A lot of my homework is difficult. (*Homework* determines that *a lot* is singular.)

A lot of chairs are missing. (*Chairs* determines that *a lot* is plural.)

None of his advice is good. (*Advice* determines that *none* is singular.)

None of the students are ready. (*Students* determines that *none* is plural.)

Singular or Plural Indefinite Pronouns	
a lot	more
all	most
any	none
lots	some

Practice 6   Underline the correct verb in the following sentences.

1. None of my questions (has/have) been answered.

2. Most of my homework (is/are) due on Monday.

3. A lot of your advice (is/are) good.

4. Most of your missing files (has/have) been found.

5. Some of your ideas (is/are) excellent.

COLLECTIVE NOUNS

5.1 Collective nouns refer to a group of people or things. Collective nouns are usually singular and take a verb with an -s ending.

Our team practices twice a week.

The club meets on Friday.

Common Collective Nouns		
a band	a family	an audience
a faculty	a team	a crowd
a number	a committee	a jury
a class	a group	

Practice 7   Underline the correct verb in parentheses.

1. The team (<u>practices</u>/practice) every afternoon.

2. My family (<u>believes</u>/believe) in celebrating birthdays.

3. A group of us (<u>is</u>/are) going to the movies together.

4. The crowd (<u>surges</u>/surge) forward.

5. My brother's band (<u>plays</u>/play) in our garage.

FIELDS OF STUDY

6.1 Fields of study are singular subjects and take a verb with an -s ending.

     S   V
Economics <u>requires</u> an understanding of math.

     S   V
The news <u>comes</u> on at six o'clock.

Fields of Study	
home economics	news
mathematics	statistics
politics	music
physics	history
Note: When *statistics* refers to numbers, it is plural.	
The statistics are deceiving.	

Practice 8   Underline the correct verb in parentheses.

1. Music (<u>calms</u>/calm) my nerves.

2. The news (<u>is</u>/are) shocking.

3. Statistics (is/are) a difficult course.

4. History (teaches/teach) us many lessons.

5. Politics (is/are) a noble profession.

COMPOUND SUBJECTS

7.1 Compound subjects are two subjects joined by *and.* Compound subjects are plural and take a verb with no ending.

S   S   V
Sarah and Aaron <u>ride</u> the bus to school.

S   S   V
My aunt and uncle <u>travel</u> to Europe every summer.

Practice 9 Circle the subject, and label it as singular (S) or plural (P). Then underline the correct verb.

1. China and crystal (is/<u>are</u>) easily broken.

2. My brother and sister (does/<u>do</u>) their homework together.

3. Eloise and Sean (takes/<u>take</u>) turns washing the dishes.

4. Jake and Sarah (has/<u>have</u>) the flu.

5. My resume and letter (shows/<u>show</u>) my work experience.

GERUNDS

8.1 A gerund (an -ing word used as a noun) is singular and takes a verb with an -s ending.

S   V
Walking <u>is</u> great exercise.

If two gerund subjects are joined by *and*, they are plural.

S   V
Studying and reviewing <u>are</u> difficult skills.

Practice 10 Circle the subject, and label it as singular (S) or plural (P). Then underline the correct verb.

1. Walking briskly (burns/burn) calories and (tones/tone) the muscles.

2. Playing tennis and reading (is/are) my favorite hobbies.

3. When I was younger, paying attention in classes (was/were) difficult for me.

4. Gardening (relaxes/relax) me.

5. Studying with my friends (helps/help) me prepare for tests.

SUBJECTS JOINED BY *OR* OR *NOR*

9.1 When subjects are joined by *or* or *nor,* only one of the subjects performs the action, so the verb **agrees with the closest subject.**

     S   S   V
My coach **or** my friends <u>are coming</u> to the game.

          S   S V
Neither the puppies **nor** the cat <u>has</u> fleas.

Practice 11   Circle the subject, and label it as singular (S) or plural (P). Then underline the correct verb.

1. Either Aunt Sarah or my friends (drives/drive) me to school every morning.

2. Neither his teachers nor his father (knows/know) how to control his behavior.

3. Either Tom or Lisa (has/have) my books.

4. Neither my attorneys nor the judge (wants/want) the case to go to trial.

5. My brothers or my best friend (is/are) going to the game.

Problem Verbs

COMPOUND VERBS

10.1 When a subject has more than one verb, it is called a compound verb. Be sure that that both verbs agree with the subject.

      S   V   V
The father <u>cooks</u> on Saturday and <u>does</u> the laundry on Sunday.

      S   V   V
My friends <u>study</u> in the library and <u>eat</u> in the cafeteria.

Practice 12   Underline the verbs in the following sentences.

1. The students in the back row read and write quietly.

2. My brother plays football after school and studies at night.

3. My best friend types and takes shorthand.

4. The farmer plants corn and weeds between the rows.

5. Jose runs downstairs, grabs his backpack, and races for the bus.

VERBS FOLLOWING *HERE* OR *THERE*

11.1 When a sentence begins with *there* or *here,* the subject comes **after** the verb. Remember that *here* and *there* are never the subject of a sentence.

       V   S
There <u>are</u> three broken chairs in my classroom.

     V   S
Here <u>comes</u> the bride.

Practice 13 In the following sentences, circle the subject and underline the correct verb.

1. There (is/are) only four questions on the test.

2. Here (is/are) my assignment.

3. There (is/are) one piece of advice my father gave me.

4. There (comes/come) a time to admit defeat.

5. Here (is/are) your paycheck.

VERBS IN QUESTIONS

12.1 The subject comes after the verb in questions.

      V   S
When <u>are</u> the boys leaving?

      V   S
What <u>is</u> your answer?

Practice 14 Circle the subject and underline the correct verb.

1. What (is/are) you doing after class?

2. Where (has/have) the time gone?

3. When (does/do) they want to leave?

4. Why (has/have) your brother called?

5. How long (is/are) the drive to the mountains?

RELATIVE PRONOUNS

13.1 The relative pronouns *who, that,* and *which* take a verb that agrees with their antecedent (the word *who, that,* or *which* refers to in the sentence).

       S   V   V

The window that was broken <u>has been</u> replaced.
                relative clause

       S   V   V

The people who run the presses <u>are</u> on strike.
               relative clause

Practice 15   In the following sentences, circle the subject and underline the correct verb.

1. The <u>test</u> that I passed (<u>was</u>/were) hard.

2. Many of the songs that (is/<u>are</u>) played in band (is/<u>are</u>) difficult.

3. The <u>man</u> who (sits/<u>sit</u>) in front of me on the bus (is/<u>are</u>) a banker.

4. The <u>classes</u> that (is/<u>are</u>) required (is/<u>are</u>) all three credits.

5. <u>Anyone</u> who (<u>studies</u>/study) (<u>passes</u>/pass) the class.

COMMON IRREGULAR VERBS

14.1 The verbs **to be, to do**, and **to have** are common irregular verbs. These irregular verbs should be conjugated correctly.

To Be

	Singular		Plural
1st person	I *am*		We *are*
2nd person	You *are*		You *are*
3rd person	**He/She/It**	*is*	They *are*
	A student	*is*	Students *are*

To Do

	Singular		Plural
1st person	I *do*		We *do*
2nd person	You *do*		You *do*
3rd person	**He/She/It**	*does*	They *do*
	A student	*does*	Students *do*

To Have

	Singular		Plural
1st person	I *have*		We *have*
2nd person	You *have*		You *have*
3rd person	**He/She/It**	*has*	They *have*
	A student	*has*	Students *have*

Practice 16   Underline the correct verb in the following sentences.

1. Shane sometimes (is/be) late for class.

2. Ron and Kay (has/have) my CD player.

3. Reading spy novels (is/are) fun.

4. (Does/Do) you know when our test is?

5. Everyone (is/are) running late for school.

6. (Has/Have) everyone finished dinner?

7. Steve and Maria (is/are) best friends.

8. The student who (has/have) the most votes will win.

9. There (is/are) two reasons why I won't go to the movies.

10. (Does/Do) Tony have a car?

MODALS

15.1 Modal auxiliaries (can, could, will, would, shall, should, may, might, must, had better, would rather, have to, ought to, have got to) and the verbs that follow them take no endings to show agreement or tense.

Jordan <u>can walk</u> five miles. (No endings on *can walk*)

Alex <u>could pass</u> the test if he studied. (No endings on *could pass*)

My boss <u>might fire</u> me if I'm late. (No endings on *might fire*)

Practice 17   Identify the verbs in the following sentences as correct or incorrect, and correct any verb errors.

_C_   1. My brother can play the guitar.

_I_   2. Tony might regrets his mistake. *it should be regret* *Sub is single*

_I_   3. Jody ought to wins the race. *it should have been win the* *Subj is single*

_C_   4. My high school buddy may open his own business.

_I_   5. My best friend will arrives from New York tonight.
Subj is single so the verb should have been arrive.

CD Connection

Power of Language

On *Writer's Resources* CD-ROM, see *Subject–Verb Agreement* in Grammar/Punctuation/Mechanics for more information and practice with subject–verb agreement.

Practice 18   *Working Together*

Working in groups of two or three, write a sentence (in the present tense) using each of the following as a subject.

Either my teachers or my coach
The jury
Everyone
The news
Studying in study groups

Practice 19   Trade the sentences you wrote in Practice 18 with another group, and check the subject–verb agreement in the other group's sentences. Share any subject–verb agreement corrections with the other group.

REVIEW EXERCISE 1

Working alone or in groups of two or three, edit the following sentences for subject–verb agreement. First, identify each subject as singular or plural. Next, apply the subject–verb agreement rule for third-person present tense (singular subject—s on the verb; plural subject—no s on the verb), and underline the correct verb.

1. There (has/have) been three book reports this term.

2. Classes at the gym (is/are) free.

3. Swimming without lifeguards (is/are) dangerous.

4. Most of my friends (has/have) part-time jobs.

5. Everyone (loves/love) spring break.

6. How many miles (does/do) he have to hike?

7. Neither my aunts nor my mother (knows/know) how to speak French.

8. The team (is/are) late.

9. The student who (wins/win) the essay contest (competes/compete) at the state level.

10. Mathematics (is/are) my hardest subject.

REVIEW EXERCISE 2

Circle the subject, and label it as singular (S) or plural (P). Then underline the correct verb.

1. Where (is/are) the papers that I typed yesterday?

2. The students in the school play (rehearses/rehearse) every day.

3. Colds in the summer (is/are) uncommon.

4. Reading books (improves/improve) one's vocabulary.

5. Anything you want to do (is/are) all right with me.

6. There (is/are) five parts to the test.

7. None of your answers (is/are) correct.

8. Either Erlene or her students (is/are) touring the capital.

9. The audience (is/are) restless.

10. Economics (is/are) no longer offered at my school.

SUBJECT–VERB AGREEMENT EDITING TEST 1

Working alone or in groups of two or three, edit the following passage. First, identify every subject as singular or plural. Next, apply the subject–verb agreement rule for third-person present tense (singular subject—*s* on the verb; plural subject—no *s* on the verb).

Almost everyone have had the experience of being criticized. Most people doesn't like being criticized even when they know that they has done something wrong. Criticism make many people feel inadequate or angry. Even if your boss don't give criticism in a positive way, it is a good idea to listen to what he or she have to say. First, employees shouldn't get angry when they is criticized but ask themselves what they can learn from the observations their boss is making. There is usually some work behaviors that we can improve upon. Next, employees should never argues with their boss. Instead, they should listen to what their boss says and try to agree with something he or she say.

SUBJECT–VERB AGREEMENT EDITING TEST 2

Correct the subject–verb agreement errors in the following paragraph.

Genetically engineered foods is foods that has been altered or changed by introducing genes from other plants or animals. The tomato was the first genetically engineered food, and it was introduced in 1994. Now, most of the soybeans grown in this country is genetically engineered, as is almost half of our nation's corn. Some scientists believes that introducing genes that carries a desirable characteristic such as resistance to insects or herbicides will improve the foods we eat. Not everyone are so excited about genetically altered foods. Some groups worries that introducing fish genes into a plant could produce unintended results such as allergies or harmful foods. There is a number of suggestions such groups have made. One of the suggestions are mandatory labeling of products that contain biotech foods. Labeling of biotech products are still voluntary.

Practicing Your Writing Power

Power of Language

© Thomson Corporation/Heinle Image Resource Bank

1. What do you think about genetically engineered foods? Do you have concerns about the quality or safety of the food that we eat? After you write your response, review the subject–verb agreement in what you have written. You might try to circle the subjects and underline the verbs.
2. Choose a favorite recipe and explain how your family fixes this dish and when you eat it.

Name _____

Section _____   Score _____

SUBJECT–VERB AGREEMENT TEST 1

Identify the subject–verb agreement in the following sentences as correct (C) or incorrect (I). Correct the verb errors in the incorrect items. There could be more than one error in a sentence.

_____   1. Many animals found in the jungle are helping prevent and cure illnesses.

_____   2. One of the creatures that help scientists are the vampire bat.

_____   3. Their saliva contain powerful anticoagulant chemicals.

_____   4. These chemicals keeps the blood of the animals they bites from

coagulating.

_____   5. There is many possible benefits from these chemicals.

_____   6. Stroke patients needs these chemicals to stay alive.

_____   7. These drugs could be given to stroke victims as long as nine hours after

they has a stroke.

_____   8. There are many other animals that scientists are studying.

_____   9. Choosing which animals to study are challenging.

_____   10. Each animal could provide a treasure trove of useful information.

Name _____

Section _____   Score _____

SUBJECT–VERB AGREEMENT TEST 2

Identify the subject–verb agreement in the following sentences as correct (C) or incorrect (I). Correct the verb errors in the incorrect items.

_____   1. Cheating on tests are common in many high schools today.

_____   2. Most high school students say they has cheated at least once.

_____   3. Students who cheat feel very little guilt in doing so.

_____   4. Adults who cheats on their income taxes set a bad example.

_____   5. There are serious consequences for cheating in the work world.

_____   6. Either the teachers or the principal need to discuss the importance of

   honesty.

_____   7. One way to discourage cheating on school assignments are for parents

   to review homework with their children.

_____   8. Most colleges have honor codes that spell out the consequences of

   cheating.

_____   9. The consequences of cheating in college is more serious than most

   students think.

_____   10. A student who cheats can be expelled from school.

Name _____

Section _____   Score _____

SUBJECT–VERB AGREEMENT TEST 3

Identify the subject–verb agreement in the following sentences as correct (C) or incorrect (I). Correct the verb errors in the incorrect items.

_____   1. Everyone who have been to a wedding knows how difficult it is to

make small talk.

_____   2. Talking with someone that you don't know is a difficult task.

_____   3. There is several tips that can help people feel more comfortable with

small talk.

_____   4. One of the most important tips to remember are that you don't have to

be clever, just nice.

_____   5. Asking a simple question help draw the other person out.

_____   6. Many people feel uncomfortable making small talk.

_____   7. Talking about the location of the gathering is another possibility.

_____   8. One of the safe questions to ask are "How do you know the host?"

_____   9. Silence in conversations is not necessarily a bad thing.

_____   10. Being a good listener to other people's stories are important, too.

Name _____

Section _____   Score _____

SUBJECT–VERB AGREEMENT TEST 4

Identify the subject–verb agreement in the following sentences as correct (C) or incorrect (I). Correct the verb errors in the incorrect items.

_____ 1. These days, just about everyone seem to be running late.

_____ 2. More and more people suffer from chronic tardiness.

_____ 3. There is lots of reasons why people show up late.

_____ 4. One of the most significant reasons are the amount of work people

have to do.

_____ 5. Punctuality is not as important to many people as it once was.

_____ 6. In the business world, people who is late cause millions of dollars in lost

productivity.

_____ 7. Cell phones at work seem to make the problem worse.

_____ 8. Being consistently late for work often cost people their jobs.

_____ 9. Either meetings or a social event are disturbed by someone who walks

in late.

_____ 10. Getting places on time is about gaining control of yourself and your life.

Chapter 8   Verb Tenses

In this chapter you will

☛ Review verb tenses

☛ Learn to form the past tense and past participle of regular and irregular
verbs

☛ Review the uses of the present and past perfect tenses

☛ Learn to recognize passive constructions and avoid unnecessary passives

☛ Learn to use the past participle as an adjective

☛ Learn not to shift tenses unnecessarily

Skill Preview

    Verb tense in a sentence indicates the time when something takes place. As
you learned in the previous chapter, adding an -s or -es ending to third-person singular verbs signals present tense, and no ending is added to verbs other than for
third-person singular.

    Past tense is signaled in several ways. Regular past-tense verbs are formed by
adding -ed. Irregular verbs, however, are more complicated because their forms
change.

Working alone or in pairs, read the passage below and circle errors in the use of
verbs. The errors in the passage have to do with the writer's failure to indicate past
tense through verb endings and the writer's addition of past-tense endings to
words that do not need them.

```
    Starting school was the best thing that ever happen to me.
In elementary school, all my teachers pay close attention to
their students. If I have a question, there was always
someone there to help me with my work. In middle school,
things change. Because classes were bigger, I learn nothing.
I feel too shy to raised my hand and asked a question when
I won't understand. The teachers always look like they just
want students to listen.
```

Compare your circles with the corrected verbs in the following passage.

> Starting school was the best thing that ever happened to me. In elementary school, all my teachers paid close attention to their students. If I had a question, there was always someone there to help me with my work. In middle school, things changed. Because classes were bigger, I learned nothing. I felt too shy to raise my hand and ask a question when I didn't understand. The teachers always looked like they just wanted students to listen.

Which verb errors did you miss?

Spotlight on Writers

Power of Language

Chuck D

"Music is how I express my politics, but culture and music are headlines, a short cut to learning. You've got to concentrate on learning. You've got to read. It's a simple, fundamental exercise that allows you to leave your situation."

Chuck D (1960–), founder of the band Public Enemy, is one of the originators of hip-hop. He feels that hip-hop is an art form that gives Public Enemy a chance to speak out on political and social issues. In addition to speaking out in the lyrics of his songs, he has released five books and maintains a Web site (http://www.publicenemy.com) that allows him to spread his vision. Chuck D maintains that while the media glamorizes the "gangsta" lifestyle, real thugs and gangstas do not want to live the life they are living. Chuck D encourages people to focus on their education, to get involved in politics, and to realize their potential because "corporations just want you to be robots and be programmed."

Verb Tense Review

Verb tense in a sentence indicates when something takes place. As you can see in the table below, the endings on verbs generally indicate agreement or tense.

Tense	Form	Use	Example
Present	verb verb + *s*	Current fact, opinion, or habit	I love chocolate. Kevin studies hard.
Present Progressive Past	(am, is, are) + verb + *ing* verb + *ed* Irregulars	Event or condition happening right now Past fact, opinion, habit	It is raining. He is studying. The cat scratched me. The meal was excellent. I went out last night.

Tense	Form	Use	Example
Past Progressive	(was, were) + verb + *ing*	Action in progress in past, especially one interrupted by another past action	She was cooking when we arrived.
Present Perfect	(has, have) + past participle	Action that occurred at unspecified time in past, several times in past, or that began in the past and continues in the present	Tony has already left. We have completed our work. I have lived here since 1995.
Past Perfect	had + past participle	The first of two past actions (the second is in past tense)	He had left by the time we arrived. We had finished when the bell rang.
Future	will + verb (am, are, is) + going to + verb	Action that is expected to happen in future	I will study tonight. I am going to study tonight.

Although the endings on verbs generally indicate agreement or tense, some words take **no endings to show agreement or tense.**

Infinitives (to run, to talk, to write), **modal auxiliaries** (can, could, will, would, shall, should, may, might, must, had better, would rather, have to, ought to, have got to), and **the verbs that follow them** take no endings to show agreement or tense.

Sandra **would like to win** the lottery. (No endings on *would like to win*)
My friends **should arrive** at nine. (No endings on *should arrive*)
Tom **can study** tonight. (No endings on *can study*)
Benny **would rather walk** than run. (No endings on *would rather walk*)

Forming the Past Tense and Past Participle
Regular Verbs

1.1 To form the past tense or past participle of regular verbs, add **-ed** or **-d** to the verb. The past tense and past participle of regular verbs have the same form.

He talk**ed** to Ramon yesterday. (past)
He has talk**ed** to Ramon every day this week. (past participle)
I dream**ed** that I was a rock star. (past)
I have dream**ed** the same dream since I was a child. (past participle)

Irregular Verbs

2.1 The past and past participle of irregular verbs are not formed by adding -ed or -d.

Cynthia **buys** her lunch at school every day. (present)
Yesterday, Cynthia **bought** her lunch at school. (past)
Cynthia **has bought** her lunch at school every day this week. (past participle)

Use Your Dictionary If You Are Unsure of the Verb Form

Good dictionaries list the past tense forms of irregular verbs. A typical dictionary entry for an irregular verb looks like this:

verb	past tense	past participle	present participle
go (go) v.	went	gone	going

If only two forms are listed, then the past and past participles are the same.

Practice 1   Use a college-level dictionary to look up the following verbs. Write the three verb forms listed after the base form of the verb, and label each as the past, past participle, and present participle.

begin: _____

take: _____

drive: _____

COMMON IRREGULAR VERBS

To be, to do, and *to have* are three frequently used verbs that cause errors for students.

The Verb *to be*

Present	Past	Past Participle
I am	I was	I have been
You are	You were	You have been
He/She/It is	He/She/It was	He/She/It has been
We are	You were	You have been
You are	We were	We have been
They are	They were	They have been

Practice 2   Write the correct form of the verb *to be* in the space.

1. My brother _____ late for school yesterday.

2. I _____ already taller than my mother.

3. Sam _____ president of his class last year.

4. Julie and Sarah _____ trying out for the cheerleading squad.

5. Novalis _____ a beautiful city in Oregon.

6. Last year, my friends _____ on the track team.

7. You _____ already late.

8. The coaches _____ pushing us all week.

9. I _____ a senior last year.

10. Tim and Andrew _____ lifeguards last year.

The Verb *to do*

Present	Past	Past Participle
I do	I did	I have done
You do	You did	You have done
He/She/It does	He/She/It did	He/She/It has done
We do	You did	You have done
You do	We did	We have done
They do	They did	They have done

Practice 3   Write the correct form of the verb *to do* in the space.

1. Yolanda _____ her homework on the city bus every day.

2. My mother _____ my hair this way last night.

3. _____ you think you have a fever?

4. Shante _____ me a favor by breaking off our engagement.

5. Have you _____ your work?

6. The twins _____ their exercises every morning.

7. My uncle _____ the crossword puzzle in the Sunday paper all his life.

8. My friends and I _____ not like the smell of cigarette smoke.

9. _____ George pass his test?

10. I'll bet you _____ not know the answer.

The Verb *to have*

Present	Past	Past Participle
I have	I had	I have had
You have	You had	You have had
He/She/It has	He/She/It had	He/She/It has had
We have	You had	You have had
You have	We had	We have had
They have	They had	They have had

Practice 4 Fill in the correct form of the verb *to have.*

1. My father _____ a new job.

2. I have _____ to recopy the assignment twice.

3. Jarrina _____ a fever since she woke up this morning.

4. _____ you ever won the lottery?

5. They have _____ trouble with their car before.

6. _____ he ever asked you out?

7. Murdock _____ a seven o'clock appointment with his instructor yesterday.

8. The best student in my algebra class has _____ a B average all term.

9. My six-year-old son _____ three missing teeth.

10. My parents _____ worked hard to send me to college.

2.2 Because there is no set pattern to form the past or past participle of **irregular verbs,** you must memorize the forms, especially if you are not allowed to use a dictionary on skill tests.

Irregular Verbs

Present	Past	Past Participle	Present	Past	Past Participle
arise	arose	arisen	light	lit /lighted	lit /lighted
awake	awoke	awakened	lose	lost	lost
bear	bore	born	make	made	made
beat	beat	beaten	mean	meant	meant
become	became	become	meet	met	met
begin	began	begun	pay	paid	paid
bend	bent	bent	quit	quit	quit
bet	bet	bet	read	read	read
bind	bound	bound	ride	rode	ridden
bite	bit	bitten	ring	rang	rung
bleed	bled	bled	rise	rose	risen
blow	blew	blown	run	ran	run
break	broke	broken	see	saw	seen
bring	brought	brought	seek	sought	sought
build	built	built	sell	sold	sold
burn	burned	burned/burnt	send	sent	sent
burst	burst	burst	set	set	set
buy	bought	bought	shake	shook	shaken
cast	cast	cast	shave	shaved	shaved
catch	caught	caught	shine	shone	shone
choose	chose	chosen	shoot	shot	shot
cling	clung	clung	show	showed	shown/ showed
come	came	come			
cost	cost	cost	shrink	shrank	shrunk
creep	crept	crept	shut	shut	shut
cut	cut	cut	sing	sang	sung
dare	dared	dared	sink	sank	sunk
deal	dealt	dealt	sit	sat	sat
dig	dug	dug	sleep	slept	slept
do	did	done	slide	slid	slid
draw	drew	drawn	slit	slit	slit
dream	dreamed	dreamed/dreamt	speak	spoke	spoken
drink	drank	drunk	speed	sped	sped
drive	drove	driven	spend	spent	spent
eat	ate	eaten	spin	spun	spun
fall	fell	fallen	split	split	split
feed	fed	fed	spread	spread	spread
feel	felt	felt	spring	sprang	sprung
fight	fought	fought	stand	stood	stood
find	found	found	steal	stole	stolen
fling	flung	flung	stick	stuck	stuck

Irregular Verbs

Present	Past	Past Participle	Present	Past	Past Participle
fly	flew	flown	sting	stung	stung
forget	forgot	forgotten	strike	struck	struck
forgive	forgave	forgiven	string	strung	strung
freeze	froze	frozen	swear	swore	sworn
get	got	gotten/got	sweep	swept	swept
give	gave	given	swim	swam	swum
go	went	gone	swing	swung	swung
grind	ground	ground	take	took	taken
grow	grew	grown	teach	taught	taught
hang	hung/hanged	hung/hanged	tear	tore	torn
have	had	had	tell	told	told
hear	heard	heard	think	thought	thought
hide	hid	hidden	throw	threw	thrown
hit	hit	hit	understand	understood	understood
hold	held	held	wake	woke	woke
hurt	hurt	hurt	wear	wore	worn
keep	kept	kept	weave	wove	woven
know	knew	known	wed	wed	wed
lay	laid	laid	weep	wept	wept
lead	led	led	wet	wet	wet
leave	left	left	win	won	won
lend	lent	lent	wind	wound	wound
let	let	let	wring	wrung	wrung
lie (to relax)	lay	lain	write	wrote	written

Practice 5   Read through the list of irregular verbs on pages 177–178 and put an asterisk by the verbs that don't sound right to you. These are the forms you are not familiar with and will have to memorize.

Practice 6   To help you focus on the verbs that cause you problems, you should keep a list of the verb forms you miss on practices, on tests, and in your writing. Most students miss the same verb forms time and time again. Keeping a list of your errors (and having them easily accessible in one place) will help you avoid making the same verb error again.

Verb Error   **Correct Form**

he gone   *he went*

1. _____   2. _____

3. _____   4. _____

5. _____   6. _____

7. _____   8. _____

9. _____   10. _____

11. _____   12. _____

13. _____   14. _____

15. _____   16. _____

17. _____   18. _____

19. _____   20. _____

Practice 7   Fill in the correct past or past participle of the verb in parentheses.

1. Lester _____ (to break) his collar bone when he was ten.

2. I have _____ (to ride) my bike to the beach three times.

3. When it got dark, I _____ (to lose) my way in the woods.

4. My mother _____ (to sing) opera when she was in college.

5. I have never _____ (to go) to the movies by myself before.

6. My music teacher _____ (to teach) me the scales when I was ten.

7. The deer have _____ (to wear) a path through the meadow.

8. My English class _____ (to write) a play together last year.

9. Have you _____ (to speak) with your instructor about your questions?

10. The car was _____ (to steal) on Friday night.

IRREGULAR VERBS THAT DO NOT CHANGE FORM

3.1 Some irregular verbs keep the same form in the present tense, past tense, and past participle.

Michael always **puts** his books on the kitchen table. (Present)
Yesterday, Michael **put** his books on the kitchen table. (Past)
For as long as I can remember, Michael **has put** his books on the kitchen table. (Past participle)

Irregular Verbs That *Do Not Change Forms*		
bet	hurt	shut
burst	let	slit
cast	put	split
cost	quit	spread
cut	read	wet
hit	set	

Practice 8   Fill in the correct form of the verb.

1. Cindy _wore_ (to wear) that dress to the prom.

2. I _sleep_ (to sleep) late on Saturdays.

3. Jerome _split_ (to split) the watermelon open with a knife.

4. Yesterday I _spent_ (to spend) all my money at the mall.

5. I have _road_ (to read) all the Harry Potter books.

6. Hank Aaron _hit_ (to hit) the ball out of the park.

7. We have _met_ (to meet) them in the park before.

8. I _quit_ (to quit) my job today.

9. Have you _set_ (to set) the table yet?

10. When I _shut_ (to shut) the door, the dog howled.

Using the Past Participle

The Present Perfect Tense

4.1 The present perfect tense expresses an action that began in the past and is continuing in the present. The present perfect tense is made with the present tense of *to have* and the past participle.

Ricardo **has ridden** his bike to school since he was ten.
Marilyn **has lived** in the same house for five years.

4.2 The present perfect tense can also describe an action that has just been completed or an action that was completed at an undetermined time in the past.

We **have just finished** our homework.
Luis **has visited** Spain.

Practice 9   Underline the correct verb.

1. My husband (made/has made) pancakes on Saturday every day since the kids were little.

2. I (had always lived/have always lived) on Laurel Street.

3. Sean (wore/has worn) the same shirt every day this week.

4. My handwriting (was/has been) hard to read since I was a kid.

5. The doorbell (was broken/has been broken) since we moved in.

6. I (ate/have eaten) all the calories I can for today.

7. Giorgio's hair (was/has been) blond for as long as I can remember.

8. My sister (studied/has studied) astrology for years.

9. Ever since she was a child, Martina (wanted/has wanted) to visit Spain.

10. Rene (is/has been) president of our class for three months.

The Past Perfect Tense

5.1 The past perfect tense is used when an action occurred in the past before another past action or point in time. It is always used when *already* or *just* is in a sentence in which one action occurred in the past before another past action. The past perfect tense is made with the past tense of *to have* and the past participle.

I **had** already **bought** my ticket when Ming Na called.
Latasha **had** just **begun** her homework when the phone rang.

Practice 10   Underline the correct verb.

1. The game (started/had just started) when the power went out.

2. Kim-Le (passed/had already passed) his swimming test when he joined
   the pool.

3. Wendy (read/had just read) the book when the movie came out.

4. My little brother (ate/had eaten) the last piece of cake by the time we returned
   from the movies.

5. By the time I arrived, Kimberly (left/had left) for school.

6. Mrs. Dalloway (picked up/had just picked up) the mail when it started
   to rain.

7. My mother (went/had just gone) through a red light when the officer pulled her
   over.

8. I (took/had already taken) the medicine when the pharmacy called to tell me there
   had been a mistake.

9. By the time I finished my homework, my friends (went/had already

   gone).

10. When I arrived at the theater, the movie (started/had just started).

Active and Passive Voice

In the **active voice,** the subject of the sentence performs the action of a verb. In the **passive voice,** the subject of the sentence receives the action of the verb.

The passive voice is made with a form of the verb *to be* and the past participle.

Active	Passive
Tonya won the race.	The race was won by Tonya.
My brother broke the window.	The window was broken by my brother.

The **passive voice is acceptable** when the doer of the action is unknown or unimportant or is less important than the receiver of the action.

My car **was burglarized** last night. (No one knows who committed the crime.)

The results of the vote **will be released** after the meeting. (Who will release the results is unknown or unimportant.)

6.1 In most writing, the **active voice is clearer** and more acceptable than the passive voice.

✗   The test was passed by Enrique.

✓   Enrique passed the test. ⚬⚬

✗   The bone was buried by the puppy.

✓   The puppy buried the bone.

Practice 11   Underline the passive verb forms in the following sentences. Next, rewrite the sentences in active voice if the passive is not appropriate.

1. The magazine is printed in New York.

   C _____

2. The cake was baked by my mother.

   My mother baked a cake _____

3. The athlete was awarded a gold medal.

   C _____

4. My new shoe was destroyed by the puppy.

The puppy destroyed my new shoe

5. The sandwiches were devoured by the hungry hikers.

The hungry hikers devoured the sandwiches

6. The letter must be postmarked by four o'clock.

_C_ _____

7. The exam was graded by the substitute teacher.

The substitute teacher graded the exams.

8. An unwritten rule was broken by the new student.

The new student broke the unwritten rule.

9. The winning lottery numbers are announced at midnight.

_C_ _____

10. The man had been convicted of several crimes.

_C_ _____

Using the Past Participle as an Adjective

7.1 The past participle form of the verb may be used as an adjective (a modifier).

✓ **mashed** potatoes	✗ **mash** potatoes
✓ an **abandoned** house	✗ an **abandon** house
✓ the **exhausted** runner	✗ the **exhaust** runner

Practice 12 Correct all errors with past participles used as adjectives.

1. The rust [_rusted_] fender fell off my car on the way home.

2. My broke [_broken_] arm aches when it rains.

3. We threw away the burn [_burnt_] toast.

4. The children were exhausted after the party. [_C_]

5. The rotten tomatoes stank. [_C_]

6. The convict [_convicted_] man was sentenced to jail.

7. We moved out of the dilapidate[_d_] house.

8. Her neatly comb[_ed_] hair shone in the sunlight.

9. Baked apples are my favorite dessert.

10. My sister's puppy isn't housebroken.

Consistent Verb Tense

8.1 Do not shift tenses unnecessarily.

Shifting unnecessarily between the past and the present will confuse the reader.

✗ When I *arrive,* the band *had* stopped playing and the crowd was leaving.

(The tense shifts from past to present to past.)

✓ When I *arrived,* the band *had* stopped playing and the crowd was leaving.

(Past tense is used consistently.)

Practice 13   Correct the shifts in verb tense in the following sentences by putting all the verbs in the same tense, present or past.

1. When lighting struck, the lights ~~go~~ went out.

2. By the time I finished shopping, I ~~am~~ was hungry.

3. The sky is blue and the leaves ~~were~~ are green.

4. I finished class and I ~~go~~ went out for pizza.

5. Because I like chocolate cake, I ~~ate~~ eat it all the time.

6. Miguel likes to listen to music while he ~~mowed~~ mowes the yard.

7. The corridors are empty when the alarm ~~went~~ goes off.

8. My brother got his license when he ~~turns~~ turned sixteen.

9. My best friend lives next door and ~~went~~ goes to school with me.

10. I go shopping when the sale pages ~~came~~ come out on Wednesday.

CD Connection

Power of Language

On *Writer's Resources* CD-ROM, see *Verb Tenses* in Grammar/Punctuation/Mechanics for more information and practice with word choice.

Practice 14 *Working Together*

Working alone or in groups, write five sentences that contain the following verb errors. Write one sentence for each verb error.

1. An incorrect irregular past tense (rule 2 or 3)

2. An incorrect irregular past participle (rule 2 or 3)

3. An inappropriate use of passive voice (rule 6)

4. An incorrect adjective form (rule 7)

5. A shift in verb tense from present to past (rule 8)

Practice 15 *Working Together*

Trade the sentences you wrote in Practice 14 with another group, and correct the errors in tense.

REVIEW EXERCISE 1

Working alone or in groups of two or three, correct all verb errors in the following sentences. Rewrite sentences in the passive voice to put them in the active voice. (Note: Some verbs are correct and should not be changed.)

1. My neighbors' grass is green because they have ~~water~~ *watered* their lawn every day this

   week.

   My neighbors grass is green because they have watered their lawn
   everyday this week!

2. The sunk boat was raised by the recovery crew.

   Correct.

3. The fifty-yard dash was won by my brother.

   My brother won the fifty-yard dash.

4. Five hundred workers were ~~lay~~ *layed:* off yesterday.

5. The boat was damaged by the storm.

6. I was treated by a well-train doctor.

catered

7. The party was ~~cater~~ by my aunt.

_____

baked

8. My favorite Italian meal is ~~bake~~ lasagna.

_____

tired

9. I am ~~tire~~ of listening to complaints.

_____

disgusted

10. The woman was ~~disgust~~ by what she saw.

_____

REVIEW EXERCISE 2

Identify the verbs in the following sentences as correct (C) or incorrect (I), and correct the verb errors.

__C__   1. The man was arrested outside our house.

__I__   2. The child was ~~overcame~~ *overcome* with grief.

__I__   3. The car was being ~~tow~~ *towed* by a truck when the accident occurred.

__I__   4. My son had two ~~broke~~ *broken* bones after his fall.

__C__   5. The candy has been hid in the closet since Halloween.

__I__   6. The ~~stole~~ *stolen* bike was recovered by the police.

__C__   7. My son has watched TV for two hours today.

__C__   8. My best friend has rode his bike to school for years.

__C__   9. The teacher extended the deadline because many students were sick.

__I__   10. When I was five, my family ~~move~~ *moved* to New York City.

EDITING FOR VERB TENSE 1

Working alone or in groups of two or three, correct all errors with verb tenses and past participle forms used as adjectives in the following paragraph.

The Statue of Liberty

The Statue of Liberty was a gift from the French people to the United States. The man who come up with the idea of

building a monument to democracy in the United States is
Edouard de Laboulaye. The sculptor he hired to build the
statue was name Bartholdi. When Bartholdi visit New York in
1871, he seen Bedloe's Island guarding the entrance to New
York Harbor. He knew he had found the perfect home for his
statue. The 151-foot-high statue was based on Libertas, the
ancient Roman goddess of freedom. It was completed in 1884,
but it is more than two years later before it was dedicated
to the American people. Millions of immigrants have pass by
this symbol of American freedom on their way to a new life.
As a thank-you to France, Joseph Pulitzer, for whom the
Pulitzer Prize is named hired Bartholdi to build a statue
called *Washington and Lafayette,* which was ~~gave~~ given to France. To
celebrate her 100th birthday in 1986, a major restoration of
the statue was ~~undertook~~ undertaken. Six million visitors ~~came~~ Come to visit
this famous landmark every year.

EDITING FOR VERB TENSE 2

Correct all errors with verb tenses and past participle forms used as adjectives in the
following paragraph.

The Origin of Critical Thinking

The ancient Greeks believed that events such as earthquakes
were caused by the Olympic gods. If an earthquake ~~destroy~~ destroyed a
city, it was because Poseidon was angry. When the Greeks
encountered the advanced cultures of Egypt and Mesopotamia,
their way of thinking ~~begun~~ began to change. They discovered that
different people worshiped different gods. Contact with
different cultures ~~brung~~ brought the Greeks many new ideas. They

borrowed the idea of an alphabet from the Phoenicians and coined money from the Lydians. Around the sixth century, the Greeks began to question many ideas. Their reasons for accepting or rejecting ideas were stated openly and could be examined and debated. Making reasoned choices was the beginning of critical thinking. Even though many of their conclusions are not ~~took~~ taken seriously today, critical thinking lay the groundwork for the development of modern science.

Practicing Your Writing Power

Power of Language

© Thomson Corporation/Heinle Image Resource Bank

Write about a place you have visited or would like to visit. After you have written the journal entry, go back and reread it, paying particular attention to the verb tenses.

3rd person

Name _Leighona Bowda_
Section _____ Score _____

VERB TENSE TEST 1

Identify the verbs in the following sentences as correct (C) or incorrect (I), and correct the verb errors.

C 1. On August 13, 2004, Hurricane Charley struck Florida.

I 2. In the high winds, trees were uprooted, and power lines were ~~snap~~ *snapped* like matchsticks.

C 3. Unfortunately, many residents were unable to evacuate before the storm struck.

I 4. As a result, the storm ~~cause~~ *caused* thirteen deaths.

C 5. During the storm, flood water rose, the streets were flooded, and many homes and businesses were damage.

C 6. Winds swept many homes off their foundations.

I 7. When residents returned to their homes, they realized they ~~have lost~~ *had lost* everything.

I 8. Family photographs that held ~~treasure~~ *treasured* memories were hardest to lose.

I 9. Repair crews were ~~bringed~~ *brought* in from all over the country to repair the downed power lines.

C 10. It was months before power was restored to some areas.

Name _____

Section _____   Score _____

VERB TENSE TEST 2

Identify the verbs in the following sentences as correct (C) or incorrect (I), and correct the verb errors.

_I_ 1. The Olympic Games were ~~began~~ *begun* in Olympia in Greece in 776 B.C.

_I_ 2. The games were ~~dedicate~~ *dedicated* to Zeus, the most powerful Greek god.

_C_ 3. During the celebration, Greeks make offerings to the gods and watched athletic contests.

_I_ 4. The celebration was always ~~hold~~ *held* in the summer and lasted for five days.

_C_ 5. Athletes arrived one month early in order to be selected for the competition.

_C_ 6. The ancient Greeks valued physical strength.

_I_ 7. Winners were ~~crown~~ *Crowned* with a wreath of olive leaves.

_C_ 8. Many contests were held in stadiums that seated more than 20,000 people.

_C_ 9. Strict rules govern the competition.

_C_ 10. Athletes who did not obey the rules were punished.

Name _____

Section _____   Score _____

VERB TENSE TEST 3

Identify the verbs in the following sentences as correct (C) or incorrect (I), and correct the verb errors.

_____I_____   1. The Napa Valley, an hour north of San Francisco, has been ~~call~~ *Called* California's Garden of Eden.

_____C_____   2. The climate and soil of the Napa Valley are ideal for cultivation of grapes.

_____I_____   3. This region ~~produces~~ *Produced* wine since the 1800s.

_____I_____   4. Wine production was temporarily ~~brung~~ *brought* to a halt by Prohibition.

_____I_____   5. Since then, the California wine industry has ~~growed~~ *grown* to nearly 200 wineries.

_____I_____   6. In the 1970s, several Napa Valley wines were ~~rank~~ *ranked* the best in the world by French judges.

_____C_____   7. Most wineries provide guided tours of the winery.

_____C_____   8. At the end of the tour, wine can be tasted by visitors.

_____C_____   9. Visitors to the valley can also enjoy fine food in many of the renovate wineries.

_____C_____ 10. Many visitors have also took advantage of outdoor activities such as hiking, biking, and hot-air balloon rides.

Name _____

Section _____   Score _____

VERB TENSE TEST 4

Identify the verbs in the following sentences as correct (C) or incorrect (I), and correct the verb errors.

___C___   1. The *Titanic* was the largest ship ever builded.

___I___   2. On April 10, 1912, it was ~~launch~~ launched in Southampton, England.

___C___   3. The ship held 1,324 passengers and 899 crew.

___I___   4. Because everyone ~~believe~~ believed the ship was unsinkable, it did not have

enough lifeboats for all the passengers.

___C___   5. The owners wanted to beat the speed record for crossing the Atlantic.

_____   6. Therefore, the captain did not to slow the ship's speed at night in spite

of the danger of icebergs.

___C___   7. At 11:40 at night, when most of the passengers had went to bed, the

ship struck an iceberg.

___C___   8. The captain quickly realized the impossible was about to happen; the

Titanic was sinking.

___I___   9. Less than three hours later, the *Titanic* ~~sinked~~ sunk beneath the water.

___I___ 10. More than 1,500 lives were ~~losed~~ lost.

Chapter 9 — Adjectives and Adverbs

In this chapter you will learn about

- ☞ Adjectives
  - • Comparative and superlatives
  - • With linking verbs
- ☞ Adverbs
- ☞ Adjective/adverb confusion

Skill Preview

Adjectives and adverbs are descriptive words. We use them all the time in our speaking and writing. There are two kinds of mistakes we make with adjectives and adverbs. The following passage illustrates the choices we make in using adjectives and adverbs.

Circle the correct word or words in each sentence.

I felt *bad/badly* yesterday. Last night I went to bed with an *awful/awfully* headache. I didn't sleep *good/well* either. I woke up with a *real/really* bad sore throat this morning. My throat hurts *terrible/terribly* right now. I hope I will feel *better/more better* tonight.

Adjectives

Adjectives describe or modify nouns (persons or things) and pronouns. Writers use adjectives to make nouns and pronouns more specific.

ADJ ADJ ADJ N   ADJ   ADJ ADJ   N
The old gray dog **became** wet **when it was left outside in** a fierce rainstorm.

The adjectives *the, old,* and *wet* describe dog, and *a* and *fierce* describe rainstorm. You will be encouraged to use adjectives in your college writing because they help readers understand what or which nouns you are writing about.

1.1 Usually an adjective comes before the noun it describes.

An adjective may be an **article** (*a, an, the*) or a descriptive word. Often a noun will have more than one adjective to describe or modify it.

ADJ ADJ ADJ N
the big red balloon

ADJ ADJ N
some scary dreams

ADJ ADJ N
many different beliefs

Practice 1 Underline the adjectives in each sentence, and draw a line to the noun each adjective describes or modifies. Then write the adjectives in the blanks after each item.

1. A little girl sat on the leather couch. _____ _____ _____ _____

2. The playful puppy chewed on an old towel. _____ _____ _____ _____

3. Some elderly couples move to retirement communities. _____ _____
_____

4. Inexpensive computers are available at my favorite store. _____ _____
_____

5. Few students enjoy completing long assignments. _____ _____

1.2 Adjectives follow linking verbs.

Linking verbs may link a subject (noun) to an adjective that describes the subject.

The **child** seems **sad**.
The **soup** tastes **good**.

Practice 2   Fill in the blank with an adjective.

1. The teacher seems _____.

2. The test that we took on Monday was _____.

3. Some students look _____ about the test.

4. One student sounded _____ when he received his score.

5. Another student became _____ when she got her test back.

Linking Verbs	
is/are	look
was/were	seem
appear	smell
become	sound
feel	taste

Spotlight on Writers

Power of Language

Bob Dylan

"How many times must the cannon balls fly before they're forever banned?"

Through his poetry and music, Bob Dylan (1941–) has articulated the feelings of a generation about war, peace, and love. In the song "Blowin' in the Wind," Dylan asks questions that are still relevant today. This song was sung during the March on Washington, where Martin Luther King, Jr., delivered his "I Have A Dream" speech. Dylan's words inspired a generation to question injustice and to become involved in changing the world.

Using Adjectives to Compare Nouns

Adjectives are used to compare two nouns (comparative form of the adjective) or show that a noun is the best (superlative form) of three or more nouns.

Sarah is **faster** than Megan, but Zoe is the **fastest** girl in the class.

1.3 For most adjectives of one or two syllables, add -er to form the comparative and -est to form the superlative.

Comparative: The chocolate icing is **sweeter** than the vanilla icing.
Superlative: The chocolate icing is the **sweetest** icing in the bakery.

1.4 For adjectives of three or more syllables, add *more* before the adjective to form the comparative, and add *most* before the adjective to form the superlative.

MacDonald's second book is the **more interesting** book of the two she has written.
The **most beautiful** painting in our house was painted by my sister.

1.5 Some common adjectives are irregular in the comparative and superlative forms.

Common Irregular Adjectives		
	Comparative	**Superlative**
good	better	best
bad	worse	worst
many	more	most

1.6 Do not use a combination of -er or -est with *more* and *most*.

✗   Jorge's test results are **more better** than Ali's results.
✓   Jorge's test results are **better** than Ali's results.

Practice 3   Fill in the blank with the correct form of the adjective.

1. Josh is the (tall) _____ of all the kids in his class.

2. Our dog seems to be (gentle) _____ than our neighbors' dog.

3. The valedictorian of our graduating class is the (intelligent) _____ student in the school.

4. I couldn't answer the (difficult) _____ problem on the test.

5. The answer to the last question was (obvious) _____ than the answer to the first question.

Adverbs

2.1 Adverbs describe or modify *verbs, adjectives,* and *other adverbs.* Many adverbs end in -ly.

      ADV   ADJ   N   *V*   ADV ADV
The extremely old man <u>spoke</u> really softly.

The adverbs answer the question *How?* about the adjective, verb, and adverb.
How old is the man? Extremely old.
How did the man speak? Softly.
How softly? Really softly.

Practice 4   Underline the adverbs in each sentence, and draw a line to the word each adverb modifies or describes. Then write each adverb on the line provided.

1. A nurse carefully tended to the badly wounded accident victim. _____

    _____

2. The driver turned the corner hesitantly because she was not exactly sure where

    she was going. _____ _____

3. The audience sat quietly and patiently as the musicians quickly tuned their instru-

    ments. _____ _____ _____

4. There was a really bad accident that occurred shortly after noon yesterday.

    _____ _____

5. The consumer happily paid the shipping charges when the company generously sent

    a replacement part for the car. _____ _____

Adjective and Adverb Confusion

2.2 Confusing adjectives and adverbs creates errors with these descriptive words.

   ✗ My arm hurt **bad** after the accident.
   ✓ My arm hurt **badly** after the accident.
     (*Badly* is an <u>adverb</u> that describes how my arm hurt.)

   ✗ Jack felt **badly** about our argument.
   ✓ Jack felt **bad** about our argument.
     (Felt is a <u>linking verb</u> that links Jack to the *adjective bad*.)

2.2.1 Real and **really** create the most common errors. *Real* is an adjective that describes a noun (person or thing), and *really* is an adverb that describes a verb, adjective, or adverb.

   ✘ The exam was **real** difficult.
   ✓ The exam was **really** difficult.

2.2.2 Good and **well** also are commonly confused. *Good* is an adjective, and *well* is an adverb.

   ✘ The marching band performed **good** at the game.
   ✓ The marching band performed **well** at the game. (*Well* is an <u>adverb</u> that describes how the band *performed*.)

Practice 5   Circle the correct adjective or adverb, and draw a line to the word it describes or modifies. Then write the correct answer on the lines provided.

_____ 1. The weather was real/really hot.

_____ 2. The motorist felt terrible/terribly about the accident.

_____ 3. The student complained that her test wasn't graded fair/fairly.

_____ 4. The child acted brave/bravely when she confronted the barking dogs.

_____ 5. The team played good/well in its final game.

CD Connection

Power of
Language

On *Writer's Resources* CD-ROM, see *Parts of Speech* in Grammar/Punctuation/Mechanics for more information and practice with adjectives and adverbs.

REVIEW EXERCISE 1

Write the correct form of the modifying word in the blanks.

1. The Jefferson family was (incredible/incredibly) _____ worn out after the long drive across the state.

2. The trip was the (miserablest/most miserable) _____ journey the Jeffersons had ever taken.

3. First, everyone was already (real/really) _____ tired before the trip even started.

4. The night before, the baby had cried (loud/loudly) _____ throughout the night, so no one slept (good/well) _____.

5. Then Mr. Jefferson had to work (real/really) _____ late, and the family didn't leave town until midnight.

6. Mrs. Jefferson was (exhausteder/more exhausted) _____ than her husband, so she rested with the baby while her husband drove.

7. Their son, Kevin, sat in front with his father and read (quiet/quietly) _____.

8. The first part of the trip went (quick/quickly) _____.

9. However, the traffic moved (more slow/slowly) _____ when it began to snow.

10. The trip took five hours (longer/more long) _____ than the same drive the year before.

REVIEW EXERCISE 2

Write the correct form of the modifying word in the blanks.

1. Because the actor looked (older/more old) _____ than he was, he got the part of Granddad on the soap opera.

2. The part was the first (real/really) _____ good role he had gotten since graduating from college.

3. The director told him that the soap opera's writers had created Granddad to be the (meanest/most mean) _____ man on the show.

4. The actor didn't mind being a villain, but he felt (sick/sickly) _____ about being asked to dye his hair white.

5. He was afraid that he would look strange/strangely _____.

6. The show's makeup artist assured him (confident/confidently) _____ that she would preserve his good looks.

7. She studied his face (close/closely) _____ before applying makeup that gave him the lines and creases of old age.

8. When the actor went home, his next-door neighbor (near/nearly) _____ fainted when she saw him.

9. When he looked in the mirror, the actor was (complete/completely) _____ unnerved by his white hair.

10. The actor wasn't handling his new look very (good/well) _____.

ADJECTIVES AND ADVERBS EDITING TEST

Alone or in pairs, correct all adjective and adverb errors in the following passage. (There are 20 errors.)

An Exciting Night

Saturday night I witnessed the most strange accident I have ever seen. A real popular band had just given a concert, and my friends and I were leaving the large parking garage where most of the audience had parked. A car was following close behind us. It pulled around our car and started driving wild through the crowded parking area. The driver was honking his horn insistent and waving his arms furious as he passed us. The young driver appeared upset. I thought I heard his passenger crying loud as they sped away. I was driving slow because the traffic was total congested. As I left the parking area, I saw clear the crazy driver plow into a car that had stopped sudden to pick up some concertgoers. A man got out of the car and began shouting excited and pointing angry at his car. The reckless driver jumped out of his car and ran quick to the passenger side. I was real worried because the girl who got out looked badly. She was walking painful, and I sudden realized that she was obvious pregnant. A crowd had gathered, and an elderly woman ran up quick to the couple and led them away. Later, I heard that a healthy baby boy was delivered in the back of the retired nurse's car.

Practicing Your Writing Power

Power of
Language

© Thomson Corporation/Heinle Image Resource Bank

Write an account of an accident you have been involved in, witnessed, or heard about. Be sure to use lots of adjectives and adverbs that describe what happened and how people felt. Check your use of adjectives and adverbs carefully after you have finished writing.

Name _____

Section _____ Score _____

ADJECTIVES AND ADVERBS TEST 1

Write the correct form of the modifying word in the blanks.

1. Fishermen swear that fishing is a real/really _____ fun sport.

2. However, I find getting up at 4 A.M. is the baddest/worst _____ part
   of our fishing trips.

3. Also, my nails get awful/awfully _____ dirty digging in the dirt to
   find worms for bait.

4. My nails look nasty/nastily _____ for the rest of the day.

5. Even the perfect/perfectly _____ still lake is a problem because of all
   the mosquitoes.

6. I row awkward/awkwardly _____ while my dad is casting his bait
   into the reeds.

7. He can cast his bait smooth/smoothly _____ without losing his
   balance.

8. I always feel good/well _____ when he catches fish.

9. Cleaning the fish can be a real/really _____ smelly job.

10. Dead fish don't smell good/well _____.

Name _____

Section _____ Score _____

ADJECTIVES AND ADVERBS TEST 2

Write the correct form of the modifying word in the blanks.

1. A house is probably the expensivest/most expensive _____ purchase
   a consumer will ever make.

2. Unfortunately, many home buyers must make a decision on a house they see very
   rapid/rapidly _____.

3. Often a good buy will not stay on the market for longer/more long
   _____ than a couple of days.

4. Therefore, home buyers must study the housing market careful/carefully
   _____ in order to make a fast decision.

5. First of all, home buyers should calculate exact/exactly _____ how
   much they can afford to pay for a house.

6. They must look close/closely _____ at different areas they may want
   to live in to find just the right neighborhood.

7. Home buyers would do good/well _____ to study how much houses
   in their choice neighborhood have sold for in the past year.

8. Of course, retaining a competent real estate agent can help make the process eas-
   ier/more easier _____.

9. Probably the importantest/most important step _____ in the process
   is making a decision to make an offer on a house.

10. When homebuyers feel good/well _____ about a house, they should
    write a contract as soon as possible.

Chapter 10 Sentence Parts and Types

In this chapter, you will learn about

- ☞ The parts of sentences: clauses and phrases
- ☞ The types of sentences: simple, compound, complex, and compound-complex
- ☞ The purposes of sentences: declarative, interrogative, imperative, and exclamatory

Skill Preview

Even though it may seem like there are thousands of ways to put together words into sentences, there are only four types of sentences. Every sentence has the same basic parts and ingredients. This chapter will introduce you to the sentence and its parts, types, and purposes. You will learn the vocabulary that writers use to talk about sentences, and you will learn about the sentence structures used in college writing.

The Main Ingredients of a Sentence

1.1 A sentence has three main ingredients: a **subject** (who or what the sentence is about) and a **complete verb** (the action or state of being of the subject) that express a **complete thought**.

         S   V
My bank <u>has notified</u> me that my paycheck was deposited on the first day of the month.

1.2 The **simple subject** is the noun or pronoun that the sentence is about without any of the words that modify or describe the subject. The **complete subject** includes the simple subject and all the modifying words. The subject of the sentence can also be a verbal, a phrase, or a clause that is used as a noun. (For more about subjects, see Chapter 6.)

Spotlight on Writers

Power of Language

Sandra Cisneros

"At one time or another, we all have felt other. When I teach writing, I tell the story of the moment of discovering and naming my otherness. It is not enough simply to sense it; it has to be named, and then written about there. Once I could name it, I ceased being ashamed and silent. I could speak up and celebrate my otherness as a woman, as a working-class person, as an American of Mexican descent. When I recognized the places where I departed from my neighbors, my classmates, my family, my town, my brothers, when I discovered what I knew that no one else in the room knew, and then spoke it in a voice that was my voice, the voice I used when I was sitting in the kitchen, dressed in my pajamas, talking over a table littered with cups and dishes, when I could give myself permission to speak from that intimate space, then I could talk and sound like myself, not like me trying to sound like someone I wasn't. Then I could speak, shout, laugh from a place that was uniquely mine, that was no one else's in the history of the universe, that would never be anyone else's, ever."

Sandra Cisneros (1954–) writes from her background as a Mexican-American woman. In this excerpt from the Introduction to *The House on Mango Street*, she explains the power writers feel when they establish their unique identity, or voice, through their writing.

1.3 The **simple predicate** is the main verb and any auxiliary (or helping) verbs. The **complete predicate** contains the complete verb and all the words that modify the verb. The subject and the predicate together express a complete thought.

Complete subject and complete predicate

S   V
My bank <u>has notified me that my paycheck was deposited on the first day of the month.</u>

In this textbook, you will see the simple subject and simple predicate (complete verb) identified in sample sentences.

Practice 1 Underline the complete subject with one line, and underline the complete predicate with two lines.

1. The computer network has been shut down for maintenance.

2. Modeling offers many advantages as a career.

3. A legal secretary has filed all the law firm's correspondence from last month.

4. The sleek sailboat glided into the cove.

5. Mario and his friends did not want to turn down the music at the party.

The Parts of a Sentence

A sentence contains two kinds of word groups. **Clauses** contain subjects and verbs. **Phrases** do not include both a subject and verb. Every sentence will have at least one clause, and most sentences include phrases, too.

Clauses

There are two kinds of clauses: **independent clauses** and **dependent clauses.**

2.1 An independent clause is *independent* because it can stand alone as a sentence.

My bank has notified me.

Joaquin will attend the party.

I love the room.

2.2 A dependent clause includes a subject and a verb but cannot stand alone as a sentence.

The dependent clause is *dependent* on an independent clause in the same sentence for its meaning.

that my paycheck was deposited.

2.3 Dependent clauses can appear anywhere in a sentence, but they always begin with a subordinating conjunction or relative pronoun.

Subordinating Conjunctions		
after	even though	until
although	if	when
as	since	whereas
because	though	whether
before	unless	while

Relative Pronouns	
that	whoever
which	whom
whichever	whomever
who	whose

2.4 A dependent clause is a sentence fragment, and it must be joined to an independent clause to form a complete sentence.

My bank <u>has notified</u> me that my paycheck was deposited.
Because the game will end by ten, Joaquin <u>will attend</u> the party.
I <u>love</u> the room, which was painted yesterday.

Phrases

2.5 Phrases are groups of related words. Phrases do not include both a subject and verb.

Verb phrase: was walking quickly
Noun phrase: a mysterious stranger
Prepositional phrases: in the middle of the night

noun phrase   verb phrase   prepositional phrase
My bank has notified me that my paycheck was deposited on the first day of the month.

We learn most of the rules for putting clauses and phrases together when we learn to speak the language. In this writing class, you are reviewing the rules to learn how to combine ideas clearly and effectively and how to punctuate them correctly. Although sentences contain both clauses and phrases, the four types of sentences are defined by how many independent clauses and how many dependent clauses they include.

Practice 2   Identify each word group as an independent clause (IC), dependent clause (DC), or phrase (PH).

_____   1. While it rained yesterday morning.

_____   2. A big puddle in the driveway.

_____   3. We got our feet wet going to the car.

_____   4. If the rain didn't stop.

_____   5. The game was cancelled.

The Four Sentence Types

3.1   A **simple sentence** contains one independent clause.

The delivery truck <u>was</u> late.

3.2   A **compound sentence** contains two independent clauses.

independent clause   *independent clause*
The newspaper <u>arrived</u> late, so I <u>didn't read</u> it this morning.

You will learn to write compound sentences when you learn about the compound sentence comma rule.

3.3   A **complex sentence** contains one independent clause and at least one dependent clause.

independent clause   *dependent clause*
The newspaper <u>arrived</u> late because it was raining.

3.4   A **compound-complex sentence** contains two independent clauses and at least one dependent clause.

independent clause   *dependent clause*   *independent clause*
The newspaper <u>arrived</u> late because it was raining, so I <u>didn't read</u> it this morning.

You will learn more about using the different types of sentences in your writing in Chapter 11, Chapter 12, Chapter 13, and Chapter 18.

Practice 3   Identify the type of each sentence: simple (S), compound (CD), complex (CX), or compound-complex (CD-CX).

_____   1. When the pizza arrived, the children were happy.

_____   2. The kids ate the pizza, and they watched the movie.

_____   3. While they ate, the kids were quiet, so the parents were able to spend time together.

_____   4. The parents went to their room to watch a movie.

_____   5. The children were satisfied until they finished the pizza.

Sentence Purposes

Sentences can be classified by the purpose of their communication.

4.1 A **declarative** sentence makes *a statement* and ends with a period.

The bus stops at the corner.

4.2 An **interrogative** sentence asks *a direct question* and ends with a question mark.

Does the bus stop at the corner?

4.3 An **imperative** sentence makes *a command* and ends with a period.

Stop the bus.

4.4 An **exclamatory** sentence expresses *strong emotion* and ends with an exclamation point.

If this bus doesn't stop, I will scream!

Practice 4   Identify the sentence purpose: declarative (DEC), interrogative (INT), imperative (IMP), or exclamatory (EXC).

_____   1. I wish that I got help around the house.

_____   2. Take the garbage out.

_____   3. I mean now!

_____   4. Why don't you want to do your chores?

_____   5. The chores are more fun when someone else helps.

Practice 5   *Working Together*

Alone or in pairs, write a simple sentence, compound sentence, complex sentence, and compound-complex sentence on the topic of *school* or *eating at a restaurant*. Then exchange papers with another group and identify that group's sentences as simple, compound, complex, or compound-complex sentences.

CD Connection

On *Writer's Resources* CD-ROM, see *Sentence Types* in Writing Elements for more information on sentence parts, types, and purposes.

Practicing Your Writing Power

© Thomson Corporation/Heinle Image Resource Bank

Introduce a good friend. Describe your friend physically, and explain why you like this person. Also, give some examples of the things you and your friend do together.

Chapter 11 Sentence Fragments

In this chapter you will learn about the different kinds of sentence fragments and how to correct them

- ☞ Missing-subject fragments
- ☞ Missing-verb fragments
- ☞ Missing-subject-and-verb fragments
- ☞ Dependent-clause fragments

Skill Preview

Even though a group of words starts with a capital letter and ends with a period, it is not a sentence unless the word group expresses a complete thought. Imagine someone handing you a note with the words below written on it. You would have questions about the words' meaning.

Try writing sentences from these fragments by adding words so that each word group expresses a complete thought.

Students on the first day of the new school year.

_____

Opens its doors.

_____

By the end of the first day of class.

_____

　　Sentence fragments occur when writers leave out part of the sentence. When the missing part is added, the sentence expresses a complete thought. The hard part of getting rid of fragments in your writing is recognizing when you are writing sentence fragments. You will use the skill of identifying subjects and complete verbs to distinguish fragments from sentences, and you will learn how to make fragments into complete sentences.

Spotlight on Writers

Power of Language

Mary J. Blige

"I always want to be a messenger, a person that, you know, that's not afraid to pass on wisdom."

R&B/rap artist and songwriter Mary J. Blige (1971–) knows about the power of language. She dropped out of high school in the eleventh grade and reads on only an eighth-grade level, so she has sometimes had difficulties understanding business contracts. However, Blige developed the courage to admit when she doesn't understand something and ask for an explanation. In her songs, Blige inspires people by writing about how she overcame her low self-esteem and the difficult life she had growing up in a housing project in Yonkers, New York.

What Is a Sentence Fragment?

A sentence fragment is a group of words that does not make sense by itself. A fragment is only part of a sentence because it does not have all three main ingredients of a sentence: ***a subject*** and ***a complete verb*** that express ***a complete thought.***

Fragment: Received a bonus for working overtime last week.

(Who received a bonus check? The subject is missing.)

Sentence: I received a bonus for working overtime last week.

Fragment: The paycheck for this month.

(What about the paycheck for this month? The verb is missing.)

Sentence: The paycheck for this month was larger than for last month.

Fragment: If I earn as much money next month.

(What will happen then? The subject and the verb are missing.)

Sentence: If I earn as much money next month, my credit card can be paid off.

A sentence fragment is a major writing error because it leaves the reader with questions. To correct a sentence fragment and make it a complete sentence, you must add the missing part of the sentence. There are four types of fragments:

missing-subject fragments, missing-verb fragments, missing-subject-and-verb fragments, and **dependent-clause fragments.** After we introduce and explain each kind of fragment, you will practice identifying the subject and complete verb in word groups and correcting sentence fragments by adding the missing part of the sentence.

Missing-Subject Fragments

1.1 When the subject of the sentence is missing, the reader does not know who or what the sentence is about.

To correct a missing-subject fragment, ask who or what the fragment is about, and add a noun (a person, place, thing, or idea) as the subject of the verb.

   ✗ Took the A train on Saturday afternoon. (Who took the A train?)
        S   V
   ✓ The band took the A train Saturday afternoon.

1.2 In a command sentence, the subject *you* is not stated but is implied.

   ✓ Take the A train to get to the ballpark.

This sentence gives directions, and the subject ***you*** is understood but not stated.

Practice 1   Identify each word group as a sentence (S) or fragment (F) by circling the subject and underlining the complete verb. To identify the subject, ask *who or what the word group is about,* and if the subject is missing, add a noun and related words to make the fragment into a sentence.

_____ 1. Will be eating at seven tonight.

_____ 2. Your grandmother will have dinner with us.

_____ 3. Cooked her favorite dish, which is chili.

_____ 4. Also, have made a chocolate cake.

_____ 5. It's her birthday.

_____ 6. Get a birthday card for her.

_____ 7. Has math class tonight.

_____ 8. Possibly may stop by after class.

_____ 9. It's the last meeting of the class.

_____ 10. Please arrive by seven tonight.

Missing-Verb Fragments

2.1 A sentence must contain a complete verb. The verb expresses the action or the state of being of the subject.

To correct a missing-verb fragment, add a complete verb.

   ✗   My tuition and books this term. (What about my tuition and books?)

          S   S   V

   ✓   My tuition and books this term <u>cost</u> over two thousand dollars.

Practice 2   Identify each word group as a sentence (S) or fragment (F) by circling the subject and underlining the complete verb. To identify the complete verb, ask *what word states the action or state of being of the subject,* and if the complete verb is missing, add a complete verb and related words to make the fragment into a sentence.

    _____   1. Richard's friend from his last job in Montana.

    _____   2. A tall man with green eyes and a beard.

    _____   3. He is moving to Wyoming.

    _____   4. His wife got a job there.

    _____   5. Their house with a view of the mountains.

    _____   6. Deer and elk in the front yard.

    _____   7. The weather can be pretty extreme.

    _____   8. Ten feet of snow or more in the winter.

    _____   9. Skiing is a lot of fun.

    _____   10. The fresh air and beautiful surroundings.

2.2 Some fragments contain a verb that is not complete.

Present participles (verbs ending in –ing, such as *taking*) and **past participles** (such as *taken*) always need a helping verb (such as *is, are, has, have, can,* and *will*), or another complete verb must be added to the fragment to make it complete. (For a review of verb forms, see "Parts of Speech," p. A-9.)

   ✗   The utility bill sitting on the table. (What about the utility bill? Add a helping verb or a complete verb.)

              S   V

   ✓   The utility bill <u>is sitting</u> on the table. (A helping verb is added.)

              S   V

   ✓   The utility bill sitting on the table <u>must be paid.</u> (A complete verb is added.)

✗ The movie shown this afternoon.

             S   V

✓ The movie <u>will be shown</u> this afternoon.

Or

            S   V

✓ The movie shown this afternoon <u>started</u> at 4 P.M.

Practice 3 Identify each word group as a sentence (S) or fragment (F) by circling the subject and underlining the complete verb. If the verb is not complete, add a helping verb or complete verb and related words to make the fragment into a sentence.

_____ 1. The kids from the neighborhood gathering in the driveway.

_____ 2. They are getting ready to play basketball.

_____ 3. The ball found in the garage.

_____ 4. An air pump needed to inflate the ball.

_____ 5. The game will start soon.

_____ 6. Everyone hopes to be on Jamal's team.

_____ 7. The boy standing by the car.

_____ 8. He has grown over six inches in the past year.

_____ 9. All the shorter boys including Jeffrey.

_____ 10. One kid gone home early.

Missing-Subject-and-Verb Fragments

3.1 Sometimes the subject and verb of the sentence are missing.

A subject and a complete verb must be added to correct these fragments.

✗ On the ledge above the front door. (Who or what is on the ledge, and what action or state of being is taking place?)

           S   V

✓ A key <u>has been hidden</u> on the ledge above the front door.

Practice 4 Identify each word group as a sentence (S) or fragment (F) by circling the subject and underlining the complete verb. If the subject and verb are missing, add them and related words to make the fragment into a sentence.

___F___ 1. By seven every morning, even in rain and snow.

___F___ 2. Delivered to our front door.

___S___ 3. The newspaper is usually wrapped in plastic.

_____F_____   4. To keep it dry and clean.

_____S_____   5. With a thud, the paper announces its arrival.

_____F_____   6. During breakfast while drinking a cup of coffee at the dining room table.

_____S_____   7. On the other hand, some readers wait to read the paper until later in the day.

_____S_____   8. Everyone has a favorite part of the paper.

_____S_____   9. Some like the comics and the sports section.

_____F_____   10. Others the movie listings and advice columns.

3.2 When the subject and the verb are missing, the fragment can often be corrected by adding it to the sentence before or after the fragment.

   ✗ **Incorrect:** The store gets deliveries every day at 2 P.M. Except on Mondays. (This fragment should be added to the sentence before it.)

   ✓ **Correct:** The store gets deliveries every day at 2 P.M., except on Mondays.

   ✗ **Incorrect:** I like Mexican food. Such as tacos, burritos, and guacamole.

   ✓ **Correct:** I like Mexican food such as tacos, burritos, and guacamole.

Practice 5   Add the underlined fragment to a word group before or after it.

Stressful Life

We all know what it feels like to experience stress. <u>In school, at work, or at home</u>. Schoolwork can be especially stressful. <u>Such as big tests or oral presentations in front of the class</u>. <u>Even while meeting with a teacher after class</u>. Students will feel some anxiety. Also, stress is produced in the workplace. <u>By demanding bosses and difficult co-workers</u>. Many workers will rest the entire weekend. <u>To recover from the work week</u>. Surprisingly, our home life can also be stressful. <u>From all the demands placed on us</u>. The stress comes from the people we care about. <u>For example, children,</u>

<u>spouses, neighbors, and friends</u>. All our important relation-
ships come with demands. <u>And expectations about how we should
act</u>. We are a nation under stress.

Practice 6  *Working Together*

Alone or with a partner, correct the fragments in the passage by adding words or
adding the fragment to the sentence before or after it.

Ways to Reduce Stress

With all the demands of daily life, we need to manage the
stress in our lives. Habits as simple as taking a walk to
unwind after a hard day at work. Can be effective in
reducing stress. Also, refraining from drinking too much
coffee. Lifestyle modifications are definitely the most
effective methods, for reducing stress and anxiety in our
daily life. Start with everyday habits. Such as smoking and
drinking. Any substance that puts more stress on our bodies
will not help us reduce stress. We must try to replace bad
habits with good ones. For instance, aerobic exercise such as
walking, jogging, or biking. Eating healthy foods in moderate
amounts and avoiding refined sugar and fatty foods. Fruits
and vegetables eaten with every meal. And lots of water every
day. Getting exercise and eating right make a big difference.
Never too late to change our lives!

Dependent-Clause Fragments

4.1 Dependent clauses contain a subject and a verb but do not express a complete
thought.

To correct a dependent-clause fragment, add an independent clause contain-
ing a subject and a verb. (Remember that an independent clause is the grammatical name for a sentence.)

S   V
✗ Because school starts in August.
     dependent clause

(Even though this word group contains a subject and verb, we are still left with a question. What will happen because school starts in August?)

S   V   S   V
✓ Because school starts in August, our family <u>will take</u> our vacation in July.
     dependent clause   **independent clause**

Or

S   V   S   V
Our family <u>will take</u> our vacation in July because school starts in August.
     independent clause   *dependent clause*

Practice 7   Correct each dependent-clause fragment by adding an independent clause with a subject and a verb.

1. When consumers buy new electronic products such as computers or televisions,

   <u>They should research all the products</u>

2. Before buyers choose a particular brand,

   <u>They must consider their needs</u>

3. After researching different features and options,

   _____

4. Although the prices can be similar for different brands,

   _____

5. If there is a manufacturer's rebate or in-store discount,

   <u>Cost less</u>

6. Since many consumers want to pay with a credit card,

   <u>they should choose a store that takes th</u>

7. While many stores offer extended warranties on the products they sell,

   <u>Some stores have no warranties</u>

8. Even though most electronics stores sell the same brands.

   _____

9. As the holiday buying season begins after Thanksgiving,

   <u>deals get better</u>

10. Because electronics are so popular with consumers,

    <u>most stores have sales.</u>

Complex sentence - dependent clause followed by an independent clause.

4.2   Dependent-clause fragments are easy to recognize because most start with a subordinating conjunction.

Common Subordinating Conjunctions		
after	in order that	until
although	since	when
as	so that	where
because	that	whereas
before	though	while
if	unless	

4.2.1   When a dependent clause *begins* a sentence, separate the dependent clause from the independent clause with a comma. When a dependent clause *follows* a sentence, **do not** use a comma to separate the dependent clause from the independent clause.

(For more information and practice using commas with dependent clauses, see "Commas," page 325.)

After class is over, I usually go to the library.
dependent clause   **independent clause**

(The dependent clause begins the sentence, and a comma separates it from the independent clause that follows.)

I usually go to the library after class is over.
independent clause   *dependent clause*

(No comma separates the independent clause from the dependent clause that follows.)

Practice 8   Circle the subordinating conjunctions in the following dependent-clause fragments. Then write a sentence using each of the dependent clauses. If the dependent clause begins the sentence, use a comma to separate the dependent clause from the independent clause, but if the dependent clause follows the independent clause that you add, do not use a comma.

1. (Before) the Thanksgiving holiday begins,

   ~~I start planning the menu~~

2. (Because) there is usually a lot of traffic the day before Thanksgiving,

   ~~I do all my shopping early.~~

3. (When) the cooks begin to prepare the Thanksgiving feast,
there is alot of chaos created.

4. (While) the turkey is cooking,
the family play games together.

5. (As) the family arrives for dinner,
we began setting the table.

6. (Since) everyone is hungry,
we all dig in.

7. (If) someone wants to carve the turkey,
here is the knife and fork.

8. (When) dinner is served,
we all began waiting.

9. (Although) everyone is full,
we all still want dessert.

10. (Unless) there is a football game on television,
we all play games.

4.2.2   Dependent clause fragments can sometimes be corrected by taking out the subordinating conjunction that begins the dependent clause. However, this method of correction changes the meaning of the word group.

   ✗ **Fragment:** Since the school term is almost over.

   ✓ **Sentence:** The school term is almost over.

   Or

   $$\text{S} \qquad \text{V}$$
   ✓ Since the school term is almost over, I must prepare for exams.

4.3   Dependent clause fragments can start with a relative pronoun.

   These kinds of dependent clauses generally come after an independent clause. Often these fragments can be added to the sentence that comes before them.

   ✗ My last class is history. Which is my strongest subject.
   $$\text{S} \quad \text{V}$$
   ✓ My last class is history, which is my strongest subject.

Relative Pronouns	
that	whoever
which	whom
whichever	whomever
who	whose

Practice 9  *Working Together*

Alone or with a partner, add the dependent clauses to the sentence before or after them.

Finding a Primary Care Physician

It is important to have a primary care physician, Who can treat you and your family. This doctor must be a person with a personality. That makes him or her easy to relate to. You should think carefully about whether you are more comfortable with a male or female doctor. Because you will have to share intimate details of your life with your doctor. Also, many health experts recommend family practitioners. Who can provide comprehensive care to the entire family. Many people prefer to ask friends for their recommendations. Before they choose a physician. When you go for your first visit, You should take notes about your experience. Since you will learn a lot about the doctor and his or her office. For example, if you are kept waiting for your appointment or the receptionist is rude, You may wish to find a different doctor. Moreover, you may want to find out how you will reach your doctor. When you have an emergency. Most doctors use an answering service. That screens their calls after hours. However, some doctors can be reached on their cell phone or by e-mail. Although they may request that you contact them after hours only during an emergency. A little investigation before you choose a doctor will save you a lot of trouble later on.

Practice 10  *Working Together*

Working in groups of two or three, write one fragment for each topic using your own paper.

1. a popular band or singer   *whom is a popular band or singer.*
2. watching television   *While watching television, with my mom.*
3. a store   *When a store opens,*
4. doctors   *After the doctors' visit.*
5. crime   *Because of the crime in our neighborhood*

Practice 11   Trade the fragments you wrote in Practice 10 with another group, and correct the other group's fragments. Share your corrections with the other group.

CD Connection

Power of Language

On *Writer's Resources* CD-ROM, see *Sentence Fragments* in Grammar/Punctuation/ Mechanics for more information and practice with sentence fragments.

REVIEW EXERCISE 1

Identify each word group as a sentence (S) or fragment (F), and correct each fragment by adding or deleting words to make a complete sentence.

_____F_____ 1. More and more Americans eating on the go.

_____F_____ 2. Breakfast in the car on the way to work.

_____F_____ 3. Lunch from a fast-food restaurant. *is good*

_____S_____ 4. Pizza, the most popular dinnertime fast food for the whole family.

_____S_____ 5. Eating on the go doesn't have to be unhealthful.

_S_   6. Every meal should include vegetables or fruits.

_S_   7. Try to eat fruit twice a day.

_F_   8. Such as apples, oranges, and bananas.

_S_   9. Vegetables are important, too.

_F_   10. Because vegetables contain important vitamins and minerals. are good for you

REVIEW EXERCISE 2

Identify each word group as a sentence (S) or fragment (F), and correct each fragment by adding or deleting words to make a complete sentence.

_S_   1. Here are some ideas for eating healthful, quick meals.

_F_   2. It is Important to eat good sources of protein such as turkey, chicken, and cheese.

_S_   3. Protein curbs the appetite.

_F_   4. Eating fewer carbohydrates such as bread and chips and avoiding fried foods, will keep you healthy

_F_   5. Sugar is a big problem.

_F_   6. Because sugar adds lots of calories.

_F_   7. Hard-boiled eggs, which are the perfect choice for eating on the go. are healthy

_F_   8. Eggs have Lots of protein and easy to pack for lunch.

_F_   9. When you want something sweet for a snack, eat an apple

_S_   10. Multigrain breads and muffins are good choices for snacks, too.

FRAGMENTS EDITING TEST 1

Working alone or in groups of two or three, edit the following passage. First, underline every sentence fragment. Then correct each fragment by adding words or connecting the fragment to a sentence before or after it.

                    Study Session

    Our class held a study session last night, For the final

exam in Math 1001. Because we were still having trouble with some of the material. The professor brought some new

worksheets. ~~To~~ practice using the formulas we have learned.

Problems _were_ taken from old exams. ~~P~~racticing all the skills that

we have been taught, ~~I~~ncluding word problems and graphing

problems. The session lasted for two hours, ~~W~~hich was enough

time to practice and ask questions. Although we were all

tired, ~~We~~ _we_ were happy that we all studied together. We thanked

the professor, ~~Who~~ _who_ wished us luck on the exam.

FRAGMENTS EDITING TEST 2

Correct the fragments in the passage by adding words or connecting fragments to a
sentence before or after the fragments.

Skin Cancer

Melanoma, which is the most serious form of skin cancer.
The number of cases has doubled in the past twenty-five
years. More common in men than women. Occurs most often
in fair-skinned persons and is ten times less common in
African-Americans than in Caucasians. A melanoma can develop
anywhere on the body. But appears mainly on the legs of
women and the upper bodies of men. This deadly disease starts
with overexposure to the sun. Certain people are more vulnerable than others. For example, people with red or blond hair
and blue eyes. Also, anyone who had bad sunburns as a child
or a family history of melanoma. To detect this disease, look
for moles. That appear suddenly. That are either flat or
bumpy, with irregular borders and varied colors. Interest-
ingly, these moles located in areas not normally exposed to
the sun. Such as breasts, buttocks, and scalp. To check for

melanoma. Examine your body regularly, and look for any change in the size or color of moles. Most importantly, everyone should try to avoid overexposure to the sun.

Practicing Your Writing Power

Power of Language

© Thomson Corporation/Heinle Image Resource Bank

Write about a health-care crisis you or a family member or someone you know has gone through. Or explain how you feel about a health-care professional, such as a doctor or dentist, or a health-care facility, such as a hospital, that you have had experience with. After writing your response, check your writing for fragments.

Font 12 double space.
— no fragments.   subj + verb agreements

Name _Seighara Bowdw_

Section _____ Score _____

FRAGMENTS TEST 1

Identify each word group as a sentence (S) or fragment (F), and correct each fragment by adding words to make a complete sentence.

__F__ 1. The spicy food _is_ from Central America and South America.

__S__ 2. There are hundreds of different peppers used in cooking.

__F__ 3. _They are_ Ranging from mild banana peppers to the extremely hot jalapenos.

__F__ 4. Probably the hottest pepper, _is_ the habanero, which looks like a cherry.

__F__ 5. _We eat_ Really hot peppers in everything from eggs to salsa.

__S__ 6. Hot vinegar is used to marinate peppers.

__F__ 7. When a cook prepares peppers for cooking. _she washes them._

__S__ 8. The juices from the pepper can irritate skin and eyes.

__F__ 9. Mexican chipotle sauce added a little at a time. _makes good salsa_

__S__ 10. Serving fruit helps cool off the palate after someone eats very hot sauce.

Name _Leighana Bowen_
Section _____ Score _____

FRAGMENTS TEST 2

Identify each word group as a sentence (S) or fragment (F), and correct each fragment by adding words to make a complete sentence.

__S__ 1. Staying healthy during pregnancy is important.

__F__ 2. What an expectant mother should and should not do during the nine months. _Can be found in this book._

__F__ 3. *She* Should take prenatal vitamins that include folic acid.

__F__ 4. If a new mother smokes cigarettes. _She should stop_

__F__ 5. Regular exercise like walking or swimming. _is good for you._

__F__ 6. Alcohol and recreational drugs are prohibited. _while pregnant._

__F__ 7. Medications prescribed by a doctor and over-the-counter medicines, too, _should be okayd by your doctor._

__F__ 8. _She should_ Avoid hot tubs and saunas because of the excessive heat.

__S__ 9. Any infection should be monitored by a physician.

__F__ 10. _only_ Limited amounts of caffeine during pregnancy. _should be drank._

FRAGMENTS TEST 3

Identify each word group as a sentence (S) or fragment (F), and correct each fragment by adding words to make a complete sentence.

_____   1. As cars become more and more sophisticated.

_____   2. Computers that talk to the driver are common in high-end new cars.

_____   3. Giving directions and alerting the driver to hazards.

_____   4. Because cars use so much technology today.

_____   5. Mechanics that are factory trained to service the new cars.

_____   6. Diagnostic machines are necessary to check a new car.

_____   7. Some seats remember your favorite position.

_____   8. Even an oil change requires diagnostic tools.

_____   9. Although new cars are very expensive to buy.

_____   10. Driving is a technological adventure these days.

Name _____
Section _____   Score _____

FRAGMENTS TEST 4

Identify each word group as a sentence (S) or fragment (F), and correct each fragment by adding words to make a complete sentence.

_____ 1. A list of the most influential cars of the past fifty years.

_____ 2. Not surprisingly, the Jeep Cherokee is on the list.

_____ 3. Driving a 1953 Chevrolet Corvette in the parade.

_____ 4. Millions of people loved the Volkswagen Beetle.

_____ 5. Although the Beetle was the first popular foreign car.

_____ 6. The Dodge Caravan introduced the van to America.

_____ 7. The first popular sports sedan, the BMW 2002.

_____ 8. The Mustang was popular with young people and old people alike.

_____ 9. Including the Ford F-100 truck, which made light trucks popular.

_____ 10. The SUV became popular in the 1990s.

Chapter 12 Run-on Sentences

In this chapter, you will learn to
- ☞ Recognize fused sentences and comma splices
- ☞ Use five methods to correct run-ons

Skill Preview

Run-on sentences occur when two sentences are incorrectly fused together without a period or when two sentences are incorrectly spliced together with a comma. When writers leave out periods and misuse commas, they can create major sentence structure errors. Readers expect a capital letter at the beginning of a sentence and a period at the end. Without these signals of where a complete sentence begins and ends, writing is hard to understand.

Try to correct the run-ons in the following paragraph. Place a period between two complete sentences, and capitalize the first word of the second sentence, or add a word like *for, and, nor, but, or, yet,* or *so* before a comma to connect two complete thoughts.

Vancouver Island

Vancouver Island lies off the coast of British Columbia it is a province of Canada. The weather is very warm the temperature does not drop below freezing during some winters. The island is an unspoiled natural wonder there are vast beaches, hidden coves, rainforests, and mountains. Vancouver Island is home to bears and wolves, also whales and sea lions swim offshore. In earlier times, the island was home to many Native American tribes, they were displaced by Europeans and Asians in the 19th century. Today, the island is home to

thousands of Canadians, they love the natural beauty and
relaxed lifestyle of the island.

There is more than one way to correct the run-ons in the passage. Here is one way.

Vancouver Island lies off the coast of British Columbia.
It is a province of Canada. The weather is very warm, and
the temperature does not drop below freezing during some winters. The island is an unspoiled natural wonder. There are
vast beaches, hidden coves, rainforests, and mountains. Vancouver Island is home to bears and wolves; also, whales and
sea lions swim offshore. In earlier times, the island was
home to many Native American tribes, but they were displaced
by Europeans and Asians in the 19th century. Today, the
island is home to thousands of Canadians because they love
the natural beauty and relaxed lifestyle of the island.

You probably had to reread some sentences because they ran on past the end of the complete thought. You used your common sense about where the complete thoughts began and ended. You also probably used your knowledge of subjects and verbs to help you add periods or connecting words. Once you learn to identify and correct run-ons, you will be able to eliminate these errors from your writing.

What Is a Run-on?

A run-on sentence occurs when an independent clause (**a subject** and **a complete verb** that express **a complete thought**) is incorrectly joined to another independent clause. There are two types of run-on sentences.

A **fused sentence** *fuses*, or runs together, two independent clauses without any punctuation.

✗ The car won't start the battery is dead.

A **comma splice** *splices*, or connects two independent clauses with only a comma.

✗ The car won't start, the battery is dead.

Run-ons contain two pairs of subjects (who or what the sentence is about) and verbs (action or state of being of the subject).

Spotlight on Writers

Power of Language

Natalie Goldberg

"Often I am asked, who taught me how to write? Everything, I want to say. Everything taught me, everything became my teacher though at the time I was not aware of all the teacher shoots that helped me along, that came up in Mr. Clemente's class, in Mr. Cates's, with all the teachers I can't remember anymore, with all the blank times, the daydreaming, the boredom, the American legacy of loneliness and alienation, my Jewish background, the sky, the desk, a pen, the pavement, small towns I've driven through. The list could go on and on until I named every moment I was alive. All of it in mysterious and ordinary ways fed me. Writing became the tool I used to digest my life and to understand, finally, the grace, the gratitude I could feel, not because everything was hunky-dory, but because we can use everything we are. Actually we have no choice. We can't use what someone else had—a great teacher, terrific childhood. That is outside ourselves. And we can't avoid an inch of our own experience; if we do it causes a blur, a bleep, a puffy unreality. Our job is to wake up to everything, because if we slow down enough, we see we our everything."

Natalie Goldberg is the author of *Writing Down the Bones*, a book about using the power of creativity when writing. The above quote is from *Long Quiet Highway*, a book about her journey to becoming a writer.

Practice 1   Identify each run-on as a fused sentence (FS) or comma splice (CS).

_____ 1. The golden retriever is a medium-sized dog, it is one of the most popular pets in the world.

_____ 2. Goldens have won praise for their intelligence their disposition is very gentle and loving.

_____ 3. These dogs are great with children, they are playful and enjoy being touched.

_____ 4. Golden retrievers were first bred in Scotland hunters used them to retrieve water fowl.

_____ 5. These beautiful dogs love to swim, they also love to lie at their owner's feet and be petted.

Recognizing Run-ons

A run-on occurs when two independent clauses, or complete thoughts, are run together. Writers make run-ons when two ideas that seem to go together are incorrectly joined.

Run-ons often occur when writers **repeat the same subject** and add a new verb.

Fused sentence: I <u>don't have</u> a lot of homework I <u>should be finished</u> in an hour.

Run-ons can occur when writers try to **explain a complete thought** with a new complete thought in the same sentence.

Comma splice: I <u>enjoyed</u> the last chapter, it <u>discussed</u> the changes in our culture over the past thirty years.

1.1 To recognize run-ons, you should **identify the subject and complete verb** of the sentence.

Start at the capital letter that begins the sentence, and ask yourself **who or what the sentence is about** and **what word or words express the action or state of being of the subject.** Pay particular attention when you identify a second subject-and-verb pair. A run-on occurs when there is only a comma before the new subject and verb or when there is no punctuation.

Comma splice: The writer <u>gave</u> many examples of cultural changes, he <u>showed</u> pictures from advertising to make his point.

In this comma splice, there are two subject-and-verb pairs: *writer gave* and *he showed.*

1.2 Because a run-on contains two independent clauses, you should be able to separate a run-on into two complete thoughts. A correct sentence cannot be separated into two complete thoughts.

        independent clause   *independent clause*
Fused sentence: Cultural diversity <u>is</u> a positive development it <u>brings</u> new ideas and values to our country.

This fused sentence contains two complete thoughts: *Cultural diversity is a positive development* and *it brings new ideas and values to our country.*

        independent clause
Sentence: Cultural diversity <u>is</u> a positive development and <u>brings</u> new ideas and values to our country.

This sentence cannot be separated into two complete thoughts. *Cultural diversity is a positive development* is a complete thought, but *and brings new ideas and values to our country* is not a complete thought. This sentence contains only one independent clause with one subject and a compound verb.

independent clause   *dependent clause*
Sentence: Cultural diversity <u>is</u> a positive development that brings new ideas and values to our country.

There is only one independent clause with one subject and a verb, plus a dependent clause, *that brings new ideas and values to our country.* Remember that a dependent clause cannot stand alone as a complete thought.

Practice 2   Circle the simple subject(s) and underline the complete verb(s) and write **RO** for a fused sentence or comma splice and **S** for a sentence.

_____ 1. Americans spend a lot of time and money on trying to remain young and healthy.

_____ 2. Baby boomers are now reaching their fifties and sixties they want to stay young as long as possible.

_____ 3. Even young Americans are concerned about maintaining their health and looking good.

_____ 4. Therefore, vitamins are more popular than ever, other nutritional supplements are also gaining popularity.

_____ 5. Sales of nutritional supplements grew over 30 percent in the past five years, sales are expected to top 20 billion dollars this year.

_____ 6. However, there are areas of the nutritional supplements industry that trouble health experts because some products may harm consumers.

_____ 7. Some research has cast doubts on the usefulness of some herbal supplements such as St. John's wort and ginseng.

_____ 8. Ephedra is a supplement that is used to lose weight it has also been linked to a number of deaths.

_____ 9. Most experts agree that harmful supplements should be banned so that consumers are protected.

_____ 10. Health supplements are here to stay most supermarkets and department stores now have entire areas devoted to vitamins and other health products.

Correcting Run-ons

The five main ways to correct run-ons include using different punctuation marks and joining words, called conjunctions. You will want to use all the methods in order to give your writing variety. In later chapters covering commas, semicolons, and sentence combining, you will build on the knowledge you gain here.

Five Ways to Correct Fused Sentences and Comma Splices

Fused sentence: The presentation was very interesting it lasted for over two hours.

Comma splice: The presentation was very interesting, it lasted for over two hours.

1. Use a period **to separate the independent clauses in a run-on into two complete sentences.**

   The presentation was very interesting. It lasted for over two hours.

2. Use **a comma and a coordinating conjunction** to join the two independent clauses.

   The presentation was very interesting, **but** it lasted for over two hours.

3. Use **a semicolon** to join the two independent clauses.

   The presentation was very interesting; it lasted for over two hours.

4. Use **a semicolon and a conjunctive adverb or a transitional expression and a comma** to join the two independent clauses.

   The presentation was very interesting; **however,** it lasted for over two hours.

5. Use **a subordinating conjunction** to make one of the independent clauses into a dependent clause.

   The presentation was very interesting **although** it lasted for over two hours.

2.1 Use **a period** to separate the independent clauses in a run-on into two complete sentences. Be sure to capitalize the first word of the second sentence.

Comma splice: This country is home to people from all over the world, their different perspectives enrich our culture.

Sentence: This country is home to people from all over the world. Their different perspectives enrich our culture.

Practice 3   Identify each item as a run-on (RO) or sentence (S). Correct each run-on by placing a period between the two independent clauses and capitalizing the first word of the second sentence.

_____ 1. Experts have been studying workers' attitudes about the workplace they say workers' attitudes are changing.

_____ 2. The economy has been hard on workers, major issues include job stability and job conditions.

_____ 3. Younger workers who are in Generation X have been particularly challenged by the shifting economy.

_____ 4. Gen X workers bring different skills and values to their jobs than their older coworkers.

_____ 5. Generation X is changing the workplace because its members hold different attitudes than their older coworkers.

_____ 6. Gen X workers see themselves as free agents, they move easily from job to job.

_____ 7. Younger workers don't have the same loyalty to their employers as older employees because their jobs aren't as secure.

_____ 8. In fact, job loyalty is not even an issue for most young employees, they will change jobs four or five times during their careers.

_____ 9. These younger workers choose employers that offer good benefits a stress-free workplace is also important to these workers.

_____ 10. When Gen X workers disagree with policies, they often protest the policies that they don't like.

2.2 Use **a comma and a coordinating conjunction** to join the two independent clauses in a run-on.

Fused Sentence: Our culture includes many different religions we learn to be tolerant of others' beliefs.

Sentence: Our culture includes many different religions**, so** we learn to be tolerant of others' beliefs.

2.2.1 Remember that a comma alone cannot join two independent clauses. A coordinating conjunction <u>and</u> a comma create a **compound sentence**.

Comma splice: Music <u>is influenced</u> by different cultures, popular musicians <u>use</u> rhythms from Africa, the Middle East, and Latin America.

Sentence: Music is influenced by different cultures, **and** popular musicians use rhythms from Africa, the Middle East, and Latin America.

2.2.2 Coordinating conjunctions express the relationship between two ideas. Use the coordinating conjunction that makes clear the relationship between independent clauses when correcting run-ons.

Coordinating Conjunctions

For suggests *because*.
I must leave, **for** I have an appointment.

And means *plus*.
I have class today, **and** the lab is tomorrow.

Nor means *neither idea*.
I don't like broccoli, **nor** do I enjoy cauliflower.
(Notice that the verb comes before the subject in the second independent clause in compound sentences using *nor*.)

But means *contrast*. The second idea is different from the first.
I love to walk, **but** I hate to run.

Or means *either*.
You can take classes in the morning, **or** you can enroll for afternoon classes.

Yet means *but*.
I enjoy fishing, **yet** I don't own a boat.

So means *as a result*. The second idea is an effect of the first.
It's supposed to rain today, **so** I must take my umbrella.

Practice 4   Correct each comma splice by adding a coordinating conjunction after the comma.

1. People from all over the world watch the Super Bowl, it is the most popular show on television.

2. Advertisers pay over a million dollars for each minute of commercials, companies compete to produce the most memorable commercial each year.

3. It is an honor to entertain during halftime, some singers are afraid to sing the national anthem.

4. The football game between the year's two best teams can be exciting, sometimes the game is a boring blowout by one team.

5. Many people invite friends over for a Super Bowl party, some people prefer to watch the game alone or with their family.

Practice 5   Correct each fused sentence by adding a comma and the appropriate coordinating conjunction, and correct each comma splice by adding only the coordinating conjunction.

1. Migraine headaches attack approximately 28 million people 70 to 80 percent of the victims have a family history of migraines.

2. Migraines can be triggered by something external like the weather, they can be caused by something internal like hormones.

3. Nerves surrounding blood vessels in the brain are set off, inflammation is the result.

4. More than fifty different drugs are used to treat migraines none of the drugs are 100 percent effective.

5. One family of drugs can prevent the onset of a migraine, another family of drugs is used once an attack occurs.

6. A drug like Elavil can help reduce the frequency of a migraine, this drug is taken daily.

7. Other therapies for migraines include biofeedback, acupuncture, and vitamin supplements someone who suffers from migraines should consult a doctor for the appropriate treatment.

8. Some herbs may also help a migraine, they sometimes prevent inflammation of the brain.

9. Some people's brains are more sensitive to the stimulants that trigger migraines the goal for these people is to stop pain messages from reaching their brain.

10. Chronic migraine sufferers may need to consider other remedies these therapies include injections of painkillers.

2.3 Use **a semicolon** to join the two independent clauses in a run-on.

(This method is recommended only when the two independent clauses are closely related.)

Fused sentence: I love Italian food my favorites include lasagna and ravioli.

Sentence: I love Italian food; my favorites include lasagna and ravioli.

Practice 6   Identify each item as a run-on (RO) or sentence (S). Correct each run-on by placing a semicolon between the two independent clauses and crossing out unnecessary commas.

_____ 1. Headaches are very common 90 percent of Americans have had at least one headache in the past year.

_____ 2. There are different kinds of headaches, the four most common are tension-type, migraine, cluster, and chronic headaches.

_____ 3. Tension-type headaches affect both sides of the head, and they can last 30 minutes to several days.

_____ 4. Cluster headaches are severe but last only a couple of hours, attacks occur in groups for weeks or months.

_____ 5. Chronic headaches may be the worst because these attacks can occur daily for up to a month at a time.

2.4 Use **a semicolon and a conjunctive adverb or a transitional expression and a comma** to join the two independent clauses in a run-on.

Comma splice: Our fashions are influenced by other cultures, caftans come from the Middle East.

Sentence: Our fashions are influenced by other cultures; **for example,** caftans come from the Middle East.

Conjunctive Adverbs and Transitional Expressions

Also and **moreover** mean the second idea is in **addition** to the first.

However and **on the other hand** mean the second idea **contrasts** with the first.

Therefore and **as a result** mean the second idea is an **effect** of the first.

For example and **for instance** mean the second idea is an **illustration** of the first.

Later and **then** show a relationship in time between the two ideas.

Practice 7   Identify each item as a run-on (RO) or sentence (S). Correct each run-on by using a semicolon, conjunctive adverb, or transitional expression, and a comma between the two independent clauses.

_____ 1. Dog bites are on the rise, it is more important than ever for canines and humans to understand one another.

_____ 2. More than four million people are bitten each year many of them are children.

_____ 3. Dogs communicate by their body language, therefore people need to know what dogs are saying with their bodies.

_____ 4. Dogs will communicate when they are tired of playing, they will walk away and lie down out of reach.

_____ 5. A wagging tail has as many meanings as a human smile the position of the tail is a better indicator of a dog's intentions.

_____ 6. A straight-up tail that is stiff means the dog is alert and confident, however a tail tucked under means that a dog is fearful and stressed.

_____ 7. A dog that has its ears back and tail wagging is saying hello and is usually safe to pet.

_____ 8. When a strange dog becomes still with tail raised and mouth closed, it is warning you to back off.

_____ 9. A dog will communicate that it wants to play by putting its front end on the ground with its rear in the air and barking at you.

_____ 10. Understanding dogs is the best way to prevent dog bites, parents should try to explain canine body language to their children.

2.5 Use **a subordinating conjunction** to make one of the independent clauses in a run-on into a dependent clause.

Fused sentence: Our most popular foods are as American as apple pie we also enjoy foods from other cultures.

dependent clause

Sentence: Although our most popular foods are as American as apple pie, we

independent clause

also enjoy foods from other cultures.

independent clause

Sentence: Our most popular foods are as American as apple pie even though we

dependent clause

also enjoy foods from other cultures.

Note: When a subordinating conjunction begins a sentence, a comma separates the dependent clause from the independent clause. When a subordinating conjunction is in the middle of a sentence, no comma is used to separate the independent clause from the dependent clause that follows. See Chapter 18 for the comma rule when using dependent clauses.

Subordinating Conjunctions

although	after
even though	as
because	before
since	until
if	when
unless	while

For definitions of the subordinating conjunctions, see Chapter 13, page 263.

Practice 8   Underline the appropriate subordinating conjunction to correct the run-on sentence.

1. Exercising doesn't have to be inconvenient (until/because) you can keep a pair of athletic shoes in your car and walk or jog anywhere when you have time.

2. (Before/Since) people spend a lot of time on the phone and in the kitchen, they can put a stationary bike or treadmill nearby to use.

3. (After/Even though) watching television is usually done while resting, it's easy to stretch, do sit-ups, or jump rope while viewing a favorite program.

4. (Although/If) we want to burn more calories, all we have to do is our daily chores.

5. Our daily routine activities are good exercise (because/until) we can burn 150 calories during a half hour of running, walking, or shoveling snow.

6. Many people think that only strenuous exercise counts (although/because) studies show that as little as 30 minutes of moderate activity can help us manage our weight.

7. (After/If) we eat lunch each day, we could walk for half an hour.

8. (Even though/Since) coaching a son's or daughter's sports team can add exercise to our daily routine, many parents benefit physically from making the commitment.

9. (Although/When) we want to have fun, a game of touch football or hide-and-go-seek provides fun exercise.

10. We should think about opportunities to ride a bike such as going to the store or running errands in the neighborhood (since/until) biking is one of the best low-stress forms of exercise.

Practice 9  *Working Together*

Working in groups of two or three, write a fused sentence and a comma splice for each topic using your own paper.

1. paying bills
2. homework
3. parents

Practice 10  *Working Together*

Trade the run-ons you wrote in Practice 9 with another group, and correct the other group's run-ons. Share your corrections with the other group.

CD Connection

Power of Language

On *Writer's Resources* CD-ROM, see *Run-ons* in Grammar/Punctuation/Mechanics for more information and practice with run-ons.

REVIEW EXERCISE 1

Identify each item as a run-on (RO) or sentence (S). Correct each run-on by using one of the five methods.

_____ 1. A stealthy enemy is lurking inside the bodies of millions of Americans, some experts fear this foe will prove as devastating as AIDS.

_____ 2. This silent killer is dangerous because it can sit in the body before any symptoms appear.

_____ 3. The name of this killer is Hepatitis C it is a virus.

_____ 4. Although the virus may hide unnoticed for decades, the disease can eventually cause permanent liver damage.

_____ 5. Each year in the United States, between 8,000 and 10,000 people die.

_____ 6. 35,000 new cases are being reported in this country each year, the dangers are much greater in less-developed countries.

_____ 7. The virus is transmitted by blood, then it may go undetected for years.

_____ 8. People who are infected may feel perfectly healthy, however the disease is destroying their liver.

_____ 9. Infected people often don't recognize the symptoms, these include fatigue, joint aches, and loss of appetite.

_____ 10. The virus eventually develops into active liver disease, and liver cancer or cirrhosis can result.

REVIEW EXERCISE 2

Identify each item as a run-on (RO) or sentence (S). Correct each run-on by using one of the five methods.

_____ 1. There was no standard screening for the hepatitis C virus before 1992, people who received blood transfusions in the 1970s and 1980s are at particular risk for having the disease.

_____ 2. Many victims of hepatitis C are now in their forties and fifties they have no idea that they are infected.

_____ 3. People who received transfusions in the 1970s and 1980s should be tested for the virus.

_____ 4. Others at risk include people who were exposed to needles through IV drugs, also anyone who has gotten a tattoo or body piercing is at risk.

___/___ 5. Hepatitis C can be transmitted through sexual activity people who have had multiple partners are at greater risk.

_____ 6. Hepatitis C becomes active within 20 years of contracting it, eventually many victims need a liver transplant to survive.

_____ 7. If the infection is caught early, the vast majority of patients can live very comfortably with the disease.

_____ 8. There is about a 55 percent cure rate for the disease, moreover many victims go back to leading normal lives.

_____ 9. Drug therapy has begun to be successful, and a combination of two drugs has been proven to control the disease.

_____ 10. Scientists are now testing a vaccine, it is designed to prevent infection.

RUN-ONS EDITING TEST 1

Working in groups of two or three, edit the following passage. First, underline every run-on sentence. Then use one of the five methods to correct each run-on.

Bullying

Children's picking on other children has never before gotten the attention it is getting today. Bullying was always shrugged off as kids just being kids, now it is seen as a factor in deadly school shootings. Parents, school

administrators, and the federal government are all focusing
on the problem and looking for ways to stop it. Schools have
begun bullying prevention classes, also authorities have
reached out to parents. Everyone agrees that bullying hampers
learning and contributes to school violence it is very common
in public schools. Bullying is defined as aggressive and
repeated behavior it is based on an imbalance of power
between students. This behavior varies from taunting and name
calling to harassment through the Internet, for example -
students might use e-mail to intimidate other students. -
Millions of kids are affected, about 30 percent of students
report being victims. Even more students witness instances of
bullying they experience fear of reporting it or fear that
the bully may turn on them. While students who are bullied
miss more school than the average student, bullies are more
likely to carry weapons and to be violent on school grounds.
The federal government is funding a campaign to combat
bullying, the government will look for support from law
enforcement and civic and religious groups. If we all work
together, maybe we can change children's attitudes and bring
bullying to a halt.

RUN-ONS EDITING TEST 2

Correct any run-ons in the following passage.

Combating Bullying

Most experts agree that eradicating bullying will take the
intervention of school authorities and parents, they must be

supported by law enforcement and the government. Parents will be the most effective adults in the campaign to stop bullying. They must teach their children to be assertive when confronted by a bully, children should avoid violence and get help from adults. When parents take an interest in day-to-day school activities, their kids are more likely to reveal incidences of bullying. School children should keep records of bullying, then they will have evidence to show authorities. Children who witness harassment should go to an adult immediately if anyone is in danger of being harmed. They shouldn't watch the bullying attention just encourages the bully. Also, children shouldn't laugh at kids who are being picked on because it just makes the situation worse. Most importantly, children who are victims should be respected everyone should refuse to believe rumors and avoid spreading them. Empowering children to do the right thing will require the efforts of all of us and all of our wisdom.

Practicing Your Writing Power

Power of
Language

© Thomson Corporation/Heinle Image Resource Bank

Explore one memory you have of elementary school. In one page, describe what you remember of that one exact time in elementary school. Try to recall what people and things looked like, and try to express how you felt during that time of your life. After writing, check each sentence to make sure it is not a run-on.

Name _____

Section _____   Score _____

RUN-ONS TEST 1

Identify each item as a run-on (RO) or sentence (S). Correct each run-on by using one of the five methods.

_____ 1. We all want to eat more healthfully, smart eating can help.

_____ 2. When ordering at a restaurant, diners can ask for half the usual amount in order to cut calories.

_____ 3. The sauces on pasta make a big difference tomato-based sauces have less fat and fewer calories than cream sauces.

_____ 4. White bread provides extra carbohydrates, it should be avoided.

_____ 5. We should limit our intake of white bread, then we will cut hundreds of calories from our meal.

_____ 6. Soups are a great way to fill up without taking in unhealthful fat or unwanted calories.

_____ 7. Fried foods should be avoided or limited, the fat content is always high and unhealthful.

_____ 8. Simply reading the labels of foods we buy will help us to avoid caloric catastrophes, for example little cookies with hundreds of calories won't taste as good once we know their contents.

_____ 9. We should eat more vegetables, too they provide necessary nutrients with very few calories.

_____ 10. Fruits are nutritious, and tasty fruits are often overlooked as a healthful substitute for dessert.

Name _____
Section _____ Score _____

RUN-ONS TEST 2

Identify each item as a run-on (RO) or sentence (S). Correct each run-on by using one of the five methods.

_____ 1. Cutting calories is the key to a healthy diet, there are a number of easy steps we can take to control our caloric intake.

_____ 2. Dieticians recommend trading a dinner plate for a salad plate we will wind up eating smaller portions.

_____ 3. Instead of ordering a super-size or large portion when ordering fast food, we can ask for a kid-size portion.

_____ 4. Studies show that we can trick our stomachs into thinking we are full, so we should start with a large salad with very little dressing.

_____ 5. When we cook meats, we should broil or bake since those methods are much more healthful than frying.

_____ 6. Cooking oils add a lot of calories, therefore we should measure oil carefully or use cooking sprays.

_____ 7. A tablespoon of oil contains 120 calories, a tablespoon of butter contains 100 calories.

_____ 8. Nibbling on snacks is a bad idea, instead it is better to wait for a full meal when hungry.

_____ 9. Because some specialty coffees carry lots of calories, coffee lovers should consider drinking black coffee or coffee with skim milk.

_____ 10. Finally, keep high-calorie foods like cookies out of sight it is better to have fruits on display in case you want a snack.

Name _____

Section _____   Score _____

RUN-ONS TEST 3

Identify each item as a run-on (RO) or sentence (S). Correct each run-on by using one of the five methods.

_____ 1. All of us want to save money, there are some easy ways available to help us.

_____ 2. Over 10 percent of all gift certificates go unredeemed, so be sure to use that free movie pass that your grandmother gave you for your birthday.

_____ 3. Most of us would do well to set financial goals, then we need to make a budget and stick to it.

_____ 4. The first step is to record all of our expenditures, however it is easy to forget to write down every purchase we make or bill we pay.

_____ 5. One place we can look for savings is in our credit card purchases since late fees alone add up to significant money.

_____ 6. More than 50 million Americans don't pay their credit-card balance in full each month, they must pay high interest charges of 15 percent or more.

_____ 7. Although Americans pay more than 70 billion dollars in credit-card interest payments every year, this money buys nothing but time to pay off the credit debt later.

_____ 8. It is a good idea to examine monthly bills for charges we can reduce or eliminate such as membership dues for a health club we don't use.

_____ 9. Also, cell phone and Internet service payments should be examined, maybe we can do without some of our conveniences if we need to cut our expenses.

_____ 10. It's a good idea to look at our spending patterns because common sense and a little restraint can add up to large savings.

Name _____

Section _____ Score _____

RUN-ONS TEST 4

Identify each item as a run-on (RO) or sentence (S). Correct each run-on by using one of the five methods.

_____ 1. Our daily lives and habits change over time, many common everyday objects eventually become extinct.

_____ 2. As technology improves our lives, some gadgets we use every day may disappear.

_____ 3. Today, we all carry cell phones when away from home, in the past we all used phone booths.

_____ 4. It is hard to find a phone booth today because public phones have given way to private cell phones.

_____ 5. Another common tool we no longer use is the typewriter, today almost everyone uses a computer to word process a document.

_____ 6. Along with the public telephone and the typewriter, carbon paper is a thing of the past.

_____ 7. Even in the computer age, certain common objects are becoming extinct, for example the floppy disk has been replaced by the CD.

_____ 8. Even though VCR tapes are still available, they may disappear as more people use DVDs.

_____ 9. Incredibly, eyeglasses are endangered, laser surgery someday will make glasses unnecessary.

_____ 10. Life goes on pretty much as it always has only the objects we take for granted sometimes disappear.

Chapter 13 Sentence Combining

In this chapter, you will learn to combine ideas using the techniques of coordination and subordination with

- Compound sentences
- Compound predicates
- Complex sentences
- Compound-complex sentences

Skill Preview

Sentence combining is a powerful way to improve our writing. Because we often begin writing the way we speak, we rely on simple sentences. However, there are a number of drawbacks to writing sentences that contain only one independent clause. Simple sentences don't convey as much information as the other sentence types, and the information is not connected by conjunctions that help the reader understand the relationship between ideas. In this chapter, you will use sentence-combining techniques to create varied sentence patterns that connect ideas and show the relationship between them.

Compare the following two paragraphs.

```
                    The Samurai

    Samurai were traditional soldiers in Japan. They were born
into the warrior class. The samurai protected feudal lords
from 1000 to 1850. This warrior class lived by a strict code
of conduct. The code of contact was called Bushido. Loyalty,
self-control, and honor all motivated the samurai. These
values made them incredibly dedicated soldiers. Samurai were
```

extremely loyal to their master. They would fight to the death. They would not surrender. The samurai felt great shame when they lost in battle. Sometimes they would commit suicide rather than surrender. The samurai are gone today. Their values are still alive in Japan. Workers have lifelong loyalty to the companies they work for. Even students exhibit samurai values. Students are loyal and respectful of their teachers. They study hard to honor their teachers. They feel great shame when they don't perform well on tests. The Japanese are proud of their samurai heritage.

The paragraph above and the one below express the same ideas. The paragraph above uses all simple sentences. In the paragraph below, the writer has used sentence-combining strategies to combine sentences and connect ideas. Notice how the relationship between ideas is clearer in the second version. The bold words show the changes.

Circle the sets of sentences in the paragraph above that are combined in its revision below.

Samurai were traditional soldiers in Japan **who** were born into the warrior class**, and** the samurai protected feudal lords from 1000 to 1850. This warrior class lived by a strict code of conduct **that** was called Bushido. Loyalty, self-control, and honor all motivated the samurai**, and** these values made them incredibly dedicated soldiers. Samurai were extremely loyal to their master**, so** they would fight to the death **and** not surrender. **Because** the samurai felt great shame when they lost in battle**,** sometimes they would commit suicide rather than surrender. **Although** the samurai are gone today**,** their values are still alive in Japan. Workers have lifelong loyalty to the companies they work for**, and** even students exhibit samurai values. **Since** students are loyal and respectful of their teachers, they study hard to honor their teachers, **and** they feel great shame when they don't perform well on tests. The Japanese are proud of their samurai heritage.

Spotlight on Writers

William Zinsser

"It's not enough for a nonfiction writer to just write good, clean sentences; he must organize those sentences into a coherent shape."

William Zinsser (1922–) is a newspaper reporter, magazine writer, editor, teacher, and writing coach. He has written fifteen books, including books on jazz and professional baseball's spring training. He currently teaches at Columbia University's Graduate School of Journalism in New York.

The Sentence Combining Process

Step 1. Express ideas in simple sentences (independent clauses).

Step 2. Determine the relationship between ideas.

Step 3. Combine sentences using appropriate conjunctions into compound, complex, and compound-complex sentences to make the relationship between ideas clear.

Simple sentences: The samurai are gone today. Their values are still alive in Japan.

Compound sentence: The samurai are gone today, yet their values are still alive in Japan.

Complex sentence: Although the samurai are gone today, their values are still alive in Japan.

Compound-complex sentence: Since students are loyal to and respectful of their teachers, they study hard to honor their teachers, and they feel great shame when they don't perform well on tests.

Recognizing the Relationship Between Ideas

The first step in combining ideas is recognizing the relationship between the ideas a writer wants to combine. The most common relationships between two ideas are **addition, contrast,** and **consequence.**

1.1 **Addition** means that two ideas are **similar** in meaning. Often the second idea *adds* more information to the first.

Samurai were <u>traditional soldiers</u> in Japan. They were born into the <u>warrior class.</u>

This warrior class lived by <u>a strict code of conduct.</u> The code of conduct was <u>called Bushido.</u>

(The underlined words in each pair of sentences are similar ideas.)

1.2 **Contrast** means that two ideas are **different or opposite** in meaning. The second idea expresses an idea *contrary* to the first.

The samurai <u>are gone</u> today. Their values are <u>still alive</u> in Japan.

History 101 is an <u>interesting class.</u> Marketing 241 is a <u>boring class.</u>

(The underlined words in each pair of sentences are contrary ideas.)

1.3 **Consequence** means that one idea is a **cause or effect** of the other. The second idea is a *result* of the first idea.

Samurai were <u>extremely loyal</u> to their master. They would <u>fight to the death.</u>

The samurai felt great <u>shame when they lost in battle.</u> Sometimes they would <u>commit suicide rather than surrender.</u>

(The underlined words in each pair of sentences show a cause and effect relationship.)

Practice 1   Determine the relationship between the two ideas in each item. Write Add for Addition, Cont for Contrast, or Cons for Consequence.

_____   1. August is a hot month in Maine. September can be quite cool.

_____   2. Many campers enjoy swimming. Most campers also like hiking in the woods.

_____   3. There is no electricity at the campsites. Cooking must be done over a fire.

_____ 4. The air is fresh and clean. Sometimes there are bugs.

_____ 5. The weather is so beautiful. The campground is usually full.

_____ 6. The campground is popular with families. Groups from churches and schools stay in the group sites.

_____ 7. The showers are not popular. There is no hot water.

_____ 8. Bears sometimes visit the campground at night. There have been no reports of bear attacks.

_____ 9. Pets are allowed in the campsites. Some dog owners are afraid that the bears will attack their dogs.

_____ 10. Snakes have been seen on the trails. No snakebites have been reported.

Sentence-Combining Strategies

Once a writer determines the relationship between the ideas to combine, there are two primary strategies for combining sentences: **coordination** and **subordination.** Writers use both strategies to combine ideas and create varied sentences.

Coordination

Coordination means making equal ideas work together. The compound sentence pattern uses coordination. Writers also use coordination to combine predicates of sentences.

2.1 Writers use the compound sentence to coordinate two independent clauses with a comma and a coordinating conjunction (**for, and, nor, but, or, yet, so**).

Compound sentence = Independent clause, *coordinating conjunction* independent clause.

Japanese students study hard to honor their teachers, **and** they feel great shame when they don't perform well on tests.

2.2 When combining independent clauses with a comma and a coordinating conjunction, determine the relationship between the ideas, and choose the coordinating conjunction that best expresses the relationship.

Coordinating Conjunctions

For suggests consequence and means *because.*

The roast is burnt, **for** it was left in the oven too long.

And adds two independent clauses that are similar and means *plus.*

The peas are fresh, **and** they are cooked perfectly.

Nor negates both independent clauses and means *neither idea.*

I don't like broccoli, **nor** do I enjoy cauliflower.

(Notice that the verb comes before the subject in the second independent clause in compound sentences using *nor.*)

But contrasts two independent clauses and means *however.*

I love the taste of chicken, **but** I don't like turkey.

Or offers the two independent clauses as equal choices and means *either.*

You can order a full course dinner, **or** you can order each item separately.

Yet limits or contrasts two independent clauses and means *but.*

The fried catfish is famous at this restaurant, **yet** I don't want to eat fish tonight.

So shows consequence and means *as a result.*

Cherry pie is the special dessert today, **so** I will order a slice after dinner.

Practice 2 Combine each pair of sentences into a compound sentence. Use an appropriate coordinating conjunction that shows the relationship between the ideas. (Sometimes, more than one coordinating conjunction expresses the relationship.)

Example:

Sentence 1: Some old fitness fictions, such as "no pain, no gain," are fading fast.

Sentence 2: Lots of misconceptions about exercise still exist.

Combined: Some old fitness fictions, such as "no pain, no gain," are fading fast, but lots of misconceptions about exercise still exist.

(*But*—or *yet*—expresses the contrasting relationship between the two ideas.)

1. Some people think that only a hard workout counts as exercise.
   They don't start an exercise program until they are ready to work out hard.

   _____

   _____

2. Research shows that any exercise is better than none.
   As little as one hour of exercise per week reduces the risk of heart disease.

   _____

   _____

3. Yoga is a gentle form of exercise.
   Some styles of yoga are actually quite demanding physically.

   _____

   _____

4. Exercise does not ensure weight loss.
   Exercising does not always reduce stress.

   _____

   _____

5. Swimming is low-impact exercise.
   Water aerobics is also good for reducing wear and tear on the body.

   _____

   _____

2.3 Sometimes the predicates (the complete verb and all the words that modify it) of two sentences can be combined with a coordinating conjunction.

        predicate   *predicate*

The samurai code runs deep in Japan. It affects the behavior of almost all Japanese.

The samurai code runs deep in Japan **and** affects the behavior of almost all Japanese.

Note: When writers combine the predicates of two sentences, *no comma* is needed.

Practice 3   Combine the predicates of each pair of sentences using the appropriate coordinating conjunction. Remember that no comma is used before the coordinating conjunction.

Example:

Sentence 1: Water-fitness programs are beneficial for everyone.

Sentence 2: They are challenging and effective even for athletes.

Combined: Water-fitness programs are beneficial for everyone and are challenging and effective even for athletes.

1. Home gyms provide good exercise.
   They reduce travel time for exercise.

   _____

   _____

2. People with special needs will enjoy home gyms.
   They won't get to socialize with others at a gym.

   _____

   _____

3. The best form of exercise is the one you can do regularly.
   The best exercise is exercise you can enjoy.

   _____

   _____

4. Fast walking is rigorous enough to benefit the cardiovascular system. It is gentle enough to keep walkers from getting injured.

_____

_____

5. Most fitness experts believe that strength training is important.
   They say that working out with weights twice a week is optimal.

_____

_____

Practice 4   *Working Together*

In groups of two or three, combine the ideas in each item in Practice 1 into a compound sentence or a sentence with a compound predicate. Then compare your answers with other groups to see the different ways that the ideas can be combined.

Subordination

Subordination means to make one idea *subordinate* or less important than a second idea. The complex sentence type uses subordination. The main idea is expressed in an independent clause, and the subordinate idea is expressed in a dependent clause.

> Complex sentence = Independent clause + dependent clause.

Because the samurai felt great shame when they lost in battle, sometimes they would commit suicide rather than surrender.

This warrior class lived by a strict code of conduct that was called Bushido.

3.1 One method of subordinating one idea to another is to use a **subordinating conjunction** to make one idea into a dependent clause.

Simple sentences: The samurai are gone today. Their values are still alive in Japan.

Complex sentences: Even though the samurai are gone today, their values are still alive in Japan.

The samurai are gone today although their values are still alive in Japan.

Note: When a subordinating conjunction starts the sentence, a comma separates the dependent clause from the independent clause it introduces. When the dependent clause follows the independent clause in a complex sentence, no comma is needed. For more information and practice with commas in introductory elements, see Chapter 18, page 328.

3.2 To combine independent clauses with a subordinating conjunction, determine the relationship between the ideas, and choose the conjunction that best expresses the relationship.

Subordinating Conjunctions

One Idea Is a Contrast of the Other

although	whereas
even though	while
though	

Although the team lost, it is still in first place.

The best player scored no points **even though** she is the team's leading scorer.

One Idea Is a Consequence of the Other

as	since
because	

Since there is no food in the house, we should go out to eat.

I have to study tonight **because** there is a test tomorrow.

One Idea Is a Condition of the Other

if	unless

If it is raining outside, you should wear your raincoat.

My sister won't be able to go on vacation **unless** she saves some money for a plane ticket.

One Idea Is Related in Time to the Other

after	until
as	when
before	while

After I get off work, I will work out.

My father always reads the newspaper **while** he eats breakfast.

Practice 5   Combine each pair of ideas by using an appropriate subordinating conjunction. Be sure to separate the dependent clause from the independent clause with a comma when you start the sentence with the subordinating conjunction. Do not use a comma when the subordinating conjunction comes in the middle of the sentence.

Example:

Houses built before 1920 are very different from new houses. Old homes are usually larger but come with fewer modern conveniences.

Houses built before 1920 are very different from new houses **because** old homes are usually larger but come with fewer modern conveniences.

(*Because*—or *since*—expresses the relationship of consequence between the two ideas.)

1. An older home only costs half of what a newer home costs.
   An older home doesn't usually have a garage or pool.

   _____

   _____

2. The median price of an old home may be as little as $100,000.
   A new home will cost almost $200,000.

   _____

   _____

3. Many young home buyers are attracted to old houses.
   They like the low price and sturdy construction.

   _____

   _____

4. Many buyers move into an old home.
   They must renovate the house's electrical wiring and heating and cooling systems.

   _____

   _____

5. Home buyers want to find an old house with lots of charm.
   They should look in older neighborhoods.

   _____

   _____

3.3 Writers use relative pronouns to combine sentences into complex sentences. Use *who* to take the place of people. Use *which* and *that* to take the place of nouns that are things or ideas.

Samurai were traditional soldiers in Japan. They were born into the warrior class.
Samurai were traditional soldiers in Japan **who** were born into the warrior class.

This warrior class lived by a strict code of conduct. The code of conduct was called Bushido.
This warrior class lived by a strict code of conduct **that** was called Bushido.

Relative Pronouns

that	whoever
which	whom
whichever	whomever
who	whose

3.3.1 Commas separate a dependent clause that is nonrestrictive and interrupts the flow of the sentence. Nonrestrictive information is additional information to the sentence and does not change the meaning of the sentence when removed. Do not use commas when the information in the dependent clause is necessary information. In general, dependent clauses that begin with *which* need commas, and dependent clauses that start with *that* do not need commas.

My favorite book**, which** is entitled *Hours of the Day,* is more than four hundred pages long.

The books **that** I bought are heavy.

In the first example, "which is entitled *Hours of the Day,*" is nonrestrictive information about my favorite book that interrupts the flow of the sentence, so commas set off the clause from the rest of the sentence. In the second example, the dependent clause *that I bought* is necessary information to restrict or define which books are heavy, so no commas are needed. For more information and practice with interrupters, see Chapter 18, page 330.

Practice 6   Use a relative pronoun to combine the pair of sentences in each item.

1. Turmeric is a major spice in curry powder.
   This spice may have anticancer properties.

   _____

   _____

2. Some commonly prescribed medications such as iron and blood pressure medicines are so potent.
   Swallowing just one or two pills can kill a child.

   _____

   _____

3. Pregnant women should limit their intake of albacore tuna.
   It contains high levels of poisonous mercury.

   _____

   _____

4. It is important to keep medications away from children.
   Kids sometimes want to experiment with pills they see their parents take.

   _____

   _____

5. Medications get too old to use safely.
   They should be thrown out.

   _____

   _____

Practice 7   Use a relative pronoun or subordinating conjunction to combine the item pairs.

1. Feeling stressed at work is very common.
   Most workers don't admit their stress to co-workers.
   (Hint: Use a subordinating conjunction that shows *contrast.*)

   _____

   _____

2. Stress might come from a demanding boss or difficult employee.
   People often think that stress is just part of the job.
   (Hint: Use a relative pronoun to put the information in the first sentence into the
   second sentence.)

   _____

   _____

3. Prolonged stress can actually kill people.
   Stress should be treated as a serious ailment.
   (Hint: Use a subordinating conjunction that shows *consequence.*)

   _____

   _____

4. Most people cannot accurately judge their own stress level.
   They should get checked by a doctor or mental health professional.
   (Hint: Use a subordinating conjunction that shows *contrast.*)

   _____

   _____

5. Workers may be able to eliminate some sources of stress.
   These sources include unnecessary tasks and self-criticism.
   (Hint: Use a relative pronoun to include the ideas in the second sentence in the first
   sentence.)

   _____

   _____

Practice 8  *Working Together*

In groups of two or three, write a complex sentence for each item in Practice 1. Then
compare your answers with other groups.

Coordination and Subordination

When writers want to combine three or more ideas, they may use coordination and subordination to write compound-complex sentences.

Simple sentences: Samurai were traditional soldiers in Japan. They were born into the warrior class. The samurai protected feudal lords from 1000 to 1850.

Compound-complex sentence: Samurai were traditional soldiers in Japan **who** were born into the warrior class**, and** the samurai protected feudal lords from 1000 to 1850.

4.1 Compound-complex sentences combine dependent clauses and independent clauses in many ways. Here are some of the most common combinations.

Compound-complex sentence = Dependent clause, independent clause, coordinating conjunction independent clause.

Although our computer is broken, I must type and print my paper, so I will go to the writing lab.

Compound-complex sentence = Independent clause + dependent clause, coordinating conjunction independent clause.

I love my iMac computer, which is made by Apple, and I hope to buy the new model soon.

Compound-complex sentence = Independent clause, coordinating conjunction dependent clause, independent clause.

The plane is boarding now, and although it is snowing, we should depart on time.

4.2 To write compound-complex sentences, determine the relationship between the ideas and choose the appropriate conjunction.

	Addition	Contrast	Consequence
Coordinating conjunctions	and	but yet	so for
Subordinating conjunctions	along with in addition to	even though although while though	because since
Relative pronouns	that which who		

Practice 9   Working in groups or alone, use subordination and coordination to combine ideas in each item into one sentence.

1. Applying for a job can be challenging.
   Workers must fill out applications.
   Workers must provide accurate information.

   _____

   _____

2. Applicants are asked for detailed information.
   The information includes addresses and phone numbers of references.
   The information can be hard to get.

   _____

   _____

3. Handwriting on the application must be easy to read.
   Applicants could lose the position.

   _____

   _____

4. The information must be accurate.
   Applicants should bring their contact information with them.
   Applicants should check the accuracy of any addresses and phone numbers they provide.

   _____

   _____

5. Employers want to know background information on job applicants.
   Employers may ask about past convictions.
   They may demand explanations about any criminal convictions.

   _____

   _____

   _____

Practice 10   Working in groups or alone, use subordination and/or coordination to combine ideas in each item into one sentence.

1. The job interview is crucial to getting a job.
   Job applicants should prepare carefully.

   _____

2. Employers usually ask the applicant questions about work history.
   Applicants should try to predict the questions they might be asked.
   They should practice their possible responses to those questions.

   _____

   _____

   _____

3. The employer may not be dressed up.
   The job applicant should dress appropriately.
   Appropriate attire means clothing that would be worn on the job.

   _____

   _____

4. Applicants want to make a good impression.
   They should arrive ten minutes early for the interview.
   Being late to the interview may cost applicants the job.

   _____

   _____

5. Showing good manners during the interview is important.
   Applicants should shake hands at the beginning of the interview.
   They should thank the interviewer at the end of the interview.

   _____

   _____

   _____

CD Connection

Power of
Language

On *Writer's Resources* CD-ROM, see *Sentence Combining* in Writing Elements for
more information and practice with sentence combining.

REVIEW EXERCISE 1

Use coordination or subordination to combine the sentences in each item.

1. Very few Americans used cell phones ten years ago.
   Now almost every adult owns a cell phone.

   _____

   _____

2. We can talk to friends and family from anywhere.
   We can also use our cell phone to call for help in an emergency.

   _____

   _____

3. Motorists may want to call the police to report a drunk driver.
   Drivers of stalled cars can call a tow truck.

   _____

   _____

4. Everyone should carry a cell phone in the car.
   No one should talk on the phone while driving.

   _____

5. There is a phone for everyone.
   Cell phones come in many sizes, shapes, and colors.

   _____

   _____

REVIEW EXERCISE 2

Use coordination or subordination to combine the sentences in each item.

1. Cell phones offer everyone entertainment possibilities.
   The entertainment possibilities include games like solitaire and tic-tac-toe.

   _____

   _____

2. Mobile phones have a date book.
   Phones also provide an address book.

   _____

   _____

3. Most cell phones enable users to access the Internet.
   Callers can check the weather.

   _____

   _____

4. Some cell phone users like to send text messages.
   Text messages can be sent and received quietly without beeps and ringing.

   _____

   _____

5. Most of us wonder how we could live without cell phones.
   They provide us with so many benefits.

   _____

   _____

REVIEW EXERCISE 3

Use coordination or subordination to combine the sentences in each item.

1. Most of us love the convenience of the cell phone.
   We hate to hear a cell phone ring during class or a movie.

   _____

   _____

2. Cell phones are especially annoying during class discussions and exams.
   Most teachers forbid phones in class.

   _____

   _____

3. Taking a call while driving can be dangerous.
   The driver is not concentrating on the road.

   _____

   _____

4. Cell phone etiquette is very important.
   Having good cell phone manners means being sensitive to the time and place of our calls.

   _____

   _____

5. Cell phones can be a blessing.
   They can be a curse.

   _____

   _____

Practicing Your Writing Power

Power of Language

© Thomson Corporation/Heinle Image Resource Bank

Explain the advantages and disadvantages of owning a cell phone. If you own a cell phone, explain why you use it and when. Tell about the phone you own and calling plan you use. What features of the phone and calling plan do you like and dislike? If you do not own a cell phone, explain why you don't own one. Tell why you would like one or don't want one. Try to use the sentence-combining strategies that you practiced in this chapter, and use a variety of sentence patterns in your response.

SENTENCE-COMBINING EDITING TEST

Working in groups of two or three, identify pairs of sentences that can be combined. Then rewrite the following passage using at least one compound, one complex, and one compound-complex sentence.

Shaping Up

Researchers have studied America's eating habits. These studies have found that Americans are increasingly becoming overweight. Some companies are doing something about the problem. These companies are taking steps to get their employees to exercise more. The companies are also trying to get employees to eat less. One step is to put gyms inside office buildings. Employees can exercise during a break. They can exercise before or after work. Businesses are encouraging exercise in other ways, too. They make the elevators run slowly. Employees may find taking the stairs takes less time. Also, cafeterias are placed far away from offices. Workers must walk to eat. These tactics make people get out of their offices. People move around more. Getting into shape is the goal. Getting to know other employees is an added benefit.

_____

_____

_____

_____

_____

_____

_____

_____

_____

Chapter 14 Pronoun Agreement

In this chapter you will learn about

- 🖝 Pronoun agreement
- 🖝 Avoiding shifts in number and person

Skill Preview

Pronouns are words such as *he, they,* and *it* that take the place of nouns. Pronouns allow us to avoid unnecessary repetition of nouns.

Read the following passage and notice how repetitious it is when pronouns are not used to replace nouns. Eliminate the repetition by writing a pronoun above each italicized noun.

Alexander decided that *Alexander* wanted to buy a new car. *Alexander* asked *Alexander's* parents whether *Alexander's* parents could loan *Alexander* the money, and *Alexander's* parents agreed to loan *Alexander* the money, under one condition: *Alexander* had to keep *Alexander's* grades up or *Alexander's* parents would take *Alexander's* new car away.

Compare your changes with the ones made below.

Alexander decided that *he* wanted to buy a new car. *He* asked *his* parents whether *they* could loan *him* the money, and *they* agreed to loan *him* enough money, under one condition: *he* had to keep *his* grades up or *they* would take *his* new car away.

Pronouns help us avoid repetition. However, using the incorrect pronoun or unnecessarily shifting pronoun number or person can cause confusion.

Spotlight on Writers

Power of Language

Phillis Wheatley

Phillis Wheatley (1753–1784) was the first African-American to publish a book. She was born in Africa, but she was sold as a slave at the age of seven to the Wheatley family in Boston. The Wheatleys encouraged her gift for writing poetry, and they and their friends helped finance the publication of her book of poetry. Her fame in both the colonies and England brought her freedom from slavery in 1773. She was a strong supporter of independence during the Revolutionary War but believed that slavery was the issue that kept whites from heroism. She felt whites could not "hope to find/Divine acceptance with th' Almighty mind" when "they disgrace/And hold in bondage Afric's blameless race."

These rules will help you avoid pronoun agreement errors in your writing.

1. A pronoun must agree with its antecedent (the word or words it replaces).
2. Pronouns should not shift unnecessarily in number or person.

Pronoun Agreement

Personal Pronouns	
Singular Pronouns	**Plural Pronouns**
I	we
you	they
he	us
she	them
it	our
me	ours
him	your
her	yours
mine	their
yours	theirs
his	
hers	
its	

1.1 A pronoun must agree with the word or words it replaces (its antecedent).

If the word the pronoun replaces (its antecedent) is singular, use a singular pronoun.

If the word the pronoun replaces (its antecedent) is plural, use a plural pronoun.

Singular   Plural
My sister left her skates out in the rain, and they were ruined.

Practice 1 Circle the pronouns in the following sentences and draw an arrow back to the antecedents (the noun or nouns) to which they refer.

1. John told his mother that he was going out.

2. The campers lost their way in the forest.

3. Sue got an A on her last test.

4. The counselor announced that his schedule was full.

5. My friends are having a party at their apartment complex this Friday.

Avoiding Sexist Language

1.2 Always using *he* to refer to an unspecified individual is considered sexist and should be avoided.

 ✗ A student should attend his classes regularly.

Because we don't know whether the student is male or female, current usage discourages the use of the male pronoun. One solution is to use his or her to refer to an unspecified noun. Another option is to avoid the problem by using a plural antecedent or by using an article instead of a pronoun. It is a good idea to consult with your instructor about his or her preferences.

 ✓ A student should attend his or her classes regularly.
 ✓ Students should attend their classes regularly.
 ✓ A student should attend classes regularly.

Businesses and Agencies

1.3 Businesses and agencies are singular and take a singular pronoun (*it* or *its*).

Singular
The college should synchronize its schedule with the public schools.

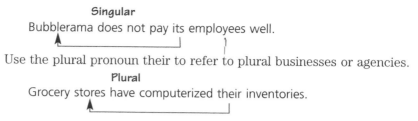

Singular
Bubblerama does not pay its employees well.

Use the plural pronoun their to refer to plural businesses or agencies.

Plural
Grocery stores have computerized their inventories.

Practice 2   Circle the correct pronoun or pronouns in each sentence.

1. Burger Barn grills (its/their) burgers.

2. Many colleges print (its/their) registration schedules on newsprint.

3. JCPenney is having (its/their) Founder's Day sale this weekend.

4. Home Depot requires that all of (its/their) employees take a drug test.

5. The FBI performs thorough background checks on all of (its/their) new recruits.

Compound Antecedents

1.4 Compound antecedents joined by *and* are plural and take a plural pronoun.

Plural
Harold and Jaime are doing their homework together.

1.5 When antecedents are joined by *or, either … or,* or *neither … nor,* the pronoun should agree with the nearest antecedent.

Plural
✓   Either Isabela or my sisters left their car keys on the table.

Singular
✓   Either my sisters or Isabela left her car keys on the table.

Practice 3   Circle the pronouns in the following sentences and draw an arrow back to the antecedent (the noun or nouns) to which they refer. Underline compound antecedents.

1. My mother and my aunt do their grocery shopping at the same store.

2. Either my coach or my parents will bring the refreshments with them.

3. Neither my friends nor my brother knows what happened to his homework.

4. My teacher or her aides grade papers during their lunch hour.

5. Beth and Mike are saving money for their summer vacation.

Practice 4   Underline the correct antecedent and choose the correct pronoun or pronouns in each sentence.

1. Either John or his friends are planning (his/their) fall schedules.

2. My mom and dad are financing (his/their) new car.

3. Neither Bob nor Sue knows what grade (he/she) is getting in algebra.

4. Either my coach or my teammates will show me (his/their) support during the final match.

5. The judge and the jury were unanimous in (his/their) decision.

Indefinite Pronouns

Indefinite pronouns refer to nonspecific nouns and can themselves serve as antecedents to personal pronouns.

1.6 Most indefinite pronouns are singular and take a singular pronoun.

No one has finished his or her homework.
Everyone is bringing his or her favorite CD to the party.

Singular Indefinite Pronouns			
"-one"	**"-body"**	**"-thing"**	**Others**
any**one**	any**body**	any**thing**	each
everyone	everybody	everything	either
no one	nobody	nothing	neither
one	somebody	something	someone

1.7 Some indefinite pronouns are plural and take a plural pronoun.

Both of my brothers passed their math tests.

Several of my friends completed their applications for summer work.

Plural Indefinite Pronouns	
both	many
few	several

1.8 Some indefinite pronouns can be either singular or plural, depending on the nouns to which they refer.

A lot of my <u>homework</u> was difficult, and I didn't finish it until ten o'clock. (Singular)

A lot of my <u>answers</u> had Xs by them because they were wrong. (Plural)

Plural or Singular Indefinite Pronouns	
a lot	more
all	most
any	none
lots	some

Practice 5   Circle the pronouns in the following sentences, and draw an arrow back to the antecedents (the noun or nouns) to which they refer.

1. Everyone regrets something in her life.

2. One of my friends got an A on his algebra test.

3. Some of these grapes have mold on them.

4. Each of the papers has a grade on it.

5. None of my seeds sprouted after I planted them.

Practice 6   Underline the correct antecedent and choose the correct pronoun or pronouns in each sentence.

1. One of my dresses has a stain on (it/them).

2. A lot of my papers have marks on (it/them).

3. Everyone loves to be recognized for (his or her/their) hard work.

4. None of my friends have finished (his or her/their) reports.

5. Anybody who wants to do well in school should attend all of (his or her/their) classes.

Collective Nouns

1.9 Collective nouns refer to a group that acts as one unit. Most collective nouns are singular and take a singular pronoun.

The jury delivered its verdict.

The team won all of its home games.

Collective Nouns	
band	committee
faculty	group
class	audience
family	crowd
team	jury

Practice 7   Circle the correct pronoun or pronouns in each sentence.

1. The business lost (its/their) license and had to close.

2. The group will make (its/their) decision tonight.

3. The band recorded (its/their) first CD in New York.

4. The faculty voted in (its/their) new president last night.

5. The crowd roared (its/their) approval when the band came onstage.

Practice 8: Pronoun Agreement Review

Circle the correct pronoun or pronouns in each sentence.

1. The team lost (its/their) first game.

2. A student left (his or her/their) books on the table.

3. Someone left (his or her/their) notebook in the classroom.

4. Tom and Martha bought (his or her/their) new car in March.

5. The IRS has (its/their) headquarters in Washington, D.C.

6. One of the viewers expressed (his or her/their) displeasure at the show.

7. Mattie's B-B-Q serves (its/their) sandwiches on paper plates.

8. My favorite TV program has (its/their) last show tonight.

9. The committee voted unanimously to cancel (its/their) spring concert.

10. Either my sisters or Elaine drops me off on (her/their) way to school.

Avoiding Unnecessary Shifts in Pronouns

While it is important to check for pronoun agreement within a sentence, it is also important to be consistent from sentence to sentence. Pronouns are classified according to person: first person (I, me, we); second person (you); and third person (he, she, it, they).

2.1 Do not shift unnecessarily from one person to another within a sentence or paragraph.

    Third-person plural
✘ Students need to establish a study routine in order to be successful in their
      Third-person singular
classes. A student who wants to succeed in his or her classes should keep several
           Second-person singular
points in mind. The first tip you should follow is to set up a study schedule that

allows you to complete your assignments.

Shifting the point of view of your pronouns from first, second, or third person or from singular to plural can confuse the reader. One way to avoid pronoun shifts is to decide at the beginning of a paragraph or piece of writing whether you will refer to your subject as singular or plural and then remain consistent throughout the entire piece.

    ✓ Students need to establish a study routine in order to be successful in their classes.
    Students   *their*
    ~~A student~~ who want to succeed in ~~his or her~~ classes should keep several points in
         students   *them*
    mind. The first tip ~~you~~ should follow is to set up a study schedule that allows ~~you~~
             their
    to complete ~~your~~ assignments.

Practice 9   Cross out any nouns and pronouns that shift in number or person and write a correct noun or pronoun above.

1. If students park on the grass, you can get towed.

2. Students should turn in all their papers on time. If you turn in a late paper, the

   instructor may not accept it.

3. Employees who want to be recognized for their efforts should follow his or her employer's instructions and recommendations.

4. Students who miss class due to illness fall behind in their work. Therefore, a student should visit the infirmary on campus to get their free flu shot.

5. Parents should make sure their child has received all his or her vaccinations. A parent who doesn't vaccinate their child can endanger his or her child's health.

2.2 Limit the use of the second person, *you.*

Although the second-person pronoun, *you,* is frequently used in speech, its use is discouraged in academic writing because it is considered vague and sometimes illogical. The use of *you* implies that the reader is being addressed personally. Replace the vague pronoun *you* with a specific noun.

✗ You should study when you are most alert.

✓ A student should study when he or she is most alert.

✓ Students should study when they are most alert.

2.3 When correcting pronoun errors, correct any related errors (such as verb errors).

✗ Every shopper should compare prices before they purchase a new product.

The pronoun *they* is incorrect because *every shopper* is singular. When you correct the pronoun error, make sure to change the verb ending if necessary to avoid a subject-verb agreement error.

✓ Every shopper should compare prices before he or she purchases a new product.

Practice 10 Revise the following sentences to eliminate the use of *you.* Think of a specific noun or pronoun to replace *you.* Be sure to correct related errors such as verbs.

1. When you shop for a new television, you should purchase the latest technology.

2. If you park on the grass, the campus police will tow your car.

3. Unless you study regularly, you will find it difficult to keep up with your classes.

4. If you want to save money on gas, you need to shop around and compare prices.

5. If you water your lawn during a drought, you can be fined.

CD Connection

Power of Language

On *Writer's Resources* CD-ROM, see *Pronoun Agreement* in Grammar/Punctuation/ Mechanics for more information and practice with pronouns.

REVIEW EXERCISE 1

Identify the pronoun agreement in the following sentences as correct (C) or incorrect (I), and correct any pronoun and related verb errors.

_____ 1. The soccer team will advance to the finals if they win their next game.

_____ 2. Either my aunts or my sister always volunteers her time at the art fair.

_____ 3. Everyone who turns their project in on time will receive an A.

_____ 4. Not one of the books has been put into its place.

_____ 5. Any student who wants to improve their grades should talk to their instructor.

_____ 6. When you miss class, you should contact your instructor or a classmate to find out what you missed.

_____ 7. Everybody who finishes the race will receive his or her award ribbon.

_____ 8. The restaurant has their big buffet on Saturday.

_____ 9. My aunt and uncle always take their vacation in July.

_____ 10. The car wash gives their regular customers a discount.

REVIEW EXERCISE 2

Identify the pronoun agreement in the following sentences as correct (C) or incorrect (I), and correct any pronoun and related verb errors.

_____ 1. My college is committed to keeping their computers up to date.

_____ 2. All of the labs on campus are scheduled to have their computers replaced.

_____ 3. The technology committee has made its decision about which computers to replace first.

_____ 4. This summer, the writing lab is replacing their computers.

_____ 5. The lab manager and her staff will supervise the replacement of the computers.

_____ 6. Neither the lab manager nor the technicians are certain of his or her responsibilities.

_____ 7. After the computers are removed, they will be available for resale.

_____ 8. Students can purchase one of the old computers if they wish to.

_____ 9. None of the computers has viruses on them.

_____ 10. Each of the computers has valuable software on their hard drive.

EDITING FOR PRONOUN AGREEMENT 1

Correct all pronoun errors and related verb errors. Substitute specific nouns for the second-person pronoun *you. Hint: Consistently refer to vacationers as plural.*

Telluride, Colorado, is a wonderful place for vacationers. Whether you visit Telluride in summer or winter, you will never be bored. If you visit in the summer, you can hike to the many waterfalls that surround the town, go fly-fishing in the one of the area rivers and lakes, or go horseback riding in the mountains surrounding the village. Another favorite activity for a vacationer is riding the gondola to Mountain Village, where you can enjoy spectacular views of the mountains and valleys. In the winter, you can ski one of the eighty-four area trails, go ice skating, or take a sleigh ride. A sightseer can also learn about the history of the area during his or her stay. The town of Telluride is proud of their long and interesting history, which involves mining booms and busts.

EDITING FOR PRONOUN AGREEMENT 2

Correct all pronoun errors and related verb errors. Substitute specific nouns for the second-person pronoun *you*. Hint: Consistently refer to students as plural.

Research shows that students who get involved in school-related activities are more successful in his or her classes than students who don't. According to the studies, if you take part in school activities, you feel more commitment to college than if you don't. Studies show that engagement helps students succeed in school, and every school wants their students to succeed. A college that is committed to their students also provides services to help them succeed. When students can see their instructors to ask questions, they are more likely to succeed. If a student hasn't gotten involved in school activities, he or she should do so to improve their chances of success.

Practicing Your Writing Power

Power of
Language

© Thomson Corporation/Heinle Image Resource Bank

Describe some of the campus activities that students at your school enjoy. Have you ever joined a student club or organization? Why or why not? What are the advantages or disadvantages of participating in school activities? When you have finished writing, go back and edit your entry for pronoun agreement.

Name _____

Section _____   Score _____

PRONOUN AGREEMENT TEST 1

Identify the pronoun agreement in the following sentences as correct (C) or incorrect (I), and then correct any noun, pronoun, or related verb errors in order to avoid pronoun agreement and unnecessary pronoun shift errors. *Hint: Consistently refer to students as plural.*

_____ 1. If students want to impress their instructor, he or she should do several things.

_____ 2. First, students should sit near the front of the room, and you should take notes during class.

_____ 3. A student should make an effort to smile at their instructor.

_____ 4. Students should read and complete the assignment before he or she comes to class.

_____ 5. When you type a paper, you should make sure you spell check for spelling errors.

_____ 6. Students should also review their notes after class.

_____ 7. A student who wants to do well should turn in all of their work on time.

_____ 8. If students must miss class, they should see the instructor to explain the absence.

_____ 9. Instructors are glad to answer any questions their students might have.

_____ 10. The college is committed to the satisfaction of their students.

Name _____

Section _____   Score _____

PRONOUN AGREEMENT TEST 2

Identify the pronoun agreement in the following sentences as correct (C) or incorrect (I), and then correct any noun, pronoun, and related verb errors in order to avoid pronoun agreement and unnecessary pronoun shift errors. *Hint: Consistently refer to a parent as singular and children as plural.*

_____ 1. Any parent who has traveled with their young children knows traveling can be difficult.

_____ 2. Young children have trouble staying in their seat for long periods of time.

_____ 3. A parent who is smart will pack lots of toys and snacks to keep their kids amused.

_____ 4. Most children don't mean to annoy their parent.

_____ 5. The most frequent question young children ask his or her parents is, "Are we there yet?"

_____ 6. A parent has to hold their breath and count to ten before he or she answers.

_____ 7. Most children enjoy tormenting his or her younger brother or sister.

_____ 8. Either the parent or the children will lose his or her patience before the end of the trip.

_____ 9. In spite of the hassles, every member of the family enjoys their vacation.

_____ 10. Still, everyone is glad when the vacation is over and the family gets back to its home again.

Name _____

Section _____ Score _____

PRONOUN AGREEMENT TEST 3

Identify the pronoun agreement in the following sentences as correct (C) or incorrect (I), and correct any noun, pronoun, and related verb errors in order to avoid pronoun agreement and unnecessary pronoun shift errors. *Hint: Consistently refer to an athlete as singular.*

_____ 1. A student athlete has to manage their time carefully.

_____ 2. An athlete must dedicate many hours to his or her practices.

_____ 3. If an athlete wishes to remain on a team, he or she must perform

athletically.

_____ 4. An athlete must also perform academically to keep their scholarship.

_____ 5. Most coaches insist that each player attend every one of their classes.

_____ 6. A coach notifies his or her players of all scheduled practices.

_____ 7. Professors generally go out of his or her way to accommodate the

needs of athletes.

_____ 8. In order to be successful, a player must set his or her personal goals.

_____ 9. A team's main goal is to win their games.

_____ 10. A student athlete has to do double duty in order to earn his or her

degree.

Name _____

Section _____ Score _____

PRONOUN AGREEMENT TEST 4

Identify the pronoun agreement in the following sentences as correct (C) or incorrect (I), and correct any noun, pronoun, and related verb errors in order to avoid pronoun agreement and unnecessary pronoun shift errors. *Hint: Refer to children as plural.*

_____ 1. Children watch thousands of hours of television in their lifetimes.

_____ 2. Most parents don't have time to supervise the programs his or her children watch.

_____ 3. Many children are allowed to choose the programs he or she watches.

_____ 4. Unfortunately, most children will witness 100,000 acts of violence on television by the time they are in middle school.

_____ 5. Either a child's parents or a relative should exert their control over the shows a child watches.

_____ 6. A television network is primarily interested in increasing their revenues.

_____ 7. PBS monitors its programs more carefully.

_____ 8. New research shows that children under the age of two who watch television damage his or her attention span.

_____ 9. The American Association of Pediatricians bases their recommendations on such findings.

_____ 10. Pediatricians now recommend that their young patients not watch television.

Chapter 15 Pronoun Reference and Case

In this chapter you will learn about

- ☞ Avoiding unclear pronoun reference
- ☞ Using correct pronoun form and case

Skill Preview

As you learned in the previous chapter, pronouns are words that take the place of nouns and allow us to avoid unnecessary repetition of nouns. However, using the incorrect pronoun or a pronoun that doesn't clearly refer to a noun can cause confusion. For example, if you were to replace all the italicized nouns in the following sentence with pronouns, the result would be confusing.

Confusing Pronoun Use

✗ Sandy asked ~~Sandy's~~ *her* mother if ~~Sandy's mother~~ *she* could loan ~~Sandy~~ *her* the money, and

~~Sandy's mother~~ *she* agreed to loan ~~Sandy~~ *her* the money, under one condition: ~~Sandy~~ *she* had to keep

~~Sandy's~~ *her* grades up or ~~Sandy's mother~~ *she* would take ~~Sandy's~~ *her* new car away.

Replacing two different singular nouns with the pronoun *she* or *her* causes confusion because the reader doesn't know whether *she* refers to *Sandy* or *her mother.*

Pronouns are used to avoid repetition, but they should always clearly refer to the noun they replace.

Spotlight on Writers

Mary McLeod Bethune

"I picked up one of the books . . . and one of the girls said to me—'You can't read that—put that down. I will show you some pictures over here,' and when she said to me 'You can't read that—put that down' it just did something to my pride and to my heart that made me feel that some day I would read just as she was reading."

Mary McLeod Bethune (1875–1955) was perhaps the most influential black educational leader in the twentieth century. Although she was born a slave, she believed passionately that education was the best road for the advancement of her people, and she founded a school for girls in Daytona Beach, which later became Bethune-Cookman College. Eleanor Roosevelt was so impressed with Bethune's work that Roosevelt brought Bethune to Washington, where she became an advisor to President Franklin Delano Roosevelt. She was later appointed Director of Negro Affairs, becoming the first black woman to hold a federal office.

These rules will help you avoid pronoun reference and case errors in your writing.

1. A pronoun must refer clearly to the noun it replaces.
2. The correct pronoun form and case should be used.

Pronoun Reference

1.1 Pronouns should always clearly refer to the nouns they replace.

Confusion occurs if one pronoun is used to refer to more than one possible antecedent. The confusion happens when there are two singular subjects or two plural subjects because the pronoun could refer to either subject.

✗ Tom told Larry that he passed the exam.

Did Tom or Larry pass the exam? Because there are two singular antecedents for *he,* we can't be sure who passed the exam. To avoid confusion, substitute a noun for the pronoun, or reword the sentence.

✓ Tom told Larry that Tom passed the exam.

✓ Tom told Larry, "I passed the exam."

✗ When the babies saw their parents, they were smiling.

Were the babies or their parents smiling? Because there are two plural antecedents for *they*, we can't be sure. To avoid confusion, substitute a noun for the pronoun, or reword the sentence.

✓ When the babies saw their parents, their parents were smiling.

✓ The babies smiled when they saw their parents.

Practice 1   Underline the pronouns in the following sentences, and circle possible antecedents. If there is more than one antecedent, label the pronoun reference Incorrect (I).

_____ 1. Edna told Rosemary that she was on restriction.

_____ 2. Schools encourage students to get involved so that they can be successful.

_____ 3. Teachers are always available to talk to students about questions they may have.

_____ 4. The newspaper editor asked the reporter what he was doing.

_____ 5. When Ted saw Mark, he was riding his bike.

Practice 2   *Working Together*

Rewrite the incorrect sentences from Practice 1 to make the pronoun reference clear.

1. Edna told Rosemary that she was on restriction.

_____

2. Schools encourage students to get involved so that they can be successful.

_____

3. Teachers are always available to talk to students about questions they may have.

_____

4. The newspaper editor asked the reporter what he was doing.

_____

5. When Ted saw Mark, he was riding his bike.

_____

1.2 Don't use a pronoun until the noun to which it refers has been named.

✗ At the pool, they won't let kids dive.

Who won't let kids dive? A pronoun must have a noun antecedent.

✓ At the pool, the lifeguards won't let kids dive.

Practice 3 **Replace the vague pronouns with specific nouns.**

1. At my college, they won't let students drop a class after midterm.

2. When we go to football games, they make us pay for parking.

3. They sell drinks at the concession stand.

4. At the airport, they check your bags.

5. They close the bars at 2 A.M.

1.3 The pronouns *it, that,* and *which* should always refer to a specific noun.

✓ The test that I took was difficult.

✓ Because the car broke down, we had to have it towed.

Pronouns cannot refer to verbs.

✗ The dogs barked most of the night, which kept me up. (The pronoun which cannot refer to the verb barked.)

Pronouns cannot refer to implied ideas.

✗ I want to be an electrician because I like doing it. (The pronoun it does not refer to electrician.)

One way to test whether or not the pronouns *it, that,* or *which* clearly refer to a specific noun is to replace the pronoun with the noun to which it is supposed to refer. If you can't replace the pronoun with a noun used in the sentence or a previous sentence, then the pronoun is unclear and is incorrect.

Test: Can you replace the italicized pronoun in the following sentences with a noun used earlier in the sentence?

✗ My dog digs holes in the yard, which irritates me.

You can't substitute *digs* for *which* or *holes* for *which,* so the pronoun is incorrect because it does not refer to a specific noun. Reword sentences to avoid unclear pronoun reference.

✓ I get irritated when my dog digs holes in the yard.

✗ My brother always teases me, and that makes me angry.

Since you can't substitute *teases* for *that,* the pronoun is incorrect because it does not refer to a specific noun.

✓ When my brother teases me, he makes me angry.

Practice 4   Circle the pronouns in the following sentences, and underline the antecedents. If there is no noun antecedent, label the pronoun reference Incorrect (I). If there is a clear noun antecedent, label the pronoun reference Correct (C).

_____ 1. I can't study when my roommate is watching TV, and that is a problem.

_____ 2. When my brother washes his car, he ruins the grass, which gets him in trouble.

_____ 3. My history test, which was given on Monday, was hard.

_____ 4. My brother broke our neighbor's window, which got him in trouble.

_____ 5. I flunked my algebra test, which disappointed me.

Practice 5   *Working Together*

Rewrite the incorrect sentences from Practice 4 to make the pronoun reference clear.

1. _____

2. _____

3. _____

4. _____

5. _____

Pronoun Case

Pronouns have different forms and different cases depending on how they are used in a sentence. Subject pronouns serve as the subject of a verb, and object pronouns serve as the object of a verb or the object of a preposition. Common errors occur when writers use the wrong form.

Subject Pronouns	Object Pronouns
I	me
you	you
he	him
she	her
it	it
we	us
they	them
who	whom

One way to remember object pronouns is that many of them have an *m* in them (me, him, them, whom).

Subject pronoun: *I* like spaghetti.

Object pronoun: Jim cooks spaghetti for *me* on Friday nights.

Practice 6 Label the pronouns in the following sentences (S) Subjects or (O) Objects.

1. He invited me to dinner.

2. He wrote a letter to her last night.

3. They are best friends with him.

4. They told him to be here at five.

5. We will surprise him with a cake.

Subject Pronouns

2.1 Use a subject pronoun when the pronoun serves as the subject of a verb. (Subject pronouns come before the verb.)

✗ Them are my friends.
✓ They are my friends.

2.2 Use a subject pronoun with a compound subject.

S   S
Dolores and I like to play tennis.
S   S
Bob and he are going to the game.
S   S
My sister and she are best friends.

> If you are not sure which pronoun to use, try using the pronoun by itself as the subject. *Note: You may have to change the verb to agree with the singular pronoun.*
>
> Dolores and I like to play tennis.
>
> ✓ I like to play tennis.
>
> ✗ Me likes to play tennis.
>
> *I like to play tennis* sounds better than *Me likes to play tennis.*

Practice 7   Underline the compound subject in the following sentences, and identify the pronoun as Correct (C) or Incorrect (I). Correct the incorrect pronouns. *Hint: Try reading the sentence with only the pronoun as the subject to see whether it is correct.*

_____ 1. Martha and her want to go swimming.

_____ 2. My mother and him are driving to Miami tonight.

_____ 3. Eduardo and I play doubles together.

_____ 4. My brother and I have always been best friends.

_____ 5. Manolo and him are going to the show at ten.

2.3 In comparisons, complete the comparison to find the correct pronoun.

✓ I played better than he (played).

✗ I played better than him (played).

✓ Dennis ran faster than she (ran).

✗ Dennis ran faster than her (ran).

Practice 8   Complete the comparison in order to determine whether the pronoun is correct (C) or incorrect (I). Correct the incorrect pronouns.

_____ 1. Susana studied longer than him.

_____ 2. My mother has studied French longer than me.

_____ 3. I can run faster than he.

_____ 4. I like chocolate more than them.

_____ 5. Can you walk as fast as he?

Object Pronouns

2.4 Use an object pronoun as the object of a verb or as the object of a preposition.

Object pronouns come after the verb or after a preposition.

S   V   O
Mike gave her a present.

Some Common Prepositions
Prepositions are words that show time or space relationship.

at	between	on
about	by	to
around	in	with

See Chapter 6, page 137 for a complete list of prepositions.

✗ Between you and I, Richard is the best player on the team.

Between is a preposition, so an object pronoun should be used.

✓ Between you and me, Richard is the best player on the team.

✗ Lydia is going to the party with he.

With is a preposition, so an object pronoun should be used.

✓ Lydia is going to the party with him.

Practice 9   Circle the subject and underline any prepositions in the following sentences to identify whether a subject or object pronoun should be used. Next, identify the pronoun as Correct (C) or Incorrect (I), and correct the incorrect pronouns.

_____ 1. Joanne plans to take Robert with her.

_____ 2. The coach will give the award to he.

_____ 3. My sister likes to drive to the beach with them.

_____ 4. The book fell on he.

_____ 5. My mother said I could go if I drive with them.

Common Errors with Pronoun Forms

3.1 Avoid common errors with personal pronouns.

Personal pronouns do not take an apostrophe.

✘ his' or her' books   ✓ his or her books

✘ it's or its' color   ✓ its color

✘ their' car   ✓ their car

✘ theirs'   ✓ theirs

3.2 Avoid common errors with demonstrative pronouns.

✘ them books   ✓ those books

✘ them there books   ✓ those books

✘ these here books   ✓ these books

3.3 Avoid common errors with reflexive pronouns.

✘ hisself   ✓ himself

✘ themself   ✓ themselves

✘ theirself   ✓ themselves

✘ theirselves   ✓ themselves

Practice 10   Identify the pronouns as correct (C) or incorrect (I), and correct any pronoun errors.

_____ 1. The boys helped theirselves to more pie.

_____ 2. The cat licked its' paws clean.

_____ 3. I'd like another one of them shirts.

_____ 4. Monty and Kirk consider themselves winners.

_____ 5. My cousin accidentally cut hisself on the arm.

_____ 6. That book is theirs.

_____ 7. My uncles consider themself to be expert swimmers.

_____ 8. Tony and Elena pay themselves to study.

_____ 9. These here puppies are cute.

_____ 10. Those chairs are broken.

CD Connection

Power of
Language

On *Writer's Resources* CD-ROM, see *Pronoun Reference and Case* in Grammar/
Punctuation/Mechanics for more information and practice with pronouns.

REVIEW EXERCISE 1

Identify the pronoun reference and case in the following sentences as correct (C) or
incorrect (I), and correct any pronoun errors.

_____ 1. Kyle told Ted that he was tired.

_____ 2. Kyle stayed up late studying for the test because he knew it would be hard.

_____ 3. Ted studied by hisself.

_____ 4. I'm sure Ted studied harder than me.

_____ 5. They put lots of hard questions on the test.

_____ 6. Between you and I, that was the hardest test I've ever taken.

_____ 7. Ted did better on the test than me.

_____ 8. Next time I will study with him.

_____ 9. Them algebra tests are hard.

_____ 10. Ted and me will study together next time.

REVIEW EXERCISE 2

Identify the pronoun reference and case in the following sentences as correct (C) or
incorrect (I), and correct any pronoun errors.

_____ 1. Larry and I flew to Denver to visit my family last week.

_____ 2. He gets more nervous than me when we fly.

_____ 3. They said our flight was delayed.

_____ 4. Larry and me decided to get a snack before our flight.

_____ 5. When they called our flight, we raced to the terminal.

_____ 6. Getting through security took thirty minutes, which was irritating.

_____ 7. They made Larry take off his shoes.

_____ 8. In spite of his embarrassment, Larry and I were both glad they were so thorough.

_____ 9. When we got there, my brother told Larry he was late.

_____ 10. Despite the delay, my family was glad that Larry and I got there safely.

EDITING FOR PRONOUN REFERENCE AND CASE

Alone or in pairs, correct all pronoun errors and related verb errors. _Hint: Refer to students as plural, and substitute specific nouns for the second-person pronoun_ you.

My twin sister and me like to do everything together. Ever since us were little, we have worn matching clothes, and everyone thinks it is cute. When we go to camp, they always put us in the same cabin because they know how much we want to be together. Even though we know how to take care of ourself, we still look after each other. I don't know what will happen when one of us gets married. Maybe her and I will both get married at the same time. I think that would be fun, but our mother says it would be too much trouble. The best part of being a twin is that they pay us lots of attention, which is fun.

Practicing Your Writing Power

Power of Language

© Thomson Corporation/Heinle Image Resource Bank

1. How do you get along with your brothers and sisters? Explain how you fit in with your brother and/or sister in your family.

2. If you are an only child, write about what you like and dislike about being an only child.

Name _____

Section _____   Score _____

PRONOUN REFERENCE AND CASE TEST 1

Identify the pronouns in the following sentences as correct (C) or incorrect (I).
Correct the pronoun errors in the incorrect items.

_____   1. My friend and I like to study together.

_____   2. Her and I make a good team.

_____   3. She remembers details well, and I remember concepts.

_____   4. She is better than me at remembering names and dates.

_____   5. I can help her put the details into perspective.

_____   6. When her and me study together, we do better on tests.

_____   7. We complement each other, which is why we do so well on tests.

_____   8. The instructor asked her and me to talk to the class about how we study.

_____   9. She and I talked about preparing, and the teacher and her talked about taking good notes in class.

_____   10. The class had lots of questions for we.

Name _____

Section _____ Score _____

PRONOUN REFERENCE AND CASE TEST 2

Identify the pronouns in the following sentences as correct (C) or incorrect (I). Correct the pronoun errors in the incorrect items.

_____ 1. My brother and me go to camp every summer.

_____ 2. He likes going to camp better than I.

_____ 3. My mother always tells us to behave ourselves.

_____ 4. She kisses us goodbye, which is embarrassing.

_____ 5. We had a two-hour bus ride, which was boring.

_____ 6. When we get to camp, they tell us to find our cabins.

_____ 7. My brother told the counselor that he was unhappy.

_____ 8. The counselor thought that was a problem.

_____ 9. The other campers and me tried to cheer him up.

_____ 10. By the second day, my brother was as happy as I.

Chapter 16 Modifiers

In this chapter, you will learn about modifiers and the errors of

- ☛ Misplaced modifiers
- ☛ Dangling modifiers

Skill Preview

Modifiers are words or phrases that describe, explain, or limit a word or words in a sentence. Modifiers can create confusion for the reader if they are misplaced or placed in a sentence that doesn't contain the word they modify.

Read the following sentences and then answer the question after each statement.

1. The truck passed the car parked at the curb with the radio blaring.

   Is it the truck or the car that has a loud radio playing? _____

2. By working hard, the class should be easy.

   Who in the sentence will be working hard? _____

Each sentence above contains a problem with a modifier. In the first sentence, a reader might think that the truck has the loud radio or that the car has the loud radio. Grammatically, the modifier *with the radio blaring* describes *the curb* because *curb* is the closest subject to the modifying phrase. In the second sentence, there is no word in the sentence that the modifier *by working hard* modifies. This sentence needs a subject such as *students* to make its meaning clear: *By working hard, students should find the class to be easy.*

> *Modifiers should be placed as close as possible to the actual word or words that they modify in the sentence.*

Spotlight on Writers

Power of
Language

Mark Twain

"The difference between the almost right word and the right word is really a large matter—it's the difference between the lightning bug and the lightning."

Samuel Langhorne Clemens (1835–1910) took his writer's name, Mark Twain—meaning *two fathoms*—as inspiration from his years as a riverboat captain. Mark Twain is arguably the finest writer America has ever produced. In his best novel, *The Adventures of Huckleberry Finn,* he explores humankind's inhumanity to humankind and asserts his belief in the equality of all people.

One of Mark Twain's greatest accomplishments was the development of a writing style that was distinctly American, rather than an imitation of the style of English writers. The loose rhythms of the language in his books give the impression of real speech. Twain's realistic prose style has influenced numerous American writers. As Ernest Hemingway stated, "All modern American literature comes from . . . *Huckleberry Finn.*"

Misplaced Modifiers

1.1 Misplaced modifiers modify the wrong word or words because of their placement. To avoid confusion, place modifiers as close as possible to the word or words they modify.

✗ The woman filled her car for the trip full of gas.

The phrase *full of gas* describes *car,* but it is closest to *trip.* A reader might misread the sentence and wonder whether the trip is full of gas.

✓ The woman filled her car full of gas for the trip.

✗ The old man crossed the street with a limp.

The street doesn't have a limp. The phrase *with a limp* should be placed closer to *man.*

✓ The old man with a limp crossed the street.

✓ With a limp, the old man crossed the street.

Often, misplaced modifiers are prepositional phrases (see Appendix 2, "Parts of Speech," beginning on page A-9, for a list of prepositions and more information about prepositional phrases). Be sure to place prepositional phrases as close as possible to the word they modify.

Practice 1   Draw a line from the misplaced modifier to its correct place in the sentence.

1. The child set the paper plane in the house *on fire*.

2. A woman entered the theater *in a long white gown*.

3. The homeowner gave a box to the mailman *wrapped in brown paper*.

4. The mechanic worked on the car *with a wrench*.

5. The movie star left the auditorium *dressed in a fur coat*.

6. The runner crossed the finished line *on one leg*.

7. The girl ran to the corner *with an ice cream cone*.

8. The state trooper clocked the speeder *using a radar gun*.

9. My secretary typed the letter *talking on the phone*.

10. The bus picked up the elderly woman *full of passengers*.

Practice 2   Write *I* next to each sentence in which the modifier is misplaced, and then circle the misplaced modifier and draw a line to where it should be placed in the sentence. If word placement in the sentence is correct, write C next to the item.

_____ 1. A couple came into the restaurant from the parking lot.

_____ 2. A band was playing in the restaurant on stage.

_____ 3. The couple looked at the specials on the menu.

_____ 4. The waiter approached the couple with a pen and pad.

_____ 5. The man and woman ordered fish from the menu broiled in wine and butter.

_____ 6. Then the couple got up to dance from their table.

_____ 7. Seeing food being served, the couple returned to their table.

_____ 8. They loved the fish that was brought to the table covered in wine sauce.

_____ 9. The man paid with a credit card for the meal.

_____ 10. The waiter gave the change to the man in small bills.

Limiting Modifiers

2.1 Limiting modifiers usually come *before* the word or words they modify. Different placements of these modifiers change the meaning of the sentence.

Limiting Modifiers	
almost	merely
even	nearly
everyday	never
frequently	only
hardly	scarcely
just	

✗   The painter almost finished painting all of the rooms.

✓   The painter finished painting almost all of the rooms.

The placement of *almost* changes the meaning of the sentence. In the first sentence, the painter painted all of the rooms but didn't finish any of the rooms. In the second sentence, the painter finished painting most of the rooms but not all of them. Do not place a limiting modifier before the verb unless you intend to modify the verb.

Practice 3   Decide whether the modifier in italics is placed next to the correct word or words. If it is, write C next to the item. If is not, write I next to the item, and draw a line from the modifier to the correct place in the sentence.

_____   1. I *hardly* have any time to study.

_____   2. The teacher explained the concept *only* one time before the test.

_____   3. The movie made *nearly* 10 million dollars the first week that it opened.

_____   4. Mary will be happy when she *just* finds the right prom dress.

_____   5. The newlywed husband cleans house and *frequently* cooks some of

   the meals.

Dangling Modifiers

3.1 **Dangling modifiers** have no word in the sentence to describe or explain. They are dangling because they are not connected to any word in the sentence. To correct dangling modifiers, add a subject after the modifier, or rewrite the dangling modifier to include a subject.

✗   Handing out the test results, the class became quiet.

Who is handing out the test results? Grammatically, the only subject in the sentence is *class*, but it isn't the class that is handing out the test results. To correct the dangling modifier, rewrite the sentence and add a subject after *handing out the test results*, or rewrite the sentence and add the subject in the dangling modifier.

✓ Handing out the test results, the teacher observed that the class became quiet.

✓ When the teacher handed out the test results, the class became quiet.

Practice 4   Rewrite each dangling modifier sentence by filling in the blank to complete the sentence.

1. When using a cell phone for a long call, the phone should be fully charged.

   When using a cell phone for a long call, _____ should charge the phone fully.

   When _____ uses a cell phone for a long call, _____

   _____

2. To charge a cell phone, the charger must be plugged into the phone for at least an hour.

   To charge a cell phone, _____

   _____

3. It is a good idea to keep the phone plugged into a charger while talking on a cell phone.

   While talking on a cell phone, _____

   It is a good idea to keep the phone plugged into a charger while _____

   _____

4. By conserving phone power, it is easy to use a cell phone all day.

   By conserving phone power, _____

5. Used with only the battery, a caller will run out of power quickly.

   Used with only the battery, _____

Practice 5 *Working Together*

Working alone or in pairs, explain what was wrong with each dangling modifier in the previous practice, and explain what you did to correct the dangling modifiers.

_____

_____

_____

3.2 In an imperative sentence (a sentence that gives a command), a modifier may describe the implied subject *you.* In this case, no modifier error occurs.

✓ When waiting in line, do not talk.

The implied subject *you* is waiting in line.

Practice 6 Rewrite sentences that contain dangling modifiers. If the sentence has no dangling modifier, write *Correct* on the blank line.

1. Working at the computer, the monitor went dead all of a sudden.

_____

2. While working at the computer, try to keep your back straight.

_____

3. Broken since last week, the old computer was put on the floor.

_____

4. To remain comfortable, the monitor should be at shoulder height.

_____

5. To be comfortable, the position in the chair should be changed every few minutes.

_____

CD Connection

Power of Language

On *Writer's Resources* CD-ROM, see *Modifiers* in Grammar/Punctuation/Mechanics for more information and practice with modifiers.

REVIEW EXERCISE 1

Write the letter of the sentence in each item that uses modifiers correctly.

_____ 1. a. The painter came down to the shore wearing a big straw hat.

b. Wearing a big straw hat, the painter came down to the shore.

_____ 2. a. She often painted beach scenes.

b. She painted often beach scenes.

_____ 3. a. Getting out her watercolors, the artist got ready to paint.

b. The artist got ready to paint getting out her watercolors.

_____ 4. a. Before setting up the picture, the wind blew over the easel.

b. Before the painter set up the picture, the wind blew over the easel.

_____ 5. a. To paint a good watercolor, a painter must use the right materials.

b. To paint a good watercolor, the right materials need to be used.

_____ 6. a. Large brushes with thick bristles help the artist fill in background colors.

b. Large brushes help the artist fill in background colors with thick bristles.

_____ 7. a. Small brushes help the painter add detail with thin bristles.

b. Small brushes with thin bristles help the painter add detail.

_____ 8. a. An artist never can have too many different brushes.

b. An artist can never have too many different brushes.

_____ 9. a. Painting outdoors, the right kind of paper must also be used.

b. Painting outdoors, the artist must also use the right kind of paper.

_____ 10. a. Used well, the materials can make the difference between a wonderful painting and a disaster.

b. Used well, an artist can make the difference between a wonderful painting and a disaster with the right materials.

REVIEW EXERCISE 2

Write the letter of the sentence in each item that uses modifiers correctly.

_____ 1. a. The World War II Memorial recently opened in Washington, D.C.

b. The World War II Memorial in Washington, D.C. recently opened.

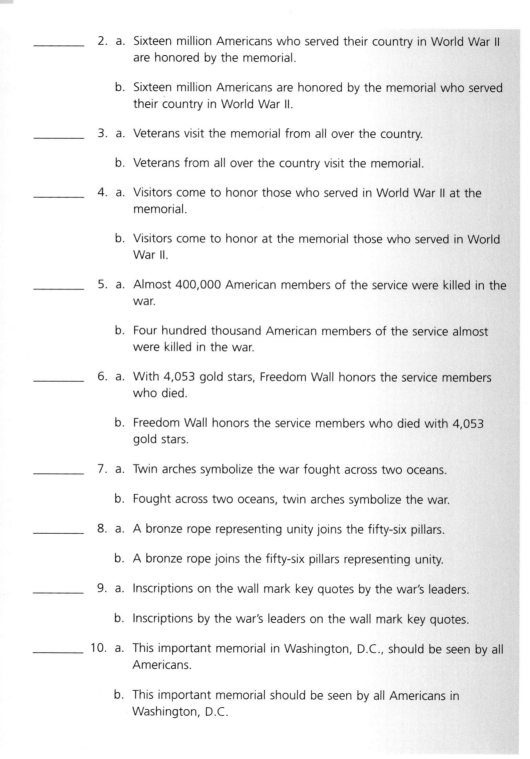

_____   2. a. Sixteen million Americans who served their country in World War II are honored by the memorial.

   b. Sixteen million Americans are honored by the memorial who served their country in World War II.

_____   3. a. Veterans visit the memorial from all over the country.

   b. Veterans from all over the country visit the memorial.

_____   4. a. Visitors come to honor those who served in World War II at the memorial.

   b. Visitors come to honor at the memorial those who served in World War II.

_____   5. a. Almost 400,000 American members of the service were killed in the war.

   b. Four hundred thousand American members of the service almost were killed in the war.

_____   6. a. With 4,053 gold stars, Freedom Wall honors the service members who died.

   b. Freedom Wall honors the service members who died with 4,053 gold stars.

_____   7. a. Twin arches symbolize the war fought across two oceans.

   b. Fought across two oceans, twin arches symbolize the war.

_____   8. a. A bronze rope representing unity joins the fifty-six pillars.

   b. A bronze rope joins the fifty-six pillars representing unity.

_____   9. a. Inscriptions on the wall mark key quotes by the war's leaders.

   b. Inscriptions by the war's leaders on the wall mark key quotes.

_____ 10. a. This important memorial in Washington, D.C., should be seen by all Americans.

   b. This important memorial should be seen by all Americans in Washington, D.C.

MODIFIERS EDITING TEST

Alone or in pairs, edit the following passage for modifier errors. Circle misplaced modifiers and draw a line to the place they should go, and rewrite the sentences with dangling modifiers. All ten sentences use a modifier incorrectly.

Bargain Hunting

Bargain hunting can be an adventure for children's clothes. There are great buys at garage sales on children's clothes. Marie found a wonderful party dress for her daughter in pink chiffon. However, carrying the dress to pay for it, her purse was missing. Marie remembered that she had left her purse in the car on the front seat. To retrieve her purse, the cashier at the sale made Marie leave the dress on a table. Returning with the money, the dress was gone! In the checkout line, Marie saw another woman holding her dress. Marie approached the woman with a smile. After explaining the situation, the woman was nice enough to give the dress back.

Practicing Your Writing Power

Power of
Language

© Thomson Corporation/Heinle Image Resource Bank

What kind of shopping do you like to do? Tell of one time when you were able to get a bargain while shopping. Read over your paper and make sure the modifiers are used correctly.

Name _____
Section _____ Score _____

MODIFIERS TEST 1

Write the letter of the sentence in each item that uses modifiers correctly.

_____ 1. a. Dietary guidelines for healthful eating by the USDA have been modified.

b. Dietary guidelines by the USDA for healthful eating have been modified.

_____ 2. a. For obesity, the government now recommends a diet that will help people lose weight.

b. The government now recommends a diet for obesity that will help people lose weight.

_____ 3. a. The panel urges dieters to exercise every day.

b. The panel urges dieters every day to exercise.

_____ 4. a. Overweight people should concentrate on counting calories to lose weight.

b. To lose weight, overweight people should concentrate on counting calories.

_____ 5. a. By eating two servings of fish each week, the heart can be protected.

b. By eating two servings of fish each week, people can protect their heart.

_____ 6. a. To lose weight, eat whole grain bread instead of white bread.

b. To lose weight, whole grain bread should be eaten instead of white bread.

_____ 7. a. Doing thirty to sixty minutes of exercise per day, dieters can lose weight.

b. Doing thirty to sixty minutes of exercise per day, weight can be lost.

_____ 8. a. Experts believe young people should exercise for at least an hour every day.

b. For at least an hour a day, experts believe young people should exercise every day.

_____ 9. a. Using the right diet, weight can be controlled.

b. Using the right diet, all of us can control our weight.

_____ 10. a. To maintain a healthy body, don't watch so much television.

b. To maintain a healthy body, television shouldn't be watched so much.

Name _____

Section _____ Score _____

MODIFIERS TEST 2

Write the letter of the sentence in each item that uses modifiers correctly.

_____ 1. a. On the Internet, some people are good at finding merchandise for sale.

b. Some people are good at finding merchandise for sale on the Internet.

_____ 2. a. When looking to buy a car, buyers can find Internet sites that will check the prices of dealers from across the country.

b. When looking to buy a car, Internet sites will check the prices of dealers from across the country.

_____ 3. a. One man found an old Corvette with a new engine and new tires for one hundred dollars.

b. One man found an old Corvette for one hundred dollars with a new engine and new tires.

_____ 4. a. However, the old car had to be shipped across the country in a crate.

b. However, the old car had to be shipped in a crate across the country.

_____ 5. a. EBay and other auction sites offer for the highest bid everything from clocks to cosmetics.

b. EBay and other auction sites offer everything from clocks to cosmetics for the highest bid.

_____ 6. a. To bid on merchandise, eBay is the most popular online site for shoppers.

b. For shoppers bidding on merchandise, eBay is the most popular online site.

_____ 7. a. Online shoppers frequently check the latest high bid on merchandise they want.

b. Online shoppers check the latest high bid on merchandise they want frequently.

_____ 8. a. With a simple click of a few computer keys, online bidders can raise their bids for merchandise.

b. With a simple click of a few computer keys, bids can be raised for merchandise.

_____ 9. a. Bidders through e-mail find out about the winner.

b. Bidders find out through e-mail about the winner.

_____ 10. a. Using a payment service like PayPal, the winning bidder can pay for the merchandise safely.

b. Using a payment service like PayPal, merchandise can be paid for safely.

Chapter 17 Parallelism

In this chapter, you will

☛ Learn to recognize and correct faulty parallelism.

Skill Preview

Writers consider parallelism when revising and polishing sentences that contain a pair of word groups or a series. The members of a pair or a series should be balanced so that all elements have the same grammatical structure.

Put a check next to the sentence in each pair that sounds better.

1. _____ a. The girls went shopping for cosmetics, perfume, and nail polish.

   _____ b. The girls went shopping for cosmetics, perfume, and hoped to find nail polish.

2. _____ a. Zena and Takela stuck to their diets faithfully and ate no fries at lunch.

   _____ b. Zena and Takela were sticking to their diets faithfully and ate no fries at lunch.

3. _____ a. Either they would find what they were looking for or there would be no prom for them.

   _____ b. Either they would find what they were looking for or they would not go to the prom.

Spotlight on Writers

Power of
Language

Ralph Ellison

"The act of writing requires a constant plunging back into the shadow of the past where time hovers ghostlike."

Ralph Ellison (1914–1994) is one of America's most famous African-American authors. His novel *Invisible Man,* published in 1952, forced Americans to confront the subtle ways in which racism has made African-Americans invisible in this culture. In his writing, he celebrated African-American contributions to American culture, particularly jazz music. Most importantly, Ralph Ellison used his writing to argue for a "unity of American experience beyond considerations of class, of race, of religion."

What Is Parallelism?

Parallelism means using the same kinds of words, phrases, and clauses when expressing a pair of ideas or a series of ideas. Writers use parallel grammatical structures to balance two ideas in a pair joined by *and, or, nor, but,* and *yet* or to balance three or more members in a series. Balanced members of pairs and series make sentences easier to read and understand.

Faulty Parallelism	Parallel Structure
✘ Ronald Reagan was **popular** but **caused controversy.**	✔ Ronald Reagan was **popular** but **controversial.** (A balanced pair of adjectives)
✘ Franklin Delano Roosevelt is honored **because he served four terms, because he brought the United States through the Depression,** and **he led the country to victory in World War II.**	✔ Franklin Delano Roosevelt is honored **because he served** four terms, **because he brought** the United States through the Depression, and **because he led** the country to victory in World War II. (A balanced series of dependent clauses)
✘ Abraham Lincoln not only **guided the country through the Civil War,** but also **slavery was ended in the United States.**	✔ Abraham Lincoln not only **guided the country** through the Civil War but also **ended slavery** in the United States. (A balanced pair of past-tense verb phrases)

> ✓ Create parallel structure by using the same part of speech to balance members of pairs and series. Use the first words of the first member of the pair or series to determine the grammatical structure for the other members.

Practice 1   Cross out the member of each list that is not in the same grammatical form as the others. Then rewrite the member in the blank to make it parallel.

1. _____

    reading   write   studying

2. _____

    to listen carefully   to question thoughtfully   clear thinking

3. _____

    in the classroom   home   on the job

4. _____

    faithful   loving   proudly

5. _____

    although he eats vegetables   since he takes medicines   while watching television

6. _____

    open door   locked the door   closed the windows

7. _____

    some kittens   a few dogs   horse

8. _____

    in the moonlight   a clear night   by the lake

9. _____

    while driving in the car   when he talks on a cell phone   if stopping for a light

10. _____

    done in the morning   taken at noon   finishing by five

Practice 2   Rewrite the italicized part of each sentence to make it parallel with the bold parts.

1. Jimmy Carter's rise to fame was remarkable **because he started as an unknown candidate from Georgia** and *because of how quickly he became president of the United States.*

   _____

2. Before becoming president, Carter was **a naval officer, a peanut farmer,** and *he was elected governor of Georgia.*

   _____

3. At the beginning of the presidential primary season in 1976, Jimmy Carter **went home to Plains, Georgia,** *asking his wife's advice about running for president,* and **decided to enter the race.**

   _____

4. Carter hoped to **meet many of the voters from around the country** and *that they would discuss events from around the world.*

   _____

5. During the presidential race, Carter was known for being **calm, reserved,** and *speaking softly.*

   _____

6. Voters came to value *him knowing world affairs* and **his personal warmth.**

   _____

7. However, during Carter's presidency, the United States faced problems both **at home** and *internationally.*

   _____

8. At home, the economy suffered from **high unemployment** and from *inflation being severe.*

   _____

9. Overseas, the United States faced crises in **Iran, Afghanistan,** and *South America was a problem.*

   _____

10. Despite these problems, Carter achieved many breakthroughs during his presidency, including **establishing diplomatic relations with China, helping to bring the hostages home from Iran,** and *bring about a peace treaty between Egypt and Israel.*

    _____

Practice 3   Complete each sentence with a word, phrase, or clause that is parallel with the other bold parts.

1. My favorite clothes store sells clothes that are **fashionable, well made,** and _____.

2. The sales staff **knows about the merchandise, makes suggestions to customers,** and _____.

3. I prefer to shop **during the weekend** rather than _____.

4. Either **waiting for a friend to try on an outfit** or _____ is my least favorite part of shopping.

5. Clothes shopping can be both **tiring** and _____.

Practice 4 *Working Together*

Alone or in pairs, cross out the unbalanced part of the sentence, and rewrite the sentence to make it parallel.

1. I find that studying for final exams can be profitable but consumes time.

   _____

2. My brother's car has wide tires, a beautiful paint job, and an engine that is powerful.

   _____

3. My mother loves to cook but hates cleaning up.

   _____

4. Either watching television or the pool for sunbathing is my sister's favorite activity.

   _____

5. My schedule this week is both hectic and demands a lot.

   _____

CD Connection

Power of Language

On *Writer's Resources* CD-ROM, see *Parallelism* in Grammar/Punctuation/Mechanics for more information and practice with parallelism.

REVIEW EXERCISE 1

Rewrite the italicized part of each sentence to make it parallel with the other bold parts.

1. President Richard Nixon had **to face almost certain impeachment for his involvement in the Watergate scandal** or *resigning from office.*

   _____

2. The Watergate scandal included **a break-in at the Democratic National Head quarters** and *employees of Nixon's 1972 reelection committee that performed other illegal activities.*

   _____

3. President Nixon's attempts to cover up these crimes became both **a major part of the scandal** and *causing him to resign.*

   _____

4. Vice President Gerald R. Ford **succeeded Nixon** and *pardons him* for any crimes he may have committed during his presidency.

   _____

5. Richard Nixon **resigned in disgrace** yet *accomplishing much.*

   _____

6. Nixon **ended the Viet Nam war, eased tensions with the Soviet Union,** and *had established relations with China.*

   _____

7. Nixon earned a reputation for **being tough on Communism** but *worked well with the Russians and Chinese.*

   _____

8. Here in the United States, Nixon **ended the military draft,** *creating an all-volunteer army,* and **encouraged other voluntary national service.**

   _____

9. Richard Nixon was **a success as president** yet *failed at governing.*

   _____

10. To explain the Nixon presidency, many historians point to Nixon's personal qualities of **painful shyness with strangers, extreme sensitivity to criticism,** and *that he was deeply suspicious of opponents.*

_____

REVIEW EXERCISE 2

Complete the following sentences using parallelism to balance the parts of the sentence.

1. Neither the employee's work with customers nor _____ made her boss happy.

2. The school's best runner trains hard during the week, runs fast at track meets, and

   _____.

3. Our dog has curly hair, sad eyes, and _____.

4. Even on the first date, the woman knew that her future husband was honest and

   _____.

5. I prefer making online payments for my credit card rather than _____.

6. Traveling by plane is faster than _____.

7. Our teacher promises to let us leave early on Friday and _____.

8. The fishermen returned home exhausted yet _____.

9. In our neighborhood, the postman always arrives early, the garbage men always arrive late, and _____.

10. Partying too hard, staying out late, and _____ can all hurt student performance on tests.

EDITING TEST 1

Alone or with a partner, revise the following paragraph by crossing out the five sentence parts with faulty parallelism and writing the correction above.

                    My Battle for Health

     Last New Year's I promised myself that I would lose weight,

begin exercising, and I had to quit smoking. Of course, all

three resolutions are not only difficult but also they are contradictory. If I exercise, I will lose weight, but if I quit smoking, more food will be eaten. Nevertheless, I am succeeding due to my wife's help and with my doctor's guidance. First, my doctor suggested a nicotine withdrawal strategy that included reducing my smoking, using nicotine patches, and a therapy group. My wife did research to find a diet that we could both live with and an exercise plan that we might even enjoy together. Now, my wife and I start the day with a brisk walk for half an hour and then a bowl of fruit and bran for breakfast. I have already lost 20 pounds and no smoking in a month!

Practicing Your Writing Power

Power of
Language

© Thomson Corporation/Heinle Image Resource Bank

Explain particular personal habits of yours that you believe will lead to a long life, and explain why or how you developed these habits. You may discuss how you keep fit or what you include or don't include in your diet.

Or

Explain some unhealthful habits you have, how you got them, and how you might change them.

Or

Tell about an experience you have had with health care, such as a doctor, dentist, or hospital you have dealt with, and explain how you feel about this experience.

Name _____

Section _____   Score _____

PARALLELISM TEST 1

Rewrite the italicized part of the sentence to make it parallel.

1. The proper lifestyle and *eating* can help ensure a healthy baby.

   _____

2. During pregnancy, expectant mothers should eat a well-balanced diet, take prenatal vitamins, and *they should exercise regularly.*

   _____

3. Also, pregnant women should abstain from alcohol, tobacco, and *drugs that are illegal.*

   _____

4. While pregnant, women should avoid not only most drugs but also *drinking coffee.*

   _____

5. Pregnant women are also advised to avoid X-rays, hot tubs, and *using saunas.*

   _____

6. For the three months after birth, babies need eight to ten hours of sleep at night and *to sleep another eight hours during the day.*

   _____

7. Doctors recommend that babies be breast-fed for one year or *a commercial iron-fortified formula.*

   _____

8. An infant's mouth needs to be cleaned with gauze after feedings and *before a baby goes to bed.*

   _____

9. Screening for defects and *tests involving the hearing* are also important.

   _____

10. Newborns should undergo tests for HIV, iron deficiency, and *poisoning by lead.*

   _____

Name _____

Section _____ Score _____

PARALLELISM TEST 2

Rewrite the italicized part of the sentence to make it parallel.

1. As we mature physically, intellectually, and *in our emotions,* we must safeguard our health.

   _____

2. Illness prevention in adults varies with our age and *what gender we are.*

   _____

3. Women are advised to get a mammogram and *that they should have a cervical exam* every year.

   _____

4. Every year, men should get a yearly physical, undergo a prostate exam, and *they should have their blood tested.*

   _____

5. When men and women reach their fifties, annual tests are more important and *cost more money.*

   _____

6. Many adults don't like going to the doctor and don't like *to visit the dentist.*

   _____

7. An annual checkup is time consuming, expensive, and *people become stressed waiting for the results.*

   _____

8. Some patients would rather see their physician than *going to a specialist.*

   _____

9. Most patients admire their doctors for their caring nature and *because they are knowledgeable.*

   _____

10. In fact, surveys consistently show that Americans trust their doctors and their religious leaders more than *their leaders of government.*

   _____

Chapter 18   Commas

In this chapter, you will learn to use the six most important comma rules

- ☛ Compound sentences
- ☛ Introductory elements
- ☛ Interrupters
- ☛ Quotations
- ☛ Series
- ☛ Dates, addresses, and numbers

Skill Preview

Commas organize information in sentences. Most of the rules for using commas follow our natural speaking rhythms.

Read the first sentence in each pair and notice how each comma punctuates a pause. Then read the second sentence in each pair, and place a comma or commas where you think the same kind of pause occurs.

A comma separates independent clauses joined by a coordinating conjunction in a **compound sentence**.

I enjoy socializing at the mall, and I even get exercise walking around the mall.
My mother loves shopping at the mall but my father does not like going to the mall.

A comma separates an **introductory element** from the independent clause that it introduces.

Because my father hates to shop, he spends as little time at the mall as possible.
When Dad does go to the mall he heads straight for the tool department.

Commas separate a word group that **interrupts** the flow of the sentence.

There was a sale last weekend at Sears, my dad's favorite store.
Dad replaced his old lawnmower a Craftsman 780.

A comma separates a **direct quote** from the rest of the sentence.

"I got a great buy on this new mower," my father reported.
Dad said "I hope this lawnmower lasts as long as the last one."

Commas separate items in a **series.**

The new lawnmower has a quiet motor, an electric choke, and a large gas tank.
Its accessories include a blade guard a grass catcher and a blade sharpener.

Commas separate items in **dates, addresses, and numbers.**

The old lawnmower was purchased on Monday, May 19, 1987, in Pontiac, Michigan.
My dad bought the new mower from the store in Madison Wisconsin.

Spotlight on Writers

Power of Language

Stephen King

"Talent is cheaper than table salt. What separates the talented individual from the successful one is a lot of hard work."

Once a high-school English teacher, Stephen King (1947–) has become one of the most popular and successful writers of horror and suspense. Many of his books—including *Carrie, The Shining,* and *The Green Mile*—and short stories, including "The Shawshank Redemption"—have become successful films and made-for-TV movies. In 2004, he wrote the ABC television series *Kingdom Hospital.*

Compound Sentences

1.1 Use a comma before a coordinating conjunction that joins an independent clause (a subject plus a complete verb that expresses a complete thought) to another independent clause. (See Chapter 13: Sentence Combining, page 259 for more information and practice using compound sentences.)

independent clause   *independent clause*
Women <u>view</u> shopping as a social event, so they <u>enjoy</u> shopping with their friends.
                        coord. conjunction

MISUSE

1.2 Do not use a comma to join a compound predicate (two verb phrases).

Use a comma only before a coordinating conjunction when it joins two independent clauses (subject and verb).

   ✗ Kids <u>meet</u> friends at the mall, and <u>walk</u> around together.
   ✓ Kids <u>meet</u> friends at the mall and <u>walk</u> around together.
   ✓ Kids <u>meet</u> friends at the mall, and they <u>walk</u> around together.

Compound Sentence Formula and Key Words
Independent clause, coordinating conjunction independent clause.

(Subject + verb)	**F**or	(Subject + verb)
	And	
	Nor	
	But	
	Or	
	Yet	
	So (when *so* does not mean *so that*)	

Practice 1   Add commas where needed. Some items may not need a comma.

1. More than 40 percent of marriages end in divorce and the average divorce costs more than $20,000.

2. A mediated divorce is much less expensive, for it typically costs only $5,000.

3. The huge savings can benefit both spouses and help them support themselves and their children.

4. Many divorces are difficult, yet a mediator can help reduce the problems.

5. The mediator negotiates differences for couples with disagreements to resolve.

6. Most divorces would be easier with a mediator, yet most couples hire lawyers instead.

7. Mediators help couples decide on how to split their belongings, and the mediator does not take sides.

8. Mediators charge the same rates as lawyers but help complete the divorce process more quickly than lawyers.

9. A mediator may need only twenty hours to complete the negotiations and prepare the couple for the divorce.

10. A couple can choose a mediator, or the couple can decide to use a divorce lawyer.

Practice 2 *Working Together*

Working with a partner or alone, write a compound sentence using each of the coordinating conjunctions. Try writing your sentences about *school* or about *relationships.* Be sure that you write a complete thought with a subject and verb on each side of the coordinating conjunction. Trade papers with other classmates and check the comma use.

Introductory Elements

2.1 Use a comma after most introductory elements. An introductory element intro-duces an independent clause and is either a dependent clause or a phrase.

Introductory elements are sentence fragments that come before the subject and verb of the sentence. (See Chapter 13: "Sentence Combining," page 262, for more information and practice using dependent clauses as introductory elements in complex sentences.)

dependent clause   *independent clause*
While their wives shop, most husbands <u>look</u> for a place to sit down and wait.

prepositional phrase   *independent clause*
In most department stores, men <u>can be found</u> sitting on benches outside the fitting areas.

infinitive phrase   *independent clause*
To pass the time while waiting, some husbands <u>bring</u> along the newspaper to read.

Introductory Element Formula

Introductory element, independent clause (subject + verb).

2.2 Most introductory elements begin with **subordinating conjunctions, preposi-tions,** and **verbals** (infinitives, past participles, and present participles).

Common Key Words That Begin Introductory Elements

Subordinating Conjunctions	Prepositions	Verbals
because	at	to go
since	in	gone
although	by	going
even though	on	to do
if	with	done
	during	doing

Common Key Words That Begin Introductory Elements

Subordinating Conjunctions	Prepositions	Verbals
unless	from	to speak
when	according to	spoken
while	except	speaking
after	throughout	
before		

MISUSE

2.3 Do not use a comma when a dependent clause or phrase follows the independent clause.

>   *independent clause*　　　　　　　　　　　　　　*dependent clause*
> ✗ Many men <u>don't like</u> to wander around the mall, when they are going to only one store.

>   *dependent clause*　　　　　　　　　　　　*independent clause*
> ✓ When they are going to only one store, many men <u>don't like</u> to wander around the mall.

Practice 3　　Add commas where needed. Some items may not need a comma.

1. Although off-road biking strengthens legs it is also great for strengthening the upper body.

2. If a rider already knows how to ride a bicycle then riding a mountain bike will be easy.

3. To find the right mountain bike a new rider should consult with a salesperson at a bike shop.

4. Riding a mountain bike through the woods a cyclist can enjoy nature and get a workout.

5. Built to withstand the shocks of off-road trails a mountain bike has shock absorbers and fat tires.

6. On mountain trails cyclists can use one of twenty-five gears to go up or down the mountain.

7. By learning how to change gears and brake correctly a rider will be able to ride safely and easily.

8. It is important to grip the handlebars tightly because a bump in the trail could throw a rider off the bike.

9. Riders should choose a trail that is on level ground when they want an easy ride.

10. After a ride is completed, riders should hose down their bikes before putting them away.

Practice 4   *Working Together*

Working with a partner or alone, write five introductory element sentences. Try writing your sentences about *movies* or about *music.* Be sure that each sentence begins with one of the key words in the list on pages 328–329 and that a complete thought follows the comma. Trade papers with other classmates and check the comma use.

Interrupters

3.1 Commas set off interrupters, which are single words or groups of words that change the flow of the sentence.

Interrupters can appear at the beginning, in the middle, or at the end of sentences. However, interrupters do not change the meaning of the sentence; they only add information.

No, I don't want to go to the mall. (small word interrupter)

Please, Maria, don't ask me to go with you. (direct address interrupter)

However, I will drive you to the mall. (transition interrupter)

Your favorite shop, The Gap, has a sale today. (appositive interrupter)

I want to eat at The Junction, which begins serving dinner at six. (nonrestrictive clause interrupter)

Small Word

3.2 Use a comma to separate **certain small words (yes, no, oh, well, hey, hi)** that begin a sentence.

✓ Yes, I enjoyed the movie.

Small Word Formula
Small word, independent clause (subject + verb).

MISUSE

3.2.1 If the small word is part of the subject of the sentence, no comma is needed.

✗ No students are absent today.

Direct Address

3.3   Separate names or titles with commas when the sentence is **directly addressing** (communicating with) the person or persons.

Sarah, stop kidding around.

MISUSE

3.3.1 If the sentence is simply communicating about the name, no commas are needed.

✗ Sarah, was asked to stop kidding around.

Transitions

3.4   Use commas to set off **transitions** that could be removed from the sentence without changing the meaning of the sentence. The most common use of this rule is when the transition begins the sentence.

Also, I want to stop at the hardware store in the mall.

I will not, however, spend much time in the hardware store.

MISUSE

3.4.1 If the transition is necessary to the meaning of the sentence, it is not an interrupter, and no commas are needed.

✗ The class is, also, taking a test today.

Appositives

3.5   Use commas to set off an **appositive,** a word or group of words that defines or explains the word or phrase that comes before it.

Susan, my oldest daughter, is in sixth grade. (my oldest daughter defines *Susan*)

The first class of the morning, History 101, meets in the library tomorrow. (History 101 explains *first class of the morning*)

MISUSE

3.5.1 An appositive must come *immediately* after the word or phrase it defines, and it must be the *same part of speech.*

✗ My last class, is Math 007. (Is is a verb and can't define the noun class.)
✗ My class, in the gym, has been cancelled. (In the gym is a prepositional phrase and cannot define the noun class.)

Nonrestrictive Information

3.6 Use commas to set off nonrestrictive (or nonessential) information. Nonrestrictive information must interrupt the sentence without changing the meaning of the sentence. The most common nonrestrictive information begins with *which* and *who*.

Jorge hates driving to the mall, which is located twenty-five miles from his house.

My father, who was born in Cuba, is now a patriotic American citizen.

MISUSE

3.6.1 Do not use commas to separate information that is restrictive (or necessary) to the meaning of the sentence.

✗ There is only one store, that has a sale today.

That has a sale today is necessary to identify the store in the sentence. Commas separate only unnecessary or additional information.

Common Interrupter Key Words		
Transitions	*Small Words*	*Nonrestrictive*
moreover	yes	which
however	no	who
on the other hand	oh	
therefore	well	
also	hey	
for example	hi	

Practice 5 Add commas where needed. Some items may not need a comma.

1. No, it is not unusual to experience stress and anxiety at work.

2. Mr. Chao, my boss at Eye Vision Associates, sometimes makes me stay late.

3. Therefore, Maria sometimes gives me a ride.

4. Call me later tonight Kari.

5. The research team is excited about its findings, which will be published next month.

6. The electricians, however, will not finish their work until tomorrow.

7. All the cars that were built at the new factory are being recalled.

8. Moreover some students will be leaving early tomorrow.

9. The town's mayor who was elected easily will begin her duties tomorrow.

10. No animals are allowed in the park.

Practice 6 *Working Together*

Working with a partner or alone, write three different kinds of interrupter sentences. Try writing your sentences about *friends* or about *jobs.* Trade papers with other classmates and check the comma use.

Quotations

4.1 Use commas to separate direct quotations from the words that identify the source of the quotation. The comma belongs inside the quotation marks when the identifying words follow the quotation.

"Stand right here," the guard directed.

The boys asked, "What did we do wrong?"

MISUSE

4.2 When the quotation ends in a question mark or an exclamation mark, no comma is needed. Also, do not use a comma when *that* comes before the quotation or when no clear, identifying source is included.

✗ "Be careful!$_,$" the children's mother called out.

✗ She warned that$_,$ "the rocks are slippery."

✗ The sign stated$_,$ "No Swimming."

✱ Practice 7   Add commas where needed. Some items may not need a comma.

1. "The warranty on this computer has expired" the technician claimed.

2. "Who will pay for the repairs?" I asked.

3. The man said "I am not responsible for the repairs."

4. "Prices will rise by 50 percent over the next ten years" the analyst predicted.

5. The local newspaper reports in today's edition that "The mayor will issue a report

on the proposal."

Series

5.1 Use commas to separate items in a series. A series is a list of at least three members.

The best bass fishing is in Florida, Georgia, and Louisiana.

5.2 Do not place a comma after the last item in the series.

✗ Mandy, Alyssa, and Takela₀ received the highest grades.

Practice 8   Add commas where needed. Some items may not need a comma.

1. Math sociology and history are all required courses.

2. The children played in the garden swam in the pool and ate lunch on the patio.

3. The restaurant serves piping hot coffee and oven-baked fruit pies.

4. Jenny's goals are graduating from college finding a good job and getting married.

5. My favorite places to study are in the library at bus stop and by the pool.

Practice 9 *Working Together*

Working with a partner or alone, write five sentences that use the series rule. Try writing your sentences about *sports* or about *television.* Trade papers with other classmates and check the comma use.

Dates, Addresses, and Numbers

6.1 Use commas to separate items in dates and addresses and to separate every three digits in numbers of 1,000 or more.

The Hillcrest Mall at 29 Peele Street, Cooperstown, North Dakota, was opened on Monday, July 1, 1992, and more than 1,200 people shopped at the mall during the first week.

6.2 Do not use commas in numbers that express years, page numbers, or addresses.

✗ Page 1₀225 of the tax records states that the house at 4₀555 Blanding Avenue was built in 1₀972.

Practice 10   Add commas where needed. Some items may not need a comma.

1. On May 2 1999, more than 2 000 trees were planted along Interstate 95 in Atlanta Georgia.

2. The police responded to a call at 759 Westphalia Street Austin Texas.

3. The report states that Room 1035 had a leak in the sink on Monday April 3.

4. Hillshire Avenue in Red Bank New Hampshire is home to more than 3000 robins each spring.

5. Our phone number is on page 1257 of the New York City phone book.

Practice 11   *Working Together*

Working with a partner or alone, write a sentence that includes the date of someone's birth, a sentence that includes an address, and a sentence that includes a number larger than 1,000. Try writing your sentences about *movies* or about *music.* Trade papers with other classmates and check the comma use.

CD Connection

Power of Language

On *Writer's Resources* CD-ROM, see *Commas* in Grammar/Punctuation/Mechanics for more information and practice with commas.

Practice 12   *Working Together*

Working in groups, create study aids to learn each rule. Use one piece of paper for each rule. Write the rule in your own words. If possible, write the formula and key words for the rule. Try to create a way to remember the rule using a drawing, key words, or an example. Each group may then teach the rules to another group.

Practice 13   *Working Together*

In groups of two or three, divide up the comma rules. Each group member will write two sentences using the rules assigned to that member. Then each member will share his or her sentences with the group and explain how the sentences fit the comma rule used.

Practice 14   *Working Together*

Each group will switch sentences written in Practice 13 with another group and then identify the rule used in each sentence.

REVIEW EXERCISE 1

Identify the comma rule used in each sentence, and place commas where needed. Use the symbols CD (compound), IE (introductory element), INT (interrupter), Q (quotation), SER (series), DAN (dates, addresses, and numbers), and NC (no comma). Remember that some sentences may not need any commas.

_____ 1. The chief executive officer the CEO is thought to be among the most successful business leaders in our country.

_____ 2. In a recent survey of successful business leaders many chief executives reported that reading was their favorite hobby during childhood.

_____ 3. "Over 80 percent of the CEOs read more than one book per week" stated the researchers.

_____ 4. Moreover fewer than 20 percent of the executives described themselves as couch potatoes.

_____ 5. Future business leaders were most likely to be involved in teams clubs and other school organizations.

_____ 6. Watching television which is many teenagers' favorite hobby was not popular with these kids.

_____ 7. On the other hand most of the CEOs were not the coolest kids in school.

_____ 8. Only 4 percent of the CEOs said that they were popular in school and over half of the CEOs described themselves as unpopular.

_____ 9. Even though reading was the most popular hobby most future business leaders were not considered the smartest students.

_____ 10. Most future leaders were motivated by fear of failure and a desire for power but money was not a major motivation for success.

REVIEW EXERCISE 2

Identify the comma rule used in each sentence, and place commas where needed. Use the symbols CD (compound), IE (introductory element), INT (interrupter), Q (quotation), SER (series), DAN (dates, addresses, and numbers), and NC (no comma). Remember that some sentences may not need any commas.

_____ 1. One queen of the cosmetics industry Helena Rubinstein led an amazing life.

_____ 2. Although she was born in Poland Rubinstein moved to Australia as a young woman.

_____ 3. Rubinstein opened her first cosmetics shop in Melbourne Australia.

_____ 4. Rubinstein quickly followed her success with new shops in London Paris and New York.

_____ 5. As her fame grew she became known simply as Madame.

_____ 6. Florence Graham was the other queen of cosmetics and she was from Canada.

_____ 7. When she was twenty-nine Florence Graham opened her first shop in New York.

_____ 8. She painted the front door to the shop red and called her business Elizabeth Arden.

_____ 9. Both women became legends in their own time and their companies are still major competitors.

_____ 10. Even though they are both dead now Rubinstein and Arden made the cosmetic industry what it is today.

COMMAS EDITING TEST 1

Working alone or in pairs, place commas where needed. (There are ten commas needed in this passage.) Above each comma, write the abbreviation for the rule you are using.

Stress

Because we all live such busy lives stress is a natural result of trying to fit everything in. Common symptoms of stress include tense muscles shortness of breath and heart flutters. All of us need to identify what causes us stress and we need to determine how to deal with the stress. A study done in May of 1994 shows that men and women have different experiences with stress. For example women report more day-to-day stress than men. Women respond differently to stress than men and they need their own strategies to cope with stress. One solution to stress is getting a good night's sleep which would be at least seven hours of uninterrupted slumber. "You must sleep enough to allow the body to relax" Dr. Alison Jenkins states. When we walk steadily for a half hour or more our bodies create chemicals that counteract stress. Also cutting down on caffeine may help reduce stress. Stress is a problem that we must deal with.

COMMAS EDITING TEST 2

Working alone or in pairs, place commas where needed. (There are ten commas needed in this passage.) Above each comma, write the abbreviation for the rule you are using.

The Causes of Stress

Most of us know that we feel stress but we often don't know why. Some common stressors in our lives include relationships jobs and self-expectations. Because relationships with loved ones are so important to our happiness we worry when there are any problems with our loved ones. Dr. Milt Jefferson an authority on stress believes that we must communicate clearly with loved ones in order to avoid conflicts. "Good communication can reduce misunderstandings and the stress that comes from conflict" reports Dr. Jefferson. Employment is another problem area in our lives. Stress from our work can come from many different sources which include demanding bosses and difficult co-workers. Finally our own expectations of ourselves can create unbearable stress. When we want to succeed in some part of our lives we put pressure on ourselves. There are many causes of stress in our lives.

Practicing Your Writing Power

Power of Language

© Thomson Corporation/ Heinle Image Resource Bank

What causes you stress in your life, and how do you handle the stress? In your one-page response, try to use the comma rules you have learned in this chapter. Use at least one compound sentence, one introductory element sentence, and one series sentence. You may use the other comma rules, too.

Name _____
Section _____   Score _____

COMMAS TEST 1

Identify the comma rule used in each sentence, and place commas where needed. Use the symbols CD (compound), IE (introductory element), INT (interrupter), Q (quotation), SER (series), DAN (dates, addresses, and numbers), and NC (no comma). Remember that some sentences may not need any commas.

_____ 1. Americans eat more than twice the salt they should but they don't get enough potassium.

_____ 2. Most of our salt intake comes from the sodium in processed food restaurant meals and soft drinks.

_____ 3. The imbalance of salt and potassium causes high blood pressure one of America's most serious health hazards.

_____ 4. Factors such as weight diet and exercise contribute to high blood pressure.

_____ 5. When we eat too much our blood pressure rises.

_____ 6. If we eat less our blood pressure drops.

_____ 7. High blood pressure is a common problem and about fifty million Americans suffer from this condition.

_____ 8. High blood pressure puts people at risk of heart attacks kidney disease and strokes.

_____ 9. "We should take in no more than a teaspoon of salt per day" the surgeon general reports.

_____ 10. Therefore heart specialists have called for a reduced level of salt in our diet.

Name _____

Section _____   Score _____

COMMAS TEST 2

Identify the comma rule used in each sentence, and place commas where needed. Use the symbols CD (compound), IE (introductory element), INT (interrupter), Q (quotation), SER (series), DAN (dates, addresses, and numbers), and NC (no comma). Remember that some sentences may not need any commas.

_____ 1. There is no cure for the common cold and the flu returns every winter.

_____ 2. Sick people spend billions of dollars on over-the-counter remedies such as aspirin cough syrup and nasal sprays.

_____ 3. Even though antihistamines have no effect on the cold virus they are one of the most popular ingredients in cold medications.

_____ 4. Also antibiotics don't work on a cold.

_____ 5. Echinacea is an herb and some doctors believe that this herb strengthens our immune system.

_____ 6. Many people swear that vitamin C blocks the common cold yet others see no benefit to vitamin C at all.

_____ 7. "My patients with colds have found zinc lozenges shorten the length of a cold" claims Dr. Carla Bensen.

_____ 8. Because children haven't built up protective antibodies they get colds more often than adults.

_____ 9. Adults catch a cold because a virus has overrun their immune system.

_____ 10. When we shake hands with a sick person we can catch a virus if we put our fingers in our mouth.

Name _____

Section _____   Score _____

COMMAS TEST 3

Identify the comma rule used in each sentence, and place commas where needed. Use the symbols CD (compound), IE (introductory element), INT (interrupter), Q (quotation), SER (series), DAN (dates, addresses, and numbers), and NC (no comma). Remember that some sentences may not need any commas.

_____ 1. While a flu shot is essential for the elderly doctors don't recommend the shot for everyone.

_____ 2. There is no guarantee that a flu shot will protect people from the flu but the effects of the flu will be milder after a flu shot.

_____ 3. The flu vaccine contains an inactive virus so a flu shot cannot give you the flu.

_____ 4. Since the flu virus changes over time a new vaccine is needed every year.

_____ 5. The best time to get a flu shot is in October or November but it is never too late to get a shot.

_____ 6. Although the shot is pretty painless it may result in a slight ache at the site of the injection.

_____ 7. If someone doesn't like needles a nasal spray is available.

_____ 8. The spray costs more than the shot and may cause the temporary side effects of a runny nose sore throat and cough.

_____ 9. "The flu should be treated in the same way as a cold" says Dr. Jackson Smithfield.

_____ 10. "Please Doctor Smithfield help my child get over the flu."

Name _____

Section _____   Score _____

COMMAS TEST 4

Identify the comma rule used in each sentence, and place commas where needed. Use the symbols CD (compound), IE (introductory element), INT (interrupter), Q (quotation), SER (series), DAN (dates, addresses, and numbers), and NC (no comma). Remember that some sentences may not need any commas.

_____ 1. To avoid catching a cold people should wash their hands frequently.

_____ 2. Although it is not always possible we should avoid unnecessary contact with sick people.

_____ 3. After contact with a sick person no one should touch his or her eyes or nose.

_____ 4. We should not touch cold-soiled tissues for used tissues carry germs.

_____ 5. When we do catch a cold there are a number of steps we can take to relieve the symptoms.

_____ 6. "Drink plenty of liquids throughout the day" recommends Dr. Smithfield.

_____ 7. Also getting plenty of rest is very important.

_____ 8. At the onset of a cold everyone should gargle with warm salt water.

_____ 9. The last time I had a cold was January 5 2004.

_____ 10. My grandmother cooks me chicken soup every week so I have avoided a cold this year.

Chapter 19 Apostrophes

In this chapter, you will learn to use apostrophes in

- Contractions
- Possessive phrases
- Letters and numerals

Skill Preview

Apostrophes indicate missing letters in contractions and possessive relationships between words. You probably know more about apostrophes and their use than you think.

Examine the contractions and possessive phrases in the left column, and then place apostrophes where you think they are needed in the contractions and possessive phrases in the right column.

Contractions	Add Apostrophes
isn't	shouldnt
can't	its
you're	theyre
that's	werent
could've	weve

Possessive Phrases	Add Apostrophes
my neighbor's fence (the fence of my neighbor)	my dogs collar (the collar of my dog)
a television's warranty (the warranty of a television)	a cars headlights (headlights of a car)
my parents' car (the car of my parents)	many doctors patients (patients of many doctors)
many voters' opinions (the opinions of many voters)	some patients problems (problems of some patients)
the children's teacher (the teacher of the children)	a few peoples favorite celebrity (favorite celebrity of a few people)

Answers:

shouldn't	the dog's collar
it's	a car's headlights
they're	many doctors' patients
weren't	some patients' problems
we've	a few people's favorite celebrity

There are probably only a few places where you weren't sure where to place the apostrophe. The hardest part of using apostrophes is recognizing when and where to place apostrophes in words that need them. This chapter will teach you the rules for apostrophe use.

Spotlight on Writers

Oprah Winfrey

"I love books! I think books open windows to the world for all of us."

Talk show host and magazine founder Oprah Winfrey (1954–) is one of the most powerful women in America. In 1996, she launched Oprah's Book Club and to date, forty-seven of the book club selections have gone to the top of the best-seller list. Oprah's Book Club and her belief in the power of reading have been credited with rejuvenating the publishing industry. She believes reading has been an important ingredient of her success, and her book club has influenced the reading habits of millions of Americans.

Contractions

1.1 Use an apostrophe to take the place of missing letters in a contraction. Be sure to place the apostrophe between the appropriate letters.

there's = there is	we will = we'll
will not = won't	would not = wouldn't

Practice 1   Make contractions out of the following phrases.

1. that is = _____

2. should have = _____

3. you are = _____

4. was not = _____

5. cannot = _____

6. they are = _____

7. were not = _____

8. he is = _____

9. does not = _____

10. would not = _____

Practice 2   Place apostrophes in the contractions in each sentence.

1. Our next-door neighbors dont have any children.

2. Ricardo and Linda arent lonely, though.

3. Theyve got two golden retrievers that they think of as their children.

4. Linda and Ricardo wouldnt think of going for a walk without their dogs.

5. Theyll even take their dogs with them on vacation.

Practice 3   *Working Together*

Alone or with a partner, make a list of twenty contractions, being careful to place apostrophes where needed. Then trade lists with another group to check apostrophes.

Possession

In writing, an apostrophe before or after an *s* usually indicates that the word group before the apostrophe owns or possesses the word group after the apostrophe. Ownership means that the word group after the apostrophe belongs to the word with the apostrophe.

One boy's friend = the friend of one boy

Some plants' dead leaves = dead leaves that belong to some plants

Many women's husbands = husbands of many women

Recognizing Possessive Phrases

You use possessive phrases all the time in your speech and in your writing. However, when you write a possessive phrase, the apostrophe makes no sound, and it is easy to forget to include it. Recognizing when you are using a possessive phrase is the most important step in learning to use possessive apostrophes.

2.1 A possessive phrase communicates that an object or objects *belong* to an owner or owners.

Both objects and owners are nouns, meaning people or things. Possessive phrases will always have the same word order.

Owner's Object	**Owners' Object**
the man's house	Many lawyers' clients
the old man's large house	Many expensive lawyers' poor clients
the wagon's wheels	some books' authors
the shiny red wagon's large wheels	some famous books' unknown authors

Notice that people can belong to people (lawyers' clients), people can belong to things (books' authors), things can belong to people (man's house), and things can belong to things (wagon's wheels). Also, the owner and the object can include descriptive words such as *some, famous,* and *unknown* (some famous books' unknown authors). You already use possessive phrases naturally in your spoken and written communication; now you must become aware of when you are using a possessive phrase and where to put the apostrophe to indicate possession.

Practice 4   Fill in the blank with the appropriate word or words.

1. a decision of a judge = a judge's _____

2. the questions of the lawyers = the lawyers' _____

3. directions of the bailiff = the _____'s directions

4. the air conditioning of the courtroom = the _____'s air conditioning

5. facial expressions of some jurors = some _____' facial expressions

Practice 5   Fill in the blank with a noun (persons or things) to make a possessive phrase.

1. most people's _____

2. a photographer's _____

3. some cars' _____

4. a house's _____

5. one plant's _____

6. some songs' _____

7. many jobs' _____

8. the women's _____

9. many vacations' _____

10. a few teachers' _____

Practice 6   *Working Together*

Alone or in pairs, make up ten possessive phrases about sports, grocery shopping, cars, or the people or objects around you.

WHEN AN S NEEDS AN APOSTROPHE

Not all words that end in *s* need an apostrophe. Most plural nouns end in *s* and need no apostrophe. Singular verbs also end in *s* and need no apostrophe.

        N   N   V

Although some <u>worker</u>s get a break every two <u>hour</u>s, my boss <u>like</u>s us to work four

  N

<u>hour</u>s without a break.

2.2 To determine whether a word ending in *s* needs an apostrophe to show possession, try to convert the word group into an obvious statement of possession.

Owner's object = object of the owner	Owners' object = object of the owners
One friend's opinion = the opinion of one friend	Two friends' opinions = opinions of two friends

2.3 Check apostrophe use by determining whether the word or word group that immediately follows the apostrophe is an object (a person or thing) that belongs to the word with the apostrophe.

✓ the player's dirty uniform

An apostrophe is needed because *dirty uniform* is an object that belongs to the *player.*

✗ the player's from the other team

An apostrophe is not needed to show possession because the next word after the apostrophe—*from*—is a preposition and cannot be owned.

✓ the players from the other team

Players ends in *s* because it is a plural noun.

✗ the player compete's today

Competes is a verb and needs no apostrophe.

✓ the player competes today

Practice 7 Determine whether the apostrophe in each item is needed to show possession. Fill in the blanks next to the phrase to check possession. Write C for Correct possessive phrases, and write I for Incorrect next to word groups where the apostrophe is incorrect.

✓ some birds' nests = <u>nests</u> of <u>some birds</u>

Nests is an object that belongs to *some birds.*

✗ some birds' fly ≠ <u>fly</u> of <u>some birds</u>

Fly is a verb and not an object that belongs to *some birds.*

_____ 1. the league's most valuable player = _____ of

   _____

_____ 2. the league's held during the summer = _____ of _____

_____ 3. some computers' in the lab = _____ of _____

_____ 4. some computers' packing cartons = _____ of _____

_____ 5. the school's faculty = _____ of _____

_____   6. the school's gymnasium = _____ of _____

_____   7. the school's with the best team = _____ of _____

_____   8. the planet's orbit = _____ of _____

_____   9. the planets' farthest from Earth = _____ of _____

_____   10. the planet orbit's the sun = _____ of _____

Placing Apostrophes in Possessive Phrases

The rules for where to place the apostrophe—before or after a final *s*—have to do with whether the owner is singular, plural, or irregular plural.

SINGULAR OWNERS

3.1   If the owner in a possessive phrase is singular (one person or thing), add **'s** to show possession.

the company's logo	one child's toys
someone's book bag	the gate's latch
my church's youth group	a classmate's notes

3.1.1 Even if the singular owner ends in -*s*, add **'s.**

Charles's father	Chris's assignments
my class's exam time	the boss's orders

Practice 8   Add apostrophes where needed. Be sure to check your answer by making sure that the word or word group immediately following the **'s** is an object or objects that belong to the word with the apostrophe. Some sentences may need no apostrophes or may need more than one apostrophe.

1. One womans idea of a good stove is a British cooker thats been around for nearly one hundred years.

2. Jade Jagger, Mick Jaggers daughter, recently added an Aga cooker to her kitchens high-tech stove.

3. The cookers two ovens and two burners are always on.

4. The stoves designer was a Swedish engineer who won the Nobel prize for another one of his inventions and became convinced he could improve on his wifes inefficient stove.

5. In todays high-tech world, the Aga cooker reminds many of an earlier era.

PLURAL OWNERS

3.2 If the owner in a possessive phrase is plural and ends in -s, add an apostrophe after the s to show possession.

many teachers' salaries   two friends' favorite movie
some dogs' owners   many companies' employees

Practice 9   Add apostrophes where needed in contractions or possessive phrases. Be sure to check your answer by making sure that the word or word group immediately following the **s'** is an object or objects that belong to the word with the apostrophe. Some sentences may need no apostrophes or more than one apostrophe.

1. Most Americans diets include too much junk food.

2. Americans dont eat right because theyre always on the run, and many families dinnertime is spent at snack bars or fast-food restaurants.

3. Experts warn that some kids health is in danger because of the foods they eat.

4. Many teenagers typical lunch consists of a soft drink and a bag of chips, and such food contains too much sugar and salt and not enough healthful nutrients.

5. Although parents cant force kids to eat healthfully, kids are influenced by their parents cooking at home, so parents should cook healthful meals full of vegetables, fruit, and protein.

3.3 Often, words around the owner will help you determine whether the owner is singular or plural.

A parent's children may misbehave, but most parents' children are well behaved. The neighbor's dog ran away from her and chased my other neighbors' cat into their garage.

Notice that the words *a, most, her,* and *their* determine whether the owner in the possessive phrase is singular or plural. A singular owner ends with an *'s,* and a plural owner ends with *s'.* The placement of the apostrophe does not depend on how many objects are owned, only on whether the owner is singular or plural.

Practice 10   Add apostrophes where needed. Words in the sentence will help you determine whether the owner is singular or plural. Some sentences may need no apostrophes or more than one apostrophe.

1. Many students study skills suffer unless they adjust to a professors teaching style.

2. A students ability to study effectively depends on the student being flexible with the amount of time and effort needed to study a courses material.

3. For example, professors assignments to their students may vary each day from as little as fifteen minutes to as long as two hours.

4. Students must also be aware of an assignments difficulty.

5. The students job is to handle whatever assignment is given them, but it is also the teachers job to be clear about the work she is assigning.

IRREGULAR PLURALS

3.4 When the owner is plural but does not end in *s*, add an *'s* to show possession. The most common irregular plural owners are *men, women, children,* and *people.*

people's opinions	children's favorite pastime
men's sizes	women's club

Practice 11   **Add apostrophes where needed in contractions or possessive phrases. Some sentences may need no apostrophes or more than one apostrophe.**

1. Many peoples idea of a good time is to take a trip to Disney World with the whole family.

2. Our childrens greatest wish is to see Mickey Mouse and to ride the Space Mountain attraction.

3. Theres a womens group that meets on Thursdays in our towns conference center.

4. Ive never seen so many mens jackets for sale.

5. One club members desire is to collect everyones dues and then buy a childrens playground.

POSSESSIVE PRONOUNS

3.5 Possessive pronouns (his, hers, theirs, ours) do not need an apostrophe to show possession.

That ball is theirs.
The dog lost its bone.

Letters and Numerals

4.1 Use *'s* to indicate that letters and numerals are plural.

Jason received all A's this term.
Temperatures will be in the 60's this week.

4.2 The use of the apostrophe with the *s* to make decades and centuries plural is optional as long as the writer is consistent.

The 80's (or 70s)
The 1700's (1700s)

Note: In all exercises in this book, use 's in decades and centuries.

CD Connection

Power of Language

On *Writer's Resources* CD-ROM, see *Apostrophes* in Grammar/Punctuation/Mechanics for more information and practice with apostrophes.

REVIEW EXERCISE 1

Add apostrophes where needed. Some sentences may need no apostrophes or more than one apostrophe.

1. Terrorism hasnt kept people from traveling by air, but its changed most peoples comfort with flying.

2. Everyones security depends upon thoroughly screening all passengers and all passengers baggage.

3. Passengers cant board planes without first going through the airports security checkpoints.

4. The security guards duties include opening bags, x-raying all travelers carry-on luggage, and searching passengers before they allow passengers to board planes.

5. Guards must even search childrens backpacks and elderly ladies handbags.

6. Along with the heightened attention to baggage, passengers behavior is also being monitored closely as they go through checkpoints.

7. Someones nervousness or profuse sweating when going through security will attract a security guards attention.

8. Screening supervisors use a score sheet that evaluates a travelers actions.

9. When a passengers score reaches the 80s, police officers are notified.

10. An airports security system is graded, and airports that receive Ds or Fs may lose federal funding.

REVIEW EXERCISE 2

Add apostrophes where needed. Some sentences may need no apostrophes or more than one apostrophe.

1. My apartment is located in one of Seattles best neighborhoods.

2. Its not an expensive area, and theres a lot of shopping within walking distance of my apartment.

3. The neighborhoods location also makes it convenient to use our countys rapid transit system.

4. All of my neighbors cooperation makes this an awesome place to live.

5. For example, when a womans cat got stuck in a tree, a young man borrowed a friends ladder and retrieved the animal.

6. Another neighbors car wouldnt start one morning, so a man helped him charge the cars battery.

7. Not surprisingly, our neighborhood won the newspapers annual award for this regions best place to live.

8. Many families decision to move here has been influenced by the areas reputation.

9. In the 1960s, our neighborhood became run down, but during the 1990s, lots of young people moved in because apartments were inexpensive.

10. Now, in many peoples eyes, theres not a better place to live.

APOSTROPHE EDITING TEST 1

Working alone or in pairs, add apostrophes where needed. Some sentences may need no apostrophes or more than one apostrophe.

```
                           Holland

    My schools requirements for graduation include spending a

term abroad at a foreign college or university. I chose to

attend the University of Amsterdam because of my parents

experience when they went to school there. Amsterdam is

Hollands capital city. Its also one of Europes primary ports.
```

The towns most famous resident is the Queen of the Netherlands. While I was living in Amsterdam, I saw the queen twice, once when she honored the countrys war dead and once when she attended a concert by the universitys orchestra. Amsterdam is famous for its canals. The city is ringed by six canals, and many peoples houses overlook a canal. Amsterdams canal houses are famous for leaning against their neighbor or leaning out over the street. The city lies below sea level, and the houses are built on sand and sink over time. Amsterdam is a charming city that seems like a small town.

APOSTROPHE EDITING TEST 2

Working alone or in pairs, add apostrophes where needed. Some sentences may need no apostrophes or more than one apostrophe.

My Year in Amsterdam

Lifes little coincidences are amazing! My parents met and married in Holland while attending a foreign exchange program during the 1980s. Naturally, their sons first name is *Dutch,* and now Im on the same exchange program twenty years later. Six months ago, I met a beautiful Dutch girl named Anika. Anikas major is English, so communication is no problem. Ive spent wonderful times here in my girlfriends hometown, and last weekend Anika took me to her familys farm outside the city. After a day of touring the farms dairy and tulip fields, I sat down with Anikas father and mother and asked her parents permission to marry Anika. They said yes, and I told them that their first grandchilds name would be

Amsterdam.

Practicing Your Writing Power

Power of Language

© Thomson Corporation/ Heinle Image Resource Bank

Explain how you met a significant other in your life. This person may be a love interest or just a friend. Be sure to describe this person and the time and place where you met. Explain what attracted you to this person and how you knew the person was right for you. If you currently don't have have a significant other, write about a past relationship that was meaningful to you. After writing a page to two pages describing your relationship, check your writing for apostrophe use.

Name _____

Section _____   Score _____

APOSTROPHE TEST 1

Add apostrophes where needed. Some sentences may need no apostrophes or more than one apostrophe.

1. John and Mary Ward started Old Man Wards Family Market in 1955.

2. During the late 1950s, this couples love for each other and passion for providing fresh food for their neighbors established a family dynasty.

3. The markets fresh produce, meat, and seafood became popular with shoppers all over the region.

4. Mrs. Ward would personally inspect all farmers produce before buying anything from them.

5. Mr. Ward spent long hours driving the countrysides bumpy back roads to inspect cattlemens beef and pork.

6. Eventually, the Wards five children all worked at the market.

7. One daughters love for sewing resulted in the market selling womens sewing supplies and hand-knit sweaters.

8. The oldest son went to the states best agricultural college, and he returned home to establish the familys own farm.

9. Another sons talent for business helped the family diversify into other businesses, including two laundries and a car dealership.

10. However, all of the businesses successes were founded on two peoples love for each other and their desire to serve their customers.

Name _____

Section _____   Score _____

APOSTROPHE TEST 2

Add apostrophes where needed. Some sentences may need no apostrophes or more than one apostrophe.

1. One of Americas most common health problems is chronic pain.

2. When someones pain lasts longer than six months, the pain is classified as chronic.

3. A chronic pains origins and possible cures are complicated.

4. To begin with, the tools dont exist that can measure pain, and pain cant be located with MRIs or X-rays.

5. In many cases, its not even possible to pinpoint the organ or tissue thats causing the pain.

6. Even a physicians most powerful drugs may not reduce the pain.

7. Often a pain sufferers best hope is a combination of medications and other therapies such as massage and physical therapy.

8. Traditional medicines answer to chronic pain is an assortment of pain blockers, ultrasound therapies, and injections of pain relievers.

9. However, alternative medicine is included in many peoples treatment plans.

10. Nontraditional healers such as acupuncturists and massage therapists address the bodys interconnected systems to help relieve chronic pain.

Name _____

Section _____   Score _____

APOSTROPHE TEST 3

Add apostrophes where needed. Some sentences may need no apostrophes or more than one apostrophe.

1. Listening to a friends troubles is one of the primary ways that we show our support.

2. In fact, the art of listening is one of the worlds most treasured skills.

3. Active listening establishes others trust in us.

4. Many professionals wouldnt be effective without good listening skills.

5. A doctors ability to listen to her patients complaints will help her to treat them.

6. Similarly, many lawyers defenses of their clients begin when the lawyers listen carefully to their clients stories.

7. One of the most effective ways to listen is to take in whats being said and then to restate a speakers thoughts.

8. For example, when listening to a family members ideas, a skillful listener will not interrupt or change the subject.

9. Instead, the listener tries to take in the loved ones words and feelings and then restate them accurately.

10. Even in todays fast-paced world, everyone values the ability to listen to others thoughts and feelings.

APOSTROPHE TEST 4

Add apostrophes where needed. Some sentences may need no apostrophes or more than one apostrophe.

1. Effective reading takes more than knowing all the words meanings.

2. A skillful readers first step in comprehending a text is to get an overall idea of the reading selections subject matter.

3. A readings main idea is the most important point that readers must understand in order to follow an authors train of thought.

4. Many articles main idea can actually be difficult to decipher, especially when authors use irony or sarcasm to get their points across.

5. The main idea can be thought of as an umbrella statement that covers a writers main points.

6. After identifying the main idea, a readers next task is to appreciate how the writer supports the main idea and how the supports are organized.

7. A skillful reader also grasps the authors purpose in writing, whether it is to report facts, make an argument, or tell a story.

8. When we read an editorial, for instance, we must also be aware of the editorials bias for or against different beliefs.

9. Reading isnt as easy as most people think.

10. Its a task that takes everyones best effort.

Chapter 20 Other Punctuation Marks

In this chapter you will learn about the

➥ Semicolon

➥ Colon

➥ Dash

➥ Hyphen

➥ Parentheses

Skill Preview

Less frequently used punctuation marks are valuable in giving writers more ways to express their ideas.

Read the following passage and circle the punctuation marks.

Hollywood star magazines—what some people call stargazers—are a great source of entertainment; however, they are not a reliable source of information. These magazines—most notably the *National Star* and the *National Sun*—are generally sold in grocery store checkout lanes and mini-markets. They are bi-monthly magazines (printed twice a month) and are known for their outlandish stories about movie stars and celebrities. One movie star (who preferred to remain nameless) said the following: "If I had a dollar for every lie told about me in the star rags, I'd be a millionaire."

Semicolon

1.1 Use a semicolon to connect two complete sentences that are closely related.

One of my classes is hard; the other class is easy.
I speak French; my brother does not.

1.2 Use a semicolon to connect two sentences joined by a conjunctive adverb or a transitional phrase.

I love to cook; therefore, I entertain regularly.
My sister loves to eat out; however, she can't afford it.
Note: Use a semicolon before the word and a comma after it.

Common Conjunctive Adverbs and Transitional Phrases	
also	meanwhile
as a result	moreover
besides	next
certainly	on the other hand
consequently	otherwise
finally	similarly
for example	subsequently
for instance	then
furthermore	therefore
however	thus

1.3 Use semicolons between items in a series when the series has internal punctuation.

This summer I will visit Halifax, Nova Scotia; Portland, Maine; and Boston, Massachusetts.

Practice 1   Identify the punctuation in the following sentences as correct (C) or incorrect (I), and then correct any punctuation errors.

_____   1. Because I speak Spanish; it is easy for me to travel in South America.

Spotlight on Writers

Power of Language

Jessica Runion

"When I wrote the hospice letter to my family and friends, I had no idea it would make such an impact. I haven't changed the entire world with my writing; I've just tried to make my little part of the world better."

Jessica Runion is a thirteen-year-old middle school student from Federalsburg, Maryland. Her mother died of ovarian cancer when Jessica was eleven years old, and Jessica has used writing as a way to work through her grief. While volunteering for a local hospice, Jessica wrote a letter to a few friends and family members asking them to sponsor her for a walk to raise money for a new hospice house. Little did Jessica know the letter would take on a life of its own. Those who received her letter either mailed or e-mailed it to their friends and family, and soon Jessica was receiving donations from people she didn't know, from as far away as California. With a single letter, Jessica was able to raise almost $1,000 for the local hospice organization.

_____ 2. My history instructor relates class material to current events; therefore, her class is interesting.

_____ 3. My instructors this term are Mr. Harris, who graduated from Harvard, Ms. Breck, who graduated from Smith, and Ms. Edwards, who graduated from UNC, Chapel Hill.

Colon

2.1 Use a colon after a complete sentence that introduces a list, definition, or quotation.

My English instructor is famous for three things: work, work, and more work.

The dictionary definition for *sepulchre* is clear: a burial vault or a tomb.

President John F. Kennedy appealed to our idealism in one of his most frequently quoted lines: "Ask not what your country can do for you but what you can do for your country."

Note: Capitalization is optional after a colon, except in a quotation. The first letter of a quotation is capitalized if it is preceded by any punctuation mark.

2.2 Use a colon after the words *the following* or *as follows.*

I plan to pack the following: three shirts, two bathing suits, and four pairs of slacks.

Practice 2   Identify the punctuation in the following sentences as correct (C) or incorrect (I), and then correct any punctuation errors.

_____   1. I was instructed to bring the following items to the party: two bags of chips, two jars of salsa, and three bottles of apple juice.

_____   2. I promised my mother I would buy: lettuce, tomatoes, and cucumbers.

_____   3. Mark had two problems: he couldn't concentrate and he couldn't read.

Dash

3.1 The dash is used to emphasize nonessential information.

My brother had to make a quick decision—flee or fight.
Modern technology—the microchip in particular—has fueled a digital revolution.

3.2 The dash can be used to signal a shift in thought or a change of tone.

My sister loves rock and roll and listens to it every day—even after she got married and had kids.

The instructor decided to give five points of extra credit on the test if the students spelled her name correctly—no kidding.

Practice 3   Identify the punctuation in the following sentences as correct (C) or incorrect (I), and then correct any punctuation errors.

_____   1. My new car—a 2004 Jeep Cherokee—was slightly damaged in the accident.

_____   2. I promised my brother—that I would take him fishing on Saturday.

_____   3. My chain saw stalled—for it was out of gas.

Hyphen

4.1 A hyphen is used to separate compound adjectives (two or more words that describe a single noun).

The player revealed her true-blue spirit.
There are many tried-and-true methods of studying.

4.2 A hyphen is used to divide a word at the end of a line. Always divide a word between syllables. (Check the dictionary for syllable divisions.)

My instructor requested that each student turn in his or her paper by the Monday following the break.

Practice 4   Identify the punctuation in the following sentences as correct (C) or incorrect (I), and then correct any punctuation errors.

_____   1. Hermione was not-so-sure of her answer.

_____   2. Ron made a half-hearted attempt to study.

_____   3. The sea was painted pale-peach by the setting sun.

Parentheses

5.1 Parentheses can be used to set off extra information that is not essential to the meaning of the sentence.

New regulations (introduced in 2004) are aimed at reducing fraud in the insurance industry.

A company's CEO (chief executive officer) is responsible for the accuracy of its financial statements.

5.2 Parentheses enclose numerals and letters in a list.

After graduation I plan to (1) get a job, (2) pay off my student loans, and (3) buy a house.

5.3 Parentheses enclose references, the sources of quoted matter, and cross-references to other parts of the same text.

According to a *Newsweek* poll, only 25 percent of young people are planning on voting (19).

Practice 5   Identify the punctuation in the following sentences as correct (C) or incorrect (I), and then correct any punctuation errors.

_____   1. Disagreement still rages over NAFTA (North American Free Trade Agreement).

_____   2. Five thousand delegates attended the Democratic National Convention in Boston [*Time* 5].

_____   3. My priorities are 1) pass my classes, 2) get my degree, and 3) go to graduate school.

CD Connection

Power of
Language

On *Writer's Resources* CD-ROM, see *Minor Punctuation Marks* in Grammar/Punctuation/
Mechanics for additional practice with dashes, parentheses, brackets, slashes, and
ellipsis points. Semicolons and colons are reviewed in *Semicolons and Colons* in
Grammar/Punctuation/Mechanics.

REVIEW EXERCISE

Identify the punctuation in the following sentences as correct (C) or incorrect (I).
Correct the punctuation errors in the incorrect items.

_____ 1. I failed my math class last term; I'm failing it again this term.

_____ 2. My favorite beaches are Waikiki, Hawaii; St. Augustine, Florida; and Sao
Paulo, Brazil.

_____ 3. My brother plays tennis, however, I do not play.

_____ 4. Barry, therefore, decided to make the best of the situation.

_____ 5. At that time of day, the restaurant serves only: sandwiches, soups, and
salads.

_____ 6. When I get up in the morning, I read the sports section first; then, I
read the comics.

_____ 7. My son has soccer practice on Tuesdays, Boy Scouts on Wednesdays,
and band practice on Thursdays.

_____ 8. She brought her favorite foods; for example, bananas and chocolate
fondue.

_____ 9. According to my mother, I will need to: get good grades and get a
good job.

_____ 10. She wanted to compete in the race, moreover, she wanted to win.

Practicing Your Writing Power

Power of Language

© Thomson Corporation / Heinle Image Resource Bank

Where would you most like to live and why? Describe the ideal location of the house of your dreams.

Name _____

Section _____ Score _____

OTHER PUNCTUATION MARKS TEST 1

Identify the punctuation in the following sentences as correct (C) or incorrect (I). Correct the punctuation errors in the incorrect items.

_____ 1. Severe summer storms have caused flooding: in many of the mid-Atlantic states.

_____ 2. The cities worst hit by the storms were Reading, Pennsylvania, Trenton, New Jersey, and Greensboro, North Carolina.

_____ 3. Some cities had to evacuate residents, for example, Greensboro evacuated more than 1,000 residents.

_____ 4. City and state officials have had to take emergency precautions such as: mobilize the National Guard, declare a state of emergency, and open shelters.

_____ 5. Some citizens have panicked; for example, they have abandoned their homes before it was necessary.

_____ 6. Others—police and fire officials, for example—have risen to the challenge.

_____ 7. Many citizens across the country (half a million by last count) have donated food and clothing to the disaster victims.

_____ 8. Some health officials fear the natural disaster could become a human disaster; if drinking water and shelter aren't provided quickly.

_____ 9. Weather forecasters are predicting the worst: more rain for the rest of the week.

_____ 10. Insurance companies will undoubtedly have to respond by raising their rates, for instance.

Name _____

Section _____ Score _____

OTHER PUNCTUATION MARKS TEST 2

Identify the punctuation in the following sentences as correct (C) or incorrect (I). Correct the punctuation errors in the incorrect items.

_____ 1. My history class is particularly demanding, for example, I often have two hours of homework a night.

_____ 2. Last night, my instructor gave three assignments: read Chapter 3, answer the discussion questions, and turn in an outline of the chapter.

_____ 3. The chapter covered the period leading up to the Revolutionary War, including tensions over taxation; the Revolutionary War, with its many battles; and the postwar period.

_____ 4. After two hours of rock-solid note taking, I took a break and made myself a snack.

_____ 5. I fixed: a sandwich, a hard-boiled egg, and a drink.

_____ 6. It was late (past midnight) when I decided to go to bed.

_____ 7. I felt I had prepared well; therefore, I felt confident that I understood the material.

_____ 8. At the beginning of class, my instructor asked us to take out: paper, pens, and dictionaries.

_____ 9. I looked around the room at the shocked faces of the students and knew two things: (1) I was the only one who had studied, and (2) I was the best prepared for the test.

_____ 10. The moral of the story is as follows better safe than sorry.

Chapter 21 Quotation Marks

In this chapter, you will learn how to

- Use quotation marks to set off the words, thoughts, and writing of others
- Punctuate quotations
- Paraphrase
- Use quotation marks to indicate the titles of short written, dramatic, and musical works

Skill Preview

The following passage contains the primary ways that college writers use quotation marks. After studying the use of quotation marks and the comments, try adding quotation marks to the second sentence.

In her article "We Are Our Words,"[1] Diane Ackerman states,[2] "Learning language can begin surprisingly early, at around 6 months, when babies start to identify the special sounds of their native tongues, like . . .[3] the squeaky e of American English's 'street'"[4] (2)[5].

[1] The titles of articles and other short works are placed inside quotation marks. The comma is also placed inside the quotation marks.

[2] The author of quoted material should be identified. A comma comes at the end of the signal phrase, and the first word of a quotation that follows punctuation must be capitalized.

[3] Ellipsis points (three spaced periods) signal that part of the quoted material has been left out.

[4] When a word is used as a word—here the word "street" is being discussed—the word should be placed in quotation marks. However, whenever quotation marks are used inside quoted material, single quotation marks are used.

[5] The page number of the article is cited at the end of the sentence.

Using the previous model, place quotation marks in the following sentence.

Based on her research findings in the research study The Part-time Student, Haley

Johnson believes, Part-time students often have more responsibilities and worries than

full-time students (3).

Answer: Based on her research findings in the research study "The Part-time Student," Haley Johnson believes, "Part-time students often have more responsibilities and worries than full-time students." (3).

Direct Quotes

1.1 When using the actual words of another person's speech, thoughts, or writing, surround the quote in quotation marks.

"Don't drive too fast," my father warned, as he handed me the keys to his brand-new Porsche, "or this will be the last time you borrow my car."

I thought to myself, "No problem."

I remembered reading in my driver's manual that "a powerful car tests the driver's skill."

Punctuating Direct Quotes

COMMAS AND PERIODS

1.2 Commas and periods should be placed inside quotation marks. (See the examples above.)

Spotlight on Writers

Power of Language

Shoshana Nisbett

"I wanted to raise awareness, and I think I managed to do that."

To draw attention to the difficulties of negotiating the campus in a wheelchair, Shoshana Nisbett sent a humorous e-mail to several prominent officials at her community college. Shoshana chose to use humor to make her point, and she succeeded in getting the attention of the school officials, who each responded to her e-mail, enabling her to open a dialogue about the difficulties she faces daily in order to attend classes. A few short weeks later, she was taking a group of school officials on a tour of the campus. The tour was successful in part because Shoshana had them all ride in wheelchairs so that they could experience firsthand the difficulties of negotiating closed doors and bumpy sidewalks.

The first word of a quotation should be capitalized if the quote follows punctuation marks. (See the second example on page 372.) If there is no punctuation before the quote, then the quotation should not be capitalized. (See the third example on page 372.)

CITATIONS

1.3 Credit the source of any material you quote or paraphrase by introducing in your text the name of the author and work. Also, provide an in-text citation of the page number where the quote can be found. The citation of the page number (and the author's name if not clear from the sentence) should be placed inside parentheses *after* the end quotation marks and *before* the period at the end of the sentence.

The plan board's report calls the proposed housing development along the river "a disturbing trend that we may regret" (6).

SHORTENING QUOTED MATERIAL WITH ELLIPSIS POINTS

1.4 Use ellipsis points (three periods) when you want to abbreviate longer quotations. Try to make the resulting passage read smoothly without the missing material.

Original Quote: Michael Pollan writes, "Late last summer, I moved from Zone 5 to Zone 9, or, to be both more and (at least to a gardener) less geographically precise, from southern New England to Northern California" (15).

Shortened Quote: Michael Pollan writes, "Late last summer, I moved from … southern New England to Northern California" (15).

Using Brackets to Add Words to Quotes

1.5 If you need to insert a word or words inside a direct quote in order to make the quote understandable or to clarify a pronoun, surround the added words in brackets.

The repairman announced, "It [the washer] is too old to fix."

Practice 1   Add quotation marks to each sentence.

1. According to Pam Deluce, The TXC microchip is the fastest processor on the market (6).

2. The professor advised, Work closely with your lab partner today.

3. I thought of my favorite line from the Grateful Dead: What a long, strange trip it's been.

4. The movie was nominated by a movie critic as funniest comedy of the year.

5. Habit is the product of a lazy mind, says my grandmother.

6. The girl blushed and replied, I'd love to go out tonight.

7. The guidebook describes the park as paradise by the sea.

8. The authors of the study note, No effects of the substance were noticeable (7).

9. I cannot go out tonight, Zia told Pete, but I am free tomorrow night.

10. In his only novel, Fred Peterson calls the main character an imitation

    cowboy . . . who wishes he had a horse and a gun (12).

Practice 2   *Working Together*

Alone or in pairs, use your own paper to practice using quotes and quotation marks. Consult the punctuation rules and examples above for models.

1. Write a sentence that uses the direct words of your teacher or another student.
2. Refer to the first twenty-five pages of this textbook, and write a sentence that quotes the authors of this text. The quotation you use should be no longer than one sentence. Be sure to mention the names of the authors and the page number where the quoted sentence can be found.
3. Using the first twenty-five pages of this textbook, try to use ellipsis points to condense a long sentence. Be sure to mention the names of the authors and the page number where the quotation can be found.

Paraphrasing

2.1 Paraphrasing means to put someone's words into your own words. Often it is preferable in college writing to paraphrase the ideas of another writer to show your understanding of the ideas. You must take care to represent the ideas fairly. You should also cite references in indirect quotations just as you would in direct quotations.

Direct Quote: "According to the travel bureau's projections, 77 percent of vacationers visit friends and relatives in the area" (Culver 9).
Paraphrase: The travel bureau estimates that 77 percent of vacationers travel to see friends and family in the area (Culver 9).

Practice 3   *Working Together*

Alone or in pairs, paraphrase the following quotations in your own words.

1. When I started college, my best friend promised, "I will write you every day."

_____

2. At the beginning of our date, I thought to myself, "I can't believe she is going out with me!"

_____

3. My favorite teacher always says, "Good grades are the product of attending every class and completing every assignment."

_____

4. "Changing the operating system on your personal computer is advisable if you are using Windows 95 or 98; however, the operation should be performed by a factory-trained technician" (Jorgenson 8).

_____

5. "Americans have always believed in hard work and in luck, and these two beliefs are at the core of our optimism" (Laskey 5).

_____

Other Uses of Quotation Marks

3.1 Use single quotation marks when placing quotation marks inside direct quotations.

My father called out, "I should never have said, 'Take the car tonight.'"

4.1 Place the titles of short works such as stories, poems, articles, chapters, songs, and episodes of television programs inside quotation marks. The titles of longer works, such as books and novels, should be underlined (or placed in italics).

"The Final Straw" is the fifth chapter in the novel <u>Beyond the Limits.</u>

5.1 When a word is used as the word itself, place the word in quotation marks (or use italics).

Our word "daughter" can be traced back to the Greek language.

Practice 4   Place double and single quotation marks where needed.

1. The first word that the baby learned was mommy.

2. Many people love the song Let It Be by the Beatles.

3. The witness testified, I told the police, Please find the criminal who robbed my neighbor.

4. In the short story The Followers, the main character states, Television is my salvation (3).

5. The patient told his wife, My doctor says, Tell your wife not to worry.

CD Connection

Power of Language

On *Writer's Resources* CD-ROM, see *Quotes* in Grammar/Punctuation/Mechanics for more information and practice with quotation marks.

REVIEW EXERCISE

Place quotation marks where needed.

1. Stay in bed and drink plenty of liquids, the doctor advised, and call me if you get worse.

2. Miser is a word that comes from Latin.

3. According to Masterson's editorial, The city commission should consider all the options before voting against the proposal.

4. As I finished the exam, I thought to myself, Don't make any careless errors.

5. The authors warn that our research should not be ignored.

6. My sister's favorite song is Salad for Sally.

7. Angela's boyfriend told her, I woke up from my dream calling out your name, Angela, Angela!

8. In today's column, the sports writer states, The similarities between the two teams are incredible.

9. The class was having trouble understanding the poem The Love Song of J. Alfred Prufrock.

10. Alright is the misspelling of two common words.

QUOTATION MARKS EDITING TEST

Alone or with a classmate, place quotation marks where needed.

First Date Fiasco

The Boy Scout motto says, Be prepared. I wish I had been a Boy Scout. Last night, I would have settled for <u>The Boy Scout Handbook</u> when I went for my first date with Lucy, a beautiful girl I met at the beach.

Lucy, Lucy who? the old woman at the front door asked.

Lucy Martinez, I answered hopefully.

She looked doubtful and called out, Lucinda, venga! Then she slammed the door in my face. It seemed like one hundred degrees out on the doorstep, and I felt perspiration running down my cheek. What is going on? I wondered.

I heard someone coming down the stairs. It was Lucy talking.

Who? What? No! she cried, throwing open the door. What are you doing here? You said, Next Saturday!

Well, well, I stammered. I was trying to remember what I had said when she slammed the door in my face. I wiped the

sweat off my face. I could hear more Spanish and the creak-
ing of stairs. I told myself, Just run for the car and don't
look back.

Then the door opened, and the old woman smiled and said,
My granddaughter is not feeling so good. You come back next
Saturday.

I drove off thinking about what I would say at school.
Then I had a happy thought: Lucy Martinez doesn't go to my
school—no one will know what a fool I have been!

Practicing Your Writing Power

Power of Language

© Thomson Corporation/Heinle Image Resource Bank

Write one to two pages telling about an interesting conversation you have had with a friend.

Or

Write one to two pages telling about an interesting date you have been on.

QUOTATION MARKS TEST 1

Place quotation marks where needed.

1. Maslow asks the question, What makes people neurotic?

2. The jury summons states, Prospective jurors must wear appropriate business clothing.

3. We have to read an article called Questions from Above.

4. Natalie Goldberg writes, There were no books in my home (23).

5. I would like you to come in early tomorrow morning, said my boss.

6. Some 25 billion tons of topsoil are now being lost each year with untold consequences to the food supply of future generations, states Thomas Berry (3).

7. Going Home Now is a song about the value of family.

8. The advertisement promised, Lowest prices or your money back.

9. In his speech, the candidate claimed, I will never say, Find someone else to deal with your problems.

10. Mississippi contains a number of double letters.

Name _____

Section _____   Score _____

QUOTATION MARKS TEST 2

Place quotation marks where needed.

1. The bumper sticker advised, Wage Peace.

2. According to Baldwin, The male eagle is a better hunter than the female (7).

3. Andersen states, Confrontations along the frontier were becoming increasingly violent (79).

4. Dwight Eisenhower first used the term military-industrial complex.

5. We Shall Overcome has had a long history as a protest song.

6. More, more, the crowd chanted as the band left the stage.

7. Murray Stein states, At midlife there is a crossing-over from one psychological identity to another (3).

8. Yes, the professor replied, your answer is correct.

9. We never had no trouble from Mister Watson, Henry Thompson says in the first chapter of Peter Matthiessen's <u>Killing Mister Watson.</u>

10. You must read the article Easy Acting for tomorrow, our drama teacher told us.

Part III   Review Tests

One of the most challenging parts of writing is editing your own writing to correct errors. To give you realistic practice in finding English errors, we provide review tests of the skills. Chapter 22 provides editing tests on the major errors of fragments and run-ons, as well as verb errors. In addition, we include editing tests that combine all the skills presented in this textbook, grouped according to skill level. Chapter 23 provides a diagnostic test of the skills and two mastery tests. All three tests cover the same skills in the same format.

Chapter 22 Combined Editing Tests

Learning grammar and punctuation skills is only the first step in writing correctly. All writers make errors when writing. Sometimes the errors are careless, meaning writers are writing so quickly that they use the wrong word, misspell a word, or create a punctuation error. Sometimes the errors occur because writers are not thinking of the rules for correct writing. Whatever the reasons, writers must proofread their finished writing by looking for common English errors.

The following exercises combine skills and give you realistic pieces of college writing to proofread for English errors. There are editing tests for the major errors of run-ons and fragments and for verb errors. In addition, there are twelve editing tests that divide all the skills taught in this textbook into basic skills, intermediate skills, and advanced skills. These last twelve tests are challenging practices that will help you sharpen your editing skills.

Name _____
Section _____ Score _____

COMBINED FRAGMENTS AND RUN-ONS EDITING TEST 1

Each of the word groups in the following passage is numbered. In the space provided, write S if a word group is a sentence, F if it is a fragment, or RO if it is a run-on. Then correct the fragments and run-ons in the passage by adding words or punctuation marks.

The First Mayor of Washington, D.C.

1. ____   [1]Washington, D.C., different from every other
2. ____   American city. [2]For over 100 years, there was no
3. ____   elected city government. [3]In 1967, President Lyndon
4. ____   Johnson appointed the city's first mayor. [4]Walter E.
5. ____   Washington, the first mayor of Washington, D.C. [5]He
            was a former administrator of housing, he became the
6. ____   first African American to head a major U.S. city.
7. ____   [6]He was a role model. [7]For African-Americans every-
8. ____   where. [8]A soft-spoken man who knew how to work with
9. ____   other leaders. [9]He was friends with Martin Luther
            King, also he preserved good relations with the
10. ____   president and Congress. [10]However, he knew where to
            draw the line, for example he refused to stop pro-
11. ____   testers. [11]Who marched on Washington during the Viet
12. ____   Nam War. [12]Mayor Washington combined a quiet confi-
13. ____   dence with an ability to set limits. [13]When he was
            first offered the position of mayor by President
14. ____   Lyndon Johnson. [14]Washington turned down the job.
15. ____   [15]Because he wasn't given control of the police

16. ____   force. [16]Later, Johnson again offered him the mayor's

17. ____   job Washington accepted the position. [17]Walter Wash-

ington led the nation's capital city during turbu-

lent times in America, and his principles and quiet

18. ____   leadership style were a perfect match. [18]For those

19 ____   difficult times. [19]In 1974, Mayor Washington was

20. ____   elected to the post of mayor. [20]After serving as the

appointed mayor for seven years.

Name _____
Section _____ Score _____

COMBINED FRAGMENTS AND RUN-ONS EDITING TEST 2

Each of the word groups in the following passage is numbered. In the space provided, write S if a word group is a sentence, F if it is a fragment, and RO if it is a run-on. Then correct the fragments and run-ons in the passage by adding words or punctuation marks.

John F. Kennedy

1. _____   ¹The 31st president of the United States.

2. _____   ²John F. Kennedy was the youngest president ever elected, he came to office at a hopeful time in

3. _____   American history. ³America had won World War II, and America was one of two superpowers, the other

4. _____   was the Soviet Union. ⁴President Kennedy governed during the cold war between the two superpowers.

5. _____   ⁵In Cuba, the Soviet Union installed missiles aimed at the United States, Kennedy insisted that

6. _____   the missiles be removed. ⁶Another foreign policy conflict, the start of the Viet Nam war in the

7. _____   early 1960's. ⁷At home, during President Kennedy's

8. _____   term in office. ⁸Civil rights were an important part of Kennedy's program for improving America.

9. _____   ⁹Tragically assassinated on November 22, 1963, at the age of 43.

10. _____   ¹⁰Historians wonder what John F. Kennedy might

11. _____   have accomplished. ¹¹If he had not been assassi-

12. _____   nated during his first term in office. ¹²Some historians believe that he would have ended the Viet

13. _____   Nam war, others are not so sure. [13]Also, in

14. _____   regards to the civil rights movement. [14]Kennedy

believed in civil rights, he opposed segregation.

15. _____   [15]Kennedy might have been able to reduce the pres-

sures of the cold war the Russians respected his

16. _____   leadership. [16]Kennedy might have been able to con-

17. _____   vince the Russians to end the arms race. [17]Most

importantly, when he started the Peace Corps,

John Kennedy inspired young people to enter pub-

18. _____   lic service. [18]A shining role model for a genera-

19. _____   tion. [19]If John F. Kennedy had not been assassi-

20. _____   nated. [20]Many people believe our nation would have

been spared much grief.

Name _____

Section _____ Score _____

VERBS EDITING TEST 1

The following passage contains ten verb errors. Next to the number for each sentence, write how many verb errors are in the sentence. Then cross out each verb error and write the correct verb form above.

My Job

1. ____   ¹I have a great boss at Grocery Line Supermar-

2. ____   ket. ²Ms. Henley supervise all the cashiers, and she

     treats every cashier the same, whether the person

     has been working at the store ten years or only ten

3. ____   days. ³There is more than forty cashiers, and my

4. ____   boss tries to give everyone a good schedule. ⁴Twenty

     years ago, Ms. Henley starts as a cashier herself,

5. ____   and she has did every job in the store. ⁵Therefore,

     she understand what the employees going through

6. ____   every day on the job. ⁶When I started at Grocery

     Line, I have a hard time adjusting to working for

7. ____   two weeks before I was payed. ⁷Ms. H. lended me

     money for my rent after my first week on the job.

8. ____   ⁸I have came to respect and to love my boss, Ms.

     Henley.

Name _____
Section _____ Score _____

VERBS EDITING TEST 2

The following passage contains ten verb errors. Next to the number for each sentence, write how many verb errors are in the sentence. Then cross out each verb error and write the correct verb form above.

Starting School

1. ____   ¹The first day of the new school year is no fun.

2. ____   ²First, getting to classes take forever because of

3. ____   the traffic. ³Also, if a student registers for

classes and buy books on the first day, there is

long lines all day long at registration and the

4. ____   bookstore. ⁴To avoid the lines, a wise student

5. ____   always register early. ⁵Most terms, I have chose

6. ____   classes that were no problem. ⁶However, this year,

my first day of classes was a nightmare for me.

7. ____   ⁷My biggest problem came when economics were can-

8. ____   celled. ⁸Either the advisors or the professor are

supposed to put up a notice on the board when a

class is cancelled, but no one told us anything

until another teacher comes in and tells us to

9. ____   return to registration. ⁹After waiting an hour for

the cancelled class, I stood in line for another

hour to register for a business course I didn't

10. ____   want to take. ¹⁰I must say that I am not happy

that the school year has began again.

Combined Skills Editing Tests

Finding our own errors is the hardest skill, and it takes practice. In this section, you will put together all that you have learned about grammar and punctuation. The twelve editing exercises that follow are divided by the level of skills being tested. In the basic exercises, you will identify and correct the first errors you learned. The intermediate and advanced exercises give you practice with the more difficult skills, as well as the basic skills.

BASIC EDITING TEST 1

Listed below are the numbers and kinds of errors in the following passage. Next to each type of error, write the number of the word group where you find this type of error. Then correct the error in the space above the error.

2	Capitalization ____ ____	1	Fragment ____
1	Adjective/adverb ____	1	Run-on ____
2	Verb tense ____ ____	2	Problem word ____ ____
1	Subject-verb agreement ____		

The Year of the Computer Virus

¹2003 was the year that computer infections became a real big problem. ²With names like Slammer and Mydoom, these infections swept across the Internet and disable thousands and thousands of computers. ³During the Summer of 2003, a computer worm named Blaster spread through computers using the Windows operating system. ⁴Which is made by Microsoft. ⁵In august, a worm called Sobig explode with even more force, it spread threw e-mail. ⁶This destructive infection stole addresses from it's victims' computer address books and e-mailed itself to all the names in the address book. ⁷At one point, the infection spread so quickly that one out of every fifteen e-mail messages carried the worm. ⁸One expert estimate the cost of computer infections in 2003 at over 80 billion dollars.

Name _____

Section _____ Score _____

BASIC EDITING TEST 2

Listed below are the numbers and kinds of errors in the following passage. Next to each type of error, write the number of the word group where you find this type of error. Then correct the error in the space above the error.

2	Capitalization ____ ____		1	Fragment ____
1	Adjective/Adverb ____		1	Run-on ____
1	Verb tense ____		3	Problem word ____ ____ ____
1	Subject-verb agreement ____			

Effective Public Speaking

[1]Most of us would rather do anything then speak in front of an audience. [2]Our principal fear is forgetting what we should say. [3]Also, we don't know what we are suppose to do with our hands. [4]We are afraid of looking foolish and sounding dumb. [5]Experts on Public Speaking offer a number of helpful hints to public speakers. [6]First, speakers should of practiced their speech three or four times before standing up in front of an audience. [7]Speakers should talk loud because a soft voice sounds boring. [8]Speakers should also establish eye contact with two or three members of the audience so that the audience feel connected to the speaker. [9]While talking, speakers should not keep their hands in their pockets, they should use their hands to gesture and emphasize points. [10]Finally, effective speakers use stories and jokes to keep the audience interested. [11]Including stories about the speaker and the speaker's family. [12]Most successful speakers have gave dozens of speeches before giving a successful speech.

Name _____

Section _____ Score _____

BASIC EDITING TEST 3

Listed below are the numbers and kinds of errors in the following passage. Next to each type of error, write the number of the word group where you find this type of error. Then correct the error in the space above the error.

1   Adjective/adverb _____   2   Fragment _____ _____

2   Verb tense _____ _____   1   Run-on _____

2   Subject-verb agreement _____ _____   2   Problem word _____ _____

Satisfaction

¹Some people feel badly no matter how successful they are. ²They may be the best baseball player at their school, yet their unsatisfied because they're not good enough to play professionally. ³Someone may be consider beautiful by everyone but still be unhappy with her looks because she is not a movie star. ⁴Everyone face the challenge of finding happiness and fulfillment. ⁵Unhappy people often judge their success against impossible standards. ⁶Such as the success of professional actors, athletes, and politicians. ⁷On the other hand, people who are happy with their lives have took a different approach, they use the standard of being just good enough to be satisfied. ⁸In fact, there is many people who are quite satisfied with there lives because they don't measure themselves against impossible standards. ⁹They are grateful to be good enough in their roles as parents, students, athletes, and workers. ¹⁰These people find satisfaction in being significant in each area of their lives. ¹¹Not trying to be the best or the greatest but just good enough to satisfy themselves and the people they care about.

Name _____

Section _____ Score _____

BASIC EDITING TEST 4

Listed below are the numbers and kinds of errors in the following passage. Next to each type of error, write the number of the word group where you find this type of error. Then correct the error in the space above the error.

2   Verb tense ____ ____   2   Capitalization ____ ____

1   Run-on ____   1   Fragment ____

4   Problem word ____ ____ ____ ____

Lucky Day

I met my girlfriend at the end of the Summer.² When my mother asks me to help her shop for school clothes for my brother Joe. ³Joe had broke his leg skateboarding, and he couldn't bear hobbling around on crutches. ⁴I wasn't doing anything accept teasing our Labrador Retriever by hiding its bone. ⁵Since I was suppose to meet my friends at the mall later anyway, I told Mom that I would help her shop. ⁶Its a lucky thing for me that I went along too. ⁷I met Natalie that day, she was the salesperson who helped us pick out clothes for my brother. ⁸It's just to bad that my brother didn't like any of the things we bought.

Name _____
Section _____ Score _____

BASIC EDITING TEST 5

Listed below are the numbers and kinds of errors in the following passage. Next to each type of error, write the number of the word group where you find this type of error. Then correct the error in the space above the error.

1 Verb tense ____	2 Fragment ____ ____
2 Run-on ____ ____	2 Subject-verb agreement ____ ____
2 Problem word ____ ____	1 Adjective/adverb ____

Community Groups

¹Joining community groups are a wonderful way to become involved in the community. ²For citizens who are looking for exercise, there is intramural sports teams in almost every popular sport. ³For example, football, basketball, soccer, and softball ⁴Leagues for every sport are organized by skill level and by gender, some leagues are co-ed to. ⁵Another great way to become active in the community is to join a governmental advisory board. ⁶These committees are made up of committed citizens who advice elected officials on the real important issues facing the community regarding land use, transportation, and the schools. ⁷Community education classes offer an ideal way to meet people and develop areas of interest such as cooking, painting, photography, and carpentry. ⁸Almost any skill a citizen may want to learn. ⁹Often classmates form bonds that last long after the class is over, in fact, many close friendships and some new marriages have began in community groups.

Name _____

Section _____ Score _____

INTERMEDIATE EDITING TEST 1

Listed below are the numbers and kinds of errors in the following passage. Next to each type of error, write the number of the word group where you find this type of error. Then correct the error in the space above the error.

1 Verb tense _____ 2 Apostrophe _____ _____

1 Subject-verb agreement _____ 3 Comma _____ _____ _____

1 Run-on _____ 2 Pronoun agreement _____ _____

Computer Infections

¹Computer viruses are a growing threat. ²In the last couple of years viruses and worms have harmed governments, industries, and individual users. ³These infections have shut down many users e-mail and companies computer networks. ⁴Many computers have lost valuable data and the damage has cost billions of dollars. ⁵Viruses and worms are two kinds of malware, which is evil software that harms computers. ⁶No one are quite sure who writes these programs, often the authors are never found. ⁷However law enforcement has began to investigate these shadowy cyber-terrorists. ⁸A virus writer may come from Europe or Asia, and they are usually young. ⁹These programmers are often brilliant but are angry at society. ¹⁰They meet online in chat spaces devoted to software writing. ¹¹Fortunately, many of these young programmers only create viruses and worms to perfect their programming skills, but the writers don't intend on releasing his creations to do harm.

Name _____

Section _____ Score _____

INTERMEDIATE EDITING TEST 2

Listed below are the numbers and kinds of errors in the following passage. Next to each type of error, write the number of the word group where you find this type of error. Then correct the error in the space above the error.

1   Adjective/adverb _____

1   Subject-verb agreement _____

1   Run-on _____

1   Fragment _____

3   Apostrophe _____ _____ _____

2   Comma _____ _____

1   Pronoun agreement _____

Computer Worms

¹Computer worms are a big problem in todays computerized world. ²A worm does not require any human interaction to spread so they can spread really quickly. ³Unlike a virus, a worm does not change or destroy a computers data. ⁴A worms biggest threat is in how fast it multiply. ⁵A worm creates traffic on the Internet that can overload the system, and shut down huge networks of computers. ⁶Some worms work quick by finding a weakness in the computer programs we all use. ⁷These digital infections can cause really serious problems, worms can cripple emergency services like the 911 emergency response network. ⁸More and more governmental organizations working together to defend against attacks. ⁹Some companies are even offering bounties for the capture of the makers of worms.

Name _____

Section _____ Score _____

INTERMEDIATE EDITING TEST 3

Listed below are the numbers and kinds of errors in the following passage. Next to each type of error, write the number of the word group where you find this type of error. Then correct the error in the space above the error.

1 Verb tense _____   1 Subject-verb agreement _____

1 Pronoun agreement _____   2 Apostrophe _____ _____

3 Comma _____ _____ _____   1 Sentence fragment _____

1 Adjective/adverb _____

Rude Behavior

¹Although air travel is still popular traveling by plane can be real stressful these days. ²Of course, passengers are fearful of terrorism and most airports have increase their security precautions. ³Because security procedures can result in waits of two hours before boarding a plane. ⁴Some passengers become impatient and abusive. ⁵Passengers swear at airport personnel and some passengers even become violent. ⁶However, there is penalties when a passengers behavior is unacceptable. ⁷A rude passenger may be ejected from the plane, or they may be arrested and prosecuted. ⁸Everyones safety depends on passengers cooperating with security and helping the airlines provide secure transportation.

Name _____

Section _____ Score _____

INTERMEDIATE EDITING TEST 4

Listed below are the numbers and kinds of errors in the following passage. Next to each type of error, write the number of the word group where you find this type of error. Then correct the error in the space above the error. **The capitalization of Hope Diamond is correct throughout the passage.**

1   Pronoun agreement _____   1   Run-on sentence _____

3   Comma _____ _____ _____   1   Sentence fragment _____

2   Apostrophe _____ _____   2   Problem word _____ _____

The Hope Diamond

¹The Hope Diamond, one of the most famous diamonds in the world. ²Mined in India, this famous gem is a blue diamond, and glows orange under ultraviolet light. ³While a typical diamond in an engagement ring is less then one carat, the Hope Diamond is 45.5 carats. ⁴Because of the diamonds size, color, and history, it has inspired many legends. ⁵One legend says that the glowing color comes from the spilled blood of French royalty during the French Revolution, another legend is about the Hope family that gave the diamond it's name. ⁶Some people believe that the diamond is cursed, because the Hope family went bankrupt. ⁷Now, the stone belongs to the Smithsonian Institute which is located in our nations capital. ⁸A visitor can view this fabulous diamond when they visit Washington, D.C.

Name _____

Section _____ Score _____

INTERMEDIATE EDITING TEST 5

Listed below are the numbers and kinds of errors in the following passage. Next to each type of error, write the number of the word group where you find this type of error. Then correct the error in the space above the error.

2   Pronoun agreement ____ ____   1   Run-on sentence ____

2   Comma ____ ____   1   Problem word ____

2   Apostrophe ____ ____   1   Adjective/adverb ____

1   Subject-verb agreement ____

Language Acquisition

[1]An infant possesses an amazing ability to learn language. [2]Learning to talk begin as early as six months. [3]All infants start by babbling, later babies acquire language by imitating grownups. [4]A baby copies the familiar sounds of their parents. [5]If an infants parents speak more than one language at home the infant can easily learn two or more languages at the same time. [6]As a child grows older, learning languages becomes difficulter for them. [7]Many childrens' schooling includes learning a second language but picking up a second language takes hard work after the age of five. [8]Adults have the hardest time, and many grownups cannot fully learn a new language. [9]What is so simple at one year of age becomes almost impossible passed the age of forty.

Name _____

Section _____ Score _____

ADVANCED EDITING TEST 1

Listed below are the numbers and kinds of errors in the following passage. Next to each type of error, write the number of the word group where you find this type of error. Then correct the error in the space above the error.

1	Fragment ____	1	Pronoun shift ____
1	Run-on ___	1	Dangling modifier ____
2	Comma ____ ____	1	Apostrophe ____
2	Pronoun agreement ____ ____	1	Parallelism ____

Digital Viruses

¹Computer viruses, the most common form of digital infection. ²When a virus comes to a computer it disguises itself really well. ³The virus might look like a copy of a song, but they are actually a tiny program. ⁴When clicked on, the computer user may reprogram the computer to do something harmful like erasing all the files, or to do something harmless like displaying a message on the screen. ⁵However, a computer virus cannot activate themselves, the computer user must click on it. ⁶Therefore, virus makers must disguise the virus as a picture, a song, or inviting the user to open a file. ⁷Computer users should take computer experts advice and not open e-mail with suspicious attachments unless you want to catch a virus.

Name _____

Section _____ Score _____

ADVANCED EDITING TEST 2

Listed below are the numbers and kinds of errors in the following passage. Next to each type of error, write the number of the word group where you find this type of error. Then correct the error in the space above the error.

2 Comma ____ ____   3 Misplaced modifier ____ ____ ____

1 Pronoun agreement ____   2 Apostrophe ____ ____

1 Pronoun case ____   1 Parallelism ____

Students and Computers

¹Using a computer almost is a necessity for todays college student. ²On the computer, a student writes papers, and checks grammar and spelling. ³The computer is a doorway to researching topics using the Internet. ⁴Furthermore, for most students, their personal computer provides they and their friends with countless hours of free entertainment. ⁵For example, a student who is bored with studying may use their computer to record and play music, watch movies, and a student can also play all sorts of video games. ⁶"The PC is essential to a students success in college", says Marc Clawson, a counselor at Valley College. ⁷Indeed, most college students don't know how they would survive without their computer.

Chapter 23

Combined Skill Tests

Name _____

Section _____ Score _____

DIAGNOSTIC TEST

Write C next to items that are correct and I next to items that are incorrect. For items with four choices, circle the correct answer. (If you are using a Scantron form, bubble in A for CORRECT and E for INCORRECT.)

Capitalization

_____ 1. My Aunt lives on Water Street.

_____ 2. The Dallas Cowboys regularly win the NFL championship.

_____ 3. Can poodles become good seeing eye dogs?

_____ 4. The FBI is investigating my Dentist.

Problem Words

_____ 5. How much was the plane fare to Boston this passed weekend?

_____ 6. I have already exercised for an hour on the stationary bike.

_____ 7. They're always late.

_____ 8. My principle concern is for your safety.

Subject-Verb Identification

9. What is the simple subject of the following sentence?

    Running in marathons requires months of training.

    A. Running

    B. Marathons

    C. Months

    D. Training

10. What is the simple subject of the following sentence?

    There are several reasons why I can't attend your party.

    A. There

    B. Reasons

    C. I

    D. Party

11. What is the complete verb of the following sentence?

    My cousin is running in the Boston Marathon.

    A. Cousin

    B. Is

    C. Is running

    D. Boston Marathon

12. What is the complete verb of the following sentence?

    What is your excuse this time?

    A. What

    B. Is

    C. Your

    D. Excuse

Subject-Verb Agreement

_____ 13. Anyone who want a good grade needs to study.

_____ 14. Neither my father nor my brothers are left-handed.

_____ 15. There are two books on the table.

_____ 16. Swimming in the Great Lakes are dangerous.

Irregular Verbs

_____ 17. John has wrote his sister a letter.

_____ 18. I was asked a question I couldn't answer.

_____ 19. How do you heal a broke heart?

_____ 20. Juan and Maria has finally finished their work.

Adjectives and Adverbs

_____ 21. Our band played good last night.

_____ 22. We were hungry, and fortunately, the pizza arrived quick.

Fragments

_____ 23. Independence Day, our national holiday on July 4th.

_____ 24. Since it was payday, Mr. Monroe took his family out to dinner.

_____ 25. Many seats at the movie were taken already.

_____ 26. The friends that Celia grew up with in Minnesota.

Run-ons

_____ 27. The test will be on Wednesday, which happens to be the teacher's birthday.

_____ 28. The new movie just came to town, it will be showing at 9 p.m. tonight.

_____ 29. Some workers are not feeling well they have gone home early.

_____ 30. When the dogs next door bark, we shut our windows to block the noise.

Commas

_____ 31. The city's best bakery, Uppercrust, sells delicious chocolate cakes, which are my favorite dessert.

_____ 32. The table is made of oak, and it was built in 1950.

_____ 33. Although, the yard needs to be mowed I can't cut the grass today.

_____ 34. Some people love the woods, and go camping whenever they can.

Pronoun Agreement, Reference, and Case

_____ 35. A child should do as they are told.

_____ 36. The teacher talked to Tamika and I.

_____ 37. My favorite restaurant treats their customers like kings.

_____ 38. John told Bob that he had failed the test.

Apostrophes

_____ 39. The women's discussion group meets on Thursdays.

_____ 40. Every year, the Barkley's give a party for the neighborhood.

_____ 41. Many kids' parents pick them up after school.

_____ 42. The department stores sign wasn't lit up last night.

Modifiers

_____ 43. To be ready for the big game, more practice is needed.

_____ 44. On the table, Jorge signed the check.

Parallelism

_____ 45. The mother told her children to stay close and that sticking together mattered.

_____ 46. The carpenter measured the space, bought the materials, and built the cabinets.

Other Punctuation Marks

_____ 47. I finished my essay; therefore, I am going out to dinner.

_____ 48. I love: apple pie, ice cream, and chocolate.

_____ 49. My instructor asked, "Why are you late for class?"

_____ 50. How old are your daughters.

Name _____

Section _____ Score _____

MASTERY TEST 1

Write C next to items that are correct and I next to items that are incorrect. For items with four choices, circle the correct answer. (If you are using a Scantron form, bubble in A for CORRECT and E for INCORRECT.)

Capitalization

_____ 1. I think German Shepherds are great dogs.

_____ 2. The Queen of England lives in buckingham palace.

_____ 3. My Brother wants to visit Yellowstone National Park.

_____ 4. Lake Michigan is one of the Great Lakes.

Problem Words

_____ 5. I have a loose tooth, but I can't bear to go to the dentist.

_____ 6. Jenny wrote a letter on blue stationary.

_____ 7. My mother won't accept any more excuses.

_____ 8. The principle told my son to finish his work and then go home.

Subject-Verb Identification

9. What is the simple subject of the following sentence?

Everything my cousin touches turns to gold.

A. Everything

B. My

C. Cousin

D. Gold

10. What is the simple subject of the following sentence?

The girls on the Greyhound bus are loud.

A. Girls

B. Greyhound

C. Bus

D. Loud

11. What is the complete verb of the following sentence?

    I have never played football.

    A. Have

    B. Have never

    C. Have played

    D. Football

12. What is the complete verb of the following sentence?

    There is no time to waste.

    A. There

    B. Is

    C. Time

    D. Waste

Subject-Verb Agreement

_____ 13. One of the books have been lost.

_____ 14. Everything is going fine.

_____ 15. Hanging out with my friends are fun.

_____ 16. There are two tests I have to study for.

Irregular Verbs

_____ 17. Jessie has took my pen.

_____ 18. I have already ate at that restaurant.

_____ 19. I have written four papers this term.

_____ 20. I have went to Disney World.

Adjectives and Adverbs

_____ 21. My sister's dog is the beautifulest poodle I have ever seen.

_____ 22. The computer finds information on the Internet real quick.

Fragments

_____ 23. Without a doubt, one of the best movies of the year.

_____ 24. The grocery cart is empty.

_____ 25. Because of the weather, the game was cancelled.

_____ 26. The red bike belonging to Lawanda.

Run-ons

_____ 27. If it snows tonight, our trip to the mountains may be postponed.

_____ 28. The band played its most famous song, then it left the stage.

_____ 29. Cell phones are not permitted in class students must turn them off.

_____ 30. Some teachers graded papers while they waited for the faculty meeting to begin.

Commas

_____ 31. In the last year of college, most students take courses that are directly related to their major.

_____ 32. The technician turned on the monitor, and adjusted the color.

_____ 33. Also, students who are graduating should see a counselor in the career center.

_____ 34. Dinner is served at 6 p.m., but snacks will be available until 11 p.m.

Pronoun Agreement, Reference, and Case

_____ 35. Sarah told Jenny that she was in trouble.

_____ 36. My brother is taller than me.

_____ 37. At school, they won't let you park on the grass.

_____ 38. Instructors have their office hours posted.

Apostrophes

_____ 39. Some peoples' mail was misplaced by the postman.

_____ 40. A neighbor's cat actually chases our dog.

_____ 41. On Monday's and Friday's, our class goes to the lab.

_____ 42. The business has its name on many teams' uniforms.

Modifiers

_____ 43. By turning the knob on and off, the television can be made to work.

_____ 44. The hostess greeted her guests with a big smile.

Parallelism

_____ 45. The police officer spoke quietly but was forceful.

_____ 46. Good students study before class, listen attentively during class, and do the homework after class.

Other Punctuation Marks

_____ 47. Ravi bought: milk, cheese, and eggs at the grocery store.

_____ 48. I love jazz; and I love blues.

_____ 49. I asked Randy, "Where he had gone last night."

_____ 50. I am twenty-one; therefore, I can vote.

MASTERY TEST 2

Write C next to items that are correct and I next to items that are incorrect. For items with four choices, circle the correct answer. (If you are using a Scantron form, bubble in A for CORRECT and E for INCORRECT.)

Capitalization

_____   1. The I.R.S. is investigating American Motors Corporation.

_____   2. Every fall, we take off for two weeks and go fishing on the Columbia river.

_____   3. There are several Universities and Colleges in the Boston area.

_____   4. According to the book *Summer Jobs,* a great way to spend a summer is to work for the United States Park Service at a national park.

Problem Words

_____   5. There is less work this semester than last semester.

_____   6. It's to late to start my homework now.

_____   7. There must of been a lot of students who missed the assignment.

_____   8. The noise in the apartment upstairs effected my ability to sleep last night.

Subject-Verb Identification

9. What is the simple subject of the following sentence?

    The neighborhood has many fine houses.

    A. The

    B. Neighborhood

    C. Many

    D. Houses

10. What is the simple subject of the following sentence?

    Yolanda and Harry ride the bus to the concert.

    A. Yolanda

    B. Harry

    C. Yolanda and Harry

    D. Concert

11. What is the complete verb in the following sentence?

    The picture of my friends was taken last month.

    A. Picture

    B. Was

    C. Taken

    D. Was taken

12. What is the complete verb in the following sentence?

    There is something wrong with the television set.

    A. There

    B. Is

    C. Something

    D. Wrong

Subject-Verb Agreement

_____ 13. Walking offers many benefits.

_____ 14. Most of my strength comes from my beliefs.

_____ 15. The books on the shelf is dusty.

_____ 16. Each of the tables need a new tablecloth.

Verb Tense

_____ 17. My son has watched TV for two hours.

_____ 18. My best friend has rode his bike to school for years.

_____ 19. The teacher extend the deadline because many students were sick.

_____ 20. When I was five, my family move to New York City.

Adjectives and Adverbs

_____ 21. The student wrote very slow during the exam.

_____ 22. I found this week's show more funny than last week's show.

Fragments

_____ 23. Because of the rain, our game is cancelled.

_____ 24. Along the side of the highway near the exit to the mall.

_____ 25. The team is playing tomorrow.

_____ 26. Jon's new car, a gold Cadillac convertible.

Run-ons

_____ 27. I love my cell phone it's easy to use.

_____ 28. We should clean the storeroom before the boss arrives.

_____ 29. The class meets until noon, later we can get something to eat.

_____ 30. Although it is supposed to rain tonight, this afternoon should be sunny and warm.

Commas

_____ 31. The professor will grade the tests tonight, and return them to us tomorrow.

_____ 32. Although, the museum is closed today, it will be open tomorrow.

_____ 33. Many citizens read the newspaper for information about the national and international news, the weather, and sports.

_____ 34. The oldest person in town, Callie Wilson, will celebrate her one hundredth birthday tomorrow.

Pronoun Agreement, Reference, and Case

_____ 35. The English department plans their Christmas party every December.

_____ 36. My brothers don't agree on who their favorite baseball players are.

_____ 37. Her and her brother tell great stories about growing up in Alaska.

_____ 38. When Ben arrived at the concert, they told him that violence had erupted inside the coliseum.

Apostrophes

_____ 39. The childrens' teacher took them on a field trip.

_____ 40. Tomorrow's meeting will be held in the auditorium.

_____ 41. The candidate didn't answer everyones questions.

_____ 42. Two teachers' exams have not been printed yet.

Modifiers

_____ 43. Floating silently overhead, the eagle eyed its prey.

_____ 44. The teacher told her students everyday to attend lecture.

Parallelism

_____ 45. Traffic congestion is a problem in many large cities but not in areas that are rural.

_____ 46. Scientists blame global warming for the increasing frequency of killer tornadoes and flooding that is severe.

Other Punctuation Marks

_____ 47. Most health clubs offer three primary types of aerobics classes: low-impact aerobics, high-impact aerobics, and step aerobics.

_____ 48. First, till the garden, then plant the seeds.

_____ 49. My mother visited Venice, Italy; Paris, France; and London, England on her vacation.

_____ 50. Most graduates have two choices—school or work.

Part IV Readings

Reading is an excellent way to boost your language power and become a more powerful writer. By reading other writers, you will be exposed to new ideas, vocabulary, and sentence structures. In addition, many of your assignments throughout college will involve reading material and then writing about it, so it's a good idea to begin practicing the reading-writing connection

Reading can also be fun. We have chosen the following reading selections from popular books and magazines. The writers come from a variety of backgrounds and walks of life, but they share the powerful use of language to communicate their experiences and beliefs. They speak in their own voices about how they and others have overcome obstacles and found inspiration. We hope that their voices will challenge you, influence you, and inspire you to develop your own writing power and achieve your dreams.

Each selection includes vocabulary exercises, comprehension questions, discussion questions, and writing topics to help you develop your language power and give you practice using your writing to respond to what you read.

© Thomson Corporation/Heinle Image Resource Bank

Readings

Preview

destiny: fate

Do you wonder what you are going to do with the rest of your life? Maybe you have been searching for the key to your **destiny.** Most of us wish we could ask someone to tell us what we should do with our lives. We even wish that what we are looking for might be as close as, say, under our bed. Read about Noah Gold-fader, who finds his calling.

Have You Looked Under Your Bed?
Po Bronson

tallied:
counted

1   Noah Goldfader didn't think he was ever going to find it. He told me that since college he's had ten jobs in eight years, spread over six cities in four states on two coasts. But when I broke it down with him, employer by employer, I **tallied** no less than *sixteen* jobs in those eight years. He never stayed anywhere long enough to move up the ladder—everything was entry-level. Two-thirds of these jobs were in the marketing and promotion. He'd given away Frappuccinos and Cuervo Gold tequila, put up placards during WNBA games and three-on-three NBA Hoop It Up tournaments, and created never-used ad campaigns for Levi's blue jeans. The highlights of his travels were pounding Coronas with Rod Stewart's band and standing on the same court with Kevin Garnett. He's thirty now. Currently unemployed. His older brother tells him to stop _ _ _ _ing around, thinks he's a slacker.

2   But Noah's no slacker. You can't fault him for not trying. My definition of a slacker is someone who thinks all jobs suck and isn't going to lift a finger. Noah would happily work sixteen-hour days if he only knew what it was he should be doing. He was all-too-desperate to find his song in life, and was panicked that there wasn't one out there for him. He didn't expect it to be easy. But he sure wanted an answer.

3   The night I went to meet Noah, he was living in old army housing in the Presidio in San Francisco, sharing an apartment with three roommates. We cracked a beer and sat in his tidy living room. He was thrilled I actually showed up. I think he might have vacuumed before I arrived—the air smelled of a tired electric motor. He was super-introverted, twisted up by his thoughts, but not a dungeon-dweller or a Web-geek—more goofy, maybe a little mentally lopsided; intuitive one moment, blind the next. He was a sports nut. His father was a football star for Brandeis University, then a minor league catcher in the Milwaukee Braves organization. His mom was a nurse for twenty years.

4   "I believe everyone has a unique gift to give the world," he agonized. "I sure as hell don't want to be one of those people who dies with the music still inside them. I wish I could find what the hell I was put on this earth to do."

5   He looked at me like maybe I'd pull the answer out of thin air. Long silence. I didn't know what to tell him. I wasn't exactly sure why I came here, why his story **piqued** my interest.

piqued: stimulated

6   He went on. "Have you ever seen or heard Dick Vitale, the college basketball commentator? He loves what he does. You could lock him in a gym for sixteen hours a day and he'd never look at his watch. Why can't we all have a passion like that?"

7   I glanced over at a coffee table book on Ben Hogan. Noah grabbed the book and leafed through it. "This book makes the hairs on my arm stand up. Hogan was the ultimate. Forget Tiger. Nobody understood Hogan. Like nobody gets me. I wouldn't even know where to start when talking about Hogan. That guy had a singular **fixation.** I wish I had that."

fixation: obsession

low-hanging fruit: something obvious

8   Noah desperately wanted my opinion. I shot at the **low-hanging fruit.** "What does your brother do?"

9   "He's in finance down in SoCal."

10   "Does he love it?"

11   "He doesn't expect to. He's stable, has his act together, and owns his house. That's what he says matters."

12   "You know, some people struggle with this question, and some people just *don't.* Look for help from people who relate. Not your brother."

13   "I don't know. I'm starting to see his point. How many years should I spend hunting for this answer, and when should I give up and get on with my life?"

14   "What would 'giving up' mean?"

15   "It'd mean admitting there is no answer for me. Not everybody gets a passion. What do you think? What have you found? Do you think everybody gets a passion?"

16   "No way." Suggesting otherwise would be irresponsible. However, there was a catch—a significant catch. I was going to regret telling him this. I was almost certainly condemning him to more years of frustration. "Some people are born into their passions. Some never get them and don't care. But I think if you're *really struggling* to find it—and I think you have, I mean, you've gone all over the country to find it—it's almost certainly for a reason. I think the depth of your struggling is the sign there's something there. Something in you that's trying to get out. People who don't have passions don't struggle." I didn't know what I believed when I started my research, but I'd heard enough stories that this was coming clear. Young people often said, "I feel an urge, a vacuum. But I'm not called to anything in particular." But those who had succeeded in finding a calling remembered that feeling as the beginning of the process. "The call was muffled and **vague** at first. That blank urge *is* the call."

vague: unclear

17   Noah nodded slowly with deep appreciation. "Wow. Yeah, my struggling *is* the sign."

18   "So keep looking."

19   "If I had something to show for these eight years, I might feel better about myself."

20   That was another interesting question. Are the years before you find your passion a waste? I hear that a lot. *My real life won't begin until I find my place.* That's bogus, and I told Noah so. "Sounds like in eight years you've learned a lot about promotion and marketing. Maybe those are tools you're going to need when you finally figure out what you're here for. So what if it's been Frappuccinos, Cuervo Gold, and Levi's? You're learning promotion. Maybe someday you'll need to promote what you really believe in."

raptly: with concentration

21   Noah was listening **raptly,** so I launched into the story of my younger brother. He's really good with people. Always has been. For this reason he was always a natural salesperson. But he never had a passion, and he had become convinced he was not a passionate person. Our family always told him not to worry, and that when he made more money he'd feel good about what he was doing. But he did worry, and one day he gave up sales, went back to school, studied medicine, and became a nurse.

22   "Does he like it?" Noah asked with some urgency, his face starting to light up.

23   "He *loves* it. He can't wait to go to work. He talks about his patients all the time. I'm telling you this story because he took this gift with people—a gift that he'd honed in those years in sales—and he brought it to nursing. And it makes him a *great* nurse. It's the same gift, the same talent—but rather than selling insurance, or selling game meat, or selling Pennzoil, he's using it to *help people.*"

24   Noah's face radiated enlightenment like I'd said the most insightful thing he had ever heard.

25   "That's what I want to do!" he blurted.

26   "You want to become a nurse?" I was confused.

27   "No, no—I want to *help people* . . ."

28   "Good . . ." I wasn't following, and I certainly didn't see this coming.

29   "I want to help people . . . *play better golf.*"

30   Play better golf! "You do?"

31   "Yeah. That's what I like more than anything. I love it."

32   In the back of my mind, I recognized this was kind of humorous, but in the moment it felt very serious. "Wait a minute! If you love golf, why haven't you been doing that? Why have you been traveling the country, going broke, and giving yourself a hard time these eight years, when all along your passion was *golf?*"

33   "I never thought of it as the way to help people before. But it is. I mean, I really feel like I'm helping people when I'm giving lessons."

guru: respected authority

entrepreneur: a person who starts a business

34   Probably every time in his life he brought up golf as a career, someone shot him down. He confirmed this. He mentioned his love of golf to his rabbi, and she didn't know what to make of it. Then he spent $100 an hour on two sessions with Patti Wilson, *the* **guru** of Silicon Valley career counselors, who is famous for helping **entrepreneurs** discover their dreams. Noah had high hopes and put a lot of stock in her advice. She asked him, "If you could do anything, what would you do?" He told her he wanted to make people better

golfers. She dismissed this quickly, as if giving lessons on the driving range were beneath someone with a college degree. The sessions were a bust.

35   "You should have stuck up for yourself."

36   "I'm not good enough to be a club pro, anyway."

37   "Golf's a ten-billion-dollar industry, Noah. Surely there's a lot of jobs that don't require a scratch handicap." Noah responded like nobody had ever acted interested before.

38   "Can I show you something?"

39   "Sure." I was trying to be supportive.

40   He went to his bedroom, reached under his bed and pulled out two hand-crafted gizmos—a swing trainer and a newfangled **putter** grip. Noah turned out to be an inventor. I couldn't believe it. This guy had been looking for his passion for eight years, and the whole time it was under his bed!

putter: a golf club used for putting

41   He said, "With a new grip like this, I can help a lot of golfers at once. It's helping people on a larger scale."

42   "Noah, why aren't you working at Ping or Wilson or Nike?"

43   He said the entry-level jobs for the manufacturers are in sales. "Would that feel good, hawking clubs to retail outlets? I don't know. I don't think I'd like it."

44   Ahhh, the Entry Level Problem. All entry-level jobs suck the big one. How do you get past that? "Noah, imagine for a moment you've become one of Ping's mad scientist inventors. Would that make you happy?"

45   "Yeah, that'd be awesome!"

46   "Well, twice a year you'd have to go to a Ping sales conference, at which you'd present your inventions to the Ping sales reps. These reps will be the voice of your putter grip to the stores and the pros. Your invention will live or die based on how they perceive it. Maybe you're going to be an inventor, but don't you think you'll be a more successful inventor if you've walked in a rep's shoes? If Ping called you tomorrow and hired you as an inventor, you'd probably fail miserably, because you don't know shit about distribution, or materials science, or manufacturing. If you're serious about nurturing your invention, you'll put in the years to learn the skills to protect your gift. So when the day comes, you'll be *ready.*"

47   "Whoa, I never thought of it like that."

48   "People have this stupid fantasy that if you're the *creator,* or the *inventor,* or the *artist,* you hand over your creation to businessmen and cash the royalty check. That's a fantasy. It's irresponsible to their gift. If you have a gift, you should take care of it."

49   "Did you do that?"

50   "Absolutely. During my late twenties I was attending writing school at night. I believed that someday I would write something worthwhile. So for five years, during the day, I put in my time at a small publishing house. I learned everything I could about the industry. I prepared the financials and paid the bills. I typeset books. I shipped orders. I designed jackets. I wrote press releases. I made publicity calls. You name it, I did it. I knew publishing wasn't

my calling, and the pay sucked, but I was determined to have the skills to protect the book I would someday write."

51   "And did it make a difference?"

52   "When my first book came out, I did at least a half-dozen unusual things that helped my publisher get the book an audience. It made a huge difference."

53   "Wow."

54   Noah was honored that I would equate his love of golf with my love of writing. (Of course I would!) He wrote me frequently afterward, remarking how much of a relief it was to tell his story and not have someone like his brother say he was wasting his time. That's all he had ever needed. A month after we met, he jumped into entry-level golf sales, becoming a merchandise manager at a Sportmart. He also reinvented his grip prototype and sent it off to the USGA, and demonstrated it at a couple of golf expos. He was on his way. Two months later he discovered a secret of the golf swing, which had eluded him his whole life. He taught it to me at a driving range. Sometimes I feel good about my little role in his life, and other times it freaks me out that I would have said something that loosened the knot in his mind, allowing him to feel his desires without guilt. I didn't say anything controversial, but that I said anything at all *was* controversial. I was on the hook.

55   "I want to help people . . . *play better golf.*"

Vocabulary Exercises

Fill in the blank with the appropriate vocabulary word from the reading.

1. The discussion _____ my interest in the subject.

2. His answer was _____ and left me wondering how he felt on the issue.

3. As the master of ceremonies _____ the votes, I held my breath.

4. The contestant said he dreamed of becoming an _____ and running his own firm.

5. The player studied the board _____ before she made her move.

Comprehension Questions

1. What did Noah Goldfader think he would never find?
   A. His purpose in life
   B. His car
   C. A girlfriend
   D. A home

2. Noah lives in
   A. Honolulu.
   B. New York City.
   C. San Francisco.
   D. Berlin.

3. Noah's past work experiences include working in
   A. pharmaceuticals.
   B. business.
   C. education.
   D. marketing.

4. When the author met Noah, Noah was
   A. employed.
   B. unemployed.

5. Noah enjoys
   A. going to the movies.
   B. watching sports.
   C. attending NASCAR races.
   D. making art.

6. According to the author, the years spent looking for our passion are wasted years.
   A. True
   B. False

7. Noah invented gadgets to help people
   A. lose weight.
   B. play better golf.
   C. type faster.
   D. hear better.

8. Noah keeps his inventions
   A. under his bed.
   B. in his garage.
   C. on his desk.
   D. in his refrigerator.

9. The author advises Noah to go
   A. to school.

   B. into sales.

   C. on vacation.

   D. to see a career counselor.

10. After being interviewed, Noah gets a job at
    A. a supermarket.

    B. a department store.

    C. a sporting goods store.

    D. a theatre.

Discussion Questions

1. What is the main idea of this selection? In other words, what does the author want us to know about finding a career path?

2. How did the writer's story about his brother help Noah Goldfader find his career path?

3. Family members told the writer's brother that when he made more money he'd feel good about what he was doing. However, it wasn't until the brother recognized that he enjoyed helping people that he found his career path. How important is money to you in choosing your career? Is it important to you that you help people by what you do?

4. Noah Goldfader realizes that he wants to help people play better golf. What do you know how to do that would help people?

5. The author asks, "Are the years before you find your passion a waste?" What do you think? Do you know now what you want to do with your life? If so, what are you doing to make your desire a reality? If you don't know what career you want to pursue, are you just wasting time while you are looking? In what ways could what you are doing now contribute to helping you find your path?

6. A career counselor rejected Noah's interest in golf as a career path for someone with a college degree. What interests do you have that others have rejected as not being important enough to spend time developing? What kinds of jobs could you do using your interest?

Writing Topics

1. The author tells Noah, "Some people are born into their passions. . . . I think the depth of your struggling is the sign there's something there. Something in you that's trying to get out." Do you have a passion in life, or are you struggling to find your passion? Write a narrative telling how and when you discovered your passion, or write a narrative telling of the struggle you have gone through finding your passion.

2. The author helped Noah Goldfader find his career path. Who has helped you realize your gifts? Whose advice do you seek in making decisions? Write a paragraph explaining why you respect this person, or write a narrative essay telling the story of a particular time you sought advice.

3. The author states, "If you have a gift, you should take care of it." Write a paragraph telling of a gift you have and how you are developing it or might develop it. Have others recognized a gift or special talent you have and brought it to your attention? Even if no one else has recognized your talent, you may sense a gift you have, something that brings you joy and that you love. You may want to generate ideas by using one of the techniques suggested on page 20.

4. Noah gets an entry-level job selling golf equipment. Choose an entry-level job you could foresee yourself taking, and explain how such a job might help you reach your goals.

5. Write a paragraph or essay about one job you've held. Explain why you liked or disliked the job.

Preview

Almost everyone has experienced a conflict with a parent. Sandra Cisneros tells of her conflict with her father and how she and her father overcame their differences during the year she started to be successful as a writer.

Only Daughter
Sandra Cisneros

contributor's note: biographical information about a writer who contributes to an anthology

anthology: a collection of writings by different writers

1   Once, several years ago, when I was just starting out my writing career, I was asked to write my own **contributor's note** for an **anthology** I was part of. I wrote: "I am the only daughter in a family of six sons. *That* explains everything."

2   Well, I've thought about that ever since, and yes, it explains a lot to me, but for the reader's sake I should have written: "I am the only daughter in a *Mexican* family of six sons." Or even: "I am the only daughter of a Mexican father and a Mexican-American mother." Or: "I am the only daughter of a working-class family of nine." All of these had everything to do with who I am today.

3   I was/am the only daughter and *only* a daughter. Being an only daughter in a family of six sons forced me by circumstance to spend a lot of time by myself because my brothers felt it beneath them to play with a *girl* in public. But that aloneness, that loneliness, was good for a would-be writer—it allowed me time to think and think, to imagine, to read and prepare myself.

destiny: fate

4   Being only a daughter for my father meant my **destiny** would lead me to become someone's wife. That's what he believed. But when I was in fifth grade and shared my plans for college with him, I was sure he understood. I remember my father saying, "*Que bueno, mi'ja,* that's good." That meant a lot to me, especially since my brothers thought the idea was **hilarious.** What I didn't realize was that my father thought college was good for girls—for finding a husband. After four years in college and two more in graduate school, and still no husband, my father shakes his head even now and says I wasted all that education.

hilarious: extremely funny

in retrospect: looking back to the past

5   **In retrospect,** I'm lucky my father believed daughters were meant for husbands. It meant it didn't matter if I majored in something silly like English. After all, I'd find a nice professional eventually, right? This allowed me the liberty to putter about embroidering my little poems and stories without my father interrupting with so much as a "What's that you're writing?"

6   But the truth is, I wanted him to interrupt. I wanted my father to understand what it was I was scribbling, to introduce me as "My only daughter, the

writer." Not as "This is my only daughter. She teaches." *El maestro*—teacher. Not even *profesora.*

7   In a sense, everything I have ever written has been for him, to win his approval even though I know my father can't read English words, even though my father's only reading includes the brown-ink *Esto* sports magazines from Mexico City and the bloody *¡Alarma!* Magazines that feature yet another sighting of *La Virgen de Guadalupe* on a tortilla or a wife's revenge on her **philandering** husband by bashing his skull in with a *molcajete* (a kitchen mortar made of volcanic rock). Or the *fotonovels,* the little picture paperbacks with tragedy and **trauma** erupting from the characters' mouth in bubbles.

8   My father represents, then, the public majority. A public who is uninterested in reading, and yet one whom I am writing about and for, and privately trying to **woo.**

9   When we were growing up in Chicago, we moved a lot because of my father. He suffered **periodic bouts of nostalgia.** Then we'd have to let go our flat, store the furniture with mother's relatives, load the station wagon with baggage and bologna sandwiches, and head south. To Mexico City.

10   We came back, of course. To yet another Chicago flat, another Chicago neighborhood, another Catholic school. Each time, my father would seek out the parish priest in order to get a tuition break, and complain or boast: "I have seven sons."

11   He meant *siete hijos,* seven children, but he translated it as "sons." "I have seven sons." To anyone who would listen. The Sears Roebuck employee who sold us the washing machine. The short-order cook where my father ate his ham-and-eggs breakfast. "I have seven sons." As if he deserved a medal from the state.

12   My papa. He didn't mean anything by that **mistranslation,** I'm sure. But somehow I could feel myself being erased. I'd tug my father's sleeve and whisper: "Not seven sons. Six! and *one daughter.*"

13   When my oldest brother graduated from medical school, he fulfilled my father's dream that we study hard and use this—our head, instead of this—our hands. Even now my father's hands are thick and yellow, stubbed by a history of hammer and nails and twine and coils and springs. "Use this," my father said, tapping his head, "and not this," showing us those hands. He always looked tired when he said it.

14   Wasn't college an investment? And hadn't I spent all those years in college? And if I didn't marry, what was it all for? Why would anyone go to college and then choose to be poor? Especially someone who had always been poor.

15   Last year, after ten years of writing professionally, the financial rewards started to trickle in. My second National Endowment for the Arts Fellowship. A guest professorship at the University of California, Berkeley. My book, which sold to a major New York publishing house.

---

philandering: cheating, as in a husband being unfaithful

trauma: shock

woo: win over

periodic bouts of nostalgia: regular times of longing for the past

mistranslation: mistake in translating from one language to another language

Fellini: Italian film director

horizontally: lying down

16   At Christmas, I flew home to Chicago. The house was throbbing, same as always; hot *tamales* and sweet *tamales* hissing in my mother's pressure cooker, and everybody—mother, six brothers, wives, babies, aunts, cousins—talking too loud and at the same time, like in a **Fellini** film, because that's just how we are.

17   I went upstairs to my father's room. One of my stories had just been translated into Spanish and published in an anthology of Chicago writing, and I wanted to show it to him. Ever since he recovered from a stroke two years ago, my father likes to spend his leisure hours **horizontally.** And that's how I found him, watching a Pedro Infante movie on Galavision and eating rice pudding.

18   There was a glass filmed with milk on the bedside table. There were several vials of pills and balled Kleenex. And on the floor, one black sock and a plastic urinal that I didn't want to look at but looked at anyway. Pedro Infante was about to burst into song, and my father was laughing.

19   I'm not sure if it was because my story was translated into Spanish, or because it was published in Mexico, or perhaps because the story dealt with Tepeyac, the *colonia* my father was raised in, but at any rate, my father punched the mute button on his remote control and read my story.

20   I sat on the bed next to my father and waited. He read it very slowly. As if he were reading each line over and over. He laughed at all the right places and read lines he liked out loud. He pointed and asked questions: "Is this So-and-so?" "Yes," I said. He kept reading.

21   When he was finally finished, after what seemed like hours, my father looked up and asked: "Where can we get more copies of this for relatives?"

22   Of all the wonderful things that happened to me last year, that was the most wonderful.

Vocabulary Exercises

Fill in the blank with the appropriate vocabulary word from the reading.

1. I am sorry, _____, for my actions because now I know how much I hurt you.

2. Some people feel that their _____ has been set since birth.

3. I find some comedians _____.

4. My grandfather loves to _____ in his workshop.

5. The young man tried to _____ the girl by sending her flowers every day for a week.

Comprehension Questions

1. How many sisters does the author have?
   A. Six

   B. One

   C. None

   D. Two

2. What nationality is the author's father?
   A. Mexican

   B. Mexican-American

   C. American

   D. Spanish

3. The author's brother
   A. played with her a lot while they were growing up.

   B. is a doctor.

   C. read many books as a child.

   D. played professional baseball.

4. The author's father wanted her to become a
   A. doctor.

   B. wife.

   C. writer.

   D. movie director.

5. The father
   A. liked the idea that the author went to college.

   B. discouraged the author from attending college.

   C. went to college with the author.

   D. stopped going to college after one semester.

6. The father believed that his daughter
   A. would never amount to anything.

   B. should go to graduate school.

    C. wasted her education.

    D. should move back home.

7. The author and her family lived mostly in
    A. New York.

    B. San Francisco.

    C. Chicago.

    D. Miami.

8. Where was the father's hometown?
    A. Guadalajara

    B. Mexico City

    C. New York

    D. Madrid

9. The author is happy when her father
    A. brags about her.

    B. gives her money for a car.

    C. reads a story she has written.

    D. gets her to autograph her story.

10. The author claims that her father represents for her
    A. the public majority.

    B. all men.

    C. a critic.

    D. authority.

Discussion Questions

1. How do the facts of the author's family, her Mexican heritage and six brothers, "have everything to do with who I am today?"

2. Explain the difference between being *an only daughter* and *only being a daughter.*

3. In what ways did the writer's upbringing help her to become a writer?

4. How has your place in your family influenced your life? Give examples of ways that you are treated differently from your brothers and sisters. Does being an only child influence the way a child grows up?

Writing Topics

1. Write a paragraph about how the author feels about being the only daughter in her family.

2. Explain three ways that the writer's upbringing has influenced her to become a writer.

3. Explain the advantages or disadvantages of being the first, middle, last, or only child in your family.

4. Explain the ways that your relationship with your father or mother is positive or negative.

Preview

All of us have been shaped by those adults who have influenced and guided us. In the preface to *Lanterns: A Memoir of Mentors,* Marian Wright Edelman describes the role mentors played in shaping her life. She describes the social, economic, and political forces that influenced her life choices and retraces her journey from a childhood in the small, segregated southern town to an adulthood in which she became a crusader for civil rights and the founder of the Children's Defense Fund.

Excerpt from the Preface to
Lanterns: A Memoir of Mentors
Marian Wright Edelman

1   It is my great joy to share some of the great lives and spirits of mentors who have **enriched,** informed, and helped shape my life. Many of them helped shape our times and national life.

enriched: made richer

2   I was born in the sturdy white wood parsonage at 119 Cheraw Street in Bennettsville, South Carolina, as the last of five children of Rev. Arthur Jerome and Maggie Leola Bowen Wright. My birth house is now a Children's Defense Fund office.

3   I have always felt blessed to be born who I was, where I was, when I was, and with the parents I had. As a Black girl child growing up in a small segregated southern town, I could never take anything for granted and never for a moment lacked a purpose worth fighting, living, and dying for, or an opportunity to make a difference if I wanted to. I was richly blessed with parents and community elders who **nurtured** me and other children and tried to live what they preached. They believed in God, in family, in education, and in helping others.

nurtured: cared for and encouraged

4   I did not come into or get through life alone. Neither did you. Our mothers had to push to get us here. And our fathers had to help too. My parents needed and got help in raising me and my sister and three brothers from our neighbors and friends in their church and community, some of whom you will meet here. They tried unceasingly to protect children from the unfair **assaults** of southern racial segregation and injustice by weaving a tight family and community fabric of love around us.

assaults: attacks

5   This book is about the **crucial** influences of the natural daily mentors in my life—my parents, community co-parents and elders, preachers, teachers, civic and civil rights leaders. It is about the **impact** of cultural, social, eco-

crucial: very important

impact: influence

perceptions: ways of seeing the world

daunting: difficult, frightening

affirm: reinforce

internalize: accept, make inward

sanctity: holiness

simultaneously: happening at the same time

prevailing: ruling, most powerful

professed: said they believed in

extrinsic: outward

intrinsic: inward

nomic, and political forces that created the external context within which my family and Black community elders lived, and about how they influenced and shaped my **perceptions** and life choices. The challenge faced by Black parents when I was growing up was **daunting.** They had to **affirm** and help us children **internalize** our **sanctity** as children of God, as valued members of our family, of the Black community, of the American community, and of the entire human community, while **simultaneously** preparing us to understand, survive in, and challenge the **prevailing** values of a legally segregated nation, with a history of slavery, that did not value or affirm us as equal citizens or practice the self-evident belief that "all men are created equal" as its founding fathers **professed.**

6   Black parents—and all parents—face these same challenges today to help children define who they are and what to value in a culture that assigns worth more by **extrinsic** than **intrinsic** measures; by racial, gender, and class rather than human values; by material rather than spiritual values; by power rather than principle; by money rather than morality; by greed rather than goodness; by consumerism rather than conscience; by rugged individualism rather than community; and that glorifies violence above nonviolence.

7   I cannot recall a single one of the mentors I share with you in this book ever talking to me about how to make a living or to get a job—worthy and necessary goals. They all stressed how to make a life and to find a purpose worth living for and to leave the world better than I found it. Their emphasis was on education, excellence, and service—not just on career. Their message was that if I were excellent I'd have less trouble securing a job—even as a young Black person. I can't remember the clothes a single one of them wore or the kind of car they drove or whether they drove a car at all. What I do remember is their **integrity,** courage in the face of **adversity,** perseverance, and shared passion for justice and a better life for children—their own and other people's—and for education as a means to the end of helping others. With one exception, Charles E. Merrill, Jr., son of the **scion** of the Merrill Lynch brokerage firm, none had much money. Some of them had none and lived hand-to-mouth by the grace of God and friends. And Charles Merrill knew that money was a means to help others and not an end. He used his to give dozens of young women and men like me and Alice Walker a chance to travel and study abroad and to experience the world he had been privileged to see.

integrity: honesty

adversity: hardship, challenge

scion: founder

8   Many of my mentors were well educated but many did not have much or any formal education. However they valued education for their children and were very **astute** about life. Some of the wisest words I have heard and most important lessons I have learned did not come from Harvard or Yale or Princeton or law school or Ph.D. trained mouths. They were from poor women and men educated in the school of life. Their books were struggle. Their pencils and pens were sharpened by poverty. Their mother wit was created by the daily battle for survival. Their inner faith was nourished by their

astute: perceptive

outer losses. Their eyes were riveted on searching for and doing God's will rather than human ways, and their standards were divine rather than human justice.

9   All of my mentors, men and women of different faiths and colors, in their own way **personified** excellence and courage, shared and instilled a vision and hope of what could be, not what was, in our racially, gender, class, and caste **constricted** country; kept America's promise of becoming a country free of discrimination, poverty, and ignorance ever before me; put the foundations of education, discipline, hard work, and perseverance needed to help build it beneath me; and instilled a sense of the here and now and forever faithful presence of God inside me.

10   In many ways, the **labyrinth** of my life is leading back to where I began and to many of the lessons learned but too easily lost in the **cacophony** of noise and clutter and **triviality** and **depersonalization** afflicting so much of modern American life and culture. With others, I seek to reweave the **frayed remnants** of family, community, and spiritual values **rent asunder** in the name of progress. That much racial, social, and scientific progress has taken place over my lifetime is evident. Millions of Black children and poor children of all races have moved into the American mainstream and are better off materially. But something important has been lost as we have thrown away or traded so much of our Black spiritual heritage for a false sense of economic security and inclusion. We are at risk of letting our children drown in the bathwater of American materialism, greed, and violence. We must regain our moral **bearings** and roots and help America recover hers before millions more children—Black, Brown, and White, poor, middle-class, and rich—self-destruct or grow up thinking life is about acquiring rather than sharing, selfishness rather than sacrifice, and material rather than spiritual wealth.

11   Finally, I look around with concern at the loneliness and neediness of so many children who are trying so hard to grow up and who need parents, and other caring, reliable adults to see, hear, listen to, and spend time with them in our too careless, too fast, too busy culture. So many children are killing themselves and others because they lack enough adults in their homes, schools, communities, public life, and culture to show them a different way and to reflect lives with positive purpose and integrity. Adults' **hypocrisy** is confusing and deadening our children's spirits and minds as they struggle through an American landmine of drugs, guns, violence, and greed **poised** to shatter their bodies, minds, dreams, and futures.

12   But I look ahead with faith and determination, firmly believing we can together build newer, healthier lives, strong families, strong communities, and strong children who are good human beings. This will require reshaping national priorities and reclaiming the enduring values of compassion, fairness, and opportunity that are the bedrock of the great experiment called America.

---

personified: were examples of

constricted: constrained

labyrinth: maze, difficult to follow passage

cacophony: inharmonious noise

triviality: superficiality

depersonalization: lack of concern for individuals

afflicting: troubling

frayed remnants: damaged remains

rent asunder: torn apart

bearings: sense of direction, balance

hypocrisy: saying one thing but doing another

poised: ready, set

Vocabulary Exercises

Fill in the blank with the appropriate vocabulary word from the reading.

1. People who love their jobs work not for _____ rewards but _____ rewards.

2. On Friday, Samantha must make a decision that is _____ to her career.

3. I admire people who have _____ and who stand up for what they believe.

4. It's difficult for children who watch hours of TV not to _____ the values portrayed on television.

5. One must be able to overcome _____ in order to survive.

6. The one characteristic I cannot tolerate in people is _____.

7. The _____ of noise coming from the building was terrible.

8. The U.S. Constitution protects the _____ of the home.

9. I had lost my _____ and didn't know which way to turn.

10. One of my friends made an _____ observation about the movie.

Comprehension Questions

1. Edelman was born and raised in
   A. New York City.
   B. Bennettsville, South Carolina.
   C. Charlottesville, North Carolina.
   D. San Diego, California.

2. Edelman's father was
   A. a construction worker.
   B. a farmer.
   C. a minister.
   D. a lawyer.

3. Edelman's childhood home is now
   A. a school.
   B. a museum.
   C. a Children's Defense Fund office.
   D. a doctor's office.

4. Edelman grew up in
   A. an immigrant society.

   B. a segregated society.

   C. an integrated society.

   D. a female society.

5. According to Edelman, mentors must be
   A. wealthy.

   B. educated.

   C. married.

   D. None of the above

6. Edelman's mentors encouraged her to
   A. find a purpose worth living for.

   B. dress professionally.

   C. make a great deal of money.

   D. get a good job.

7. Edelman feels _____ to have had the upbringing she did.
   A. angry

   B. blessed

   C. cheated

   D. guilty

8. According to Edelman, the challenges parents face today are
   A. just as difficult as those in the past.

   B. more difficult than those in the past.

   C. less difficult than those in the past.

9. What does Edelman remember about her mentors?
   A. How they dressed

   B. The cars they drove

   C. Their integrity and courage

   D. Their appearance

10. According to Edelman, modern society
    A. is too materialistic.

    B. is too violent.

    C. is too selfish.

    D. All of the above

Discussion Questions

1. Describe Edelman's upbringing.

2. What does Edelman mean when she says, " I did not come into or get through life alone. Neither did you."

3. How hard is it to instill spiritual values and a sense of self-worth in children today? What forces in our society fight against such values? What challenges do Black parents—and all parents—face today? How must they battle the forces of contemporary society?

4. What did Edelman's mentors value? What values did they encourage in her?

5. Were all of Edelman's mentors well educated? What sort of education did they have? What characteristics did Edelman's mentors share?

Writing Topics

1. "I did not come into or get through life alone. Neither did you. . . . My parents needed and got the help...." Describe what your parents or neighbors or community have done to help get you through life. What sacrifices did they make? What guidance did they provide? How did they help bring you up? What values did they encourage in you?

2. Who were your mentors? Pick one mentor and describe that person and his or her influence on you. What did your mentor(s) value? What values did they encourage in you?

3. How did the "extended context" within which you grew up—the cultural, social, economic, and political forces—influence and shape your perceptions and life choices? What roles or careers did you believe were open to you? Were you raised

to believe that you could be anything you wanted to be, or did your culture encourage you to pursue certain roles and not others?

4. "Black parents—and all parents—face the same challenges today to help children define who they are and what to value...." What challenges do parents today face? How does our society, with its emphasis on appearance and material goods, make it difficult to instill values in children?

5. If you could do one thing to improve your community, city, state, nation, or the world, what would it be?

Preview

Do you have a hobby or something you love to do? Wouldn't it be nice to earn a living doing what you enjoy doing? That's what Chad Pregracke managed to do. He turned his love of the Mississippi River and his desire to keep it clean into a full-time job.

Trash Talker: Chad Pregracke Takes Mucking Up the Mississippi River Very Personally
Steve Kemper

shrill: loud

1 After ramming his flat-bottomed aluminum boat onto the muddy band of a nameless island in the Mississippi River, near Grafton, Illinois, Chad Pregracke (pronounced pree-GRA-kee) leaps ashore with a **shrill** whoop. Within seconds, he has disappeared among logjams and high weeds, happily absorbed in his favorite outdoor pastime: collecting trash. The weather's hot, the mosquitoes are tearing him up and he's knee-deep in muck. Why is he doing this? Because he's a true-blue patriot, that's why. "As a national treasure, the Mississippi River is probably more famous than the Statue of Liberty," he says, not sounding the least bit **hokey** about it. "We wouldn't tolerate half this garbage in Yellowstone Park or on the Mall in Washington, D.C., so why should we put up with it here?"

hokey: corny

2 For Pregracke, 28, nothing beats heaping his boat with river junk and haul-ing the whole filthy mess back to one of the three 135-foot barges he uses as sorting depots. He lugs couches, cracked toilets, sinks, furnaces, microwaves, motorcycles and lawn mowers. He piles TV sets, bowling balls and freezers on top of propane tanks and huge slabs of Styrofoam. And, yes, occasionally he does come across a bottle with a message inside—usually, "return to sender."

enthusiastic: excited

crusader: someone who fights for a cause

severed: cut off

prosthetic: artificial

grisliest: goriest

3 It's hard to think of anything this boyishly **enthusiastic** clean-up **crusader** hasn't brought to light. The cooler with the **severed** horse's head inside was freaky. So were the two **prosthetic** legs and the rubber sex doll. The **grisliest** find of all turned up last summer when a Pregracke helper dis-covered a human head on an island just north of Fort Madison, Iowa. The local police eventually determined that it had belonged to a suicidal young man who had jumped from a bridge a year earlier.

4 Mary Alice Ramirez, the director of environmental outreach at Anheuser-Busch, the big beer company in St. Louis, remembers her first phone conver-sation with Pregracke this way:

5 He: "Will you give me some money?"

6 She: "Who are you?"

7 He: "I want to get rid of the garbage on the Mississippi River."

Steve Kemper, "Trash Talker," from *Smithsonian*.

proposal:
formal plan

8   She: "Can you show me a **proposal**?"

9   He: "What's a proposal?"

10   Ramirez invited Pregracke in for a meeting. When he showed up, the receptionist announced that some dead-beat was in the lobby. "He had a dirty T-shirt, ripped jeans, long hair and a sweaty cap," Ramirez says, "and he looked about 18."

irrepressible:
not to be
kept down

debris: litter

tributaries:
smaller
rivers and
streams that
lead into a
larger one

galvanized:
solidified,
brought
together

collaborate:
cooperate

agendas:
goals,
objectives

11   Anheuser-Busch gave Pregracke $25,000 to help expand his Mississippi River Beautification and Restoration Project, which he was running out of his parents' house in East Moline, Illinois. That was in 1999. By now the **irrepressible** river rat and his ragtag crew have removed and recycled more than 800 tons of **debris** from the banks of the Mississippi and several **tributaries** between St. Louis and Minneapolis. They've also **galvanized** a couple of dozen towns in Iowa, Illinois and Missouri to undertake annual cleanups of their own. Because of Pregracke, groups that don't usually **collaborate,** such as the U.S. Army Corps of Engineers and environmentalists, now often find themselves working shoulder to shoulder. "We all have our own **agendas,** but Chad brings people together," says Christine Favilla, a project manager with the Sierra Club in Illinois.

12   It won't be long, if Pregracke has his way, before his motto "Coming to a river near you" will be spoken in many languages. Last year at an environmental conference in Johannesburg, South Africa, "I worked out a deal to bring 10 to 15 Russians over here in August to teach them everything I know—the right equipment, how to organize community cleanups," he says. "Next I'll bring some people from China."

13   Pregracke grew up beside the Mississippi. From his boyhood home in East Moline, where his dad taught high school and his mom directed a child care program, he could take a few running steps and jump right in the water. He and his older brother, Brent, fished and dove for mussels. Nights they camped out like Huck Finn and Jim. Pregracke loved it, except for one thing: too many people treated the river and shoreline like a dump.

eyesores:
ugly features

14   During summers off from high school and community college, he worked as a commercial shell diver and photographed some of the Mississippi's worst **eyesores.** Brushed off by local and state officials when he tried to show them his pictures of the trash, he grabbed a phone book one day, called a company named Alcoa ("because it started with A," he says) and asked for the "top guy." He eventually talked Alcoa into giving him an $8,400 startup grant. Using an old haul boat and a salvaged pickup truck, he took more than 20 tons from the Mississippi that first year.

**mush-
roomed:**
grown,
expanded

motley: var-
ied, colorful

refurbished:
fixed up

15   Perhaps because Pregracke resembles the actor Tom Cruise and talks like a wired skateboarder ("Dude, you need to let me show you some pictures!"), a number of corporations have found his charms persuasive. Today, his annual operating budget has **mushroomed** to more than $400,000. His **motley** fleet consists of a **refurbished** 20-year-old tug, five hauling craft and a houseboat

that doubles as a dormitory and office, as well as those three big barges. Pregracke and his crew, which varies from three to six, start working in mid-February and don't quit until ice forces them off the water in December. Last year, assisted by thousands of volunteers, they got rid of more than 270 tons of trash.

16   Those who work for Pregracke, including girlfriend Margaret Abts, a recent biology graduate, make $1,500 to $1,800 a month. The boss pays himself the princely sum of $35,000 a year. They all live aboard the houseboat, where the perks will soon include plumbing and hot water; meanwhile they use portable toilets and bathe in the river. Pregracke **rouses** his **colleagues** early each morning by tugging on their toes and pushes them hard until dark.

17   Pregracke is patient as well as persistent. One day he spotted a huge raft of old Styrofoam floating downriver. He hauled it up to the marina that had dumped it. "I thought you might want this back," he told the startled owner. Next day, the same stuff came floating down the river again. "It takes a long time to change things," Pregracke says.

18   He knows trash is the least of the Mississippi's problems. "But I think getting people out removing barrels and tires is worth a lot because now they have a stake in the river. When bigger problems like **siltation** and runoff come up, they'll be interested. So half of this project is for the river and half is for the people."

19   The passion that led Pregracke to clean up the Mississippi now leaves him little time to enjoy it. Recently, he bought a new fishing pole, but his dog, Indy, chewed the handle off before he had a chance to use it. Not to worry, he says. "I really *love* my job."

rouses: wakes
colleagues: fellow workers

siltation: the buildup of silt or dirt on the bottom of rivers

Vocabulary Exercises

Fill in the blank with the appropriate vocabulary word from the reading.

1. I have a _____ to make concerning next year's bazaar.

2. He had an _____ sense of humor.

3. There are many _____ that flow into the Mississippi River.

4. Each group that attended the meeting had its own _____.

5. I have always felt that billboards are _____ on our highways.

6. It was the _____ crime ever committed in our town.

7. Would you like to _____ on our school project?

8. The bird had a _____ cry.

9. She has always been a _____ for women's rights.

10. Cheerleaders are always _____ about games.

Comprehension Questions

1. Chad Pregracke enjoys
   A. collecting trash.
   B. fishing.
   C. working for big companies.
   D. writing grants.

2. Pregracke grew up
   A. in a city.
   B. on a farm.
   C. beside the Mississippi River.
   D. on a houseboat.

3. Chad is
   A. nineteen.
   B. twenty-eight.
   C. forty-eight.
   D. sixty-eight.

4. What organization gave Pregracke his first grant?
   A. U.S. government
   B. Army Corps of Engineers
   C. Alcoa
   D. Anheuser-Busch

5. Pregracke showed up for his meeting with Anheuser-Busch representatives wearing
   A. a coat and tie.
   B. a dirty T-shirt and jeans.
   C. a sports shirt and jeans.

6. Pregracke has
   A. removed more than 800 tons of trash from the Mississippi.
   B. encouraged annual cleanups along the Mississippi.
   C. helped rival groups work together.
   D. All of the above

7. Pregracke recently attended a conference in
   A. Washington, D.C.

   B. Russia.

   C. China.

   D. South Africa.

8. He and his workers live in
   A. hotels along the river.

   B. a houseboat.

   C. comfortable homes.

   D. dormitories.

9. Today, Pregracke's budget is
   A. $8,200.

   B. $100,000.

   C. $250,000.

   D. over $400,000.

10. How does Pregracke feel about his job?
    A. He hates it.

    B. He loves it.

    C. He is bored but knows it's important.

    D. He is ready to move on.

Discussion Questions

1. Describe Chad Pregracke. What does he look like? How does he speak? How do others perceive him?

2. How did Pregracke make his dream come true? How did he get funding to support his clean-up efforts?

3. How does Pregracke feel about his work?

4. Why has he been so successful?

5. How has Pregracke expanded his one-man efforts over the years?

Writing Topics

1. If you could turn a hobby into a job the way Pregracke did, what would it be?

2. How did Pregracke make his dream come true? How did he get funding to support his clean-up efforts? Tell the story of his efforts to clean up the Mississippi.

3. Describe one thing you could do to help clean up your neighborhood or community. First, describe the problem and then what you think you could do or you think should be done to solve it.

4. Chad Pregracke became a crusader to clean up the Mississippi River because he believed strongly in what he was doing. What do you believe in strongly enough to fight for?

5. Chad Pregracke seems to have found happiness in doing something he loves to do. How important is it that you do something you love to do? How important are satisfaction and happiness in life?

Preview

Have you noticed the difference being motivated can make? Malcolm X discovered motivation when he was in prison, and he set out to teach himself to read and write by copying the dictionary. He was so successful that he rose to become an articulate and powerful leader of the Black Muslim faith during the 1960's.

From *The Autobiography of Malcolm X*
Malcolm X

acquire: get

1   It was because of my letters that I happened to stumble upon starting to **acquire** some kind of a homemade education.

convey: communicate

articulate: able to communicate effectively with words

2   I became increasingly frustrated at not being able to express what I wanted to **convey** in letters that I wrote, especially those to Mr. Elijah Muhammad. In the street, I had been the most **articulate** hustler out there—I had commanded attention when I said something. But now, trying to write simple English, I not only wasn't articulate, I wasn't even functional. How would I sound writing in slang, the way I would say it, something such as, "Look, daddy, let me pull your coat about a cat. Elijah Muhammad—"

3   Many who today hear me somewhere in person, or on television, or those who read something I've said, will think I went to school far beyond the eighth grade. This impression is due entirely to my prison studies.

stock: saved up material

emulate: take after

4   It had really begun back in the Charlestown Prison, when Bimbi first made me feel envy of his **stock** of knowledge. Bimbi had always taken charge of any conversation he was in, and I had tried to **emulate** him. But every book I picked up had few sentences which didn't contain anywhere from one to nearly all of the words that might as well have been in Chinese. When I just skipped those words, of course, I really ended up with little idea of what the book said. So I had come to the Norfolk Prison Colony still going through only book-reading motions. Pretty soon, I would have quit even these motions, unless I had received the motivation that I did.

5   I saw that the best thing I could do was get hold of a dictionary—to study, to learn some words. I was lucky enough to reason also that I should try to improve my penmanship. It was sad. I couldn't even write in a straight line. It was both ideas together that moved me to request a dictionary along with some tablets and pencils from the Norfolk Prison Colony school.

painstaking: taking pains to be careful

ragged: having rough edges

6   I spent two days just riming uncertainly through the dictionary's pages. I'd never realized so many words existed! I didn't know which words I needed to learn. Finally, just to start some kind of action, I began copying.

7   In my slow, **painstaking, ragged** handwriting, I copied into my tablet everything printed on that first page, down to the punctuation marks.

8   I believe it took me a day. Then, aloud, I read back, to myself, everything I'd written on the tablet. Over and over, aloud, to myself, I read my own handwriting.

immensely:
greatly

9   I woke up the next morning, thinking about those words—**immensely** proud to realize that not only had I written so much at one time, but I'd written words that I never knew were in the world. Moreover, with a little effort, I also could remember what many of these words meant. I reviewed the words whose meanings I didn't remember. Funny thing, from the dictionary first page right now, that "aardvark" springs to my mind. The dictionary had a picture of it, a long-tailed, long-eared, burrowing African mammal, which lives off termites caught by sticking out its tongue as an anteater does for ants.

fascinated:
greatly
interested
succeeding:
following

10   I was so **fascinated** that I went on—I copied the dictionary's next page. And the same experience came when I studied that. With every **succeeding** page, I also learned of people and places and events from history. Actually the dictionary is like a miniature encyclopedia. Finally the dictionary's A section had filled a whole tablet—and I went on into the B's. That was the way I started copying what eventually became the entire dictionary. It went a lot faster after so much practice helped me to pick up handwriting speed. Between what I wrote in my tablet, and writing letters, during the rest of my time in prison I would guess I wrote a million words.

inevitable:
could not be
avoided

11   I suppose it was **inevitable** that as my word-base broadened, I could for the first time pick up a book and read and now begin to understand what the book was saying. Anyone who has read a great deal can imagine the new world that opened. Let me tell you something: from then until I left that prison, in every free moment I had, if I was not reading in the library, I was reading on my bunk. You couldn't have gotten me out of books with a **wedge.** Between Mr. Muhammad's teachings, my **correspondence,** my visitors . . . and my reading of books, months passed without my even thinking about being imprisoned. In fact, up to then, I never had been so truly free in my life.

wedge: tool
used to split
wood
**correspon-
dence:**
letters

Vocabulary Exercises

Fill in the blank with the appropriate vocabulary word from the reading.

1. I admire _____ people who have a way with words.

2. The work I had to do was slow and _____.

3. After the race, I was _____ tired.

4. Your opponents will try to drive a _____ between you and your friends.

5. On the _____ pages, I discovered what happened to the hero.

6. The mountains looked _____ in the distance.

7. I am going to school because I need to _____ new skills.

8. Eleanor decided to take _____ of the contents of her pantry.

9. My friends and I were _____ by the speaker.

10. I have decided to _____ the best student and prepare for the next test.

Comprehension Questions

1. Why does Malcolm X call his education homemade?
   A. It helped him make a home.

   B. He was homeschooled.

   C. He taught himself.

   D. He attended a one-room schoolhouse.

2. Why did Malcolm X admire Bimbi?
   A. He controlled the supply of drugs and alcohol.

   B. He controlled other prisoners.

   C. He spoke well and was knowledgeable.

   D. He could ask the warden for favors.

3. How much formal education did Malcolm X have?
   A. None

   B. Fifth grade

   C. Eighth grade

   D. Twelfth grade

4. On the street, Malcolm was considered
   A. well spoken.

   B. well dressed.

   C. dangerous.

   D. sophisticated.

5. Malcolm X had trouble reading because
   A. he needed glasses.

   B. he didn't know the meaning of words.

   C. he didn't like reading.

6. The word _emulate_ in paragraph 4 means
   A. impress.

   B. beat.

   C. be like.

   D. take advantage of.

7. What would Malcolm X do when he encountered a word he didn't know in a book he was reading?
   A. Look it up.

   B. Skip it

   C. Ask Bimbi what it meant.

   D. Add it to a list of words he didn't know.

8. What did Malcolm X request from the prison school?
   A. Legal textbooks

   B. Crime fiction

   C. A dictionary and writing paper

   D. Adventure stories

9. What word does Malcolm X say he still remembers from his prison studies?
   A. Anteater

   B. Aardvark

   C. Dictionary

   D. Reactionary

10. What did Malcolm X spend his free time in prison doing?
   A. Playing cards

   B. Playing basketball

   C. Working out

   D. Reading

Discussion Questions

1. How does Malcolm X describe himself before he went to prison?

2. What happened to change him once he was in prison?

3. How did Malcolm X respond to his situation in prison?

4. Malcolm X says that learning to read made him feel more truly free than ever before. How could reading make him feel free even though he was in prison?

5. Does Malcolm X's story seem believable to you? Why or why not?

Writing Topics

1. Malcolm X describes how frustrating and difficult it was for him to read. Describe your experiences reading when you were younger. Was reading painful, difficult, or pleasurable? Were your experiences with reading always the same, or can you remember a time when you enjoyed reading more or less than you do now? Describe one experience you had with reading that was painful or pleasurable.

2. Describe the role reading can play in a person's life. How can reading improve a person's life? How can reading free a person from the boundaries of space and time?

3. Malcolm X set out to improve his reading and writing skills without the help of a formal education. If you could choose one skill you would like to improve, what would it be? Why would you want to improve that skill? How might you learn the skill?

4. What did you learn by reading Malcolm X's account of teaching himself to read? Pick one characteristic or value that his story illustrates, and describe how his story illustrates that value.

5. Describe Malcolm X's journey from illiteracy to literacy. What was his motivation, and how did he go about teaching himself to read and write?

Preview

We all have memories of the joys and disappointments of receiving or not receiving the gifts we wanted for Christmas. Bill Maxwell, a columnist with the *St. Petersburg Times,* recalls a Christmas disappointment that turned out to be a blessing.

A Christmas Bicycle Illuminates the Spirit of Giving
Bill Maxwell

correspondent: equal to

annual: yearly

ritual: symbolic ceremony

mandatory: required

vivid: colorful

routine: everyday

comprehend: understand

siblings: brothers and sisters

equate: realize that two things are the same

sacrifice: to give something up

appreciativeness: feeling of appreciation

confided: shared a secret

paltry: small, insignificant

recall: remember

1   December 25, 1994

2   A gift, to be true, must be the flowing of the giver unto me, **correspondent** to my flowing unto him.

Ralph Waldo Emerson

3   By now, most Americans have bought and received Christmas gifts. This **annual ritual** of **mandatory** giving and receiving has fascinated me since I was a young child.

4   Today, at age 49, I have **vivid** memories of some of my earliest gifts: cap pistols and colorful cowboy outfits; a hunting knife and bolt-action .22 caliber rifle; a yellow tricycle; baseballs and gloves; footballs and basketballs; a bugle and a guitar; a Timex watch; a pedal-operated car that I drove onto a busy street, nearly getting run over by a real car; a wind-up train set; two red wagons.

5   Although I enjoyed these gifts, none meant very much to me at the time. They were **routine,** like that other boys received. Another reason these gifts were not important then was that I had gotten them while my parents were living together, when we were a normal family, when we had extra money after the bills were paid. Even though we were poor, I had yet to **comprehend** the true meaning of poverty.

6   By my ninth birthday, however, my parents had separated. Because my mother, five **siblings,** and I had no money and lived in a two-bedroom apartment in a government housing project, I had begun to relish even the smallest gifts. For good or bad, I was learning to **equate** the value of gifts with the degree of **sacrifice** and wisdom of the giver and the **appreciativeness** of the receiver.

7   As the oldest child, I worried mostly about the cost of gift giving in our family. Because my mother **confided** in me, I was fully aware of the **paltry** wages she earned as a maid on Ft. Lauderdale Beach. My siblings and I took nothing for granted, especially gifts.

8   When I was 11, my mother gave me a bicycle for Christmas. It was my first bike. I had set my heart on a slick one in the window of the downtown Western Auto and had shown it to my mother one morning in late October as we waited for the bus. I do not **recall** the bike's price, but it was a sum that made my mother shake her head. I had no real hopes of getting the bike.

Bill Maxwell, "A Christmas Bicycle Illuminates the Spirit of Giving," pp. 11–14. MAXIMUM INSIGHT: Selected Columns. Reprinted by permission of the University Press of Florida.

expectation: belief or hope that something will happen

plundering: rummaging

9   But I was constantly encouraged when I would discover my mother secretly counting money. And my heart pounded with **expectation** after the bike was removed from the store window the week before Christmas. On Christmas Eve night, I lay awake listening to my mother **plundering** in the darkness, taking gifts out of hiding, putting them under the tree. My siblings were awake, too, whispering and giggling. As the "man of the house," I had to pretend to be asleep. At daylight, the other kids dashed into the living room and began ripping open gifts. I strolled in, fingers crossed, praying that the bike was there.

10   It was not.

11   Instead, a turquoise monstrosity that vaguely resembled an American Flyer stood near the stove. My heart sank. Aware of my disappointment, my mother said: "I couldn't afford the new bike. I had Mr. Dennis fix up one for you. He said it's just like new." Mr. Dennis was a **piddler, scavenger,** and handyman **par excellence.** With trembling hands, he could put together any **contraption.**

piddler: someone who spends time on insignificant matters

scavenger: one who finds and reuses things

par excellence: excellent

contraption: homemade or put together machine

incidentals: not important items

12   Initially, I hated the bike, a hulk of discarded parts and brush-streaked paint. The neighborhood boys laughed at it, calling it the "Mack truck." After about two weeks, though, when most of the new bikes were banged up or stolen, the laughing stopped. My turquoise monster was right at home. In fact, it was a godsend, with its three big baskets, one on the handlebar and one on each side of the rear fender. My mother did not own a car, so we rode the bus or walked everywhere. As the oldest child, I did a lot of the grocery shopping and running around for **incidentals.** When I shopped alone, I sometimes would have to walk to the store three times to collect all of the bags. With the bike, I could make one trip.

fondly: with love or affection

epitomized: symbolized, represented perfectly

dignity: pride, self-respect

13   Why, of the many gifts I have received in my life, do I remember that bicycle so **fondly?** Because, for me, the experience related to it **epitomized** the spirit of gift giving. Not only did my mother know how badly I wanted a bike, she also knew that, because of my duties as the oldest child, the bike would make life easier for me. She knew that it would give me some **dignity.** I would not have to walk everywhere or piggyback on another boy's bike. It gave me something in common with the boys whose families had more money.

jerrybuilt: built quickly from second-hand materials

self-reliant: relying only on yourself

acknowledging: recognizing

14   In the spring, that bike did let me become "the man of the house." It gave me the opportunity to become a carrier for the *Fort Lauderdale News.* I was able to earn enough money to help my mother pay several household bills each week. That **jerrybuilt** bike gave me independence—a way to become **self-reliant.** My mother knew that, even as a child, I was driven by the desire to do for myself, and her gift was her way of **acknowledging** me. She has since told me so. To this day, my mother and I exchange gifts of mutual acknowledgement—if we are inclined to exchange gifts at all.

15   I am certain that I view gift giving too seriously. Even so, I am convinced that Ralph Waldo Emerson captured its true meaning more than a century ago:

convey: give
tokens: symbols

barbarous: uncivilized

primary: first or most important

motives: reasons for doing something

signify: mean

materialism: concern for material things

16   Next to things of necessity, the rule for a gift . . . is that we might **convey** to some person that which properly belongs to his character, and was associated with him in thought. But our **tokens** of compliment and love are for the most part **barbarous.** Rings and other jewels are not gifts, but apologies for gifts.

17   The only gift is a portion of thyself. Thou must bleed for me. Therefore the poet brings a poem; the shepherd, his lamb; the farmer, corn; the miner, a gem; the sailor, a coral and shells; the painter, his picture; the girl, a handkerchief of her own sewing. This is right and pleasing, for it restores society in so far to its **primary** basis, when a man's biography is conveyed in his gift. . . .

18   Is Emerson asking too much of us? Should we, especially during the Christmas season, think more seriously about our **motives** for giving? Should we measure our feelings with greater care when we receive? If the day marking the birth of the Christian savior is important enough to honor, should the rituals related to this day **signify** more than a grand celebration of **materialism?**

Vocabulary Exercises

Fill in the blank with the appropriate vocabulary word from the reading.

1. I considered the man's rude behavior to be _____.

2. Our culture is overly concerned with money and _____.

3. From the time the author was young, he wanted to be _____.

4. The author has five _____.

5. I don't want to work for _____ wages.

6. What does the sign _____?

7. The flowers were a _____ of my affection.

8. How can you ride around town in that ridiculous _____?

9. In our school, uniforms were _____.

10. I have _____ memories of my childhood.

Comprehension Questions

1. What event marks the time after which the author remembers gifts more clearly?
   A. His fifth birthday
   B. The separation of his parents
   C. His father's return
   D. Their move to a big city

2. How old was the author when his parents separated?
   A. Three
   B. Five
   C. Nine
   D. Sixteen

3. Why does he worry about gift giving in his family?
   A. He thinks his brothers get nicer gifts than he does.
   B. He worries that his siblings are being spoiled.
   C. He worries about the cost to his mother.
   D. He worries about what others will think of their gift giving.

4. What does the author's mother do for a living?
   A. She is a maid.
   B. She is a nurse.
   C. She is a waitress.
   D. She is a teacher.

5. The author is the _____ child in his family.
   A. youngest
   B. middle
   C. oldest

6. How has the author communicated to his mother what he wants for Christmas?
   A. He has shown her a picture in a catalog.
   B. He has written a letter to Santa.
   C. He has shown her the bike in the window of the hardware store.
   D. He has told her.

7. What is the author's first reaction to the bike he gets for Christmas?
   A. Excitement
   B. Disappointment
   C. Gratitude
   D. Anger

8. What color is the bike?
   A. Red
   B. Black
   C. Turquoise
   D. Orange

9. Why was the bicycle so useful to the author?
   A. He could ride to school.

   B. He could give his friends rides.

   C. He could carry groceries home.

   D. He could go to the movies.

10. How does the bike allow the author to help support his family?
    A. By delivering groceries

    B. By delivering newspapers

    C. By mowing lawns

    D. By getting a job

Discussion Questions

1. Describe the author's life before and after his parents separate.

2. What role does the author play in his family? Why does he worry about gift giving in his family?

3. Does the author expect to get the bike he wants for Christmas? Why does he think he won't? Why does he begin to hope he might?

4. How does the bike prove to be a godsend? What does it allow him to do?

5. How does the bike illustrate what the author thinks is the spirit of gift giving?

Writing Topics

1. Do you remember a special Christmas or special Christmas gift when you were a child? Describe the gift and what it meant to you.

2. What sorts of gifts did you give to loved ones when you were a child? Did you ever give someone a special gift that you made yourself? Describe the gift, what it meant to you, and what it meant to the person who received it.

3. What role did you play in your family as a child?

4. If you could have gotten any gift you wanted as a child, what would it have been, and why would it have been important to you?

5. Agree or disagree with the author's belief that gift giving should be personal and should represent the connection between the giver and receiver.

Preview

Making a change in the pattern of your life is one of the most difficult, but sometimes necessary, steps you can take. As you begin college, consider what Mary Oliver has to say about the difficulties and rewards of embarking on a new journey.

The Journey
Mary Oliver

One day you finally knew
what you had to do, and began,
though the voices around you
kept shouting
5   their bad advice—
though the whole house
began to tremble
and you felt the old tug
at your ankles.
10   "Mend my life!"
each voice cried.
But you didn't stop.
You knew what you had to do,
though the wind **pried**
15   with its stiff fingers
at the very foundations,
though their **melancholy**
was terrible.
It was already late
20   enough, and a wild night,
and the road full of fallen
branches and stones.
But little by little,
as you left their voices behind,
25   the stars began to burn
through the sheets of clouds,
and there was a new voice
which you slowly
recognized as your own,
30   that kept you company
as you **strode** deeper and deeper
into the world,
determined to do
the only thing you could do—
determined to save
the only life you could save.

pried:
removed
something
stuck on

melancholy:
sad

strode:
walked confidently

Comprehension Questions

1. What is the speaker leaving?
   A. Work

   B. Home

   C. School

   D. A party

2. At what time of day is the speaker leaving?
   A. Morning

   B. Noon

   C. Afternoon

   D. Night

3. What word best describes the attitude of those the speaker leaves behind?
   A. Happiness

   B. Confidence

   C. Melancholy

   D. Encouragement

4. What do the voices shout as the speaker leaves?
   A. Goodbyes

   B. Cheers of encouragement

   C. Bad advice

   D. Weeping

5. What fills the road?
   A. Cheering people

   B. Children

   C. Fallen branches and stones

   D. Flowers

Discussion Questions

1. What things hold the speaker of the poem back from her journey?

2. Describe the conditions under which the speaker sets out on her journey.

3. What positive elements does the speaker experience as she sets out on the journey?

4. Where is the speaker striding (walking)?

5. At the end of the poem, what does the speaker decide to do and why?

Activity

In groups of two or three, introduce yourselves and discuss any line or image that strikes you in the poem. You might talk about what the line or image means to you or how it relates to your journey.

Writing Assignment

Answer each of the following questions in a paragraph of four to five sentences. You do not need to write the question or number your answers. Indent the first line of each paragraph.

1. What is the goal of your journey? Where are you heading?

2. What life are you leaving behind as you set out on your journey?

3. What obstacles are you likely to face on your journey, and how might you overcome them?

4. What behaviors or attitudes do you want to leave behind on your journey (because you know they will not be useful in achieving your dream)?

5. Choose an image to inspire you on your journey, and describe how that image will help keep you focused on your goals.

Preview

Have you ever wondered why men and women seem to have so much trouble communicating? Deborah Tannen is an expert in communication theory, and she has written many books and articles about the differing communication styles and purposes of men and women. This article is only one example of an entire academic field called *gender studies,* which explores the differences between males and females.

From *You Just Don't Understand: Women and Men in Conversation*
Deborah Tannen

intimacy: having a close personal relationship

negotiate: move through

networks: interrelationships or connections

minimize: to reduce to the smallest amount

consensus: agreement

status: rank in social position

primary: basic

chum: friend

1   ***Intimacy*** is key in a world of connection where individuals **negotiate** complex **networks** of friendship, **minimize** differences, try to reach **consensus,** and avoid the appearance of superiority, which would highlight differences. In a world of **status,** *independence* is key, because a **primary** means of establishing status is to tell others what to do, and taking orders is a marker of low status. Though all humans need both intimacy and independence, women tend to focus on the first and men on the second. It is as if their lifeblood ran in different directions.

2   These differences can give women and men differing views of the same situation, as they did in the case of a couple I will call Linda and Josh. When Josh's old high-school **chum** called him at work and announced he'd be in town on business the following month, Josh invited him to stay for the weekend. That evening he informed Linda that they were going to have a houseguest, and that he and his chum would go out together the first night to shoot the breeze like old times. Linda was upset. She was going to be away on business the week before, and the Friday night when Josh would be out with his chum would be her first night home. But what upset her the most was that Josh had made these plans on his own and informed her of them, rather than discussing them with her before extending the invitation.

3   Linda would never make plans, for a weekend or an evening, without first checking with Josh. She can't understand why he doesn't show her the same courtesy and consideration that she shows him. But when she protests, Josh says, "I can't say to my friend, 'I have to ask my wife for permission'!"

implies: means

underling: subordinate or someone less important

4   To Josh, checking with his wife means seeking permission, which **implies** that he is not independent, not free to act on his own. It would make him feel like a child or an **underling.** To Linda, checking with her husband has nothing to do with permission. She assumes that spouses discuss their plans with each

intertwined: connected

conse-quences: effects or results

warranted: justified

consult: talk over

conceptions: beliefs

evidence: sign

oppressed: held down

hemmed in: restrained

initiate: begin, set in motion

freewheel-ing: free and open

continual: continuing

in concert: coordinated

cogs in a wheel: people locked together

other because their lives are **intertwined,** so the actions of one have **conse-quences** for the other. Not only does Linda not mind telling someone, "I have to check with Josh"; quite the contrary—she likes it. It makes her feel good to know and show that she is involved with someone, that her life is bound up with someone else's.

5   Linda and Josh both felt more upset by this incident, and others like it, than seemed **warranted,** because it cut to the core of their primary concerns. Linda was hurt because she sensed a failure of closeness in their relationship: He didn't care about her as much as she cared about him. And he was hurt because he felt she was trying to control him and limit his freedom.

6   A similar conflict exists between Louise and Howie, another couple, about spending money. Louise would never buy anything costing more than a hundred dollars without discussing it with Howie, but he goes out and buys whatever he wants and feels they can afford, like a table saw or a new power mower. Louise is disturbed, not because she disapproves of the purchases, but because she feels he is acting as if she were not in the picture.

7   Many women feel it is natural to **consult** with their partners at every turn, while many men automatically make more decisions without consulting their partners. This may reflect a broad difference in **conceptions** of decision-making. Women expect decisions to be discussed first and made by consensus. They appreciate the discussion itself as **evidence** of involvement and communication. But many men feel **oppressed** by lengthy discussions about what they see as minor decisions, and they feel **hemmed in** if they can't just act without talking first. When women try to **initiate** a **freewheeling** discussion by asking, "What do you think?" men often think they are being asked to decide.

8   Communication is a **continual** balancing act, juggling the conflicting needs for intimacy and independence. To survive in the world, we have to act **in concert** with others, but to survive as ourselves, rather than simply as **cogs in a wheel,** we have to act alone. In some ways, all people are the same: We all eat and sleep and drink and laugh and cough, and often we eat, and laugh at, the same things. But in some ways, each person is different, and individuals' differing wants and preferences may conflict with each other. Offered the same menu, people make different choices. And if there is cake for dessert, there is a chance one person may get a larger piece than another—and an even greater chance that one will *think* the other's piece is larger, whether it is or not.

Vocabulary Exercises

Fill in the blank with the appropriate vocabulary word from the reading.

1. The teacher and the class reached _____ on the best time for the exam.

2. A large _____ of friends, family, and co-workers supported the family during their crisis.

3. The judge ruled that the police's action was _____ when they stopped the reckless driver.

4. The driver _____ the sharp turns on the mountain road skillfully.

5. A student should _____ contact with her teacher if she is having trouble learning the course material.

6. The couple had a _____ argument all evening.

7. The puddles in the road are _____ that it has rained.

8. Some people think that their lives are _____ with their parents' lives.

9. The lawyer asked to _____ with his client before the trial.

10. The class had a _____ discussion about current events.

Comprehension Questions

1. According to Deborah Tannen, intimacy in a relationship means
   A. being sexual.
   B. getting close.
   C. negotiating consensus.
   D. understanding each other.

2. According to Deborah Tannen, independence means
   A. establishing status.
   B. breaking away from others.
   C. being boss.
   D. being free.

3. The example the author gives of a couple making a decision concerns
   A. plans for going out to eat.
   B. plans for a visit from an old friend.
   C. plans for where to go on vacation.
   D. plans for the weekend.

4. Women are primarily concerned with
   A. intimacy.
   B. independence.
   C. child rearing.
   D. marriage.

5. Men are primarily concerned with
   A. intimacy.

   B. independence.

   C. jobs.

   D. friendship.

6. According to the author, women want
   A. to talk over decisions with their partner.

   B. to avoid arguments.

   C. to make the plans.

   D. to spend money.

7. According to the author, men like
   A. to have the last word in arguments.

   B. to invite friends over.

   C. to make decisions without talking to their partner.

   D. to spend time in front of the television.

8. According to the author, men and women
   A. have similar ideas about how a couple should make a decision together.

   B. can never reach agreement.

   C. don't have similar ideas about how a couple should make a decision together.

   D. like different television programs.

9. The author believes that communication between men and women is
   A. an easy task.

   B. an impossible task.

   C. an enjoyable task.

   D. a balancing act.

10. The author believes that
    A. women make decisions better than men.

    B. men make better decisions than women.

    C. no one makes good decisions.

    D. men and women must work together to make decisions.

Discussion Questions

1. Using information from the article, explain how women feel about intimacy.

2. Explain what independence means to men.

3. Explain how the values of intimacy and independence play a part in the example of the disagreement between Josh and Linda.

4. What examples does the author give of men valuing independence? What examples does the author give of women valuing intimacy?

5. Think of a disagreement you have had with a member of the opposite sex. How did the values of intimacy and independence play a part?

Writing Topics

1. Explain the different values men and women have in relationships, and give at least one example from your own life.

2. Which do you value most, intimacy or independence, and why?

3. Write a paragraph or essay explaining a value or trait that you look for in a partner. It may be different values from intimacy and independence. Explain why this trait or value is important to you.

4. Explain how the differences between men and women can cause conflicts in a relationship.

5. How can understanding the differences between men and women help partners resolve conflicts?

Preview

Most of us have had jobs we didn't particularly care for and had bosses we didn't like. Our experiences in those jobs, however mundane, often help us make up our mind what we want to do or don't want to do in life. In this short story, first published in the 1950's, John Updike introduces us to a young man with lots of personality who makes a decision that will help determine who he is. After all these years, Sammy seems remarkably modern.

A&P
John Updike

1   In walks these three girls in nothing but bathing suits. I'm in the third checkout slot, with my back to the door, so I don't see them until they're over by the bread. The one that caught my eye first was the one in the plaid green two-piece. She was a chunky kid, with a good tan and a sweet broad soft-looking can with those two crescents of white just under it, where the sun never seems to hit, at the top of the backs of her legs. I stood there with my hand on a box of HiHo crackers trying to remember if I rang it up or not. I ring it up again and the customer starts giving me hell. She's one of these cash-register-watchers, a witch about fifty with rouge on her cheekbones and no eyebrows, and I know I made her day to trip me up. She's been watching cash registers for fifty years and probably never seen a mistake before.

2   By the time I got her feathers smoothed and her goodies into a bag—she gives me a little snort in passing, if she'd been born at the right time they would have burned her over in Salem—by the time I get her on her way the girls had circled around the bread and were coming back, without a pushcart, back my way along the counters, in the aisle between the checkouts and the Special bins. They didn't even have shoes on. There was this chunky one, with the two piece—it was bright green and the seams on the bra were still sharp and her belly was still pretty pale so I guessed she just got it (the suit)—there was this one, with one of those chubby berry-faces, the lips all bunched together under her nose, this one, and a tall one, with black hair that hadn't quite frizzed right and one of these sunburns right across under the eyes, and the chin that was too long—you know, the kind of girl other girls think is very "striking" and "attractive" but never quite makes it, as they very well know, which is why they like her so much—and then the third one, that wasn't quite so tall. She was the queen. She kind of led them, the other two peeking around and making their shoulders round. She didn't look around, not this queen, she just walked straight on slowly on these long white **prima-donna** legs. She came down a little hard on her heels, as if she didn't walk in her bare feet that much, putting down her heels and then letting the weight move along to her toes as if she was testing the floor with every step, putting a little deliberate

prima-donna: someone who thinks she is special, Italian for "first lady"

extra action into it. You never know for sure how girls' minds work (do you really think it's a mind in there or just a little buzz like a bee in a glass jar?) but you got the idea she had talked the other two into coming in here with her, and now she was showing them how to do it, walk slow and hold yourself straight.

nubble: little raised bumps

3   She had on a kind of dirty-pink—beige maybe, I don't know—bathing suit with a little **nubble** all over it and, what got me, the straps were down. They were off her shoulders looped loose around the cool tops of her arms, and I guess as a result the suit had slipped a little on her, so all around the top of the cloth there was this shining rim. If it hadn't been there you wouldn't have known there could have been anything whiter than those shoulders. With the straps pushed off, there was nothing between the top of the suit and the top of her head except just her, this clean bare plane of the top of her chest down from the shoulder bones like a dented sheet of metal tilted in the light. I mean, it was more than pretty.

4   She had sort of oaky hair that the sun and salt had bleached, done up in a bun that was unraveling, and a kind of prim face. Walking into the A&P with your straps down, I suppose it's the only kind of face you can have. She held her head so high her neck, coming up out of those white shoulders, looked kind of stretched, but I didn't mind. The longer her neck was, the more of her there was.

5   She must have felt in the corner of her eye me and over my shoulder Stokesie in the second slot watching, but she didn't tip. Not this queen. She kept her eyes moving across the racks, and stopped, and turned so slow it made my stomach rub the inside of my apron, and buzzed to the other two, who kind of huddled against her for relief, and then they all three of them went up the cat-and-dog-food-breakfast-cereal-macaroni-rice-raisins-seasonings-spreads-spaghetti-drinks-crackers-and-cookies aisle. From the third slot I look straight up this aisle to the meat counter, and I watched them all the way. The fat one with the can sort of fumbled with the cookies, but on second thought she put the package back. The sheep pushing their carts down the aisle—the girls were walking against the usual traffic (not that we have one-way signs or anything)—were pretty hilarious. You could see them, when Queenie's white shoulders dawned on them, kind of jerk, or hop, or hiccup, but their eyes snapped back to their own baskets and on they pushed. I bet you could set off dynamite in an A&P and the people would by and large keep reaching and checking oatmeal off their lists and muttering "Let me see, there was a third thing, began with A, asparagus, no, ah, yes, applesauce!" or whatever it is they do mutter. But there was no doubt, this jiggled them. A few houseslaves in pin curlers even looked around after pushing their carts past to make sure what they had seen was correct.

6   You know, it's one thing to have a girl in a bathing suit down on the beach, where what with the glare nobody can look at each other much anyway, and another thing in the cool of the A&P, under the fluorescent lights, against all those stacked packages, with her feet paddling along naked over our checkerboard green-and-cream rubber-tile floor.

7   "Oh Daddy," Stokesie said beside me. "I feel so faint."

8   "Darling," I said. "Hold me tight." Stokesie's married, with two babies chalked up on his **fuselage** already, but as far as I can tell that's the only difference. He's twenty-two, and I was nineteen this April.

9   "Is it done?" he asks, the responsible married man finding his voice. I forgot to say he thinks he's going to be manager some sunny day, maybe in 1990 when it's called the Great Alexandrov and Petrooshki Tea Company or something.

10   What he meant was, our town is five miles from a beach, with a big summer colony out on the Point, but we're right in the middle of town, and the women generally put on a shirt or shorts or something before they get out of the car into the street. And anyway these are usually women with six children and varicose veins mapping their legs and nobody, including them, could care less. As I say, we're right in the middle of town, and if you stand at our front doors you can see two banks and the Congregational church and the newspaper store and three real-estate offices and about twenty-seven old freeloaders tearing up Central Street because the sewer broke again. It's not as if we're on the Cape, we're north of Boston and there's people in this town haven't seen the ocean for twenty years.

11   The girls had reached the meat counter and were asking McMahon something. He pointed, they pointed, and they shuffled out of sight behind a pyramid of Diet Delight peaches. All that was left of us to see was old McMahon patting his mouth and looking after them sizing up their joints. Poor kids, I began to feel sorry for them, they couldn't help it.

12   Now here comes the sad part of the story, at least my family says it's sad, but I don't think it's so sad myself. The store's pretty empty, it being Thursday afternoon, so there was nothing much to do except lean on the register and wait for the girls to show up again. The whole store was like a pinball machine and I didn't know which tunnel they'd come out of. After a while they come around out of the far aisle, around the light bulbs, records at discount of the Caribbean Six or Tony Martin Sings or some such gunk you wonder they waste the wax on, sixpacks of candy bars, and plastic toys done up in cellophane that fall apart when a kid looks at them anyway. Around they come, Queenie still leading the way, and holding a little gray jar in her hands. Slots Three through Seven are unmanned and I could see her wondering between Stokes and me, but Stokesie with his usual luck draws an old party in baggy gray pants who stumbles up with four giant cans of pineapple juice (what do these bums *do* with all that pineapple juice? I've often asked myself). So the girls come to me. Queenie puts down the jar and and I take it into my fingers icy cold. Kingfish Fancy Herring Snacks in Pure Sour Cream: 49¢. Now her hands are empty, not a ring or a bracelet, bare as God made them, and I wonder where the money's coming from. Still with that prim look she lifts a folded dollar bill out of the hollow at the center of her nubbled pink top. The jar went heavy in my hand. Really, I thought that was so cute.

13   Then everybody's luck begins to run out. Lengel comes in from haggling with a truck full of cabbages on the lot and is about to scuttle into that door marked MANAGER behind which he hides all day when the girls touch his eye. Lengel's pretty dreary, teaches Sunday school and the rest, but he doesn't miss that much. He comes over and says, "Girls, this isn't the beach."

14   Queenie blushes, though maybe it's just a brush of sunburn I was noticing for the first time, now that she was so close. "My mother asked me to pick up a jar of herring snacks." Her voice kind of startled me, the way voices do when you see the people first, coming out so flat and dumb yet kind of **tony,** too, the way it tickled over "pick up" and "snacks." All of a sudden I slid right down her voice into the living room. Her father and all the other men were standing around in ice-cream coats and bow ties and the women were in sandals picking up herring snacks on toothpicks off a big glass plate and they were all holding drinks the color of water with olives and sprigs of mint in them. When my parents have somebody over they get lemonade and if it's a real racy affair Schlitz in tall glasses with "They'll Do It Every Time" cartoons stenciled on.

tony: high
class

15   "That's all right," Lengel said. "But this isn't the beach." His repeating this struck me as funny, as if it had just occurred to him, and he had been thinking all these years the A&P was a great big dune and he was the head lifeguard. He didn't like my smiling—as I say he doesn't miss much—but he concentrates on giving the girls that sad Sunday-school-superintendent stare.

16   Queenie's blush is no sunburn now, and the plump one in plaid, that I liked better from the back—a really sweet can—pipes up, "We weren't doing any shopping. We just came in for the one thing."

17   "That makes no difference," Lengel tells her, and I could see from the way his eyes went that he hadn't noticed she was wearing a two-piece before. "We want you decently dressed when you come in here."

18   "We are decent," Queenie says suddenly, her lower lip pushing, getting sore now that she remembers her place, a place from which the crowd that runs the A&P must look pretty crummy. Fancy Herring Snacks flashed in her very blue eyes.

19   "Girls, I don't want to argue with you. After this come in here with your shoulders covered. It's our policy." He turns his back. That's policy for you. Policy is what the kingpins want. What the others want is juvenile delinquency.

20   All this while, the customers had been showing up with their carts but you know sheep, seeing a scene, they had all bunched up on Stokesie, who shook open a paper bag as gently as peeling a peach, not wanting to miss a word. I could feel in the silence everybody getting nervous, most of all Lengel, who asks me, "Sammy, have you rung up their purchase?"

21   I thought and said "No" but it wasn't about that I was thinking. I go through the punches, 4, 9, GROC. TOT—it's more complicated than you think, and after you do it often enough, it begins to make a little song, that you hear words to, in my case "Hello (*bing*) there, you (*gung*) hap-py *pee*-pul (*splat*)!"—

the *splat* being the drawer flying out. I uncrease the bill, tenderly as you may imagine, it just having come from between the two smoothest scoops of vanilla I had ever known were there, and pass a half and a penny into her narrow pink palm, and nestle the herrings in a bag and twist its neck and hand it over, all the time thinking.

22   The girls, and who'd blame them, are in a hurry to get out, so I say "I quit" to Lengel quick enough for them to hear, hoping they'll stop and watch me, their unsuspected hero. They keep right on going, into the electric eye; the door flies open and they flicker across the lot to their car, Queenie and Plaid and Big Tall Goony-Goony (not that as raw material she was so bad), leaving me with Lengel and a kink in his eyebrow.

23   "Did you say something, Sammy?"

24   "I said I quit."

25   "I thought you did."

26   "You didn't have to embarrass them."

27   "It was they who were embarrassing us."

28   I started to say something that came out "Fiddle-de-doo." It's a saying of my grandmother's, and I know she would have been pleased.

29   "I don't think you know what you're saying," Lengel said.

30   "I know you don't," I said. "But I do." I pull the bow at the back of my apron and start shrugging it off my shoulders. A couple customers that had been heading for my slot begin to knock against each other, like scared pigs in a chute.

31   Lengel sighs and begins to look very patient and old and gray. He's been a friend of my parents for years. "Sammy, you don't want to do this to your Mom and Dad," he tells me. It's true, I don't. But it seems to me that once you begin a gesture it's fatal not to go through with it. I fold the apron, "Sammy" stitched in red on the pocket, and put in on the counter, and drop the bow tie on top of it. The bow tie is theirs, if you've ever wondered. "You'll feel this for the rest of your life," Lengel says, and I know that's true, too, but remembering how he made the pretty girl blush makes me so scrunchy inside I punch the No Sale tab and the machine whirs "pee-put" and the drawer splats out. One advantage to this scene taking place in summer, I can follow this up with a clean exit, there's no fumbling around getting your coat and galoshes, I just saunter into the electric eye in my white shirt that my mother ironed the night before, and the door heaves itself open, and outside the sunshine is skating around on the asphalt.

32   I look around for my girls, but they're gone, of course. There wasn't anybody but some young married screaming with her children about some candy they didn't get by the door of a powder-blue Falcon station wagon. Looking back in the big windows, over the bags of peat moss and aluminum lawn furniture stacked on the pavement, I could see Lengel in my place in the slot, checking the sheep through. His face was dark gray, and his back stiff, as if he'd just had an injection of iron, and my stomach kind of fell as I felt how hard the world was going to be to me hereafter.

Vocabulary Exercises

Fill in the blank with the appropriate vocabulary word from the reading.

1. The _____ of the plane was shiny aluminum.

2. The homecoming queen paraded down the sidewalk like a _____.

3. For our anniversary, we went to a _____ restaurant.

4. The _____ of the material made it feel rough.

5. Write your own sentence with one of the above words.

_____

Comprehension Questions

1. What is Sammy's job at the A&P?
   A. Manager

   B. Cashier

   C. Stockman

   D. Butcher

2. Who comes in the A&P?
   A. A policeman

   B. Sammy's parents

   C. Three girls

   D. Sammy's two friends

3. What are they wearing?
   A. Church clothes

   B. Shorts

   C. Bathing suits

   D. Beach dresses

4. What does Sammy call the other store customers?
   A. Sheep

   B. Houseslaves

   C. Pigs in a chute

   D. All of the above

5. How much older than Sammy is Stokesie?
   A. Thirty years

   B. Twenty years

   C. Ten years

   D. Three years

6. What do the girls buy?
   A. Cookies

   B. Herring snacks

   C. Gum

   D. A magazine

7. What does Sammy do as the girls leave the store?
   A. Rings up the next customer

   B. Demands a raise

   C. Demands that Lengel apologize

   D. Quits his job

8. What does Sammy lay on the counter?
   A. A magazine

   B. His hat

   C. His apron and tie

   D. A bag of groceries

9. Why does Mr. Lengel want to give Sammy a second chance?
   A. He is Sammy's uncle.

   B. He is Sammy's friend.

   C. Sammy owes him money.

   D. He is friends with Sammy's parents.

10. What does Sammy think when he leaves the store?
    A. That his parents will be proud of him

    B. That the world will be hard on him

    C. That the girls were impressed by his gesture

    D. That Stokesie will be proud of him

Discussion Questions

1. How does Sammy feel about his job at the A&P? What is Sammy like? How do you get to know Sammy?

2. How does Sammy see the A&P customers?

3. What does he think about the girls who enter the store? What is it about Queenie and her friends that appeals to Sammy? What does Sammy realize about Queenie when he sees what she is buying?

4. How does Sammy see Stokesie, his co-worker? How does Sammy see Mr. Lengel?

5. Why do you think Sammy quit his job? Why do you think the world will be hard on him after he quits his job, as he says in the last line?

Writing Topics

1. Did you ever quit or want to quit a job? Why did you or did you not quit? Did your decision turn out to be a wise or unwise one for you?

2. Describe a good or bad job you have had. What made the job enjoyable or not enjoyable?

3. Have you ever had a particularly good or a particularly bad boss? Make a statement about your boss, and support it with concrete evidence from your experience.

4. Write an opinion statement about Sammy, and support it with evidence from the story.

5. Contrast the way Sammy sees the regular A&P customers and the way he sees Queenie and the girls who enter the store. Back up your observations with details and descriptions from the story.

Preview

Many people love to write because they use writing as a way to explore who they are and where they have come from. The memoir is a literary form used to explore our lives. William Zinsser gives some valuable advice to writers who want to write memoirs, and he offers an excerpt from Maxine Hong Kingston that illustrates what he values in a memoir.

Writing About Yourself
William Zinsser

1   Of all the subjects available to you as a writer, the one you know best is yourself: your past and your present, your thoughts and your emotions. Yet it's probably the subject you try hardest to avoid.

2   Whenever I'm invited to visit a writing class in a school or a college, the first thing I ask the students is: "What are your problems? What are your concerns?" Their answer, from Maine to California, is the same: "We have to write what the teacher wants." It's a depressing sentence.

3   "That's the last thing any good teacher wants," I tell them. "No teacher wants twenty-five copies of the same person, writing about the same topic. What we're all looking for—what we want to see pop out of your papers—is individuality. We're looking for whatever it is that makes you unique. Write about what you know and what you think."

4   They can't. They don't think they have permission. I think they get that permission by being born. . . .

        . . .

5   Why not? Wasn't America the land of the "rugged individualist"? Let's get that lost land and those lost individuals back. If you're a writing teacher, make your students believe in the **validity** of their lives. If you're a writer, give yourself permission to tell us who you are.

6   By "permission" I don't mean "permissive." I have no patience with sloppy workmanship—the let-it-all-hang-out **verbiage** of the '60s. To have a decent career in this country it's important to be able to write decent English. But on the question of who you're writing *for,* don't be eager to please. If you consciously write *for* a teacher or *for* an editor, you'll end up not writing for anybody. If you write for yourself, you'll reach the people you want to write *for.*

7   Writing about one's life is naturally related to how long one has lived. When students say they have to write what the teacher wants, what they often mean is that they don't have anything to say—so **meager** is their after-school existence, **bounded** largely by television and the mall, two artificial versions

validity:
importance or significance
verbiage:
language

meager:
lacking in richness
bounded:
set by boundaries, limited

William Zinsser, "Writing About Yourself: The Memoir" from ON WRITING WELL, 6/e by William Zinsser. Reprinted by permission of Carol Brissie.

of reality. Still, at any age, the physical act of writing is a powerful search mechanism. I'm often amazed, dipping into my past, to find some forgotten **incident** clicking into place just when I need it. Your memory is almost always good for material when your other wells go dry.

8   Permission, however, is a two-edged instrument, and nobody should use it without posting a surgeon general's warning: EXCESSIVE WRITING ABOUT YOURSELF CAN BE HAZARDOUS TO THE HEALTH OF THE WRITER AND THE READER. A thin line separates ego from egotism. Ego is healthy; no writer can go far without it. Egotism, however, is a drag, and this chapter is not intended as **license** to **prattle** just for therapy. Again, the rule I suggest is: Make sure every component in your **memoir** is doing useful work. Write about yourself, by all means, with confidence and with pleasure. But see that all the details—people, places, events, **anecdotes,** ideas, emotions—are moving your story steadily along.

9   Which brings me to memoir as a form. I'll read almost anybody's memoir. For me, no other nonfiction form goes so deeply to the roots of personal experience—to all the drama and pain and humor and unexpectedness of life. The books I remember most vividly from my first reading of them tend to be memoirs: books such as André Aciman's *Out of Egypt*, Michael J. Arlen's *Exiles*, Russell Baker's *Growing Up*, Vivian Gornick's *Fierce Attachments*, Pete Hamill's *A Drinking Life*, Moss Hart's *Act One*, John Houseman's *Run-Through*, Mary Karr's *The Liars' Club*, Frank McCourt's *Angela's Ashes*, Vladimir Nabokov's *Speak, Memory*, V.S. Pritchett's *A Cab at the Door*, Eudora Welty's *One Writer's Beginnings*, and Leonard Woolf's *Growing*.

10   What gives them their power is the narrowness of their focus. Unlike autobiography, which spans an entire life, memoir assumes the life and ignores most of it. The memoir writer takes us back to some corner of his or her past that was unusually intense—childhood, for instance—or that was framed by war or some other social upheaval. Baker's *Growing Up* is a box within a box. It's the story of a boy growing up, set inside the story of a family battered by the Depression; it takes its strength from its historical context. Nabokov's *Speak, Memory,* the most elegant memoir I know, invokes a golden boyhood in czarist St. Petersburg, a world of private tutors and summer houses that the Russian Revolution would end forever. It's an act of writing frozen in a unique time and place. Pritchett's *A Cab at the Door* recalls a childhood that was almost Dickensian; his grim apprenticeship to the London leather trade seems to belong to the 19th century. Yet Pritchett describes it without **self-pity** and even with a certain **merriment.** We see that his childhood was **inseparably** joined to the particular moment and country and class he was born into—and was an organic part of the wonderful writer he grew up to be.

11   Think narrow, then, when you try the form. Memoir isn't the summary of a life; it's a window into a life, very much like a photograph in its selective composition. It may look like a casual and even random calling up of bygone events. It's not; it's a deliberate construction. Thoreau wrote seven different

---

incident: event or occurrence

license: permission

prattle: chatter

memoir: nonfiction form of writing in which the writer remembers personal history

anecdotes: stories of particular events

self-pity: feeling sorry for oneself

merriment: good humor

inseparably: not able to be separated

drafts of *Walden* in eight years; no American memoir was more painstakingly pieced together. To write a good memoir you must become the editor of your own life, imposing on an untidy **sprawl** of half-remembered events a narrative shape and an organizing idea. Memoir is the art of inventing the truth.

sprawl:
unorganized
spreading
out

12   One secret of the art is detail. Any kind of detail will work—a sound or a smell or a song title—as long as it played a shaping role in the portion of your life you have chosen to **distill**. . . .

distill:
reduce
to the
essential

    . . .

13   For Maxine Hong Kingston, a daughter of Chinese immigrants in Stockton, California, shyness and embarrassment were central to the experience of being a child starting school in a strange land. In this passage, aptly called "Finding a Voice," from her book *The Woman Warrior,* notice how vividly Kingston recalls both facts and feelings from those traumatic early years in America:

14   When I went to kindergarten and had to speak English for the first time, I became silent. A dumbness—a shame—still cracks my voice in two, even when I want to say "hello" casually, or ask an easy question in the front of the check-out counter, or ask directions of a bus driver. I stand frozen . . .

15   During the first silent year I spoke to no one at school, did not ask before going to the lavatory, and flunked kindergarten. My sister also said nothing for three years, silent in the playground and silent at lunch. There were other quiet Chinese girls not of our family, but most of them got over it sooner than we did. I enjoyed the silence. At first it did not occur to me I was supposed to talk or to pass kindergarten. I talked at home and to one or two of the Chinese kids in class. I made motions and even made some jokes. I drank out of a toy saucer when the water spilled out of the cup, and everybody laughed, pointed at me, so I did it some more. I didn't know that Americans don't drink out of saucers . . . .

16   It was when I found out I had to talk that school became a misery, that the silence became a misery. I did not speak and felt bad each time that I did not speak. I read aloud in first grade, though, and heard the barest whisper with little squeaks come out of my throat. "Louder," said the teacher, who scared the voice away again. The other Chinese girls did not talk either, so I knew the silence had to do with being a Chinese girl.

17   That childhood whisper is now an adult writer's voice that speaks to us with wisdom and humor, and I'm grateful to have that voice in our **midst.** Nobody but a Chinese-American woman could have made me feel what it's like to be a Chinese girl plunked down in an American kindergarten and expected to be an American girl. Memoir is one way to make sense of the cultural differences that can be a painful fact of daily life in America.

midst: in the
middle of

Vocabulary Exercises

Fill in the blank with the appropriate vocabulary word from the reading.

1. Our neighborhood is _____ on the north by a highway and on east by the river.

2. The professor didn't give anyone the _____ to talk during the exam.

3. My grandfather loves to tell _____ about growing up on a farm.

4. A good student can _____ what she is learning into a few concepts that she can easily remember.

5. The town's _____ has threatened the wildlife in the surrounding countryside.

6. The class didn't know that it had an expert on the subject in its _____.

7. Studying regularly is _____ connected to learning.

8. The policeman's account of the _____ was included in his report.

9. I can't even afford to go to the movie on my _____ salary.

10. Students must believe in the _____ of what they are learning in order to remain motivated.

Comprehension Questions

1. What subject does Zinsser believe that writers try to avoid writing about?
   A. History of their country
   B. Themselves
   C. Their friends
   D. What they study in school

2. What do writing students complain about?
   A. Not getting published
   B. Having to be original
   C. Having to write what the teacher wants
   D. Finding subject matter to write about

3. Why does Zinsser think that writing students have trouble expressing their individuality?
   A. Writers don't think they have permission.
   B. Writers don't think readers want to read something unique.

    C. Writers aren't individuals.

    D. Writers want to be creative.

4. Does Zinsser believe it is important for writers to have decent English skills?
    A. Yes

    B. No

    C. Sometimes

    D. Maybe

5. Who should writers write for, according to Zinsser?
    A. Publishers

    B. Teachers

    C. Themselves

    D. Everyone

6. Zinsser believes that _____ is a powerful search mechanism.
    A. the Internet

    B. the library

    C. the physical act of writing

    D. the teacher

7. The author cautions writers against
    A. ego.

    B. egotism.

    C. greed.

    D. power.

8. Zinsser says he will read almost anybody's writing if the writing is
    A. a novel.

    B. a report.

    C. a memoir.

    D. an article or essay.

9. A memoir transports the reader to the writer's
    A. past.

    B. imagination.

    C. dreams.

    D. thoughts.

10. The writer states that memory is like a
    A. film.

    B. cartoon.

    C. painting.

    D. photograph.

Discussion Questions

1. Zinsser believes that students must be able to write "decent English" to have a "decent career." Why do you agree or disagree? What do you think Zinsser means by "decent English"? Be specific about the skills you think he means. What kinds of careers require decent English?

2. How does Zinsser define memoirs in paragraph 10? What is the difference between "summary of a life" and "a window into a life"? What memories are most intense for you? How do you think writers invent the truth when they present a picture in a memoir?

3. Why do you think Zinsser believes that the secret to effective memoirs is giving specific detail? "Any kind of detail will work—a sound or a smell or a song title—as long as it played a shaping role in the portion of your life you have chosen to distill." How do such details help the reader experience the moment being written about?

4. What details of "shyness and embarrassment" does Maxine Hong Kingston relate in her memoir? How do these details help us feel what it is like to be "a Chinese girl plunked down in an American kindergarten and expected to be an American girl"?

5. How can reading a memoir help us understand "the cultural differences that can be a painful fact of daily life in America"?

Writing Topics

1. Write a two- to three-page memoir of a meaningful experience. Choose a time in your life that was important to you, such as elementary, middle, or high school. Tell of one intense moment during this time. Concentrate on using concrete details and sensory impressions such as what things looked like or sounded like. Include your feelings and thoughts at the time.

2. Choose a family member or friend that you are interested in learning more about. Interview this person, and ask him or her to tell you about a particularly meaningful memory of a moment in the person's life. Write a one- to two-page report

explaining the memory and giving the most memorable details from the person's account.

3. Write a paragraph explaining why you think Maxine Hong Kingston didn't speak in elementary school. Put yourself in her place, and imagine what her background was like and why she had difficulties fitting in.

4. Write a one- to two-page memoir of a moment in your life when you didn't fit in. Include details of how you felt and what you remember of the sights, sounds, and people in your memory.

Appendix 1   Spelling and Dictionary Skills

A number of tools are available to help you improve your spelling. The secret is to bring awareness to how you spell words by keeping a list of your misspellings, by learning the spelling rules, by studying commonly misspelled words and the combinations of letters that make them easy to misspell, and by using a dictionary, a spell check, and/or a word processor when writing.

Personal Spelling List

Most of us have particular words in our vocabulary that we misspell. By recording every word you misspell, both your misspelling and the correct spelling, you will bring awareness to your spelling and improve your spelling dramatically. Usually your instructor will circle misspellings. You should look up the spelling of every word marked as a spelling error.

Use the "Personal Error List" on page A-50 to record your misspellings and their correct spellings. Study your personal list of misspellings every time you prepare to write a paper. Go down the list of misspellings and mentally correct the spelling, and then check your answers using the list of corrections.

Personal Spelling List		
My Misspelling	**Correction**	**Explanation/Rule**
recieve	receive	*i* before *e* except after *c*
alot	a lot	two words
1. _____		
2. _____		
3. _____		

Practice 1   Start your personal list on the lines above by adding three words you know that you have misspelled on papers. If you can't think of any misspellings, look over papers you have written in this class or another for misspellings that have been marked by your teacher.

Common Rules for Spelling

Spelling rules are needed to keep the pronunciation correct when word endings such as *–ing* and *–ed* are added to words. The rules have to do with combinations of **vowels** (*a, e, i, o, u,* and sometimes *y*) and **consonants** (all letters except vowels) and the rules for adding endings to words.

i Before e

1.1 Use **i** before **e** except after **c.**

believe
reprieve
friend

1.2 Use **e** before **i** after **c**.

receive
deceive
conceive

When the word makes a long a **(ay)** sound, use **e** before **i**.

neighbor
eight
weight
freight

1.3 Exceptions to the rule

either	height
neither	weird
foreign	leisure
seize	

Single-Syllable Word Endings

2.1 Double the final consonant of a word when adding an ending that begins with a vowel such as **-ing, -ed, -er,** and **-est** if the word is one syllable and a vowel comes before the consonant. (The last consonant is doubled to preserve the sound of the vowel.)

bat + ed = batted	sit + ing = sitting
pen + ed = penned	run + er = runner
rob + ing = robbing	slim + est = slimmest

Multisyllable Word Endings

2.2 When adding an ending that begins with a vowel such as **-ing, -ed, -er,** and **-est,** double the final consonant of multisyllable words when the final syllable is stressed and a vowel comes before the final consonant.

control + ed = controlled	begin + er = beginner
permit + ed = permitted	admit + ing = admitting
prefer + ed = preferred	commit + ing = committing
refer + ed = referred	patrol + ing = patrolling

Dropping the Final e

3.1 Drop the final **e** on a word when adding an ending that begins with a vowel.

believe + er = believer	rake + ing = raking
like + able = likable	move + able = movable

3.2 Keep the final **e** when adding an ending that begins with a consonant.

achieve + ment = achievement
rare + ly = rarely
like + ness = likeness

3.3 Exceptions to the rule

argue + ment = argument
judge + ment = judgment
true + ly = truly

Dropping the Final y

4.1 Drop the final **y** and add **i** when adding an ending if there is a consonant before the **y**.

pretty + er = prettier   reply + ed = replied
funny + est = funniest   happy + ness = happiness
try + ed = tried   beauty + ful = beautiful
rely + able = reliable

4.2 Keep the final **y** when adding an ending if there is a vowel before the **y**.

delay + ed = delayed
donkey + s = donkeys
play + er = player

4.3 Always keep the final **y** when adding **-ing** to words endings in **y**.

rely + ing = relying
reply + ing = replying
try + ing = trying

4.4 Exceptions to the rule

lay + ed = laid
pay + ed = paid
say + ed = said

Practice 2   Use the spelling rules to determine which word in each item is misspelled, and write the correct spelling of the word in the blank.

1. _____
    stepped
    prying
    payed

2. _____
   wiegh
   prayed
   dimmer

3. _____
   deceive
   controling
   friendly

4. _____
   belief
   studing
   happiest

5. _____
   cryed
   swimmer
   saddest

Frequently Misspelled Words

You can improve your spelling significantly by studying the following list of frequently misspelled words. Try to remember how they are spelled by looking at the bold letters that show what is unusual or tricky about the spelling of these words.

a**cross**	begi**nn**ing	exer**c**ise	int**er**est
actua**lly**	bel**ie**ve	exp**eri**ence	**lai**d
ag**ai**nst	br**ea**th	fav**o**rite	lib**r**ary
a lot **(two words)**	breath**e**	f**ie**ld	lik**e**ly
all right **(two words)**	business	fina**lly**	marr**ia**ge
al**m**ost	careful	f**or**ty	m**ea**nt
although	carr**ied**	f**our**th	m**ere**
alway**s**	cloth**es**	f**or**ward	natura**lly**
am**ong**	com**ing**	fr**ie**nd	n**ei**ther
an**swer**	d**ea**lt	genera**lly**	n**ie**ce
a**r**ound	de**s**troy	gr**ate**ful	nine**ty**
arti**cle**	dining	**g**uard	**ninth**
a**tt**ack	during	happi**ness**	**pai**d
befor**e**	easily	h**ei**ght	hun**gry**
	effect		pers**o**nal
			perso**nn**el

planned	roommate	sophomore	themselves
poison	safety	source	therefore
possible	science	speech	together
probably	sense	stopped	truly
proving	sentence	stories	until
quiet	several	straight	using
really	since	strength	view
receive	shining	strict	writing
regard	shoulder	studying	yield
remember	simply	supposed	

Practice 3   Alone or with a partner, review the spelling list and place a star next to words that you have misspelled in the past. Then have your partner read your words to you to spell.

CD Connection

Power of Language

On *Writer's Resources* CD-ROM, see *Spelling* in Grammar/Punctuation/Mechanics for more information and practice with spelling.

Guide to the Dictionary

Unless you are writing on a computer, the most valuable resource you have to check spelling is the dictionary. You should carry a **college-level paperback dictionary** with you to any class in which you will write. Use the headwords at the top of the page; these indicate the first and last word on the page. For example, *leadplant/ learnable* tells you that any word starting with the letters *leadplant* up to and including *learnable* is on this page. If the word you have spelled starts with "leag" and is not on the page, your spelling is incorrect. You must guess again with another spelling of the word and look up this spelling in order to confirm the spelling.

The dictionary can give you more information than the spelling about the words it lists. Depending on how large and thorough the dictionary you use is, it will also tell you the syllable breaks, pronunciation, part of speech, definitions, and history (or etymology) of the word, and irregular past tense and participle forms of verbs and irregular plural forms of nouns. In addition, the dictionary will often give related words and synonyms (words that have the same meaning).

[1]**learn** [2](lurn) [3]**v.** [4]**learned** or **learnt; learning.** [5]1. to acquire knowledge 2. to become informed of or acquainted with [6]3. *nonstandard. To teach: I'll learn him a thing or two.*

[7]ME *lern,* OE *leornian* to learn, read, ponder] [8]–**learnable,** adj.

1. **Spelling of word:** Not only does the dictionary provide the spelling, but the syllables will be separated in case you want to hyphenate the word at the end of a line of writing.
2. **Phonetic transcription:** This spelling of the word consists of the international symbols for the sounds of the letters in the word. The dictionary will provide a pronunciation guide at the beginning of the dictionary to help you pronounce words.
3. **Part of speech:** Also at the beginning of the dictionary is a guide to the abbreviations for the parts of speech. Here, **v** means that the word *learn* is a verb.
4. **Past tense, past participle,** and **present participle:** With verbs, the dictionary will give irregular past tense and participles.
5. **Definitions of word:** The definitions are in the order of most common to least common. If you are using the dictionary to understand the meaning of a word you are using, it is best to stick with the most common meanings because the less common meanings may be specialized meanings.
6. **Nonstandard usage:** The dictionary aims to give all the ways a word is used, even if the usage is not the standard or typical way the word is used. Nonstandard usage is considered unacceptable in college writing.
7. **Etymology of word:** The dictionary gives a history of the word, in other words, how the word has come into modern English. Here, *learn* comes from the Middle English *lern* and the Old English *leornian.* A guide to the abbreviations of languages such as ME can be found in the beginning of the dictionary.
8. **Related words:** At the end of an entry, the dictionary often gives related words. These words may be helpful while writing.

Practice 4   Using a dictionary, answer the following questions.

1. What part of speech is *avail?* _____

2. How many syllables does *sequester* have? _____

3. What is the first definition of *maudlin?* _____

4. What language does the word *glue* come from?

_____

5. What is the past tense form of the verb *put?* _____

Spell Checkers and Word Processors

The problem with using a dictionary to check your spelling is that you must know which words to look up. Often writers don't know which words they are misspelling. Also, you must be fairly close to the correct spelling in order to find the word listed in the dictionary. If the misspelling is very far off, such as "sickology" for *psychology,* you won't find the word.

Writing on a word processor with a spell check feature takes care of both these problems. Any word you misspell will be <u>underlined</u> in red. When you click on the word, you will get a list of words with similar spellings. It will be important that you choose the correct word to replace your misspelling. If you are in doubt, check the definition of your choice to confirm that you are using the correct word. You should also pay careful attention to the words identified as misspelled and add them to your personal list of spelling errors in order to improve your spelling.

You can also buy small spell checkers to bring to class with you. You simply type a word to get a read-out of the correct spelling. Spell checkers are recommended for poor spellers. Check with your teacher to make sure that this tool is acceptable to use.

Appendix 2 Parts of Speech

In this section, you will review the following topics:

- Nouns
- Pronouns
- Adjectives
- Verbs
- Adverbs
- Prepositions
- Conjunctions
- Interjections

The Eight Parts of Speech

The parts of speech define the eight general ways that words function in sentences. Writers use the parts of speech to understand the rules of writing and to discuss the words in their sentences.

Nouns

1.1 **Nouns** name persons, places, things, and ideas.

teacher, church, lamps, energy

Classes of Nouns

1.2 **Proper nouns** name *particular* persons, places, and things and are capitalized. **Common nouns** do not name particular nouns and are not capitalized.

Proper Nouns	Common Nouns
George Harrison	musician
Chicago	city
Niagara Falls	waterfall

1.3 **Concrete nouns** are tangible and can be touched, seen, heard, smelled, or tasted. **Abstract nouns** are ideas, conditions, or feelings and cannot be touched, seen, or heard.

Concrete Nouns	Abstract Nouns
book	theory
music	mathematics
smoke	sadness

1.4 **Collective nouns** name a group that is thought of as a single body.

audience, class, team, family, group, jury

Singular and Plural Nouns

1.5 **Singular nouns** name one person, place, thing, or idea, and **plural nouns** name more than one. To make most nouns plural, add -s (or -es, for most nouns ending in o, x, z, sh, ch, ss, and y). The most common **irregular plural nouns** (don't end in s or es) are men, women, people, and children.

book/books	class/classes	woman/women
card/cards	church/churches	child/children

Practice 1   Underline the nouns in each sentence.

1. The jacket has two patches.

2. Our class discusses politics and religion.

3. Mrs. Rogers blew kisses at her baby.

4. Winter is here, and there are leaves on the ground.

5. Some novels have unpleasant themes and characters.

Connections

Nouns are the subjects and objects of sentences. They work with verbs and prepositions. Adjectives describe or modify nouns. Pronouns take the place of nouns. Nouns are an important part of Chapter 6, "Identifying Subjects and Verbs"; Chapter 9, "Adjectives and Adverbs"; Chapter 14, "Pronoun Agreement"; and Chapter 15, "Pronoun Reference and Case."

Pronouns

2.1 **Pronouns** take the place of nouns (called antecedents) in sentences.

Like nouns, pronouns are singular or plural.

Antecedent   Pronoun   Pronoun
The **student** took **her** textbook to the library so that **she** could study.

Antecedent   Pronoun   Pronoun
The **students** asked **their** teacher to take **them** to the library.

Pronoun Case

2.2 Different pronoun forms are used in different parts of the sentence. **Subjective case** pronouns are the subject of sentences and usually come before the verb. **Objective case pronouns** come after the verb. **Possessive case** pronouns show possession.

	Subjective Case	**Objective Case**	**Possessive Case**
Singular	I	me	my/mine
	you	you	your/yours
	he/she/it	him/her/it	his/her/its
Plural	we	us	our/ours
	you	you	your/yours
	they	them	their/theirs

S V   OBJ   POS
I took **him** to **his** car.

Kinds of Pronouns

2.3 **Personal pronouns** refer to people or things.

I, me, you, it, she, her, they, them

2.4 **Possessive pronouns** indicate ownership.

my, mine, your, yours, his, hers, its, theirs, ours

2.5 **Reflexive pronouns** indicate that the doer and receiver of an action are the same.

myself, yourself, himself, themselves

The woman e-mailed **herself** a reminder.

2.6 **Relative pronouns** introduce dependent clauses and refer to a noun or pronoun that comes before them. Use *that* and *which* with things and *who* with people.

who, whom, which, that, whoever, whomever, whatever

The computer **that** is on the table belongs to the man **who** just left the room.

2.7 **Interrogative pronouns** are used in questions.

who, whom, what

What are the dates of the exam?

2.8 **Demonstrative pronouns** identify or point to nouns.

this, that, these, those

This class meets at nine every morning.

2.9 Indefinite pronouns do not refer to any particular person or thing. Most indefinite pronouns are singular and take a singular verb and a singular pronoun, but some are plural, and some can be either singular or plural.

Indefinite Pronouns	
any	neither
anybody	nobody
anyone	none
anything	no one
both	nothing
each	one
either	several
everybody	some
everyone	somebody
everything	someone
few	something
many	

Practice 2   Underline the pronouns in each sentence.

1. When she hurt herself, my wife called the doctor and asked him for a prescription.

2. Everyone should bring his or her book to class.

3. Whom should I call?

4. Something is bothering them about the way they handled the incident.

5. They suggested that their children play with ours.

Connections

Pronouns take the place of nouns (antecedents). The correct form (case) of the pronoun depends upon its relationship to other words in the sentence. Subject pronouns come before the verb, and object pronouns come after the verb and after prepositions. Learn more about pronouns in Chapter 14 and Chapter 15.

Adjectives

3.1 Adjectives describe or modify nouns and pronouns. Adjectives add detail to sentences and come before nouns. Adjectives also follow linking verbs.

Adj Adj N Adj   Adj
That young man is loud and obnoxious.

The adjectives *that* and *young* identify the noun *man. Loud* and *obnoxious* are adjectives that follow the linking verb *is* and describe the *man.*

Articles

3.2 The **articles** *a, an,* and *the* are adjectives that modify nouns.

A is used before words that begin with a consonant sound (such as *b, c, d,* and *f*).

a book, a camera, a zebra, a university

An is used before words that begin with a vowel sound (*a, e, i, o, u,* and *y*) or silent *h.*

an astronomer, an expedition, an interest, an honorary degree, an F grade

Practice 3 Underline the correct article.

1. A/An onion is called for in a/an recipe that a/an old friend gave me.

2. A/An university student received a/an A on a/an algebra test and a/an B on a/an history exam.

3. While a/an electrician worked on the wiring, a/an plumber installed a/an water pipe in a/an hour.

4. We took a/an interesting tour of a/an home in a/an new part of the city.

5. Because of a/an early departure from the tournament, a/an well-known player was a/an spectator in the stands during a/an semifinal game.

Practice 4 Underline the adjectives in each sentence.

1. A large brown bag sat next to the little child on the red park bench.

2. My tired puppy was not feeling good.

3. On a sunny day, the famous painter walked down to the deserted beach and painted the beautiful scene.

4. Paul was happy to climb the stately old tree while his worried parents looked on.

5. Bitter arguments broke out between the angry contestants.

Connections

Adjectives are like spice; they add color and flavor to sentences because they are descriptive words. Learn more about adjectives in Chapter 9.

Verbs

4.1 **Verbs** are words that express the action or state of being of a noun.

My neighbor **walks** to work.

The weather **is** hot today.

Kinds of Verbs

4.2 **Action verbs** express an action.

talk, stop, come, fall, try

The car **stopped** at the gate.

4.3 **Linking verbs** link the subject to a noun, pronoun, or adjective.

is, feel, look, seem, appear, become, smell, sound, taste

Your essay **looks** good.

The verb *looks* does not express an action; instead it links the subject *essay* to the adjective *good*. The most common linking verb is the *to be* verb in all its forms (*is, are, was, were, been*).

4.4 **Helping or auxiliary verbs** link the subject to a verb.

is, are, was, were, am, be, been, being, was, could, might, will, would, shall, should, must, can, may, have, has, had, do, did

Our car **should have been** repaired by now.

Should, have, and *been* are all helping verbs that link the subject *car* to the main verb *repaired.*

Verb Forms

4.5 There are three main forms of the verb: the **present, past,** and **past participle.**

The form of the verb changes according to its **tense** (present, past, future, present perfect, past perfect, future perfect); **number** (singular or plural); **voice** (active, passive); and **mood** (indicative, imperative, subjunctive). The chapters on subject-verb agreement and verb tenses, Chapters 7 and 8, explain the rules for verb endings in the present and past tenses.

Present: I always take a walk in the morning.
Past: Yesterday, I took a walk with my dog.
Past participle: I have not taken my walk today.

Practice 5   Underline the verbs in the following sentences.

1. My boss has been preparing the year-end report.

2. When I was driving home, there was a traffic jam on the freeway.

3. The trip takes over ten hours.

4. The crops were planted in late April.

5. The family had dinner before taking a walk.

Verbals

Verbals are verb forms that act as another part of speech.

4.6 Infinitives are verb forms introduced by *to*. Infinitives are not part of the main verb of the sentence.

Cassandra wants **to buy** a new car.

4.7 Gerunds are verb forms ending in *-ing* that act as nouns.

Running is good exercise.

4.8 Participles are verb forms usually ending in *-ing* or *-ed* that act as verbs or adjectives.

The **closed** shop was dark inside.

Connections

Verbs are action words or being words (is/are, seem). Verbs join subjects (nouns) to make sentences. Verbs are modified by adverbs. Verbs are covered in Chapters 6, 7, and 8.

Adverbs

5.1 Adverbs describe or modify *verbs, adjectives,* and other *adverbs.* Many adverbs end in *-ly.*

V   Adv   Adv   Adv Adj
The two women talked *very quietly* in the *really* old church.

The three adverbs in the example above each modify a different part of speech. *Very* modifies the adverb *quietly,* which modifies the verb *talked. Really* modifies the adjective *old.* Adverbs answer the question "how?" about a verb, an adjective, or another adverb. How did the women talk? *Quietly.* How quietly did they talk? *Very quietly.* How old is the church? *Really old.*

Practice 6   Underline the adverbs in each sentence.

1. I did very well on the test because I studied diligently.

2. The exam was really difficult.

3. The actress spoke clearly and delivered her lines convincingly.

4. The path is extremely slippery, so we must walk carefully.

5. The pedestrian shouted angrily at the motorist who was driving recklessly.

Adverb/Adjective Confusion

Because many descriptive words can be used both as adjectives and adverbs, using the adjective for the adverb is a common error.

✗ Incorrect: The workmen were **real** tired after the long day.
✓ Correct: The workmen were **really** tired after the long day.

Only adverbs can modify or describe adjectives.

Connections

Adverbs, like adjectives, add spice and detail to writing. They describe verbs, adjectives, and adverbs. The most common mistake with adverbs is using an adjective for an adverb. See Chapter 9 for more information about adjectives and adverbs.

Prepositions

6.1 A **preposition** explains the relationship between its **object** (the noun or pronoun that follows it) and another word in the sentence. Many prepositions explain time or space relationships. A preposition and its object are called a **prepositional phrase**.

Prep phrase   Prep phrase

The child on the beach is putting water in his pail.

The preposition *on* explains the relationship between *child* and *beach*.
The preposition *in* explains the relationship between *water* and *pail*.

Common Prepositions		
about	around	besides
above	as	between
according to	as far as	beyond
across	at	by
after	before	despite
against	behind	down
along	below	during
along with	beneath	except
among	beside	for
		Continued

Common Prepositions—*Continued*		
from	off	to
in	on	toward
in addition to	on account of	under
inside	on top of	until
in spite of	out	up
instead of	outside of	upon
into	over	with
like	since	within
near	through	without
of	throughout	

Practice 7   Underline the prepositional phrases in each sentence.

1. Over the weekend, some of my classmates met in the library for a study session.

2. The euro is the currency of most countries in Europe.

3. The computer in the back office has dust on it.

4. A car in the parking lot has a dent in its bumper.

5. Our family will fly to Minneapolis for Thanksgiving.

Connections

Prepositions are short words that show relationships between nouns. (Think of a cloud and a plane. Prepositions describe the relationship of the plane to the cloud: under, over, in, to, from, within.) Prepositions and their objects together form **prepositional phrases.** A prepositional phrase can appear anywhere in a sentence. Prepositional phrases will be important in Chapter 6, "Identifying Subjects and Verbs," and in Chapter 18, "Commas."

Conjunctions

7.1 **Conjunctions** join words or groups of words.

Coordinating Conjunctions

7.2 **Coordinating conjunctions** join together similar elements (a word to a word, a phrase to a phrase, or a clause to a clause).

Coordinating Conjunctions	
for	or
and	yet
nor	so
but	

Remember *fanboys: for, and, nor, but, or, yet, so*
See Chapter 13 for the meaning of each coordinating conjunction.

Jared **and** Tia will go to the party, **or** they will go to a movie.

The coordinating conjunction *and* joins two words, and the coordinating conjunction *or* joins two independent clauses.

Practice 8   Write an appropriate coordinating conjunction in each blank.

1. Either my parents _____ my grandparents will pick me up from school today.

2. Keri is excited, _____ tomorrow is her birthday.

3. I enjoyed the first movie _____ not the second one.

4. It may rain today, _____ I will carry an umbrella.

5. We got paid yesterday, _____ I am almost broke already.

Subordinating Conjunctions

7.3 Subordinating conjunctions show the relationship between ideas. Subordinating conjunctions begin dependent clauses.

Subordinating Conjunctions		
after	in order that	until
although	since	when
as	so that	where
because	that	whereas
before	though	while
if	unless	

Independent Clause   Dependent Clause
A crowd gathered **while** the firefighters put out the fire.

Dependent Clause   Independent Clause
Because the fire started on the roof, everyone got out of the building safely.

Word groups that begin with subordinating conjunctions are sentence fragments and cannot stand alone as sentences. See Chapter 13 for the meaning of each subordinating conjunction. For the rules about when to use commas in joining dependent clauses to independent clauses, see Chapter 18, "Commas."

Practice 9   Write an appropriate subordinating conjunction in each blank.

1. _____ the team played very well, it lost to its cross-town rivals.

2. The game was almost cancelled _____ it had been raining all day.

3. The players must practice hard _____ they want to win.

4. _____ the team plays next week, it must travel to another town.

5. There are only two more games _____ the season is over.

Conjunctive Adverbs

7.4 Conjunctive adverbs are used to join independent clauses.

Common Conjunctive Adverbs		
therefore	moreover	then
consequently	also	later
however	furthermore	

Final exams begin next week; **therefore,** I must study all day Sunday.

Note: When conjunctive adverbs are used to join independent clauses, a semicolon ends the first independent clause, and a comma follows the conjunctive adverb.

Connections

Conjunctions, like junctions, join word groups. The meaning of each conjunction explains the relationship between the word groups. For more information about conjunctions, see Chapter 10, "Sentence Parts and Types"; Chapter 12, "Run-on Sentences"; Chapter 13, "Sentence Combining"; and Chapter 18, "Commas."

Interjections

8.1 An **interjection** communicates a strong emotion and is separated from the rest of the sentence by a punctuation mark such as a comma or an exclamation point.

Common Interjections		
wow	hey	okay
yikes	ouch	

Ouch! That hurts.
Hey, don't eat my piece of cake.

Connections

Interjections are not used in academic writing.

CD Connection

Power of Language

On *Writer's Resources* CD-ROM, see *Parts of Speech* in Grammar/Punctuation/ Mechanics for more information and practice with the parts of speech.

Appendix 3 ESL Skills

This section of the textbook reviews common English problems experienced by students who are learning English as a second language. In this section, you will review the following topics:

- Nouns
  - Singular and plural
  - Count and noncount
- Adjectives
  - Articles
  - Determiners
  - Participles as adjectives
  - Adjective position
  - Adjective order
- Verbs
  - Modals
  - Verb tenses
  - Passives
  - Gerunds and infinitives
  - Two-word verbs
- Adverbs
  - Position
- Prepositions
  - Time
  - Location
  - Transportation
- Word Order
- Common ESL errors

Nouns

1.1 Singular nouns have no –s or –es endings.

cat, student, window, boat

1.2 Plural nouns have an –s or –es ending.

cats, students, windows, boats

1.3 Irregular plural nouns do not end in –s or -es.

men, women, children, policemen, firemen, deer, sheep

(For spelling rules, see page A-2.)

Count/Noncount Nouns

1.4 Count nouns can be counted and have plural forms.

a dog	dogs
a hat	hats

1.5 Noncount nouns cannot be counted and do not have plural forms.

Do not use *a* or *an* in front of noncount nouns. Noncount nouns may be preceded by indefinite adjectives (*some, a lot, more, any, much*) and may be preceded by units of measure.

wisdom	much wisdom	a piece of wisdom
furniture	a lot of furniture	two pieces of furniture
soup	a little soup	two bowls of soup
music	more music	three sheets of music
bacon	some bacon	three slices of bacon

1.6 Noncount nouns are singular and take singular verbs (with an -s).

My homework **is** difficult.
A lot of information ha**s** been lost.

Categories of Noncount Nouns

Abstract Nouns
  ✓ **Emotions** (love, hate, jealousy, misery, etc.)
  ✓ **Qualities** (beauty, honor, justice, wisdom, etc.)

✓ **Abstractions** (health, success, friendship, freedom, etc.)

✓ **Activities** (swimming, football, dancing, camping, baseball, etc.)

✓ **General categories** (homework, information, jewelry, furniture, machinery, music, etc.)

Mass Nouns

✓ **Liquids** (water, tea, cream, soup, gasoline, milk, etc.)

✓ **Solids** (sugar, butter, lettuce, tin, bacon, toothpaste, etc.)

✓ **Gases** (air, nitrogen, oxygen, smoke, steam, smog, etc.)

✓ **Natural phenomena or weather terms** (darkness, rain, sleet, wind, thunder, lightning, etc.)

✓ **Subject areas** (history, music, biology, politics, etc.)

Practice 1 Identify each noun as count (C) or noncount (U), and provide a plural form for each.

Noun		Plural Expression
Example: air	U	some air
1. milk	_____	_____
2. smoke	_____	_____
3. tea	_____	_____
4. lightning	_____	_____
5. politics	_____	_____
6. swimming	_____	_____
7. darkness	_____	_____
8. highway	_____	_____
9. friendship	_____	_____
10. friend	_____	_____

Adjectives

2.1 Adjectives are not made plural in English.

three **blue** suits, six **long** poles

Indefinite Articles

2.2 *A* is used before singular, nonspecific nouns or adjectives that begin with a consonant sound.

a town, a house (**h** sound), **a** unit (**you** sound), **a** university (**you** sound).

2.3 *An* is used before singular nonspecific nouns that begin with a vowel sound (*a, e, i, o, u*).

an apple, **an** owl, **an** apartment, **an** oven

2.4 *The* is used with singular or plural nouns that have been specified.

I bought **a** sandwich. (singular, nonspecific noun)
I bought **the** biggest sandwich in **the** shop. (singular specific nouns)

2.5 *The* is used before a superlative.

My uncle is **the** worst driver I know.

2.6 *The* is used before ordinal numbers.

the first, **the** third

2.7 Use *the* before political unions, groups of islands, mountain ranges, rivers, and oceans.

the United States, **the** Rocky Mountains, **the** Hawaiian Islands, **the** Amazon, **the** Atlantic Ocean, **the** Dead Sea

Pitfalls

2.8 Do not use *the* before a possessive noun.

✗ *the* Juan's car

2.9 Do not use *the* in front of the names of streets, cities, states, countries, continents, lakes, islands, and mountains.

✗ the Miami, the Florida, the Argentina, the South America, the Lake Alto, the Cuba, the Mount Rushmore

Practice 2   Write *the* in the blank if needed.

1. _____ Monica's mother is driving to _____ Lake Superior.

2. I left _____ package in _____ restaurant.

3. _____ Berkshire Mountains are lovely in _____ fall.

4. _____ Route 66 is one of _____ most scenic highways in _____ United States.

5. _____ Mexico City is _____ largest city in _____ Mexico.

6. Miranda studied _____ Spanish when she was a student at _____ University of Madrid.

7. _____ Gainesville is located in _____ north central Florida.

8. _____ Santa Fe River runs to _____ Gulf of Mexico.

9. _____ palm tree in my yard fell on _____ car parked in _____ driveway.

10. _____ Cuba has _____ beautiful beaches.

Practice 3   Write *a, an,* or *the* in each blank if needed.

1. _____ marine biology class I took last semester was _____ most interesting class I have ever taken.

2. _____ professor was a graduate of _____ Harvard University.

3. He gave _____ interesting lecture on _____ first day.

4. He used _____ computer to show _____ interactive model of _____ ocean.

5. After _____ first class, I asked him _____ question.

6. His answer was _____ five-minute lecture on _____ ocean ecosystem.

7. _____ first assignment he gave us was to study _____ plankton.

8. Plankton is _____ vital part of the food chain in _____ ocean.

9. I had to do _____ great deal of research in _____ library.

10. At _____ end of the term, I had to write _____ report and make _____ oral presentation.

Determiners

2.10 Use *this* and *that* with singular nouns. Use *these* and *those* with plural nouns.

this paper	**that** paper
these papers	**those** papers

2.11 Use *many* with plural countable nouns. Use *much* with noncount nouns.

many news stories
much advice

2.12 Use *few* (meaning not many) or *a few* (meaning several) with plural countable nouns.

few letters, **a few** roses

2.13 Use *little* (meaning not very much) or *a little* (meaning a small amount) with noncount nouns.

little information, **a little** coffee remaining

Note: Little (meaning small) can be used with countable nouns.

a little house, a little boy

2.14 Use *some* with positive statements about count or noncount nouns. Use *any* in negative statements about count or noncount nouns.

She gave me **some** good advice.
She doesn't want to hear **any** noise.

2.15 Use *another* with singular nouns. Use *other* with plural nouns.

another sandwich, two **other** sandwiches

Practice 4   Write phrases with the following words.

Example: some   <u>some houses   </u>

1. any   _____
2. a few   _____
3. this   _____
4. little   _____
5. some   _____
6. other   _____
7. another   _____
8. many   _____
9. those   _____
10. much   _____

Participles Used as Adjectives

2.16 Present participles (*-ing* form) and past participles can be used as adjectives.

shining sun, fried chicken, dried fruit, broken window

Adjective Position

2.17 Adjectives are generally placed before the noun or pronoun they modify, but they follow a linking verb.

       adj.   N   *adj.*   N
I won a gold trophy at the tennis tournament.
   N   L.V.   *adj.*
Milan is crowded.

Adjective Order

2.18 Adjectives generally appear in front of the noun they modify, and when there are several adjectives in a row, they appear in the order listed below.

Order of Adjectives

1. Determiners (a, an, the, that, those, some, his, her, our, etc.)
2. Evaluation (subjective) adjectives (perfect, beautiful, ugly, interesting, etc.)
3. Size and shape adjectives (tiny, enormous, square, triangular, etc.)
4. Age (antique, old, young, etc.)
5. Color (blue, rosy, dark, light, etc.)
6. Nationality (American, English, Spanish, etc.)
7. Religion (Baptist, Buddhist, Jewish, Islamic, etc.)
8. Material (glass, stone, plastic, wooden, etc.)
9. Qualifying adjectives that are often seen as part of the noun (beach chair, sports car, baby carriage, love letter, etc.)

Example: We had *a long, cold* winter. *The pine* trees were covered with *glistening white* snow. We took *long, leisurely* walks through *the silent, snowy* woods, and sipped *steaming hot* chocolate beside *a blazing* fire.

For comparative and superlative forms, see "Adjectives and Adverbs," page 193.

Verbs

Modals

3.1 Modal auxiliaries (**can, could, will, would, shall, should, may, might, must, had better, would rather, have to, ought to, have got to**) take **no** endings to show agreement or tense.

Juan **can walk**. (No ending on walk)
Eliza **would rather run** than **walk**. (No ending on run or walk)

Verb Tenses

For a review of the principal tenses, see Chapter 8, "Verb Tenses," page 171.

Practice 5   In each blank, write the correct tense of the verb in parentheses.

1. Last month, I _____ (accept) a new job.

2. My father _____ (buy) a briefcase yesterday.

3. I promise that I _____ (come) to your party on Friday.

4. By six o'clock I had already _____ (eat) too much pie.

5. Ramon _____ (exercise) on Mondays.

6. Lola _____ (take) a nap right now.

7. My brother _____ (flunk) his math test.

8. She _____ (jog) when she fell.

9. I _____ (see) that movie twice already.

10. Last week, Susana _____ (break) her arm.

Passives

3.2 English speakers prefer the use of active voice rather than passive voice. Avoid using the passive construction.

In **active voice,** the subject performs the action.

      S   V   Obj.

✓ Antonio played golf.

✓ Tang-Li won the award.

✓ I wrecked the car.

In **passive voice,** the subject receives the action.

S + be + past participle

✗ Golf was played by Antonio.

✗ The award was won by Tang-Li.

✗ The car was wrecked by me.

Passives are acceptable if the doer of the action is unknown or unimportant.

✓ Susana was elected class president.

✓ The program was cancelled.

Gerunds and Infinitives

A **gerund** is a verb + -*ing* used as a noun (reading, swimming, running).

3.3 Use a gerund after a preposition (a word like *by, of, in,* or *about*).

Elena won the race **by swimming** the fastest.

3.4 Use a gerund after these phrases:

to be accustomed to _____ing
to be used to _____ing
to look forward to _____ing
to object to _____ing

3.5 Use a gerund after these verbs:

finish	keep/keep on (continue)
stop (cease)	enjoy
quit (give up)	appreciate
avoid	mind
postpone (put off)	consider (think about)
delay	discuss (talk about)
go	

He stopped smoking last week.
I will consider playing the piano for you.

An **infinitive** is to + the simple form of the verb (to run, to sit, to play). Infinitives can be used as a subject or an object:

To play tennis in college would be fun. (Subject)
I would like **to play** tennis in college. (Object)

3.6 Use an infinitive after these verbs:

hope	offer
promise	refuse
decide	remember
agree	forget
ask	expect
seem	want
appear	need
demand	claim

Sung-ling **decided to go** shopping.
The boys **appear to be** innocent.

When using a negative form, put not before the infinitive.

I decided not to play tennis.

3.7 Use a noun or pronoun and an infinitive after these verbs:

tell	allow
remind	require
advise	force
encourage	order
warn	ask
permit	except
want	need

My coach **reminded me to get** a good night's sleep before the game.
My mother **warned my brother not to stay** out late.

3.8 Certain verbs may be followed by either a gerund or an infinitive.

start	hate
begin	can't stand
continue	intend
like	try
prefer	remember
stop	regret
forget	

I **prefer to stop** every hour when I'm driving.
I **prefer stopping** every hour when I'm driving.
I **hate to lose.**
I **hate losing.**

Most verbs that can take either a gerund or an infinitive have no change in meaning. However, "stop," "remember," and "forget" are different. Although either a gerund or an infinitive can be used with these verbs, the meaning changes.

I stopped to water the flowers.
I stopped watering the flowers.

3.9 Both gerunds and infinitives may be used as singular subjects.

Reading is a great pastime.
To learn a second language is difficult.

Practice 6   Circle the correct gerund or infinitive.

1. The teacher offered (to give/giving) me extra time on the test.

2. Marco finished (to study/studying) at nine o'clock.

3. I avoid (to study/studying) late at night.

4. My mother expects (to win/winning) the lottery.

5. The coach warned me not (to swim/swimming) at night.

6. Sarah refused (to participate/participating).

7. My friends encouraged me (to apply/applying).

8. I need (to study/studying) tonight.

9. Norm agreed (to run/running) for class president.

10. Santiago enjoys (to ski/skiing).

Two-Word Verbs

Two-word verbs are a verb and a preposition that have special meaning.

3.10 Nonseparable two-word verbs cannot be separated by a noun or pronoun.

call on	come across	get along with
catch up	drop by	get in (into), get
check into	drop in	off, get on, get
check out of	drop off	over, get through

go over	look into	run into
grow up	look out for	run out of
keep up with	pass away	show up
look after	put up with	take after

3.11 Separable two-word verbs can be separated by a noun or pronoun.

call ___ back	find ___ out	put ___ away
call ___ off	give ___ back	put ___ off
call ___ up	give ___ up	take ___ off
cheer ___ up	hand ___ in	take ___ out
clean ___ up	hang ___ up	take ___ over
cross ___ out	look ___ over	tear ___ down
cut ___ out	look ___ up	think ___ over
do ___ over	make ___ up	try ___ on
drop ___ off	pick ___ out	turn ___ in
figure ___ out	pick ___ up	turn ___ off
fill ___ out	point ___ out	turn ___ up

Practice 7   Circle the correct verb phrase. For some items, both answers may be correct.

1. My mother asked me to (look out for my sister/look my sister out for).

2. Tenday wanted to (keep his brother up with/keep up with his brother).

3. My teacher told me to (figure out the answer/figure the answer out).

4. This weekend I plan to (catch up on my homework/catch my homework up on).

5. My friend wants to (look into the offer/look the offer into).

6. I will (call on my friend/call my friend on) today.

7. Maria promised to (pick me up/pick up me) at eight.

8. I don't have to (put up with you/put you up with) any longer.

9. I told him to (take the trash out/take out the trash).

10. My mother told me to (clean my room up/clean up my room).

Practice 8
EDITING FOR VERB ERRORS

Correct the twenty verb errors in the passage below. Do not make any unnecessary changes.

My friends has study in the United States for three years. They come to this country after they graduate from high school because they wanted studying English and engineering. The school they choose attending is the University of California at Berkeley. After they have been in school several months, they decide taking a vacation and visiting other parts of California. They wanted seeing Disneyland and Hollywood. They drive for several hours before they are reaching their destination. They stay in southern California for two nights and then they driving up the coast to see Big Sur and Carmel. They didn't arrived home until one in the morning. The next day they was sleepy, and they haven't remembered doing their homework.

Adverbs

Adverbs modify verbs, adjectives, and other adverbs.

Adverb Position

4.1 Adverbs may be placed before or after the verbs, adjectives, or adverbs they modify.

Rosario answered the question.
Quietly, Rosario answered the question.
Rosario answered the question **quietly.**
Rosario **quietly** answered the question.

Adverbs generally come before the verb, adjective, or adverb they modify.

ADV   verb
Germaine **quickly** answered the question.

ADV adj
Parvati is a **very** hard worker.

ADV adv
The house was **quite easily** painted.

4.2 Many adverbs may be placed after the object or verb.

Germaine answered the question **quickly.**
The house was painted **quite easily.**

4.3 Frequency adverbs (often, always, never, usually, sometimes, seldom, frequently, never, occasionally) are placed before most verbs, but they are placed after a *be* verb and between a helping verb and a main verb.

We **never** go to the beach in August. (Before main verb)
Montoya is **usually** late. (After *be* verb)
The dogs have **always** barked at night. (Between helping verb and main verb)

Pitfalls

4.4 Do not place an adverb between a verb and its object.

✘ They answered **quickly** the question.
✘ Ramon ran **quickly** the race.

Practice 9   **Place the adverb correctly in the sentence.**

1. Antonio mows the lawn. (never)

2. Paolo and Roberta are talking. (always)

3. He prepared for the conference. (quickly)

4. My baby sister fell asleep. (easily)

5. Kim-le is reading. (always)

6. My brother is wrong. (often)

7. I like to cook dinner. (sometimes)

8. They boarded the plane. (slowly)

9. My mother travels by car. (seldom)

10. The instructor distributed the tests. (quietly)

Prepositions

Prepositions show relationships between things. They indicate where something is in relation to something else (over, under, through, by, with). They can also indicate direction, time, or origin (to, toward, by, at, from, of). For a more complete list of prepositions, see "Parts of Speech," pages A-17–A-18.

Prepositions of Time

5.1 Use *on* for a day of the week, a holiday, and a calendar date.

on Monday, **on** the Fourth of July, **on** August 2

5.2 Use *in* for a year or a part of a day.

in 2004, **in** the morning

5.3 Use *at* for a specific time and for the phrase "at night."

at one o'clock, **at** noon

Practice 10   Write *in, on,* or *at* if needed in the blanks.

1. Maria was born _____ August 6 _____ Miami, Florida.

2. I am having a party _____ 7 o'clock _____ Saturday.

3. The boat will dock _____ midnight _____ the 7th.

4. My brother always wants to arrive _____ the movies _____ time.

5. My speech is _____ two o'clock _____ Tuesday.

6. _____ December 21, we will have our office party _____ the end of the day.

7. I always jog _____ 6 o'clock _____ the morning.

8. Paula likes to wake up _____ 5 o'clock _____ the morning.

9. The play will begin promptly _____ 8 o'clock _____ the evening.

10. _____ three _____ the afternoon, the bell rings.

Prepositions of Location

5.4 Use *at* for a specific place.

at the store, **at** the movies

5.5 Use *by* for beside.

by the fireplace, **by** the pool

5.6 Use *in* for inside of.

in a car, **in** a store, **in** a building

5.7 Use *in* with a city, state, or country.

in Paris, **in** France, **in** Europe

5.8 Use *near* for close to.

near the house, **near** the chair

5.9 Use *on* for a surface.

on the floor, **on** the table, **on** the roof

Practice 11 Write *in, on, at, by,* or *near* if needed in each blank.

1. Marta left her homework _____ the table _____ her room.

2. My homework is _____ the bag _____ the floor.

3. The party is _____ the largest house _____ Gainesville.

4. We went shopping _____ Harrods, the biggest store _____ England.

5. I live _____ the pool, so I can swim every day.

6. They placed the peaches _____ a bowl _____ the table.

7. The phone is _____ the chair _____ the door.

8. He passed _____ the school _____ his car.

9. I parked _____ the gate.

10. My aunt lives _____ the fire station.

Prepositions of Transportation

5.10 Use *on* if the means of transportation carries one person or many people.

on a bike, on a horse, **on** roller skates, **on** a motorcycle
on a plane, **on** a boat, **on** a train, **on** a bus

5.11 Use *in* if the means of transportation carries four to six people.

in a car, **in** a taxi, **in** a small plane

Practice 12   Fill in the blank with *on* or *in.*

1. _____ an automobile
2. _____ a bike
3. _____ a motorcycle
4. _____ a plane
5. _____ a bus

6. _____ a battleship
7. _____ a convertible
8. _____ a canoe
9. _____ a sailboat
10. _____ a ferry

Practice 13   Fill in the blank with the appropriate preposition (*in, on, by, at, of, near, to*) if needed.

1. We get _____ the plane _____ 6 o'clock.

2. _____ Christmas, you give gifts _____ your friends and family.

3. I was born _____ Germany _____ January 1, 1985.

4. Americans celebrate their independence _____ the Fourth of July.

5. My report is _____ the table _____ the hall.

6. My mother won't ride _____ a subway _____ night.

7. I get up early _____ the morning and walk _____ the park.

8. The accident happened _____ the racetrack.

9. The test is _____ 9 o'clock _____ Friday.

10. We were married _____ St. Louis _____ December.

Word Order

Basic Sentence Patterns

6.1 Subject–Verb

    S   V
The sun <u>rises</u>.

Other words and phrases may be added to modify or describe the subject or verb.

    Adj   S   V   **prepositional phrase**
The golden sun <u>rises</u> through the fog.

6.2 Subject–Verb–Direct Object

    S   V   D.O.
Wanda <u>watched</u> TV.

Other words and phrases may be added to modify or describe the subject, verb, or direct object.

S   V   D.O.

After passing her exam, Wanda watched TV for several hours.

6.3 Subject–Verb–Indirect Object–Direct Object

S   V   I.O.   D.O.

Sarah sent her sister a card.

Other words and phrases may be added to modify or describe the subject, verb, or direct object.

S   V   I. O.   D.O.

Sarah sent her older sister a postcard from Spain.

If *to* or *for* appears before the object, then the sentence ends in a prepositional phrase rather than a direct object.

S   V   I.O.   prep phrase

Sarah drove her older sister across town to school.

Do not use the words *to* or *for* before an indirect object.

S   V (No *to*) I.O. D.O.

Maria sent ↑ Juan a letter.

S   V (No *for*) I.O.   D.O.

My sister bought ↑ me an ice cream cone.

6.4 Subject–Linking Verb–Adjective or Noun

S   L.V.   Adj.

Alfonso seems unhappy.

S   L.V.   Noun

My father is an architect.

6.5 Questions

In questions, the subject comes after the verb.

L.V.   S

Where is your sister?

L.V.   S

When is the show?

V S V

Why are you crying?

Not only . . . but also phrases require the inverted word order of questions in the first clause.

V   S   V   S   V
Not only <u>does</u> Andy <u>know</u> how to sing, but he also <u>knows</u> how to dance.

6.6 Sentences that begin with *There* or *Here*

In sentences that begin with *there* or *here,* the subject comes after the verb.

L.V.   S
There <u>are</u> three reasons I can't go.

L.V.   S
Here <u>are</u> the flowers you ordered.

6.7 Use either a noun or a pronoun as a subject, but do not follow a noun with a pronoun.

✗ Sarah she sings beautifully.

✓ Sarah sings beautifully.

✓ She sings beautifully.

Practice 14 **Correct the faulty word order in the following sentences.**

1. My brother answered slowly my question.

   _____.

2. Santiago has seen many times the movie.

   _____.

3. I have been never to Spain.

   _____.

4. Uncle Eduardo gave to me a book.

   _____.

5. When the party is?

   _____?

6. Here the book you ordered is.

   _____.

7. Mario sad seems today.

   _____.

8. The clerk the book placed on the counter.

   _____.

9. Marta she cooks well spaghetti.

   _____.

10. My dog is tired never of playing.

_____.

Common ESL Errors

7.1 Independent clauses need a subject (except for command sentences that have an understood *you* subject).

   ✗ Is a pretty day.
   ✓ It is a pretty day.

7.2 One of _____s (plural noun) _____s (verb with –s ending)

   ✗ One of the chairs seems broken.

7.3 Do not use double negatives in English.

   ✗ Sandra does**n't** want **no** shrimp.
   ✓ Sandra doesn't want any shrimp.
   ✓ Sandra doesn't want shrimp.

Practice 15 Correct the common errors in the following sentences.

1. My sister doesn't eat no spinach.

2. Is cloudy today.

3. Because the car is broken, needs to be fixed.

4. Clara doesn't know nothing about the test.

5. One of the book is lost.

Practice 16
EDITING FOR "S"

In the passage below, correct words with missing –s endings. Also, correct the words that have unnecessary –s endings.

My two bests friend are taking tennis lesson. They takes private lesson twice a weeks and group lesson once a week. They says that the lesson are expensives but they is worth it. Some peoples don't believes in paying moneys to learns to play tennis, but my friends wants to be ables to impresses their friends and family when they returns to Argentina this summers.

Practice 17
EDITING FOR "S"

In the passage below, correct words with missing –s endings. Also, correct the words that have unnecessary –s endings.

Student have many distraction while they is in college. The biggest distraction is friends who wants to go out and party at the locals clubs. Some club doesn't opens until 11 o'clock at nights and they don't closes until 2 o'clock in the mornings. Students who stays out late hurts their performances in school. They may forgets to do their homeworks, and they may does poorly on test. They may feel sleepy, but if they falls asleep in class, their instructors will be unhappys.

Practice 18
EDITING FOR BASIC ERRORS

Correct all the errors in the passage below. Do not make any unnecessary changes. Watch for different kinds of errors, such as mistakes with run-ons, fragments, verbs, spelling, homonyms, capitals, and common ESL errors.

Many student who comes to the United State want study in American college. Since the September 11 attacks, it has became more difficult for international student to obtains the student visas needed to study in these country. Some student reports having to wait several month for their visas to be issue. Once student is here, he or she cannot returns home to visits his or her family, or he or she may not be allow back into the country. Many Americans universities are protesting these difficulties experience by their students.

Practice 19

EDITING FOR BASIC ERRORS

Correct all the errors in the passage below. Do not make any unnecessary changes. Watch for different kinds of errors, such as mistakes with run-ons, fragments, verbs, spelling, homonyms, capitals, and common ESL errors.

Studys in foreign country are exciting but difficult. Is interesting to lives in another culture for a period of times. Students who does study abroad discovers another way of livings. At first, is difficult to adjusts to another languages. Everyday activities such as driving, shoppings, or doing the laundry became more difficult if a student don't speak the languages. However, by participating in daily activity and getting to know native speaker, one can makes the adjustment to a foreign cultures.

Appendix 4 Paragraph Writing Checklists

This appendix provides

- Paragraph writing process prompts
  - Map template
  - Outline template
- Paragraph revision checklist
- Editing checklist
- Personal error list
- Editing symbols

Paragraph Writing Process Prompts

The following prompts will guide you in writing paragraphs. You may wish to consult these prompts each time you write a paragraph until the process becomes second nature.

1. **Understanding the Assignment**

   Assignment: _____

   Length: _____

   Due date: _____

2. **Narrowing the Topic**
   Use one or more brainstorming methods to narrow your topic.

3. **Determining the Writing Context**
   Decide on your purpose, audience, and tone. Then choose a tentative main idea.

   Purpose: _____

   Audience: _____

   Tone: _____

   Tentative main idea: _____

4. **Generating Ideas**

   Generate ideas by brainstorming, free writing, listing, clustering, or dividing. You may find it helpful to use scratch paper. Come up with as many ideas as possible. Keep your purpose and audience in mind as you generate ideas to support your topic sentence.

5. **Organizing Ideas**
   A. Examine the ideas you have generated, and revise your tentative topic sentence.
   B. Select your strongest support ideas, and place them in the map or outline template in the order in which you would like to use them. Do more brainstorming if you do not have enough supports to develop your topic sentence.
   C. Generate specific details for each of your supports.
   D. You may wish to state how each support relates to or proves the topic sentence.

Map Template

Topic sentence:

_____

_____

Area of Support	Specific Details	Relation to Topic Sentence
1. _____		
2. _____		
3. _____		
4. _____		
5. _____		

Outline Template

Topic sentence:

_____

I. Support 1

_____

A. Specific details

_____

B. Explain how idea supports topic sentence

_____

II. Support 2

_____

A. Specific details

_____

B. Explain how idea supports topic sentence

_____

III. Support 3

_____

A. Specific details

_____

B. Explain how idea supports topic sentence

_____

IV. Support 4

_____

A. Specific details

_____

B. Explain how idea supports topic sentence

_____

6. **Drafting**

Write a draft of the paragraph by creating a sentence or sentences for each area of support on your map or outline. Incorporate your specific details and, where appropriate, the relation to the topic sentence.

7. **Revising**

If possible, get feedback on your paragraph from peers or your instructor. If feedback is not available, analyze the strengths and weaknesses of your paragraph using the "Paragraph Revision Checklist" below.

8. **Editing**

Use the "Editing Checklist" on the next page and the suggestions of your peer editors to find and correct errors in your paragraph.

Paragraph Revision Checklist

1. Form

Title: Are the major words (including the first and last words) capitalized?

Does the title reveal the topic and slant of the paragraph?

Does it catch the reader's attention?

Is the first sentence indented?

Does the paragraph have the required number of sentences?

Does the paragraph have the required organizational pattern?

2. Topic Sentence

Does the topic sentence fit the assignment?

Is it appropriate for the intended audience and purpose?

Is the main idea clear?

3. Support

Is there enough support (three to five supports, depending on the assignment) to explain or prove your topic sentence?

Does each support clearly relate to or develop the topic sentence?

Are there enough specific details, facts, and examples to convince the reader?

Are any supports repeated?

Does anything in the paragraph not relate to the main idea?

Is the relationship between support sentences clear?

Are there clear transitions within and between sentences?

Is the order of supports clear and logical?

Are the sentences varied in length and structure?

Is appropriate vocabulary used?

Is the language clear and precise? (Are there strong verbs, specific nouns, and colorful adjectives and adverbs?)

4. Conclusion

Does the conclusion tie together the paragraph?

Does it introduce any new ideas or arguments that might confuse the reader?

Editing Checklist

As you learn about the following skills, add them to your editing checklist.

1. Check for run-ons and fragments. Is there one complete sentence—and no more than one complete sentence—between every two periods? (Identify the subject and the verb, and make sure the word group makes sense.)

2. Check every verb. Do subjects and verbs agree? Is proper verb tense used? Be sure to check the problem phrases such as *there is/there are* and pay attention to singular subjects such as *everyone*.

3. Check pronouns. Do they agree with their antecedents?

4. Use the dictionary or computer spell check to catch capitalization errors and misspellings. Remember, however, that the spell check will not catch errors with problem words such as *there/their*.

5. Remember your personal list of errors. Check your writing for any of these errors.

6. Look for any missing words or letters by reading the writing slowly from the last sentence to the first.

7. Check for apostrophes in contractions and possessives.

8. Check commas.

Personal Error List

Keep a list of the errors you make in your writing. Be sure to record the error just as you made it. Then write the correction and any explanation that will help you remember the correction.

Error	*Correction*
Example: This fine bike shop are	This fine bike shop is
Example: recieve	receive

1. _____
2. _____
3. _____
4. _____
5. _____
6. _____
7. _____
8. _____
9. _____
10. _____
11. _____
12. _____
13. _____
14. _____
15. _____
16. _____
17. _____
18. _____
19. _____
20. _____

Guide to Editing Symbols

Major Errors		Strategy to Correct Errors
Run-on Chapter 12	**RO**	Two independent clauses must be separated by a period or punctuated properly using a comma and a coordinating conjunction, a semicolon, or a semicolon and a transition and a comma. *Never* use a comma alone to join two sentences (comma splice).
Fragment Chapter 11	**FRAG**	Be certain that each sentence has a subject and a complete verb and makes sense.
Verb Chapter 7	**VE**	Verb errors are serious problems and require careful proofreading.
Chapter 8	**S/V AGR**	Subject/Verb Agreement: In the present tense: Single Subject + Verb with -s ending Plural Subject + Verb without -s ending Be sure to use the correct form of the verb.
	TENSE	Check the spelling of irregular verbs. Also, maintain verb tense consistency. Use present tense or past tense—don't shift tenses unless you have a good reason.

Minor Errors		Strategy to Correct Errors
Spelling Appendix	**sp**	Review the spelling rules; keep an ongoing list of misspelled words to add to and to study.
Problem Word Chapter 4	**pw**	Review lists, and use memory hooks to remember the meanings.
Wrong Word Chapter 5	**ww**	Check definition to be sure you have chosen the correct word.
Missing Word Chapter 5	**?**	Proofread to avoid leaving out words.
Capitalization Chapter 3	**cap**	Review capitalization rules, and write capitals and lowercase letters clearly.
Singular Plural Parts of Speech	**sing/pl**	Spell singular or plural nouns correctly. In general, a singular noun does not end in -s (one boy), and a plural noun does end in -s (two boys). Irregular plural nouns do not end in -s (men, women, children, people).

Awkward	**awk**	Sentence is not constructed well. Try reading sentence aloud to make sure ideas are put together clearly.
Article Parts of speech	**art**	Check your articles (a, an, the). In general, use *a* before words that start with a consonant (a cat). Use *an* before words that start with a vowel (an egg) or vowel sound (an hour). Use *the* to indicate a particular person or thing (the book).
Pronoun Chapter 14	**pron**	Be sure pronouns agree in gender and number with the words they rename.
Apostrophe Chapter 19	**apost**	Possessives: The owner of the object comes before the object (owner's object). In general, *'s* means a single owner; *s'* means more than one owner. Use *'s* with irregular plural owners such as men, women, children, people (children's toys). Contractions: Spell contractions correctly.
Comma Chapter 18	**com**	Compound = Independent clause, coordinating conjunction independent clause. Coordinating conjunctions: for, and, nor, but, or, yet, so Introductory element = Dependent clause or phrase, independent clause. Introductory elements are fragments that start with subordinating conjunctions, prepositions, and verbals. An independent clause (subject and a complete verb that make sense) should follow the comma. When a dependent clause or phrase follows an independent clause, no comma is needed. Transition = Transition, independent clause. Transitions: also, first, finally, for example, moreover, however, therefore Series = A, B, and/or C Dates and addresses: Friday, July 7, 1906, in Springfield, Illinois, was hot.

Answer Key

Chapter 1: The Paragraph

Practice 1, page 17

1. B, <u>wonderful</u>
2. A, <u>favorite</u>
3. B, <u>great</u>
4. A, <u>terrible</u>
5. B, <u>great</u>

Practice 2, page 18

1. B
2. A
3. B
4. A
5. C

Practice 3, page 19

Answers will vary.

Practice 4, page 19

Answers will vary.

Practice 5, page 23

Answers will vary.

Practice 6, page 26

I. 1. D
   2. B
   3. C
   4. A
   5. E

II. 1. B
    2. D
    3. E
    4. C
    5. A

III. 1. B
     2. A
     3. C
     4. D
     5. E

Practice 7, page 28

1. D
2. B
3. C

Practice 8, page 30

Answers will vary.

Practice 9, page 31

Answers will vary.

Practice 10, page 33

1. 3
2. 4

Practice 11, page 37

1. C
2. B
3. A

Practice 12, page 38

1. First, Next, Then, Eventually
2. First, Second, Most importantly
3. Moreover, Also, Another, Finally

Practice 13, page 41

I.	2	IV.	1
II.	1	V.	1
III.	2		

Practice 14, page 42

Answers will vary.

Practice 15, page 43

1. B	4. B
2. A	5. A
3. B	

Chapter 2: The Essay

Practice 1, page 63

Answers not shown.

Practice 2, page 66

1. B
2. C
3. B

Practice 3, page 67

1. D, A, C, B
2. D, A, C, B
3. C, A, B, D

Chapter 3: Capitalization

Practice 1, page 78

1. Joaqin asked me if I had seen the latest movie.
2. Rooney asked me out on a date.
3. When I returned to class, Mr. Peabody asked, "Where were you yesterday?"
4. Jean Paul offended me when he said, "What happened to your hair?"
5. My mother looked at me and said "Where have you been?"

Practice 2, page 79

Ron Weasley
my favorite uncle
Sandy Perkins
Aunt Sarah
Prince William

doctor
my father
Mrs. Sandros
Professor Snape

Practice 3, page 80

Altuna River
southern Canada
Grand Canyon
Times Square
France

the polluted river
Sangre de Cristo Mountains
California
Berlin

Practice 4, page 81

Montgomery Middle School
Federal Bureau of Investigation (FBI)
my favorite barbecue restaurant
Buckingham Palace
the Toronto Blue Jays

Tide detergent
University of California
community college
the Jefferson Memorial
the mall

Practice 5, page 81

November
Sunday
winter snowstorm
June
fall

Saturday
Fourth of July
Thanksgiving
holiday
spring

Practice 6, page 82

Portuguese
the Spanish Civil War
my favorite situation comedy
The Washington Post
jazz

the Vietnam War
history
a punk rock group
The Supremes
Drawing 101

Practice 7, page 82

bottlenose dolphin
Florida panther
hammerhead shark
pansies
sugar snap peas

shrimp cocktail
daffodils
chestnut trees
English bull dog
black bear

Chapter 4: Problem Words
List 1 (pages 93–99)

1. accept, except
2. accept, except
3. An, an, and
4. An, an, and
5. It's, its
6. It's, its
7. know, no
8. no, know
9. past, passed
10. past, passed
11. peace, piece
12. peace, piece
13. principal, principle
14. principal, principle
15. write, right
16. Write, right
17. steal, steel

18. steel, steal
19. suppose, supposed
20. suppose, supposed
21. then, than
22. than
23. They're, their
24. their, there
25. through, thorough
26. through, thorough
27. threw, throw
28. throw, threw
29. thought, though
30. though, thought
31. to, two
32. too, to, to
33. used to
34. use, used to

35. whether, weather
36. weather, whether
37. woman, women's
38. woman, women's
39. of, have
40. have, of
41. You're, your
42. You're, your

List 2 (pages 102–106)

1. advised, advice
2. advice, advises
3. effect, affected
4. affected, effects
5. already, all ready
6. already, all ready
7. all together, altogether
8. altogether, all together
9. bear, barely
10. barely, bear
11. blew, blue
12. blew, blue
13. break, brake
14. break, brakes
15. by, buy
16. by, buy
17. capital, capitol
18. capital, capitol
19. choose, chose
20. chose, choose
21. complements
22. compliment, complements
23. fair, fare
24. fare, fair
25. hear, here
26. here
27. hole, whole
28. whole, hole
29. lay
30. lie
31. lose, loose
32. loose, lose
33. stationary, stationery
34. stationery, stationary
35. weak, week
36. week, weak

Chapter 5: Word Use and Choice
Practice 1, page 115

1. courthouse
2. crow
3. owns
4. Rocky Mountains
5. studies
6. Irish setter
7. politician
8. goldfish
9. Wyles Elementary
10. ladybug

Practice 2, page 115

Answers will vary.

Practice 3, page 117

1. were, were
2. We'll
3. want
4. our, were

5. Where
6. mind
7. respectable

8. encouraged
9. want
10. regrettable

Practice 4, page 118

1. I'm *going to* go *regardless* of what my parents say.
2. Jerome *doesn't want to* go to school *because* he *doesn't* feel good.
3. *Because* we won the game, *we are going to* go to the drive *through and* buy shakes.
4. *Because* I didn't have *any idea* how long the project was *going to* take, I *underestimated* how much time I would need.
5. I *couldn't* care less if they *aren't going to* pay for *themselves.*

Practice 5, page 119

1. Jerome doesn't have *any* time to waste.
2. Sandy won't go to *any* (or *an*) office party.
3. I'm not interested in *any* (or *a*) date.
4. The teacher won't give us *any* extra credit.
5. Don't bring *any* problems around here.

Practice 6, page 119

Answers will vary.

1. Pedro wanted to *relax at his house.*
2. I want to *drive* in a *fantastic car.*
3. The *professor* introduced us to a *fascinating* idea.
4. I'm *disappointed* over my low grade.
5. The *man* claimed he was *the most important person* of the *neighborhood.*

Practice 7, page 121

Answers will vary.

1. When I study history, what interests me is learning about where events took place.
2. Every time I make plans, some surprise changes everything.
3. I would like to work for two or three years in business.
4. It will take me more than two years to complete my degree because I need to take several college prep classes.
5. My advisor recommended that I not take more than three classes each term because I have to work.

Practice 8, page 121

Inserted letters and words are in italics.

1. Many of my friend*s* work at the same time *as* they go *to* school.
2. When *I* have to work late during the week, I'm sleepy in class *the* next day.
3. Since no one *is* supporting me, I have to work to pay my bills.
4. I work twenty hour*s* during *the* week and eight hours on Saturday.
5. It is hard to complete all *my* homework when I have *to* work so many hour*s*.

Chapter 6: Identifying Subjects and Verbs

Practice 1, page 135

1. service is becoming
2. Companies have lowered
3. communities are paying
4. Competition has helped
5. Companies have reduced
6. Consumers pay
7. Everyone may give up
8. plans make
9. Consumers have
10. service is

Practice 2, page 136

1. homeowners have found
2. They are getting
3. banks have been lending
4. This is called
5. homeowners will watch
6. they may call
7. experts recommend
8. consumers have saved
9. You should consult
10. anyone can benefit

Practice 3, page 136

1. Taking can be
2. Remembering can help
3. You Don't wait
4. You Try
5. You take

Practice 4, page 137

1. A number of stores in town have begun to stay open all night long.
2. Along with a grocery store and a drug store, a department store in the shopping mall offers late night hours to customers.
3. People in my family enjoy shopping late at night instead of watching television.
4. Shoppers in the deserted aisles can appear mysterious.
5. In addition to people who work late, students from the local college shop during the wee hours of the morning.
6. At one store in the mall, employees play progressive music after 10 P.M.
7. By the end of the night, customers can be seen dancing in the aisles.

8. ~~On Halloween,~~ trick-or-treaters ~~from every neighborhood~~ come ~~to the mall for a party after closing time.~~

9. ~~From midnight until two in the morning,~~ older kids ~~in costume~~ are allowed to skateboard ~~along the walkways of the mall.~~

10. ~~For many people,~~ shopping ~~at all-night stores~~ can be amusing.

Practice 5, page 138

1. ~~As early as May,~~ fans ~~from around the country~~ look forward ~~to the college football season.~~

2. ~~Throughout the summer,~~ followers ~~of the different teams~~ get ready ~~for the first game.~~

3. Articles ~~about the top teams~~ appear ~~in newspapers and magazines.~~

4. National polls ~~of sportswriters~~ rank the top teams ~~in each conference.~~

5. ~~Along with guessing the top teams,~~ everyone ~~with an interest in football~~ tries to guess who will be the best players ~~in the country.~~

6. ~~Throughout the season,~~ games ~~between the best teams~~ will be broadcast ~~on television.~~

7. The most loyal fans will travel ~~with their team to games~~ all ~~over the nation.~~

8. ~~Between August and December,~~ college teams will play ~~over five thousand football games.~~

9. ~~Near the end of the season,~~ teams ~~with the best records~~ will be invited ~~to bowl games.~~

10. ~~After the season,~~ the best players ~~of the year~~ are chosen ~~for special recognition.~~

Practice 6, page 139

1. Many people love to travel to foreign countries, but they should remember to take their passports.

2. Also, some countries require shots for diseases and recommend certain medications to bring along on the trip.

3. Magda and Johan are visiting from Holland and are touring America for three months.

4. They take their passports everywhere and also carry their international driver's licenses.

5. Tourists everywhere must carry picture identification, and everyone also should carry an international credit card for emergencies.

Practice 7, page 140

1. Have you ever traveled to a foreign country?

2. Here are a few reasons to visit a foreign country.

3. There is a different culture to study.

4. There will be new foods and customs to explore.

5. Where can we find American food?

Practice 8, page 141

1. There <u>is</u> a digital revolution in America's schoolrooms.
2. Wireless phones and handheld digital assistants <u>are</u> now <u>seen</u> as essential back-to-school supplies for students across America.
3. Most students now <u>carry</u> cell phones, so schools <u>are beginning</u> to change their policies regarding phones in the classroom.
4. Students who own cell phones and personal digital assistants (PDAs) <u>are bringing</u> them to class and <u>are using</u> them during class.
5. Because cell phones can be disruptive, many teachers <u>have prohibited</u> them in class.
6. However, PDAs and laptop computers <u>can be</u> useful to students who want to take notes or complete research assignments.
7. Here <u>are</u> some of the best ways for students to use their electronic devices.
8. Cell phones <u>can be used</u> to record assignments, and laptops <u>can be used</u> to take notes or compose papers in class.
9. Also, because many cell phones connect to the Internet, they <u>can be used</u> to research information.
10. Probably within five years, there <u>will be</u> teachers who require students to bring cell phones and laptops to class, and electronic devices <u>will be</u> as common in the classroom as paper and pencil.

Practice 9, page 141

Answers will vary.

Chapter 7: Subject–Verb Agreement

Practice 1, page 151

1. P
2. S
3. S
4. P
5. P
6. S
7. P
8. S
9. P
10. P

Practice 2, page 152

The modern American supermarket <u>has become</u> a one-stop shopping center for the entire family. While the neighborhood supermarket still <u>sells</u> the usual groceries, it also now <u>offers</u> a variety of choices from around the world such as Italian olive oils and pastas, Asian noodles, and South American plantains. The store bakery <u>bakes</u> everything from breads to donuts and birthday cakes, and because we <u>can fill</u> prescriptions while we <u>shop</u>, supermarkets <u>have become</u> our primary drug stores.

<u>P</u>   <u>P</u>   <u>P</u>

(Videos), (flowers), and even (perfumes) <u>are</u> a few of the expanded lines of merchandise
                                            <u>P</u>
that grocery (stores) <u>stock</u>. Also, most (stores) <u>provide</u> stamps, check cashing, and photo
                                            <u>P</u>
processing, and (they) <u>house</u> a deli that makes sandwiches and salads for busy
                    <u>S</u>
workers on the go. (Shopping) <u>is becoming</u> a pleasure at supermarkets these days.

Practice 3, page 153

1. The (leaves) <s>on the tree</s> (is/<u>are</u>) turning brown.

2. The (cars) <s>on the freeway</s> (creates/<u>create</u>) pollution.

3. (One) <s>of my classes</s> (<u>is</u>/are) difficult.

4. The (clouds) <s>in the sky</s> (moves/<u>move</u>) quickly.

5. The (student) <s>in the front</s> <s>of the room</s> (<u>belongs</u>/belong) <s>to my drama club</s>.

6. The (teachers) <s>at my school</s> (is/<u>are</u>) strict.

7. The (dents) <s>on my car</s> (looks/<u>look</u>) terrible.

8. The (papers) <s>in my notebook</s> (is/<u>are</u>) well organized.

9. (Each) <s>of the boys</s> (<u>plays</u>/play) soccer.

10. (Some) <s>of my answers</s> (is/<u>are</u>) correct.

Practice 4, page 154

1. goes
2. is
3. pleases

4. belongs
5. is

Practice 5, page 154

1. assign
2. are
3. work

4. are
5. want

Practice 6, page 155

1. have
2. is
3. is

4. have
5. are

Practice 7, page 156

1. practices
2. believes
3. is
4. surges
5. plays

Practice 8, page 156

1. calms
2. is
3. is
4. teaches
5. is

Practice 9, page 157

1. (China and crystal) (is/<u>are</u>) easily broken.

2. My (brother and sister) (does/<u>do</u>) their homework together.

3. (Eloise and Sean) (takes/<u>take</u>) turns washing the dishes.

4. (Jake and Sarah) (has/<u>have</u>) the flu.

5. My (resume and letter) (shows/<u>show</u>) my work experience.

Practice 10, page 157

1. (Walking) briskly (<u>burns</u>/burn) calories and (<u>tones</u>/tone) the muscles.

2. (Playing) tennis and (reading) (is/<u>are</u>) my favorite hobbies.

3. When I was younger, (paying) attention in classes (<u>was</u>/were) difficult for me.

4. (Gardening) (<u>relaxes</u>/relax) me.

5. (Studying) with my friends (<u>helps</u>/help) me prepare for tests.

Practice 11, page 158

1. Either (Aunt Sarah) or my (friends) (drives/<u>drive</u>) me to school every morning.

2. Neither his (teachers) nor his (father) (<u>knows</u>/know) how to control his behavior.

3. Either (Tom) or (Lisa) (<u>has</u>/have) my books.

4. Neither my (attorneys) nor the (judge) (<u>wants</u>/want) the case to go to trial.

5. My (brothers) or my best (friend) (<u>is</u>/are) going to the game.

Practice 12, page 158

1. read, write
2. plays, studies
3. types, takes
4. plants, weeds
5. runs, grabs, races

Practice 13, page 159

1. There (is/__are__) only four ⌀questions⌀ on the test.
2. Here (__is__/are) my ⌀assignment⌀.
3. There (__is__/are) one ⌀piece⌀ of advice my father gave me.
4. There (__comes__/come) a ⌀time⌀ to admit defeat.
5. Here (__is__/are) your ⌀paycheck⌀.

Practice 14, page 159

1. What (is/__are__) ⌀you⌀ doing after class?
2. Where (__has__/have) the ⌀time⌀ gone?
3. When (does/__do__) ⌀they⌀ want to leave?
4. Why (__has__/have) your ⌀brother⌀ called?
5. How long (__is__/are) the ⌀drive⌀ to the mountains?

Practice 15, page 160

1. The ⌀test⌀ that I passed (__was__/were) hard.
2. ⌀Many⌀ of the songs that (is/__are__) played in band (is/__are__) difficult.
3. The ⌀man⌀ who (__sits__/sit) in front of me on the bus (__is__/are) a banker.
4. The ⌀classes⌀ that (is/__are__) required (is/__are__) all three credits.
5. ⌀Anyone⌀ who (__studies__/study) (__passes__/pass) the class.

Practice 16, page 161

1. is
2. have
3. is
4. Do
5. is
6. Has
7. are
8. has
9. are
10. Does

Practice 17, page 162

1. C
2. I (regret)
3. I (win)
4. C
5. I (arrive)

Practice 18, page 162

Answers will vary.

Practice 19, page 162

Answers will vary.

Chapter 8: Verb Tenses

Practice 1, page 174

begin: began (past), begun (past participle), beginning (present participle)
take: took, taken, taking
drive: drove, driven, driving

Practice 2, page 175

1. was
2. am
3. was
4. are
5. is

6. were
7. are
8. have been
9. was
10. were

Practice 3, page 175

1. does
2. did
3. Do
4. did
5. done

6. do
7. did
8. do
9. Did
10. do

Practice 4, page 176

1. has
2. had
3. has had
4. Have
5. had

6. Has
7. had
8. had
9. has
10. have

Practice 5, page 178

Answers will vary.

Practice 6, page 178

Answers will vary.

Practice 7, page 179

1. broke
2. ridden
3. lost
4. sang
5. gone
6. taught
7. worn
8. wrote
9. spoken
10. stolen

Practice 8, page 180

1. wore
2. sleep
3. split
4. spent
5. read
6. hit
7. met
8. quit
9. set
10. shut

Practice 9, page 180

1. has made
2. have always lived
3. has worn
4. has been
5. has been broken
6. have eaten
7. has been
8. has studied
9. has wanted
10. has been

Practice 10, page 181

1. had just started
2. had already passed
3. had just read
4. had eaten
5. had left
6. had just picked up
7. had just gone
8. had already taken
9. had already gone
10. had just started

Practice 11, page 182

1. C, <u>is printed</u>
2. My mother baked the cake. (<u>was baked</u>)
3. C, <u>was awarded</u>
4. The puppy destroyed my new shoe. (<u>was destroyed</u>)
5. The hungry hikers devoured the sandwiches. (<u>were devoured</u>)
6. C, <u>must be postmarked</u>
7. The substitute teacher graded the exam. (<u>was graded</u>)
8. The new student broke an unwritten rule. (<u>was broken</u>)
9. C, <u>are announced</u>
10. C, <u>had been convicted</u>

Practice 12, page 183

1. rusted
2. broken
3. burned
4. C
5. C

6. convicted
7. dilapidated
8. combed
9. C
10. housebroken

Practice 13, page 184

1. struck, went or strikes, go
2. finished, was or finish, am
3. was, were or is, are
4. finished, went or finish, go
5. liked, ate or like, eat

6. liked, mowed or likes, mows
7. were, went or are, goes
8. got, turned or gets, turns
9. lived, went or lives, goes
10. went, came or go, come

Practice 14, page 185

Answers will vary.

Practice 15, page 185

Answers will vary.

Chapter 9: Adjectives and Adverbs

Practice 1, page 194

1. a, little, the, leather
2. the, playful, an, old
3. some, elderly, retirement

4. inexpensive, my, favorite
5. few, long

Practice 2, page 195

Answers will vary.

Practice 3, page 196

1. tallest
2. gentler
3. most intelligent

4. most difficult
5. more obvious

Practice 4, page 197

1. carefully, badly
2. hesitantly, exactly
3. quietly, patiently, quickly

4. really, shortly
5. happily, generously

Practice 5, page 198

1. really
2. terrible
3. fairly

4. bravely
5. well

Chapter 10: Sentence Parts and Types

Practice 1, page 206

1. The computer network has been shut down for maintenance.
2. Modeling offers many advantages as a career.
3. A legal secretary has filed all the law firm's correspondence from last month.
4. The sleek sailboat glided into the cove.
5. Mario and his friends did not want to turn down the music at the party.

Practice 2, page 208

1. DC
2. PH
3. IC

4. DC
5. IC

Practice 3, page 209

1. CX
2. CD
3. CD-CX

4. S
5. CX

Practice 4, page 210

1. DEC
2. IMP
3. EXC

4. INT
5. DEC

Chapter 11: Sentence Fragments

Practice 1, page 215

_____F_____ 1. (We) Will be eating at seven tonight.

_____S_____ 2. Your (grandmother) will have dinner with us.

_____F_____ 3. (She) Cooked her favorite dish, which is chili.

_____F_____ 4. Also, (We) have made a chocolate cake.

_____S_____ 5. (It's) her birthday.

_____S_____ 6. <u>Get</u> a birthday card for her.
_{You}

_____F_____ 7. <u>Has</u> math class tonight.
_{Your brother}

_____F_____ 8. Possibly <u>may stop</u> by after class.
_{He}

_____S_____ 9. <u>It's</u> the last meeting of the class.

_____S_____10. Please <u>arrive</u> by seven tonight.
_{You}

Practice 2, page 216

_____F_____ 1. Richard's friend from his last job in Montana.
is visiting

_____F_____ 2. A tall man with green eyes and a beard.
came with him

_____S_____ 3. He <u>is moving</u> to Wyoming.

_____S_____ 4. His wife <u>got</u> a job there.

_____F_____ 5. Their house with a view of the mountains.
sits in the valley

_____F_____ 6. Deer and elk in the front yard.
roam

_____S_____ 7. The weather <u>can be</u> pretty extreme.

_____F_____ 8. Ten feet of snow or more in the winter.
is not unusual

_____S_____ 9. Skiing <u>is</u> a lot of fun.

_____F_____10. The fresh air and beautiful surroundings.
make me happy

Practice 3, page 217

_____F_____ 1. The kids from the neighborhood gathering in the driveway.
are

_____S_____ 2. They <u>are getting</u> ready to play basketball.

_____F_____ 3. The ball found in the garage.
was

_____F_____ 4. An air pump needed to inflate the ball.
is

_____S_____ 5. The game <u>will start</u> soon.

_____S_____ 6. Everyone <u>hopes</u> to be on Jamal's team.

_____F_____ 7. The boy standing by the car.
is

_____S_____ 8. He <u>has grown</u> over six inches in the past year.

_____F_____ 9. All the shorter boys including Jeffrey.
need gloves

_____F_____10. One kid gone home early.
has

Practice 4, page 217

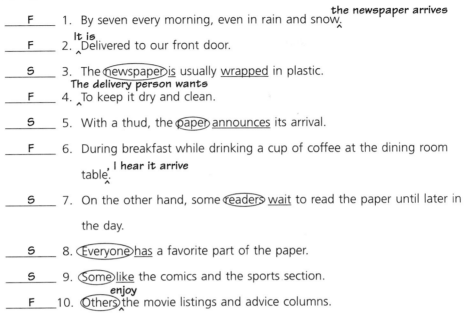

   F 1. By seven every morning, even in rain and snow. *the newspaper arrives*

   F 2. *It is* Delivered to our front door.

   S 3. The newspaper is usually wrapped in plastic.

   F 4. *The delivery person wants* To keep it dry and clean.

   S 5. With a thud, the paper announces its arrival.

   F 6. During breakfast while drinking a cup of coffee at the dining room table. *I hear it arrive*

   S 7. On the other hand, some readers wait to read the paper until later in the day.

   S 8. Everyone has a favorite part of the paper.

   S 9. Some like the comics and the sports section.

   F 10. Others *enjoy* the movie listings and advice columns.

Practice 5, page 218

We all know what it feels like to experience stress in school, at work, or at home. Schoolwork can be especially stressful, such as big tests or oral presentations in front of the class. Even while meeting with a teacher after class students will feel some anxiety. Also, stress is produced in the workplace by demanding bosses and difficult co-workers. Many workers will rest the entire weekend to recover from the work week. Surprisingly, our home life can also be stressful from all the demands placed on us. The stress comes from the people we care about, for example, children, spouses, neighbors, and friends. All our important relationships come with demands and expectations about how we should act. We are a nation under stress.

Practice 6, page 219

Answers will vary.

  With all the demands of daily life, we need to manage the stress in our lives. Habits as simple as taking a walk to unwind after a hard day at work can be effective in reducing stress. Also, refraining from drinking too much coffee is good. Lifestyle modifications are definitely the most effective methods for reducing stress and anxiety in our daily life. Start with everyday habits like smoking and drinking. Any substance that puts more stress on our bodies will not help us reduce stress. We must try to replace bad habits with good ones, for instance, aerobic exercise like walking, jogging, or biking. Eating healthy foods in moderate amounts and avoiding refined sugar and fatty foods can help. Fruits and vegetables should be eaten with every meal and lots of water drunk every day. Getting exercise and eating right make a big difference. It is never too late to change our lives!

Practice 7, page 220

Answers will vary.

Practice 8, page 221

Answers will vary.

Practice 9, page 223

It is important to have a primary care physician who can treat you and your family. This doctor must be a person with a personality that makes him or her easy to relate to. You should think carefully about whether you are more comfortable with a male or female doctor because you will have to share intimate details of your life with your doctor. Also, many health experts recommend family practitioners who can provide comprehensive care to the entire family. Many people prefer to ask friends for their recommendations before they choose a physician. When you go for your first visit, you should take notes about your experience since you will learn a lot about the doctor and his or her office. For example, if you are kept waiting for your appointment or the receptionist is rude, you may wish to find a different doctor. Moreover, you may want to find out how you will reach your doctor when you have an emergency. Most doctors use an answering service that screens their calls after hours. However, some doctors can be reached on their cell phone or by e-mail, although they may request that you contact them after hours only during an emergency. A little investigation before you choose a doctor will save you a lot of trouble later on.

Practice 10, page 224

Answers will vary.

Practice 11, page 224

Answers will vary.

Chapter 12: Run-on Sentences

Practice 1, page 235

1. CS
2. FS
3. CS
4. FS
5. CS

Practice 2, page 237

_____ S _____ 1. (Americans) spend a lot of time and money on trying to remain young and healthy.

_____ RO _____ 2. Baby (boomers) are now reaching their fifties and sixties (they) want to stay young as long as possible.

_____ S _____ 3. Even young (Americans) are concerned about maintaining their health and looking good.

_____ RO _____ 4. Therefore, (vitamins) are more popular than ever, other nutritional (supplements) are also gaining popularity.

_____ RO _____ 5. (Sales) of nutritional supplements grew over 30 percent in the past five years, (sales) are expected to top 20 billion dollars this year.

_____ S _____ 6. However, there are (areas) of the nutritional supplements industry that trouble health experts because some products may harm consumers.

_____ S _____ 7. Some (research) has cast doubts on the usefulness of some herbal supplements such as St. John's wort and ginseng.

_____ RO _____ 8. (Ephedra) is a supplement that is used to lose weight (it) has also been linked to a number of deaths.

_____ S _____ 9. Most (experts) agree that harmful supplements should be banned so that consumers are protected.

_____ RO _____ 10. Health (supplements) are here to stay most (supermarkets) and department (stores) now have entire areas devoted to vitamins and other health products.

Practice 3, page 239

1. RO, workplace. They
2. RO, workers. Major
3. S
4. S
5. S

6. RO, agents. They
7. S
8. RO, employees. They
9. RO, benefits. A stress-free
10. S

Practice 4, page 240

1. for
2. and, so
3. but, yet

4. but
5. or

Practice 5, page 241

1. people, and
2. weather, or
3. off, and or off, so
4. migraines, but or migraines, yet
5. migraine, and

6. migraine, and or migraine, so
7. supplements, and
8. migraine, for
9. migraines, so
10. remedies, and

Practice 6, page 242

1. RO, common; 90 percent
2. RO, headaches; the four
3. S

4. RO, hours; attacks
5. S

Practice 7, page 243

Answers will vary.

1. RO
2. RO
3. RO
4. RO
5. RO

6. RO
7. S
8. S
9. S
10. RO

Practice 8, page 244

1. because
2. Since
3. Even though
4. If
5. because

6. although
7. After
8. Since
9. When
10. since

Practice 9, page 245

Answers will vary.

Practice 10, page 245

Answers will vary.

Chapter 13: Sentence Combining

Practice 1, page 258

1. Cont
2. Add
3. Cons
4. Cont
5. Cons

6. Add
7. Cons
8. Cont
9. Cont
10. Cont

Practice 2, page 260

1. Some people think that only a hard workout counts as exercise, so they don't start an exercise program until they are ready to work out hard.
2. Research shows that any exercise is better than none, for (or and) as little as one hour of exercise per week reduces the risk of heart disease.

3. Yoga is a gentle form of exercise, yet (or but) some styles of yoga are actually quite demanding physically.
4. Exercise does not ensure weight loss, nor does exercising always reduce stress.
5. Swimming is low-impact exercise, and water aerobics is also good for reducing wear and tear on the body.

Practice 3, page 261

1. Home gyms provide good exercise and reduce travel time for exercise.
2. People with special needs will enjoy home gyms but won't get to socialize with others at a gym.
3. The best form of exercise is the one you can do regularly and is exercise you can enjoy.
4. Fast walking is rigorous enough to benefit the cardiovascular system yet is gentle enough to keep walkers from getting injured.
5. Most fitness experts believe that strength training is important and say that working out with weights twice a week is optimal.

Practice 4, page 262

Answers will vary.

1. August is a hot month in Maine, but September can be quite cool.
2. Many campers enjoy swimming and also like hiking in the woods.
3. There is no electricity at the campsites, so cooking must be done over a fire.
4. The air is fresh and clean, but sometimes there are bugs.
5. The weather is so beautiful, so the campground is usually full.
6. The campground is popular with families, and groups from churches and schools stay in the group sites.
7. The showers are not popular, for there is no hot water.
8. Bears sometimes visit the campground at night, but there have been no reports of bear attacks.
9. Pets are allowed in the campsites, and some dog owners are afraid that the bears will attack their dogs.
10. Snakes have been seen on the trails, but no snakebites have been reported.

Practice 5, page 263

1. An older home only costs half of what a newer home costs because an older home doesn't usually have a garage or pool.
2. The median price of an old home is around $100,000 while a new home will cost almost $200,000.
3. Many young home buyers are attracted to old houses because they like the low price and sturdy construction.

4. When many buyers move into an old home, they must renovate the house's electrical wiring and heating and cooling systems.
5. If home buyers want to find an old house with lots of charm, they should look in older neighborhoods.

Practice 6, page 265

1. Turmeric, which is a major spice in curry powder, may have anticancer properties.
2. Some commonly prescribed medications such as iron and blood pressure medicines are so potent that swallowing just one or two pills can kill a child.
3. Pregnant women should limit their intake of albacore tuna because it contains high levels of poisonous mercury.
4. It is important to keep medications away from children, who sometimes want to experiment with pills they see their parents take.
5. Medications that get too old to use safely should be thrown out.

Practice 7, page 266

Answers will vary.

1. Although feeling stressed at work is very common, most workers don't admit their stress to co-workers.
2. People often think that stress, which might come from a demanding boss or difficult employee, is just part of the job.
3. Since prolonged stress can actually kill people, stress should be treated as a serious ailment.
4. Because most people cannot accurately judge their own stress level, they should get checked by a doctor or mental health professional.
5. Workers may be able to eliminate some sources of stress, which include unnecessary tasks and self-criticism.

Practice 8, page 266

Answers will vary.

1. Although August is a hot month in Maine, September can be quite cool.
2. While many campers enjoy swimming, most campers also like hiking in the woods.
3. Since there is no electricity at the campsites, cooking must be done over a fire.
4. Even though the air is fresh and clean, sometimes there are bugs.
5. Because the weather is so beautiful, the campground is usually full.

6. While the campground is popular with families, groups from churches and schools stay in the group sites.
7. The showers are not popular because there is no hot water.
8. Bears sometimes visit the campground at night though there have been no reports of bear attacks.
9. Because pets are allowed in the campsites, some dog owners are afraid that the bears will attack their dogs.
10. Snakes have been seen on the trails although no snakebites have been reported.

Practice 9, page 268

Answers will vary.

1. Applying for a job can be challenging because workers must fill out applications and provide accurate information.
2. Applicants are asked for detailed information, which includes addresses and phone numbers of references, and the information can be hard to get.
3. Handwriting on the application must be easy to read, or applicants could lose the position.
4. The information must be accurate, so applicants should bring their contact information with them and check the accuracy of any addresses and phone numbers they provide.
5. Because employers want to know background information on job applicants, employers may ask about past convictions, and they may demand explanations about any criminal convictions.

Practice 10, page 268

Answers will vary.

1. Since the job interview is crucial to getting a job, job applicants should prepare carefully.
2. Employers usually ask the applicant questions about work history, so applicants should try to predict the questions they might be asked and practice their possible responses to those questions.
3. Although the employer may not be dressed up, the job applicant should dress appropriately, and appropriate attire means clothing that would be worn on the job.
4. If applicants want to make a good impression, they should arrive ten minutes early for the interview because being late to the interview may cost applicants the job.
5. Showing good manners during the interview is important, so applicants should shake hands at the beginning of the interview and should thank the interviewer at the end of the interview.

Chapter 14: Pronoun Agreement

Practice 1, page 275

1. John told (his) mother that (he) was going out. *his and he refer to John*

2. The campers lost (their) way in the forest. *their refers to campers*

3. Sue got an A on (her) last test. *her refers to Sue*

4. The counselor announced that (his) schedule was full. *his refers to counselor*

5. My friends are having a party at (their) apartment complex this Friday. *their refers to friends*

Practice 2, page 276

1. its
2. their
3. its

4. its
5. its

Practice 3, page 276

1. My mother and my aunt do (their) grocery shopping at the same store. *their refers to mother and aunt*

2. Either my coach or my parents will bring the refreshments with (them). *them refers to parents*

3. Neither my friends nor my brother knows what happened to (his) homework. *his refers to brother*

4. My teacher or her aides grade papers during (their) lunch hour. *their refers to aides*

5. Beth and Mike are saving money for (their) summer vacation. *their refers to Beth and Mike*

Practice 4, page 277

1. Either John or his <u>friends</u> are planning (his/their) fall schedules.

2. My <u>mom</u> and <u>dad</u> are financing (his/their) new car.

3. Neither Bob nor <u>Sue</u> knows what grade (he/she) is getting in algebra.

4. Either my coach or my <u>teammates</u> will show me (his/their) support during the final match.

5. The <u>judge</u> and the <u>jury</u> were unanimous in (his/their) decision.

Practice 5, page 278

1. Everyone regrets something in his life.

2. One of my friends got an A on his algebra test.

3. Some of these grapes have mold on them.

4. Each of the papers has a grade on it.

5. None of my seeds sprouted after I planted them.

Practice 6, page 278

1. <u>One</u> of my dresses has a stain on (it/them).

2. <u>A lot of my papers</u> have marks on (it/them).

3. <u>Everyone</u> loves to be recognized for (his or her/their) hard work.

4. <u>None of my friends</u> have finished (his or her/their) reports.

5. <u>Anybody</u> who wants to do well in school should attend all of (his or her/their) classes.

Practice 7, page 279

1. its
2. its
3. its
4. its
5. its

Practice 8, page 279

1. its
2. his or her
3. his or her
4. their
5. its
6. his or her
7. its
8. its
9. its
10. her

Practice 9, page 280

1. If students park on the grass, *they* can get towed.
2. Students should turn in all their papers on time. If *they* turn in a late paper, the instructor may not accept it.
3. Employees who want to be recognized for their efforts should follow *their* employer's instructions and recommendations.
4. Students who miss class due to illness fall behind in their work. Therefore, *students* should visit the infirmary on campus to get their free flu shot.
5. Parents should make sure their child has received all his or her vaccinations. *Parents* who don't vaccinate their child can endanger *their* child's health.

Practice 10, page 281

1. When consumers shop for a new television, they should purchase the latest technology.
2. If a student parks on the grass, the campus police will tow his or her car.
3. Unless students study regularly, they will find it difficult to keep up with their classes.
4. If drivers want to save money on gas, they need to shop around and compare prices.
5. If homeowners water their lawn during a drought, they can be fined.

Chapter 15: Pronoun Reference and Case

Practice 1, page 291

$\underline{\quad I \quad}$ 1. (Edna) told (Rosemary) that she was on restriction.

$\underline{\quad I \quad}$ 2. (Schools) encourage (students) to get involved so that they can be successful.

$\underline{\quad I \quad}$ 3. (Teachers) are always available to talk to (students) about questions they may have.

$\underline{\quad I \quad}$ 4. The newspaper (editor) asked the (reporter) what he was doing.

$\underline{\quad I \quad}$ 5. When (Ted) saw (Mark) he was riding his bike.

Practice 2, page 292

1. Edna told Rosemary that Edna (or Rosemary) was on restriction.
2. Schools encourage students to get involved so that students can be successful.
3. Teachers are always available to talk to students about questions students may have.
4. The newspaper editor asked his reporter what the reporter was doing.
5. When Ted saw Mark, Ted (or Mark) was riding his bike.

Practice 3, page 292

1. At my college, the security officers won't let you drop a class after midterm.
2. When we go to football games, the attendants make us pay for parking.
3. Parents sell drinks at the concession stand.
4. At the airport, security guards check your bags.
5. Owners close the bars at 2 A.M.

Practice 4, page 293

__I__ 1. I can't study when my roommate is watching TV, and (that) is a problem.

__I__ 2. When my brother washes his car, he gets soap on the grass, (which) is a

problem.

__C__ 3. My history test, (which) was given on Monday, was hard.

__I__ 4. My brother broke our neighbor's window, (which) got him in trouble.

__I__ 5. I flunked my algebra test, (which) got me in trouble.

Practice 5, page 293

Answers will vary.

1. My roommate interferes with my ability to study when he watches TV.
2. My brother causes problems when he gets soap on the grass while washing his car.
3. C
4. My brother got in trouble when he broke our neighbor's window.
5. I got in trouble when I flunked my algebra test.

Practice 6, page 294

1. He invited me to dinner.
   S   O
2. He wrote a letter to her last night.
   S   O
3. They are best friends with him.
   S   O
4. They told him to be here at five.
   S   O
5. We will surprise him with a cake.
   S   O

Practice 7, page 295

__I__ 1. Martha and ~~her~~ *she* want to go swimming.

__I__ 2. My mother and ~~him~~ *he* are driving to Miami tonight.

_C_ 3. Eduardo and I play doubles together.

_C_ 4. My brother and I have always been best friends.

                        he
_I_ 5. Manolo and ~~him~~ are going to the show at ten.

Practice 8, page 295

                                he (did)
_I_ 1. Susana studied longer than ~~him~~.

                                      I (have)
_I_ 2. My mother has studied French longer than ~~me~~.

                            he (can)
_C_ 3. I can run faster than he.

                               they (do)
_I_ 4. I like chocolate more than ~~them~~.

                             he (can)
_C_ 5. Can you walk as fast as he?

Practice 9, page 296

_C_ 1. (Joanne) plans to take Robert <u>with</u> her.

                             him
_I_ 2. The (coach) will give the award <u>to</u> ~~he~~.

_C_ 3. My (sister) likes to drive to the beach <u>with</u> them.

                         him
_I_ 4. The (book) fell <u>on</u> ~~he~~.

_C_ 5. My (mother) said I could go if I drive <u>with</u> them.

Practice 10, page 297

_I_ 1. themselves   _C_ 6.

_I_ 2. its   _I_ 7. themselves

_I_ 3. those   _C_ 8.

_C_ 4.   _I_ 9. cross out *here*

_I_ 5. himself   _C_ 10.

Chapter 16: Modifiers

Practice 1, page 305

Misplaced modifiers have been correctly placed here.

1. The child set the paper plane *on fire* in the house.
2. A woman *in a long white gown* entered the theater.
3. The homeowner gave a box *wrapped in brown paper* to the mailman.
4. The mechanic worked *with a wrench* on the car.
5. The movie star *dressed in a fur coat* left the auditorium.

6. *On one leg,* the runner crossed the finish line.
7. The girl *with an ice cream cone* ran to the corner.
8. *Using a radar gun,* the state trooper clocked the speeder.
9. *Talking on the phone,* my secretary typed the letter.
10. The bus *full of passengers* picked up the elderly woman.

Practice 2, page 305

Misplaced modifiers have been correctly placed here.

  I   1. A couple came *from the parking lot* into the restaurant.
  C   2. A band was playing in the restaurant *on stage.*
  C   3. The couple looked at the specials *on the menu.*
  I   4. The waiter *with a pen and pad* approached the couple.
  I   5. The man and woman ordered *from the menu* fish broiled in wine and butter.
  I   6. Then the couple got up *from their table* to dance.
  C   7. *Seeing food being served,* the couple returned to their table.
  I   8. They loved the fish *covered in wine sauce* that was brought to the table.
  C   9. The man paid *with a credit card* for the meal.
  I   10. The waiter gave the change *in small bills* to the man.

Practice 3, page 306

Misplaced modifiers have been correctly placed here.

  I   1. I have *hardly* any time to study.
  C   2. The teacher explained the concept *only* one time before the test.
  C   3. The movie made *nearly* 10 million dollars the first week that it opened.
  I   4. Mary will be happy when she finds *just* the right prom dress.
  C   5. The newlywed husband cleans house and *frequently* cooks some of the meals.

Practice 4, page 307

Answers will vary.

1. When using a cell phone for a long call, callers should charge the phone fully.
   When a caller uses a cell phone for a long call, the phone should be fully charged.
2. To charge a cell phone, a user must plug the charger into the phone for at least an hour.
3. While talking on a cell phone, a caller should keep the phone plugged into a charger.
   It is a good idea to keep the phone plugged in to a charger while a caller talks on the cell phone.
4. By conserving phone power, a user can talk on a cell phone all day.
5. Used with only the battery, a cell phone will run out of power quickly.

Practice 5, page 308

The subject (who or what the modifier is about) was not present in the sentence. To correct each dangling modifier, the writer must include the subject of the modifier in the sentence, either in the modifying phrase or immediately after.

Practice 6, page 308

Answers will vary.

1. *Working at the computer,* the owner found that the monitor went dead all of a sudden.
2. Correct
3. Correct
4. *To remain comfortable,* a user should adjust the monitor to shoulder height.
5. *To be comfortable,* workers should change positions every few minutes.

Chapter 17: Parallelism

Practice 1, page 319

1. writing
2. to think clearly
3. at home
4. proud
5. while he watches television
6. opened the door
7. a horse
8. on a clear night
9. when talking on a cell phone
10. finished by five

Practice 2, page 318

1. because he quickly became president of the United States
2. a governor of Georgia
3. asked his wife's advice about running for president
4. discuss events from around the world
5. soft-spoken
6. his knowledge of world affairs
7. around the world
8. severe inflation
9. South America
10. bringing about a peace treaty between Egypt and Israel

Practice 3, page 319

Answers will vary.

Practice 4, page 319

Answers will vary.

1. I find that studying for final exams can be profitable but time consuming.
2. My brother's car has wide tires, a beautiful paint job, and a powerful engine.
3. My mother loves to cook but hates to clean up.
4. Either watching television or sunbathing by the pool is my sister's favorite activity.
5. My schedule this week is both hectic and demanding.

Chapter 18: Commas

Practice 1, page 327

1. divorce, and
2. expensive, for
3. C
4. difficult, yet
5. C

6. mediator, yet most
7. belongings, and
8. C
9. C
10. mediator, or the

Practice 2, page 328

Answers will vary.

Practice 3, page 329

1. legs, it
2. bicycle, then
3. bike, a
4. woods, a
5. trails, a

6. trails, cyclists
7. correctly, a
8. C
9. C
10. completed, riders

Practice 4, page 330

Answers will vary.

Practice 5, page 332

1. No, it
2. Mr. Chao, my boss at Eye Vision Associates, sometimes
3. Therefore, Maria
4. tonight, Kari
5. findings, which

6. electricians, however, will
7. C
8. Moreover, some
9. mayor, who was elected easily, will
10. C

Practice 6, page 333

Answers will vary.

Practice 7, page 333

1. expired," the
2. C
3. The man said, "I am not responsible for the repairs."
4. years," the
5. C

Practice 8, page 334

1. Math, sociology, and history
2. played in the garden, swam in the pool, and ate lunch on the patio.
3. C
4. graduating from college, finding a good job, and getting married.
5. in the library, at the bus stop, and by the pool.

Practice 9, page 334

Answers will vary.

Practice 10, page 335

1. May 2, 1999, more than 2,000 trees . . . Atlanta, Georgia.
2. 759 Westphalia Street, Austin, Texas.
3. Monday, April 3.
4. Red Bank, New Hampshire, . . . 3,000 robins
5. C

Practice 11, page 335

Answers will vary.

Practice 12, page 335

Answers will vary.

Practice 13, page 335

Answers will vary.

Practice 14, page 335

Answers will vary.

Chapter 19: Apostrophes

Practice 1, page 346

1. that's
2. should've
3. you're
4. wasn't
5. can't

6. they're
7. weren't
8. he's
9. doesn't
10. wouldn't

Practice 2, page 347

1. don't
2. aren't
3. They've

4. wouldn't
5. They'll

Practice 3, page 347

Answers will vary.

Practice 4, page 348

1. decision
2. questions
3. bailiff

4. courtroom
5. jurors

Practice 5, page 348

Answers will vary.

Practice 6, page 348

Answers will vary.

Practice 7, page 349

  C   1. the league's most valuable player = most valuable player of the league
  I   2. the league's held during the summer = held of the league
  I   3. some computers' in the lab = in of some computers
  C   4. some computers' packing cartons = packing cartons of some computers
  C   5. the school's faculty = faculty of the school
  C   6. the school's gymnasium = gymnasium of the school
  I   7. the school's with the best team = with of the school
  C   8. the planet's orbit = orbit of the planet
  I   9. the planets' farthest from Earth = farthest of the planets
  I   10. the planet orbit's the sun = the of orbit

Practice 8, page 350

1. One woman's idea . . . that's
2. Mick Jagger's daughter . . . kitchen's high-tech stove.
3. The cooker's two ovens
4. The stove's designer . . . wife's inefficient stove
5. In today's high-tech world

Practice 9, page 351

1. Most Americans' diets
2. don't . . . they're . . . many families' dinnertime
3. some kids' health
4. Many teenagers' typical lunch
5. can't . . . parents' cooking

Practice 10, page 351

1. Many students' study skills . . . a professor's teaching style.
2. A student's ability . . . a course's material.
3. professors' assignments to their students
4. an assignment's difficulty.
5. The students' job . . . the teacher's job

Practice 11, page 352

1. Many people's idea
2. Our children's greatest wish
3. There's a women's group . . . our town's conference center.
4. I've . . . men's jackets
5. One club member's desire . . . everyone's dues . . . a children's playground.

Chapter 20: Other Punctuation Marks

Practice 1, page 363

__I__ 1. Because I speak Spanish, it is easy for me to travel in South America.
__C__ 2. My history instructor relates class material to current events; therefore, her class is interesting.
__I__ 3. My instructors this term are Mr. Harris, who graduated from Harvard; Ms. Breck, who graduated from Smith; and Ms. Edwards, who graduated from UNC, Chapel Hill.

Practice 2, page 364

<u>C</u> 1. I was instructed to bring the following items to the party: two bags of chips, two jars of salsa, and three bottles of apple juice.

<u>I</u> 2. I promised my mother I would buy lettuce, tomatoes, and cucumbers.

<u>C</u> 3. Mark had two problems: he couldn't concentrate and he couldn't read.

Practice 3, page 364

<u>C</u> 1. My new car—a 2004 Jeep Cherokee—was slightly damaged in the accident.

<u>I</u> 2. I promised my brother that I would take him fishing on Saturday.

<u>I</u> 3. My chain saw stalled for it was out of gas.

Practice 4, page 365

<u>I</u> 1. Hermione was not so sure of her answer.

<u>C</u> 2. Ron made a half-hearted attempt to study.

<u>I</u> 3. The sea was painted pale peach by the setting sun.

Practice 5, page 365

<u>C</u> 1. Disagreement still rages over NAFTA (North American Free Trade Agreement).

<u>I</u> 2. Five thousand delegates attended the Democratic National Convention in Boston (*Time* 5).

<u>I</u> 3. My priorities are (1) pass my classes, (2) get my degree, and (3) go to graduate school.

Chapter 21: Quotation Marks

Practice 1, page 373

1. According to Pam Deluce, "The TXC microchip is the fastest processor on the market" (6).
2. The professor advised, "Work closely with your lab partner today."
3. I thought of my favorite line from the Grateful Dead: "What a long, strange trip it's been."
4. The movie was nominated by a movie critic as "funniest comedy of the year."
5. "Habit is the product of a lazy mind," says my grandmother.
6. The girl blushed and replied, "I'd love to go out tonight."
7. The guidebook describes the park as "paradise by the sea."
8. The authors of the study note, "No effects of the substance were noticeable" (7).
9. "I cannot go out tonight," Zia told Pete, "but I am free tomorrow night."
10. In his only novel, Fred Peterson calls the main character "such an imitation cowboy . . . who wishes he had a horse and a gun" (12).

Practice 2, page 374

Answers will vary.

Practice 3, page 375

Answers will vary.

1. When I started college, my best friend promised that she would write every day.
2. At the beginning of our date, I couldn't believe that she was going out with me.
3. My favorite teacher always says that good grades are the product of attending every class and completing every assignment.
4. Jorgenson believes that a trained technician should change the operating systems on computers with Windows 95 or 98 (8).
5. Hard work and luck are two core beliefs Americans have always held (Laskey 5).

Practice 4, page 376

1. The first word that the baby learned was "mommy."
2. Many people love the song "Let It Be" by the Beatles.
3. The witness testified, "I told the police, 'Please find the criminal who robbed my neighbor.'"
4. In the short story "The Followers," the main character states, "Television is my salvation" (3).
5. The patient told his wife, "My doctor says, 'Tell your wife not to worry.'"

Appendix 1: Spelling and Dictionary Skills

Practice 1, page A-2

Answers will vary.

Practice 2, page A-4

1. paid
2. weigh
3. controlling
4. studying
5. cried

Practice 3, page A-6

Answers will vary.

Practice 4, page A-7

1. verb
2. three
3. emotional or sentimental
4. Middle English or Old French or Greek
5. put

Appendix 2: Parts of Speech

Practice 1, page A-11

1. jacket, patches
2. class, politics, religion
3. Mrs. Rogers, kisses, baby
4. Winter, leaves, ground
5. novels, themes, characters

Practice 2, page A-13

1. she, herself, my, him
2. Everyone, his, her
3. Whom, I
4. them, they
5. They, their, ours

Practice 3, page A-14

1. An onion, a recipe, an old friend
2. A university student, an A, an algebra test, a B, a history exam.
3. an electrician, a plumber, a water pipe, an hour
4. an interesting tour, a home, a new part
5. an early departure, a well-known player, a spectator, a semifinal game

Practice 4, page A-14

1. A large brown, the little, the red park
2. My tired, good
3. a sunny, the famous, the deserted, the beautiful
4. happy, the stately old, worried
5. Bitter, the angry

Practice 5, page A-15

1. has been preparing
2. was driving, was
3. takes
4. were planted
5. had

Practice 6, page A-16

1. very well, diligently
2. really
3. clearly, convincingly.
4. extremely, carefully.
5. angrily, recklessly.

Practice 7, page A-18

1. Over the weekend, of my classmates, in the library, for a study session.
2. of most countries, in Europe.
3. in the back office, on it.
4. in the parking lot, in its bumper.
5. to Minneapolis, for Thanksgiving.

Practice 8, page A-19

1. or
2. for
3. but
4. so/and
5. yet/but/and

Practice 9, page A-20

1. Even though/Although
2. because/since
3. if
4. When/After/Before
5. before

Appendix 3: ESL Skills
Practice 1, page A-25

Answers will vary

1. milk	U		some milk
2. smoke	U		some smoke
3. tea	U		some tea
4. lightning	U		some lightening
5. politics	U		a lot of politics
6. swimming	U		more swimming
7. darkness	U		much darkness
8. highway	C		highways
9. friendship	U		some friendship
10. friend	C		friends

Practice 2, page A-26

1. 0,0 (no article in either blank)
2. the, the
3. The, the
4. 0, the, the
5. 0, the, 0
6. 0, the
7. 0, 0
8. The, the
9. The, the, the
10. 0, 0

Practice 3, page A-27

1. The, the
2. The, 0
3. an, the
4. the, an, the
5. the, a

6. a, the
7. The, 0
8. a, the
9. a, the
10. the, a, an

Practice 4, page A-28

Sample answers (Answers will vary.)

1. any   Negative statement about count or noncount noun (homework)
2. a few   Plural countable noun (books)
3. this   Singular countable noun (purse)
4. little   Noncount noun (hope)
5. some   Plural countable noun (books)
6. other   Plural countable noun (stories)
7. another   Singular countable noun (headache)
8. many   Plural countable noun (cookies)
9. those   Plural countable noun (cars)
10. much   Noncount noun (concern)

Practice 5, page A-29

1. accepted
2. bought
3. will come
4. eaten
5. exercises

6. is taking
7. flunked
8. was jogging
9. have seen
10. broke

Practice 6, page A-32

1. to give
2. studying
3. studying
4. to win
5. to swim

6. to participate
7. to apply
8. to study
9. to run
10. skiing

Practice 7, page A-33

1. look out for my sister
2. keep up with his brother
3. figure out the answer or figure the answer out
4. catch up on my homework
5. look into the offer
6. call on my friend

7. pick me up
8. put up with you.
9. take the trash out or take out the trash
10. clean my room up or clean up my room.

Practice 8: Editing for Verb Errors, page A-34

My friends **have studied** in the United States for three years. They **came** to this country after they **graduated** from high school because they wanted **to study** English and engineering. The school they **chose to attend was** the University of California at Berkeley. After they **had** been in school several months, they **decided to take** a vacation and **to visit** other parts of California. They wanted **to see** Disneyland and Hollywood. They **drove** for several hours before they **reached** their destination. They **stayed** in southern California for two nights and then they **drove** up the coast **to see** Big Sur and Carmel. They didn't **arrive** home until one in the morning. The next day they **were** sleepy, and they **hadn't** remembered **to do** their homework.

Practice 9, page A-35

1. Antonio **never** mows the lawn.
2. Paolo and Roberta are **always** talking.
3. He **quickly** prepared for the conference. (or He prepared for the conference **quickly.**)
4. My baby sister **easily** fell asleep. (or My baby sister fell asleep **easily.**)
5. Kim-le is **always** reading.
6. My brother is **often** wrong.
7. I **sometimes** like to cook dinner. (or I like to cook dinner **sometimes.**)
8. They **slowly** boarded the plane. (or They boarded the plane **slowly.**)
9. My mother **seldom** travels by car.
10. The instructor **quietly** distributed the tests. (or The instructor distributed the tests **quietly.**)

Practice 10, page A-36

1. on, in
2. at, on
3. at, on
4. at, on
5. at, on
6. On, at
7. at, in
8. at, in
9. at, in
10. At, in

Practice 11, page A-37

1. on, in
2. in, on
3. at, in
4. in or at, in
5. near or by
6. in, on
7. on, by
8. by, in
9. near or by
10. near

Practice 12, page A-38

1. in
2. on
3. on
4. on
5. on

6. on
7. in
8. in
9. in
10. on

Practice 13, page A-38

1. on, at
2. On, to
3. in, on
4. on
5. on, in

6. in, at
7. in, in
8. at
9. at, on
10. in, in

Practice 14, page A-40

1. My brother slowly answered my question. (or My brother answered my question slowly.)
2. Santiago has seen the movie many times.
3. I have never been to Spain.
4. Uncle Eduardo gave me a book. (or Uncle Eduardo gave a book to me.)
5. When is the party?
6. Here is the book you ordered.
7. Mario seems sad today.
8. The clerk placed the book on the counter.
9. Marta cooks spaghetti well.
10. My dog is never tired of playing.

Practice 15, page A-41

1. My sister doesn't eat **any** spinach.
2. **It** is cloudy today.
3. Because the car is broken, **it** needs to be fixed.
4. Clara doesn't know **anything** about the test.
5. One of the book**s** is lost.

Practice 16: Editing for "S," page A-41

My two **best friends** are taking tennis **lessons.** They **take** private **lessons** twice a **week** and group **lessons** once a week. They **say** that the **lessons** are **expensive** but they **are** worth it. Some **people** don't **believe** in paying **money** to **learn** to play tennis, but they **want** to be **able** to **impress** their friends and family when they **return** to Argentina this **summer.**

Practice 17: Editing for "S," page A-42

Students have many **distractions** while they **are** in college. The biggest distraction is friends who **want** to go out and party at the **local** clubs. Some **clubs don't open** until 11 o'clock at **night** and they don't **close** until 2 o'clock in the **morning.** Students who **stay** out late **hurt** their **performance** in school. They may **forget** to do their **homework,** and they may **do** poorly on **tests.** They may feel sleepy, but if they **fall** asleep in class, their instructors will be **unhappy.**

Practice 18: Editing for Basic Errors, page A-42

Many **students** who **come** to the United **States** want **to** study in American **colleges.** Since the September 11 attacks, it has **become** more difficult for international **students** to **obtain** the student visa needed to study in **this** country. Some **students report** having to wait several **months** for their visas to be **issued.** Once **a** student is here, he or she cannot **return** home to **visit** his or her family, or he or she may not be **allowed** back into the country. Many **American** universities are protesting these difficulties **experienced** by their students.

Practice 19: Editing for Basic Errors, page A-43

Studying in **a** foreign country **is** exciting but difficult. **It** is interesting to **live** in another culture for a period of **time.** Students who **do** study abroad **discover** another way of **living.** At first, **it** is difficult to **adjust** to another **language.** Everyday **activities** such as driving, **shopping,** or doing the laundry **become** more difficult if a student **doesn't** speak the **language.** However, by participating in daily **activities** and getting to know native **speakers,** one can **make** the adjustment to a foreign **culture.**

Index

Credits

This page constitutes an extension of the copyright page. We have made every effort to trace the ownership of all copyrighted material and to secure permission from copyright holders. In the event of any question arising as to the use of any material, we will be pleased to make the necessary corrections in future printings. Thanks are due to the following authors, publishers, and agents for permission to use the material indicated.

Chapter 1. 13: Used by permission of the author. **41:** Used by permission of the author. **46:** Used by permission of the author. **50:** Natalie Knight, "Bad Break-up." Used by permission of the author. **51:** Evan Locker, "Laptops: Portable Gifts." Used by permission of the author. **52:** Nicole Budget, "Healthy Choice." Used by permission of the author. **53:** Sparky Vilsaint, "Cheating Doesn't Help" (aka "Academic Dishonesty"). Used by permission of the author. **54:** Phil Trautwein, "Dis-Owning a Dog." Used by permission of the author. **55:** Cornelius Ingram, "The Oldest Child." Used by permission of the author. **56:** Used by permission of the author. **57:** Used by permission of the author.

Chapter 2. 59: Used by permission of the author. **73:** Chris Vaughn, "My Journey." Used by permission of the author.

Readings. 419: "What Should I Do With My Life?" by Po Bronson, ©2002 by Po Bronson. Used by permission of Random House, Inc. **428:** Sandra Cisneros, "Only Daughter," ©1990 by Sandra Cisneros. First published in GLAMOUR, Nov. 1990. Reprinted by permission of Susan Bergholz Literary Services, New York. All rights reserved. **434:** "Lanterns: A Memoir of Mentors" by Marian Wright Edelman. ©1999 by Marian Wright Edelman. Reprinted by permission of Beacon Press, Boston. **441:** Steve Kemper, "Trash Talker," from SMITHSONIAN. **447:** From THE AUTOBIOGRAPHY OF MALCOLM X by Malcolm X and Alex Haley, ©1964 by Alex Haley and Malcolm X. ©1965 by Alex Haley and Betty Shabazz. Used by permission of Random House, Inc. **452:** Bill Maxwell, "A Christmas Bicycle Illuminates the Spirit of Giving," pp.11–14, MAXIMUM INSIGHT: Selected Columns. Reprinted by permission of the University Press of Florida. **457:** "The Journey" from DREAM WORK by Mary Oliver. ©1986 by Mary Oliver. Used by permission of Grove/Atlantic, Inc. **460:** Deborah Tannen, "You Just Don't Understand," ©1990 by Deborah Tannen. Reprinted by permission of HarperCollins Publishers, Inc. **465:** John Updike, "A&P" from PIGEON FEATHERS AND OTHER STORIES by John Updike, © 1962 and renewed 1990 by John Updike. Used by permission of Alfred A. Knopf, a division of Random House, Inc. **473:** William Zinsser, "Writing About Yourself: The Memoir" from ON WRITING WELL, 6/e by William Zinsser. Reprinted by permission of Carol Brissie.

Photos: © Thomson Corporation/Heinle Image Resource Bank.